Accounting:
A Management
Perspective

Accounting: A Management Perspective

LYMAN A. KEITH

Northeastern University

Prentice-Hall, Inc., Englewood Cliffs, N.J.   07632

Library of Congress Cataloging in Publication Data

Keith, Lyman A
    Accounting, a management perspective.

    Includes index.
    1. Accounting.   2. Managerial accounting.
I. Title
HF5635.K27   658.1'511   79-19552
ISBN   0-13-001214-9

Editorial/production supervision and interior design by Kim Gueterman
Cover design by Jerry Pfeifer
Manufacturing buyer: Edmund W. Leone

Printed in the United States of America

10   9   8   7   6   5   4   3   2   1

PRENTICE-HALL INTERNATIONAL, INC., *London*
PRENTICE-HALL OF AUSTRALIA PTY. LIMITED, *Sydney*
PRENTICE-HALL OF CANADA, LTD., *Toronto*
PRENTICE-HALL OF INDIA PRIVATE LIMITED, *New Delhi*
PRENTICE-HALL OF JAPAN, INC., *Tokyo*
PRENTICE-HALL OF SOUTHEAST ASIA PTE. LTD., *Singapore*
WHITEHALL BOOKS LIMITED, *Wellington, New Zealand*

Contents

Preface

A basic premise underlying the design and preparation of this text is that more students of business administration will, in their careers, look at accounting from their positions as managers rather than as practicing accountants. Managers are frequently required to interface with accounting and accountants but this is only one facet of their managerial role. There are significant differences between the understanding an accountant must have of many accounting issues and the understanding needed by managers. The manager needs to understand what the accountant does and why but does need the depth and breadth of knowledge that is necessary for an accountant.

Accounting: A Management Perspective presents those aspects of the accounting process that are of primary concern to managers at all levels of business and other institutions. It was written with the accounting needs of managers in mind rather than the needs of an accounting theorist. Many of the concepts developed are the same, as regards their title, as those developed in a number of management accounting texts. The principle difference between this and other texts in the field is the manner in which the various concepts are developed, explained, and used. We are primarily concerned for the basic issues yet the materials in this text have provided many students with the background needed for advanced study in the areas of cost accounting and financial control.

We show how the accounting system serves the operating manager and how in certain instances it *fails* to provide the information needed in many decision-making areas. Our concern is for the overall accounting process with emphasis on an understanding of costs, cost behavior, cost systems, and how this understanding can enable managers to perform more effectively.

We have intentionally made our discussions as direct and uncomplicated as possible, appreciating the fact that these materials can be presented in much greater depth and detail. This is a non-mathematical text that places greater emphasis on numerical relationships than on mathematics and equations. This, in our opinion, makes the subject matter easier to master and more palatable. At the end of each chapter we list key words or terms that were used and the meaning of them is given in the Glossary.

We begin with an overview of the accounting process and explain why all managers must be involved with it and understand how it operates. We emphasize the difference between a firm's accounting department and the accounting process which is a part of the firm's information system. In Chapter 2 we explain the rudiments of financial accounting and develop the process that leads to the preparation of financial statements. In Chapter 3 we explain how managers can use accounting data in the area of financial analysis.

The second section of this text discusses costs and cost behavior. In Chapter 4 the various types of cost inherent in business operation are discussed with emphasis on the behavior of cost when volumes of activity change. With this background we enter, in Chapter 5, into a discussion of break-even analysis and profit planning. In Chapter 6 we explore practical application in the broad area of cost-volume-profit relations.

The third section of this text is devoted to budgets and budgeting. We include these topics at this point because cost-volume-profit relationships are an integral part of budgeting and budget preparation. Chapter 7 covers operating budgets such as the sales and production budgets, and Chapter 8 covers financial budgets and pro forma financial statements.

The fourth section of this text is concerned with assigning costs to jobs or units of production. The assigning process involves a number of steps. Chapter 9 explains how the various costs of production flow into process and are assigned to the various departments of the firm. Chapter 10 explains how certain indirect costs are allocated to the various departments. After costs are accumulated for each production department we are ready, in Chapter 11, to determine the cost of jobs or units of production. Chapter 12 explains how cost control can be achieved through the use of standards and standard costs.

The last section of the text deals with four specific areas.

Chapter 13 treats the problems associated with short-term decisions, and Chapter 14 concerns long-term or capital budgeting decisons. Chapter 15 covers a number of problem areas associated with the management of inventory. The text concludes with a chapter that emphasizes organization concepts and responsibility accounting. We include this chapter to show that the entire accounting system in general and the management of cost in particular is conditioned by the organization structure. Whether the concepts developed throughout this text will work depends on the organizational environment in which managers must operate.

ACKNOWLEDGMENTS

Special thanks are due Professor Richard L. Keith of Northeastern University for his critical evaluations and contributions to this text; to the hundreds of students who have studied and commented on much of the material presented here; and to Donna and Martha for their nimble and accurate fingers.

Thanks are also due to reviewers whose helpful suggestions are incorporated in the text: Professor David Buehlmann (University of Nebraska, Omaha), Professor Ron Burrows (Northern Illinois University), Professor Anthony DiFrancesco (San Francisco State University), and Professor Sanford C. Gunn (SUNY at Buffalo).

PART 1

An Accounting Overview

1 Accounting and Management

The purpose of this chapter is to shed new and different light on the accounting process. It shows that there is considerable difference between the role of an accounting system and the work done by people in a firm's accounting department. It shows that all managers are a part of a firm's accounting process and that the work of an accounting department depends largely on decisions that managers make. It shows that the accounting experience you have had to date is but one part of a firm's accounting process.

This chapter shows how a firm's approach to its organization impacts on its accounting process and the firm's information system. And we show how approaches to organization can facilitate or deter the process of planning and control.

QUESTIONS FOR CONSIDERATION

1. From a manager's point of view, what is accounting and what does it involve?
2. What are the different fields of accounting and what does each accomplish?
3. What should an operating manager know about accounting?
4. Why is an understanding of a firm's organization necessary for an understanding of a firm's accounting process?
5. Can management determine what it actually costs to produce a product?

Most students of business seem to have a distorted view of accounting and, thus, may be completely turned off by the mere mention of accounting. To many students of business and people in general—accounting is nothing more than debits, credits, journals, adjusting entries, and the like. But this, the mechanics of an accounting system, is only a small part of the accounting process, a part that we will pay little attention to.

We get a different picture of accounting and can see why it is a part of the management process from the following definitions:

> Accounting is a service activity. Its function is to report quantitative information, primarily financial in nature, about economic entities that is intended to be useful in making economic decisions.[1]
>
> Accounting is the recording, accumulation, and dissemination of information relevant to various decision makers.

Note that neither definition makes reference to journal entries, working papers, or even financial statements. The accounting process in most firms extends well beyond the activity that takes place in a firm's accounting department and involves every responsible manager. The key word in each definition is *information,* information that can originate anywhere in the organization. Some of this information is gathered by the accounting department and made into a variety of reports that management may use in its decision-making activity. The specific types of information that are involved may depend in part on management decisions. A management decision to sell on credit gives rise to certain information—accounts receivable—that the accounting people gather and process. At certain time intervals the accounting people will report the amount and age of accounts receivable to the manager responsible. If management decides instead to use only American Express credit cards for credit sales, there will be no accounts receivable information and no job for the accounting people in this area of activity. Thus we emphasize again that accounting is but one segment of a firm's information system and that the types of information involved will depend to a degree on management decisions.

---

[1] Accounting Principles Board, *Statement No. 4: Basic Concepts and Accounting Principles Underlying Financial Statements of Business Enterprises* (New York: American Institute of Public Accountants, 1970), p. 17.

THE FIELDS OF ACCOUNTING

Accounting systems must have the capacity to serve different people and different purposes. They should have the capacity to provide the information managers need to establish objectives; they should have the capacity to provide the information managers need to monitor and control operations—to compare actual performance with the objective; and they must be able to provide information to groups outside the firm such as banks, stockholders, and government agencies. Accounting has both internal and external purposes and involves many different types of activity. In the following paragraphs we will point out how each field of accounting serves different people and different purposes.

Financial Accounting

This field of accounting encompasses a broad range of activity dealing with a firm's assets, liabilities, owner (stockholder) equity, revenues, and expenses. This function records all business transactions such as sales, purchases, payroll, and the like, classifies transactions into the proper accounts, summarizes these transactions, and, after making appropriate adjustments, presents the results of business operations in the form of an income (profit and loss) statement and a statement of financial position (balance sheet) and other records of financial activity.

This is a most necessary and important function, but its purpose is to simply record and present a summary of what has happened. It deals with history that may never be repeated. But a more significant characterization of the end products of financial accounting is that they are designed to communicate financial data to external users such as investors, potential investors, creditors, and government agencies. The financial accounting system is not specifically designed to provide operating managers with much of the information they need to carry out their basic tasks of planning and control.

More specifically, financial statements are prepared for stockholders, creditors, financial analysts, and the like, and the interests and concerns of these groups may be quite unlike those of operating managers. Statements are prepared for outside agencies such as the Securities and Exchange Commission and the Internal Revenue Service. The former is largely interested in whether "generally accepted accounting principles" were applied in the accounting process. The latter agency is primarily concerned for the adherence to the Internal Revenue Code. In other words, groups outside the firm may establish standards for reporting revenue and expense plus other data, and these standards may or may not allow for a realistic reporting of effective or ineffective management within a given business firm.

Most operating managers are not directly involved with the financial accounting process, and they do not understand the intricacies of the process. This process, as just noted, is governed by generally accepted accounting principles that are subject to countless often-disputed interpretations plus a multitude of ever-changing rules and regulations promulgated by a variety of government agencies at the federal and state levels. Financial accounting is in a constant state of flux and it is difficult for a certified public accountant to keep abreast of these changes. Operating managers, as a rule, should not try to maintain expertise in this area of activity. They should, however, be generally familiar with the processes and understand what the end results of the processes are, as discussed in Chapter 2.

Cost Accounting

Cost accounting and costing techniques are most closely identified with the manufacture of goods, but they are also necessary functions in other areas of activity such as

the construction industry where bidding for jobs is common

the medical care industry where rate schedules for the delivery of services must be prepared for governmental agencies and Blue Cross-Blue Shield

government agencies where cost-benefit analyses must be conducted before projects are funded

retail stores where markups on merchandise must be established; in retailing, markup (gross margin) must cover operating costs and profit

a dean's office where the dean is trying to get the administration to approve a new off-campus management development program

Cost accounting and financial accounting can be separate functions, yet they are interdependent. Considerable data generated by the cost accounting system feeds into the financial accounting system.

In manufacturing, the basic purpose of the cost accounting system is to ascertain the cost involved in the creation of a unit of production and to provide information needed in the planning and control functions. There are different types of cost accounting systems just as there are different types of manufacturing systems. The cost accounting system must serve the manufacturing system. The two most common types of manufacture are job-order, or custom, production and process, or homogeneous, production. A machine shop that provides various machining services for its customers is a job shop. The manufacture of automobile tires is done on a process-oriented basis. In a job-order situation, the aim of the cost accounting system is to determine the cost of each job completed. In a sense, the job is the unit of production. In a job-order situation, the cost accounting system must permit estimating what the cost of each job will be because frequently selling prices must be established before production begins. In process production, the process-cost system determines the average cost to produce one unit such as an automobile tire.

Both job-order and process cost accounting systems deal with the past; they record what has happened. They leave unanswered several important questions such as, Is the cost what it should be? Is the cost reasonable or unreasonable? Are costs under control? Are costs going to increase or decrease? Control over cost cannot be maintained in the absence of standards or norms. What has occurred (actual) must be compared with what should have happened (standard) to determine whether the situation is under control. A third aspect of cost accounting that concerns us is standard costing. As the title implies, standard costing uses established targets for material cost, labor cost, and other manufacturing costs. This provides a benchmark of "what should be." If actual costs are in agreement with planned costs, costs are considered to be under control. If actual costs are not reasonably in agreement with what was expected, the system provides a means for alerting managers to the exception and corrective action can be initiated. Standard cost systems are used in both job-order and process manufacturing, but these systems are more easily applied to process manufacturing.

Cost Accounting and the Manager

As a generalization, the components of cost accounting are more stable and subject to far less regulation from outside groups than are the components of financial accounting, as cost accounting and costing systems are largely internal; that is, they are designed primarily to provide operating managers with data they need in a number of decision areas.[2] An understanding of cost is needed in such areas as product design, the design of production processes, equipment selection, and inventory management. It is both proper and necessary for all managers to develop a basic understanding of cost and costing as it applies to their area of concern. For example, marketing managers should understand distribution costs and production managers should understand manufacturing cost.

Every business function involves cost, and managerial performance is frequently judged, at least in part, by cost performance. Costs that are out of control or are excessive are common reasons for firing, reassigning, or demoting managers. Managers therefore should understand what constitutes "out of control" or "excessive." These are relative terms and have meaning only when compared with some benchmark such as a plan or a standard. But, if a manager does not understand how benchmarks are established or the process by which costs are assigned to his area of responsibility, he is in a poor position to defend himself if charged with poor cost performance in his department. Costs can be manipulated, and it might be possible for the manager of one department, who understands cost, to present a good cost picture at the expense of another department. If for no other reason than self-preservation, a manager should understand the basics of cost and costing. Later in this chapter we will identify some of the problems involved in cost management and suggest ways of coping with them.

Managerial Accounting

Managerial accounting is a means of communicating to managers certain information that they as decision makers must have—information that is not provided by conventional accounting records. Conventional accounting records may show that a profit was made during a particular period of time, but, unless management fully understands the combination of ingredients that produced profit, it will be less able to decide what should be done to ensure a continuation of profit. The specific uses of managerial accounting are variable because the specific problems needing solution are variable. Manager-

[2]The Cost Accounting Standards Board, established by Congress to determine and to publish cost accounting principles to be applied to government contracts, could change this because of the large number of firms doing business with agencies of the federal government.

ial accounting comes into play when specific problems arise. It may involve such considerations as dropping a product line as GAF (film) and Gillette (digital watches) have done, adding to a product line as Polaroid has done so successfully, or purchasing a machine for the foundry.

Managerial accounting differs from financial and cost accounting in a number of respects:

> It is not a specific function as is financial accounting. All managers from time to time may be involved with managerial accounting, with involvement depending on problems that arise and decisions that must be made.

> It is not a mandatory function. It is visualized by some top managers as an aid in the decision-making process. The intent is to obtain all relevant inputs from whatever sources so that the best possible decisions can be made.

> It does not have a common body of knowledge as does financial accounting. The activity that is called managerial accounting in one business may be called managerial finance in another.[3]

> It is generally concerned with specific decisions in specific segments of the firm and relies heavily on future, not historical, costs.

Much of the material in this text after Chapter 2 deals with managerial accounting issues.

ORGANIZATION AND MANAGEMENT ISSUES

Businesses, hospitals, universities, and the like are organizations, and every manager and employee works within an organizational environment. The specific features that management incorporates into its organization structure can have a significant impact on each segment of the firm. We organize because through organization a firm can achieve objectives more effectively and efficiently. Organizations are therefore facilitative, yet they also restrict. They demand conformity in varying degrees, they identify what a manager can and cannot do, they establish hierarchies and chains of command.

The essence of organization is its functions and their relationships. That is, management identifies those things that must be done

---

[3]The National Association of Accountants has instituted a Certified Management Accounting program (CMA). As more accountants are certified in this area, a common body of knowledge may develop.

to achieve objectives and then establishes the desired relationships between functions. Through organization management divides and subdivides the total task into segments. Figure 1-1 shows how management has divided and subdivided the overall task at the Hypothetical Company. Here management has divided the total job into seven major departments and thus has created seven major cost centers and seven major information centers. Seven is neither a magic number of divisions nor necessarily the ideal number of divisions.

Another top management group might view the ideal organization structure differently. For example, it could make purchasing and maintenance subdivisions of the plant manager function. Management's decision to assign a function in one spot rather than another can have a significant impact on the managerial process. If these two functions were subdivisions of the plant manager, he would not only be responsible for the costs of these functions but he would be in a position to control what they do. As it now stands, these functions are supervised by the vice president who decides what these functions will do and the costs they will incur. The plant

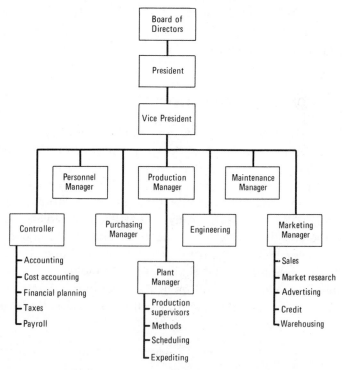

FIGURE 1-1.   The Hypothetical Company

manager uses these functions yet he cannot control the level of service they will provide him and he does not have control over the cost he must absorb. Note also in Figure 1-1 that the marketing manager has control over the credit function. Might a credit department function differently if it came under the controller's jurisdiction? Good jobs and poor jobs, easy and difficult situations to manage depend to a great extent on organizational design.

Organization Emphasis

Organization emphasis has a bearing on the types of accounting information that will flow through the firm and on the planning and control of cost. Figure 1-2 shows two approaches to organization. Each is an approach that an organization could use to achieve its objectives.

Figure 1-2A depicts the organization by function; that is, functions such as production, marketing, and personnel are major cost centers. (This approach to organization is also shown in Figure 1-1.) Figure 1-2B depicts organization by product; that is, products such as cosmetics, soaps, and detergents are major cost centers. To a degree these are reverse organizations.

In firm A, the manager of each functional department must be concerned with each of the four products, and in firm B the manager of each product must be concerned with each functional area. However, there can be considerable difference in information needs and the cost-control process between these two approaches to organization. In firm A, the cost of each function must be allocated to each product, and this, as we shall see, is a subjective process. In firm B, every dollar spent by the Manager, Soap is spent for that product and there is no need for allocations. Thus the Manager, Soap could be running a separate business, generating revenue, incurring costs, and perhaps showing a profit. In firm B, the vice president is not particularly concerned with the dollars spent by the Manager, Soap because ineffective use of resources impacts on profit. In firm A, the vice president is concerned for the dollars spent by each function because he cannot apply a profit yardstick to each function.

Cost Centers and Profit Centers

A cost center is simply a segment of an organization that has the authority to incur cost. The grinding department in a foundry could be a cost center, or the entire foundry could be a cost center.

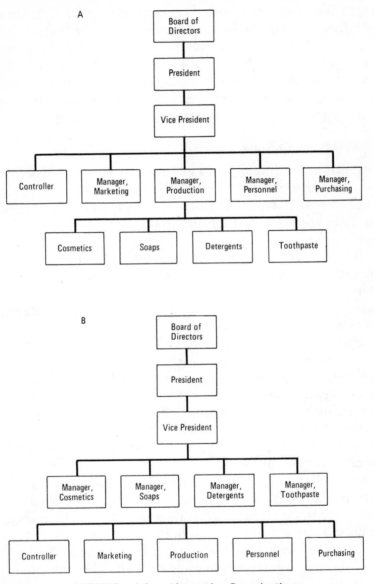

FIGURE 1-2. Alternative Organizations

A profit center, on the other hand, has the authority to incur cost, but it also generates revenue. Thus the soap department in Figure 1-2 could be a profit center. The advantages of using profit centers should be obvious. Here managerial performance can be evaluated based on the "residue" between revenue and expense. Product managers must focus their attention on all factors that make for profitable operations, not simply production, or marketing, or personnel.

Chevrolet is a natural profit center because it brings revenue into the firm, but the profit center concept can be applied to departments whose customers are other departments in the firm. A maintenance department could be a profit center because it could generate revenue by serving other departments. For example, a department manager wants a bulletin board outside his office. He calls maintenance and is told that it will cost him $150. If the price is reasonable the department manager will have the job done and have $150 transferred from one of his accounts to maintenance. Thus over a period of time the maintenance department generates revenue that can be compared with the cost of operating the function. If, over a period of time, the maintenance department's "revenue" is substantially below its cost of operation, it may signal that the maintenance department is too big or too inefficient.

Line and Service Functions

Most organizations have two types of functions. Some functions are directly involved with the generation of income; other functions exist to facilitate this primary function by providing a variety of specialized services. Line functions and line managers are directly involved with the production and distribution of goods and services. Often these managers are concerned for measureable units of output such as the manufacture of 5,000 room air conditioners. Here it is relatively easy to determine the amount of material, labor, and other manufacturing cost that should go into a unit of production. Here it is relatively easy to measure waste or the impact of change on the cost of production.

Managers of service divisions such as accounting, personnel, and purchasing or other divisions not directly involved with the production and distribution functions see the consequences of their decisions indirectly as they impact on the departments or divisions they serve. The personnel department, for example, cannot make the unit labor costs of production decline. It may serve the production (line) department with such effectiveness that production managers can bring about cost reductions. This bifurcation of effort between line and service functions makes it very difficult to place credit or blame for management action or inaction. Thus it is difficult to determine which type of function is making what contribution toward achieving enterprise objectives. If the production foreman utilizes one more or less production line worker, the impact may be measured almost immediately. There may be no measureable gain or loss of effectiveness if one more or one less employee is used in the personnel department. We should expect that planning and controlling costs will be more difficult in those firms that rely heavily on service functions.

The concepts developed here apply also to American business in general. Until recently, in historical terms, economic activity in America primarily concerned the production and distribution of goods. Today, a very high percentage of economic activity involves service-related functions. More people are now employed in the service sector of our economy than in manufacturing. The consequence of this shift is extremely important to those who must plan and control costs. Assembly lines move at precisely regulated speeds and output per labor-hour can easily be predicted, but at the local bank it is far more difficult to determine the number of customers that one teller should serve per hour or per day or the number of loans a loan officer should complete each day. In service industries and with service functions within the firm, there is apt to be a great imbalance between the demand for a specific service and the firm's capacity to supply the service.

Centralization and Decentralization

An organization chart such as that presented in Figure 1-1 tells us very little about managerial roles and responsibilities. We cannot tell from this chart whether production supervisors have a great deal or very little authority and responsibility. We cannot tell the extent to which individual managers are decision makers or suppliers and users of information. The types of decisions that managers must make and their information needs depend on the amount of authority that they have. In organizations described as centralized, the bulk of all authority rests at high organization levels, and we should expect that most decisions of any consequence are also made at high organization levels. With centralization low-level managers have little authority and little involvement in the decision-making process.

If the reverse is true and low-level managers have significant authority, the organization is considered decentralized. Here managers are decision makers, sources of information and users of information. A centralized organization uses fewer managers to operate a business entity than would a dentralized organization. Thus there would be fewer major cost centers and fewer suppliers and users of information. Decentralization has many advantages, but unless properly developed and monitored it can be a wasteful approach to organization.

MANAGEMENT ISSUES

The primary tasks of all managers are planning and control. However, the specific planning and control problems that a manager must handle depends on a number of factors. Planning of any sort at the lowest management levels is characterized by a relatively short time span, a relatively narrow range of activity such as the assembly of a product, and the involvement of a relatively small portion of the firm's total resources. As we move up the organization ladder, the nature of planning changes with longer time spans, broader areas of activity, and larger portions of the firm's total resources. The type of planning and manager information needs varies at each level of organization. At low levels of the organization, for example, for a production foreman, planning can be quite specific because it relates to work currently being done. Information needs at this level of activity are also quite specific, for the same reason. As we move up the organization hierarchy, activities are less related to current happenings and more related to future events. Planning and control become more difficult at higher organization levels because the wisdom of the plan and its associated costs and benefits will not be known until some time in the future.

The Information Problem

All aspects of management depend on information and information flow; they cannot function without it. It serves little purpose to design an accounting system without first assessing the information and information flow requirements of the firm and the firm's capacity to deliver the information. A standard cost system, for example, cannot achieve its potential for assisting in the planning and control function unless information relating to actual costs of operation is available to the responsible manager on a timely basis—the sooner the better. If actual cost data is not available until two months after production has taken place, control is absent for two months, and this lack of information precludes the possibility to take corrective action.

Despite the computer and its potential for processing data, information problems still rank high on the list of organizational weaknesses. For a multitude of reasons managers in well-known companies are making decisions based on data that turns out to be incomplete or inaccurate. It may be hard to believe that today large firms that appear to be prospering are actually on the verge of bankruptcy. Many managers today do not know how close to bankruptcy they may be simply because they do not know the state of the firm's financial affairs. When a firm experiences increased sales and profits, there is a tendency for managers to assume that everything is fine. It is quite possible for sales and profits to increase while the firm's financial status is deteriorating. Recently, a good-sized retail discount chain went into bankruptcy, at least in part because of faulty information regarding such basic activity as accounts receivable, accounts payable, inventory, and, believe it or not, the cash-in-the-bank balance. Management did not realize how bad the situation was until payroll checks started to bounce. Upon examination it was found that the computer printouts showed cash, receivables, and inventory balances much larger than they proved to be.

An objective of any information system should be to provide information that is (1) accurate, (2) complete, (3) relevant, and (4) timely. On the surface this may seem to be an easily obtained set of objectives, but this may not be so because of the many trade-offs that are usually made. The time objective can impact on the accuracy and completeness objective, for example, and there is the overriding consideration that the cost of obtaining information must not exceed the benefits that are likely to be derived. Information that is more accurate, complete, relevant, and timely may also be more costly.

It is also quite possible to provide a manager with so much information that it cannot be used effectively. This is called an information overload. Also, there can be a great difference between information flow and the movement of paper with numbers and words on it. It is essential, therefore, that the specific information needs of each manager be spelled out in detail and then reviewed periodically.

Every organization has a built-in information system whether it is formally recognized or not. A basic purpose of any organization structure is to establish channels for communication through which the desired information will flow. But no organization structure by itself can ensure that information will flow in such fashion that information needs will be satisfied. Whether this happens depends in large measure on the people involved and their concern and willingness to provide others with the information they need. Some people by nature seek to hold for themselves as much information as possible; they have a "let the other guy find out" attitude. This condition can arise because a manager has failed to meet the objectives set for him and wants to hide the fact as long as possible; or he may be a loner; or it could be caused by other factors.

Jones was promoted to the position of production manager last September when Smith, the production manager for the past five years, violated company policy once too often. Through hard work and effective management, Jones actually shipped over $1 million in orders during the month, the best monthly volume ever. When Jones received the September results, he noticed that he had been given credit for only $550,000 of orders shipped. Upon investigation it was found that Smith had reported shipments in August amounting to $450,000 that were never made. Smith had a policy of doing the paper work associated with a shipment when the job in question was about 80 percent completed and hoped that shipments would be made before anyone checked on his activity. Whatever the information system, it must be monitored continuously (by another part of the information system) to ensure that it is providing accurate data.

In a highly decentralized organization that uses many service functions, there can be a significant time lag between events happening and the time others find out about the events.

ACCOUNTING AND MANAGEMENT— A CONCLUSION

Much of the material in this text relates to planning, measurement, and control—the planning, measurement, and control of cost. We need to understand at the outset what we, the managers, can expect the accounting system to produce in terms of accurate and meaningful information. From an outside point of view, accounting seems to be a very scientific and precise process. It is not. We cannot expect that an accounting system will always provide the information needed with complete accuracy. Most accounting information is historical, and judgments must be made as to its usefulness in decision making.

Frequently management decisions are based on estimates, and this does not preclude either good management or profitable operation. We will use the following example to illustrate. As the first Monte Carlo Chevrolet rolled off the assembly line at the start of a model year, General Motors determined the cost of the car to be $5,149.21. But just what does this figure mean? Is this what the actual cost of a Monte Carlo will be, or is it the average cost of a Monte Carlo, or is it the average cost provided total cost and total production go according to plan? If it is any of these it is the last. Realistically, there is no way that G.M. can determine at the start of a model year what the cost of a car will be. There are so many factors that effect cost that it is impossible to pinpoint what costs will be in the future. The most that we can expect from an accounting system is reasonable accuracy and this goal can be achieved.

KEY TERMS

centralization

cost accounting

cost center

decentralization

financial accounting

information overload

line function

managerial accounting

organization by function

organization by product

profit center

service function

staff function

QUESTIONS

1. Explain what accounting involves.
2. Distinguish between the role of accounting and the role of the accounting department in a business organization.
3. Illustrate how management decisions can impact on the accounting process.

4. Accounting systems must have the capacity to serve different people and different purposes. Discuss.

5. What is the primary purpose of a financial accounting system?

6. From management's point of view, is the financial accounting system a good source of information? Explain why or why not.

7. Should operating managers be directly involved with the financial accounting process? Explain why or why not.

8. Cost accounting techniques have application only in manufacturing businesses. Do you agree with this statement? Explain.

9. How does job-order cost accounting differ from process cost accounting?

10. How does standard costing differ from job-order or process cost accounting?

11. Should operating managers be involved with cost accounting and cost concepts? Explain why or why not.

12. With what types of situations do we consider managerial accounting?

13. How does managerial accounting differ from financial and cost accounting?

14. How does the assignment of organization functions impact on cost and cost control?

15. Would you expect the broad area of cost management—planning and control—to be different when organization by function is used as opposed to organization by product? Explain.

16. Distinguish between a cost center and a profit center.

17. Can the profit center concept be applied to the service departments of a firm? Explain why or why not.

18. Distinguish between a line function and a service function.

19. Planning and control will be more difficult in those firms that rely heavily on service functions. Why is this so?

20. It is easier to determine the number of workers needed in a factory than in a bank. Why is this so?

21. How would a foreman's planning job differ from that of the company president?

22. Distinguish between centralization and decentralization in an organization.

23. How might the accounting function differ in a centralized versus a decentralized organization?

24. What problems are involved in achieving the objectives of an information system?

25.   When General Motors says that the cost of a car is $5,149.21, just what does this figure mean?

PROBLEMS _____

The following situations are presented to focus attention on the types of situations that managers may face. You will not find any answers directly in the chapter material, but the chapter material should get you thinking about accounting issues from a manager's point of view.

1.   You know the number of students enrolled in this class. This is one of four courses you are taking this term. Your tuition for this term is $1,200. Your instructor will be paid $6,000 for this quarter and teaching this course comprises one-third of the teaching load. Does the class break even? Explore.

2.   The Argyle Corporation is a relatively young firm and, as of this date, has but two major functions as shown in Figure 1-3. All the things that must be done to achieve objectives are now the responsibility of these two managers. These managers have asked the president to add the following service functions: accounting, purchasing, personnel, credit, and market research.

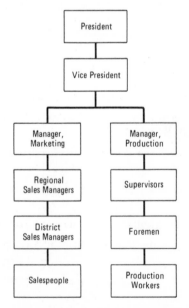

FIGURE   1-3.   Argyle Corporation Organization Chart

Required:

a. Where would you place each of these functions on the organization chart? What is your reasoning for this?

b. Has this assignment limited what each function can do? Explain.

c. Would a different assignment change the role of each function? Explain.

3. A new Chevy Nova which had a sticker price of $5,328.92 cost the dealer $4,169.98. The dealer sold this car for $3,300 plus a three-year-old Chevy Nova having a red book value of $1,650. The salesman's commission was 7½ percent.

Required:

a. How much profit (gross margin) did the dealer make on this sale? Explain.

b. How much commission would the dealer pay the salesman? When would the dealer pay him?

2 Financial Accounting

CHAPTER OVERVIEW

The purpose of this chapter is to discuss the rudiments of the financial accounting process. We do this by explaining the basic financial statements and the various accounts that are included in these statements. We show where the numbers come from and what they mean.

Financial accounting is a process through which business transactions are recorded in the appropriate accounts. The manner in which transactions are recorded is often governed by generally accepted accounting principles. We show in an elementary way how the process of recording transactions leads to the end result—the financial statements. Managers generally are more concerned with the statement of financial position or balance sheet and the income statement than they are the accounting process, but a look at the process makes the numbers in the statements more meaningful.

QUESTIONS FOR CONSIDERATION

1. What is an income statement and what does it tell management?
2. What is a balance sheet and what does it tell management?
3. What steps are involved in the accounting process?
4. How can management cope with the problem of credit risks?
5. In what way does management recover the costs of its investment in buildings and machinery?

A society can use many approaches to supply the goods and services that its members want and need. In some societies, as on a remote South Sea island, this task is left to the individual. In others, as in the Soviet Union or in Cuba, the task is assumed by government. In the United States, this task is left largely to free (private) enterprise that is motivated by the possibility of generating a profit.

In our illustration, the South Sea islander probably has no interest in or use for accounting in any form. In a totalitarian state, on the other hand, all property is owned by the state, all workers are employed by the state, and all purchases of goods and services are made from the state; whether a given activity is "profitable" or wasteful may be of no concern to state officials. And in the United States the only privately owned businesses that can continue to serve society are those that earn a profit for their owners. This is as true for the shoe repair shop as it is for General Motors.

In our society an accounting system must serve a number of purposes. It must have the capacity to present an accurate picture of the firm's profitability, the firm's financial position, and it must provide operating managers with information needed in the decision-making process. And, because there are parties apart from the operating managers—stockholders and government agencies, for example—who are concerned with the firm's finances, the system must have the capacity to communicate with these groups also. Thus, in our society, accounting is a multipurpose activity.

Financial accounting concerns the recording, classifying, and summarizing of business transactions. It is also a process that is governed by generally accepted accounting principles. These have been developed by the accounting profession to ensure, to a degree, that the accounting process will yield consistent and meaningful results. It would be asking too much to expect business managers to have a full understanding of the accounting process and the accounting principles that are applied. Some understanding of process and principles is necessary for the outputs of the process to be accurately interpreted. This, an understanding of the outputs, will be our emphasis.

The users of accounting information are vitally concerned for two accounting reports, two results of the accounting process. They are the statement of financial position, also referred to as the balance sheet, and the income statement, also referred to as the profit and loss statement. The balance sheet presents a picture of the firm's financial position as of a given point in time. The income statement shows whether a firm made a profit or incurred a loss over a particular time period. We begin our discussion of financial accounting with an examination of these two major "outputs," because, once the reader understands them, it will be much easier to visualize the process that led to these results.

THE BASIC FINANCIAL STATEMENTS

It has been noted that financial accounting is the process of recording, classifying, and summarizing business transactions. Virtually all business transactions affect, in one way or another, the two basic financial statements just referred to. More specifically, the transactions affect one or more of the accounts that comprise these statements. We will first identify these accounts through sample financial statements (Tables 2-1 and 2-2) and then proceed to explain their meaning.

Table 2-1 is a statement of financial position for the Paramount Corporation. Notice that the only accounts included in this statement are assets, liabilities, and owner equity. Notice, too, that there are a variety of asset and liability accounts and several components of owner equity.[1]

Table 2-2 is an income statement for the Paramount Corporation. Note that the income statement summarizes activity for a particular period of time, whereas the statement of financial position relates to a specific point in time. This income statement shows revenue from the sale of goods. From this the cost to the firm of goods sold is deducted, and the balance is referred to as gross margin. Operating expenses are deducted from the gross margin to produce the net income (profit) or loss for the period. Table 2-2 is a condensed income statement. In practice the composition of revenues and expenses may be shown in greater detail. Note that there is a relationship between the income statement and the statement of financial position. The net income after taxes of $32,500 is an addition to the owner equity account in the statement of financial position. Also, the December 31 merchandise inventory of $600,000 which

---

[1] In a corporation owner equity may be called stockholder equity.

TABLE 2-1

The Paramount Corporation
Statement of Financial Position,
December 31, 19X4

Assets		
Current Assets:		
Cash	$100,000	
Accounts recievable, net	300,000	
Inventories	600,000	
Total Current Assets		$1,000,000
Long-term Assets:		
Land and buildings, net	$500,000	
Machinery, net	250,000	
Furniture and fixtures, net	50,000	
Total Long-term Assets		800,000
Total Assets		$1,800,000

Liabilities and owner equity:		
Current liabilities:		
Accounts payable	$550,000	
Taxes payable	17,500	
Accrued wages payable	12,500	
Total Current Liabilities		580,000
Long-term Liabilities:		
Mortgage		200,000
Total Liabilities		$ 780,000
Ownership Equity:		
Capital stock (150,000 shares)	$750,000	
Retained earnings, Jan. 1	237,500	
Net income for the year	32,500	
Retained earnings, Dec. 31	$270,000	
Total Owner Equity		1,020,000
Total Liabilities and Owner Equity		$1,800,000

TABLE 2-2

The Paramount Corporation
Income Statement,
For the year ended December 31, 19X4

Sales revenue	$2,025,000	
Less sales returns and allowances	25,000	
Net Sales		$2,000,000
Less: Cost of goods sold		
Merchandise inventory, Jan. 1	$ 440,000	
Merchandise purchases, net	1,320,000	
Cost of goods available for sale	1,760,000	
Merchandise inventory, Dec. 31	(600,000)	
Cost of Goods Sold		1,160,000
Gross margin		$ 840,000
Less: Operating expenses		
Salaries and wages	300,000	
Office expenses	120,000	
Selling and promotion expense	320,000	
Rent, light, and utilities	50,000	
Total Operating Expenses		790,000
Net income before taxes		50,000
Income tax		17,500
Net income (to retained earnings)		$ 32,500

was subtracted from the cost of goods available for sale is shown as a current asset in the statement of financial position.

TYPES OF ACCOUNTS

The two basic financial statements illustrated identify the basic types of accounts used in financial accounting. They are assets, liabilities, owner equity, revenues, and expenses. In the following paragraphs we will describe what the numbers in Tables 2-1 and 2-2 mean and what they do not mean.

The total of assets shown in Table 2-1 is $1,800,000, but we should not assume that this is the market value of the items listed. Rather, it depicts expected future benefits as measured by generally accepted accounting principles. Frequently financial reports will contain footnotes that describe how the size of individual account balances was obtained. This provides a basis for determining the meaning of each account balance.

Assets

An asset is something of value owned by a firm that is expected to provide future benefit and can be measured objectively in terms of money. Buildings and machinery are examples of tangible assets; trademarks, patents, and goodwill are examples of intangible assets. Assets have value to a firm, but each of the numbers in the asset section of Table 2-1 needs to be described so that its size will be more meaningful to the reader of the statement. We will look at each of these assets.

Cash.   Does this firm have $100,000 to spend? We cannot tell because cash includes checks that could prove to be worthless. Thus the amount of cash on hand is, to a degree, estimated.

Accounts receivable.   The term "net" tells us that $300,000 is not the total of accounts receivable on the firm's books. It is the gross amount of receivables reduced by the amount that management believes will not be collectable. Thus $300,000 is the estimated amount of cash management expects to collect from accounts receivable outstanding on December 31.

Inventory.   The actual benefit of this asset will not be known until it is sold. Obviously management hopes to sell the inventory for much more than $600,000, but there is no way to tell on December 31 the amount of revenue that this inventory will generate.

Long-term assets.   Long-term or fixed assets are generally expressed at their acquisition cost less any depreciation that has been taken. Land generally cannot be depreciated and must be carried on the books at the price actually paid for it. Thus the $800,000 of long-term assets at the Paramount Corporation may or may not be a meaningful expression of economic value. The land, if purchased many years ago, is probably shown considerably below its current market value. Buildings may for a time appreciate in value yet are carried on the books at cost minus depreciation. On the other hand, if the long-term assets in question were recently purchased, their economic value and book value could be about the same.

If the only knowledge we have of machinery, for example, is that its net book value (cost minus depreciation) is $250,000, we know far too little about this asset. The book value could, for example, be either A or B:

	A	*B*
Cost	$900,000	$260,000
Accumulated depreciation	650,000	10,000
Net Book Value	$250,000	$250,000

In case A the machinery is more than 70 percent depreciated, and we can conclude that on an average it is old and early replacement may be necessary. In case B the machinery is less than 4 percent depreciated, and we can conclude that on an average it is relatively new.

Classification of Assets

Assets can be classified in many ways, but one of the most useful approaches is based on their liquidity. Most assets can be classified as either current or long term (fixed). A current asset is either cash or an item of property that normally becomes cash or is consumed in the operation of the business within a year. Thus accounts receivable and inventories also belong in the current asset category. The sum of current assets is crucial to a firm because it provides a measure of the firm's ability to pay current liabilities. Fixed assets include such items as land, buidings, and machinery. As a generalization these assets will provide benefit to the firm for more than one year. As already indicated, it is common practice to depreciate (decrease) the book value of fixed assets (except land) as they are used up. For example, a building costs $400,000, it has an estimated useful life of 40 years, and it has no scrap or salvage value. If straight-line depreciation is used, the book value of the building is decreased $10,000 per year. The process of depreciating fixed assets is discussed later in this chapter.

The relation between total current assets and total long-term assets is important, but there are no standard ratios that apply across the board to all firms or all industries. A petroleum or steel producer will have a high percentage of fixed assets, whereas a retail chain that utilizes leased facilities should have a relatively low fixed investment.

It may take ten years or more for a steel producer to recapture its investment in facilities; a retail store may recapture its investment in a matter of months.

Liabilities

As the term implies, these are obligations to pay or perform arising from business operation. As with assets, liabilities are classified as current or long term. Current liabilities are obligations that normally will have to be paid within one year's time. Accounts payable, short-term notes, wages payable, and taxes payable are common current liabilities.

We can now see the need for comparing current assets and current liabilities. If the current assets on December 31 are less than current liabilities, the firm may be in jeopardy of meeting these short-term obligations. This may be a signal for corrective action.

Long-term liabilities are obligations that will come due more than one year from the date in question. Long-term notes, mortgages, and bonds fall into this category. The portion of a long-term liability that will become due in a given year is considered a current liability for that year.

Owner Equity

Owner equity or net assets is always the difference between the total of a firm's assets and its total liabilities. Owner equity is expressed differently in proprietorships and partnerships than in corporations where it is commonly called stockholder equity. Proprietors and partners actually own the assets of the firm, and they can withdraw funds from the business whenever they choose. Under these forms of ownership the net income of the business is the net income of the owner(s).

In a corporation the owners do not own the firm's assets; the corporation itself owns the assets. The owners of a corporation own shares of stock which give them certain rights. These rights allow stockholders to vote on certain issues and to share in the firm's profits, provided that the board of directors declares a dividend.

As a generalization, owner equity in a corporation arises from two sources: the amount that the owners (stockholders) paid for their shares of stock when they were issued by the corporation and the amount of retained earnings. Retained earnings is the cumulative amount of net income after taxes that has remained in the firm. In a sense, all income after taxes is retained earnings until such time a dividend is paid or other uses are made of it. The payment of dividends reduces the amount of retained earnings. In Table 2-1, stockholders contributed $750,000 for their shares of stock, and over the years a total of $237,500 in retained earnings has accumulated. This year's net income after taxes of $32,500 increased retained earnings to $270,000. In many businesses the amount of retained earnings is greater than the owner's contribution.

A proprietor's or partner's capital is the amount that the individual invested in the firm plus any profit that has been earned, less any losses incurred or monies withdrawn from the business.

The Significance of Owner Equity

The statement of financial position of the Paramount Corporation (Table 2-1) shows stockholder equity to be $1,020,000. Just what does this mean? What does it tell management? The owners? It is simply the difference between two numbers on a given date. By itself it may provide relatively little information. Changes in the individual balance sheet items over time can provide more information about the firm's financial health than an isolated look at stockholder equity.

Revenues

Revenues, or the inflow of assets, for our purposes come mainly from the sale of goods and services. It is commonly shown on the income statement as "sales revenue." It may be useful to divide sales into their gross and net amounts as shown in Table 2-2.

Expenses

Expenses, or the outflow of assets associated with sales revenue, need no explanation at this point. It is necessary to distinguish between a cost and an expense. An expense is an expired cost. For example, the Paramount Corporation (see Table 2-2) had merchandise available for sale that cost $1,760,000, but only $1,160,000 of this was an expense because $600,000 of merchandise remained in inventory at year's end. This concept is explored in greater detail in later chapters.

BUSINESS TRANSACTIONS

The amounts shown in the various accounts of Tables 2-1 and 2-2 are the totals or balances resulting from various business transactions. The $100,000 balance in the cash account equals the cash balance at the start of the period plus all receipts of cash and less all cash payments. The net sales figure in Table 2-2 is the total of all sales recorded during the year less any returns and allowances. All accounts come into being because of transactions. If the Paramount Corporation had nothing but cash sales, there would be no need for an accounts receivable account. Transactions are activities that directly affect the balances of assets, liabilities, and owner equity such as the purchase or sale of goods. The hiring of an employee is not a transaction in the accounting sense, but the payment of wages to an employee is.

The Double-entry System

There are always at least two components to an accounting transaction. One way to view this is that in every transaction something is given and something is received. For example,

1. Merchandise is purchased for cash. Merchandise is received, cash is given.
2. Wages are paid. Worker services are received, cash is given.
3. Merchandise is sold on account. A promise to pay is received, merchandise is given.

The Basic Accounting Equation

Assets equal liabilities plus owner equity; this is the basic accounting equation. We know that there are two basic components of owner equity so the basic accounting equation can be expressed as

Assets = Liabilities + capital stock + retained earnings

For our purposes, retained earnings increases with revenues and decreases with expenses. Therefore we can express the accounting equation as

Assets = Liabilities + capital stock + retained earnings + revenue − expenses

or

$$A = L + CS + RE + R - E$$

Illustrative Problem

The impact of business transactions on the elements of the accounting equation is shown in Table 2-3. Fred Smith, a sole proprietor, opened a store on May 1. Using receipts, invoices, and memos, he reported the following summarized activity for the month.

1. Withdrew $15,000 from his savings account and invested it in the business.

2. Paid rent for the month, $500.

3. Purchased merchandise inventory for cash, $14,000.

4. Purchased merchandise inventory on account, $4,000.

5. Sold merchandise for cash, $15,000.

6. Sold merchandise on account, $3,700.

7. Paid cash for heating oil, $250.

8. Withdrew cash for personal use, $900.

9. Paid cash for light bill, $140.

10. Paid wages to part-time help, $100.

11. Purchased equipment for cash, $1,500.

12. $8,000 of merchandise was on hand at the end of the month.

Thus the cost of merchandise sold was $10,000 ($18,000 − $8,000). Table 2-3 shows the impact of these transactions on assets, liabilities, and owner equity.

Notice that assets equal liabilities plus owner equity. During the month owner capital increased from $15,000 (item 1) to $21,810, or by $6,810. However the profit earned for the month is $900 more, or $7,710. When a proprietor withdraws cash from the business, it is not a business expense. Rather, such withdrawals reduce owner capital.

Financial Accounting—Additional Issues

The previous illustration explains the initial impact of business transactions on the accounting equation, but this explanation could be deficient in two respects. First, accounting records are kept on either a cash basis or an accrual basis as is explained in the following paragraphs. In addition, the recording of data, as presented, may be incomplete in several respects. Assets such as equipment depreciate in value over time, and this should be recorded. There may be

TABLE 2-3

Fred Smith's Business Activity, For month ended May 31

Item		Cash	+ Receivables	+ Inventory	+ Equipment	=	Payables	+ Capital	+ Revenue	− Expenses
1	+	$15,000						+ $15,000		
2	−	500								$ 500
3	−	14,000		+ $14,000						
4	+			+ 4,000			$4,000			
5	+	15,000							$15,000	
6			$3,700						3,700	
7	−	250								250
8	−	900						− 900		
9	−	140								140
10	−	100								100
11	−	1,500			$1,500					
12	−			10,000						10,000
Bal.		$12,610 +	$3,700 +	$ 8,000 +	$1,500	=	$4,000 +	$14,100 +	$18,700 −	$10,990
		$25,810					$25,810			

N.B.: Owner equity was increased by Smith's investment and was decreased when he withdrew cash for his personal use. The sale of merchandise, whether for cash or on account, increased owner equity, and expenses decreased owner equity.

expenses incurred or revenues earned that have not yet been recorded and either could cause a misstatement of net income for the period. Adjustments such as these are the subject of this section.

CASH AND ACCRUAL BASES FOR ACCOUNTING

The basic difference in these two approaches to accounting lies in the treatment of revenue and expense. Under the cash basis, revenue is recorded and is considered earned not at the time goods are sold or services rendered but at the time payment is received. Similarly, bills are not considered an expense until they are paid.

The cash method of accounting is very simple because, basically, it is "checkbook" accounting. Many businesses, especially service businesses such as doctors, lawyers, authors, consultants, and the like, frequently use this approach.

This method of accounting provides some flexibility to the businessman when it comes to measuring income for a particular period. He may ask customers to speed up payment or to postpone payment based on the impact that either action would have on his annual income and income taxes. Over an extended time, ten years, for example, the total income shown via the two methods would probably be about the same but the income for each year could vary considerably.

The basic question involved here can be best presented via an illustration. Suppose that you do some consulting work for a client in the months of November and December and bill the client on December 26 for $2,500. You actually get your money on January 15 of the following year. To which year should the income of $2,500 be credited? If the cash basis were used, the revenue would be recorded on January 15, but, if the accrual basis were used, the revenue would be recorded on December 26. Under the accrual basis, revenue is recorded when earned, and expenses are recorded when incurred.

In accounting, every attempt is made to match revenue and expense (matching concept). If the expenses associated with the consulting work are charged to one year, and the revenue credited to another, a lopsided picture of profit for the two years will result.

THE NEED FOR ADJUSTMENTS

The accrual basis of accounting requires a number of adjustments to revenue and expense at year's end so that all revenues earned and all expenses incurred for a period are accounted for. There is nothing automatic about adjusting entries. The accountant and management must review what has happened at year's end and determine what must be done to present a realistic picture of income.

There may be certain revenues earned that have not been received on the day that the books are closed as shown in case 1. There may be revenues received and not yet earned on the day that the books are closed as shown in case 2. Similarly, there may be expenses incurred that have not been recorded as shown in case 3. Finally, expenses may have been paid in advance as shown in case 4.

1. On December 1 the firm received a $10,000 60-day 10 percent interest-bearing note from a customer. Both the interest and the principal are due on January 29. However, 31 days' interest was earned during the current year and should be recorded as follows:

DEBIT Accrued interest receivable $84.93
CREDIT Interest revenue $84.93

2. The business rents out a portion of its buiding. On October 1 a payment of $5,000 was received to cover the next six months' rent. When the payment was received the following entry was made:

DEBIT Cash $5,000
CREDIT Prepaid rent $5,000

Through December 31, half the prepaid rent has been earned and the following entry should be made to reflect this fact:

DEBIT Prepaid rent $2,500
CREDIT Rent revenue $2,500

3. The pay period for the firm runs from December 29 through January 2. Normally, payroll expense would be recorded on January 2. The payroll for three days should be charged to the current year and the remaining two days' payroll to the next year. The following adjustment should be made on December 31:

DEBIT Payroll expense xxxx
CREDIT Accrued payroll payable xxxx

4.   On January 2 the company paid $6,000 for a three-year fire insurance policy and made the following journal entry:

DEBIT   Prepaid insurance $6,000
CREDIT   Cash $6,000

During the year one-third of this policy expired, and the following entry should be made to show this as an expense:

DEBIT   Insurance expense $2,000
CREDIT   Prepaid insurance $2,000

Prepaid insurance and other prepaid expenses are assets and are generally shown in the balance sheet under the current asset category.

ASSET VALUATION

It has already been mentioned that it might be advisable to question or verify the value of every asset owned by the firm to assure that its value was properly presented. Because of the passage of time or because of new information, it may be necessary to restate the book value of certain assets. The manner in which the value of these assets might be adjusted is discussed in the following paragraphs.

Accounts Receivable

It is inevitable in business that certain customers will not or cannot pay their bills. Because credit losses are a fact of life, business-men plan for this inevitability. Each year an analysis should be made of the accounts receivable to determine which if any are likely to be uncollectable. Both the age of accounts receivable and the financial position of customers are factors in this analysis. In addition, a con-tinuous study of all accounts receivable should be made to determine what percentage of the accounts go bad over a period of time. If you could identify in advance which accounts will be uncollectable, you would not make the sale. Not knowing which accounts will be un-collectable, however, an overall adjustment must be made. Suppose that over the past five years one-half of 1 percent of accounts receivable have been uncollectable, but, because of current economic conditions, management estimates that 1 percent of the current accounts receivable will probably go bad. If accounts receivable on December 31 total $500,000, and there was no balance in the allowance for uncollectable accounts account, the following adjustment is in order:

> DEBIT   Est. uncollectable sales revenue $5,000
> CREDIT   Allowance for uncollectable accounts $5,000

$5,000 is charged as a decrease in revenue for the year even though none of these accounts has yet gone bad. In a way, a reserve is created against which accounts can be charged if they go bad. If one of this year's accounts receivable should go bad in a future year the following entry is made:

> DEBIT   Allowance for uncollectable accounts   xxxx
> CREDIT   Accounts receivable   xxxx

Because there is no effect on revenue and expense at the time of write-off, the write-off does not affect net income for the year when the write-off is made. It is quite unlikely that exactly $5,000 of these accounts receivable will go bad. Should the amount of the allowance account become too large or too small, it can be easily increased or decreased.

Allowance for uncollectable accounts is a permanent account and is shown in the balance sheet as a deduction from the gross amount of accounts receivable as follows:

Accounts receivable	$500,000	
Less: Allowance for uncollectable accounts	5,000	
Net Accounts receivable		$495,000

Inventory

Inventory management, which includes inventory valuation, is covered in some detail in Chapter 15. At this point we will simply show the impact of different approaches to inventory valuation.

Common sense dictates that a physical count of inventory be made at least once a year. Determining the physical count of items in inventory is the first step in the valuation process. The second step involves the costing of inventory items—putting a price tag on these items. Most businessmen prefer to show a low inventory valuation, because, as we have seen, inventory valuation has a direct impact on net income.

In most instances it is impossible to determine the cost value of inventory items. Frequently an inventory is made up of items purchased at different times and at different prices. Consequently, various cost flow assumptions are made. Two of the more common assumptions are discussed in the paragraphs following.

First in, first out (FIFO).   Under this assumption, as goods are sold they are expensed at the oldest price actually paid. This means that those items remaining in inventory at year's end will carry the most recent price. During periods of rising prices this approach results in an inventory valuation more in line with current cost.

Last in, first out (LIFO).   Under this assumption, as goods are sold they are expensed at the latest price actually paid. Note that here we are discussing cost flow and not the physical movement of goods. Logic dictates in many instances that the oldest goods be used first. The goods that remain in inventory will carry the oldest price. During periods of rising prices this approach results in a relatively low inventory valuation when compared with FIFO.

Long-term Assets

These are long-life assets and their cost should be spread over their useful life as an expense. It would be unrealistic to charge the cost of a $100,000 machine to one year's operation if its useful life is estimated to be ten years.

Business firms are allowed to charge off a portion of their long term assets each year by a process called depreciation. Land cannot be depreciated, but buildings, machinery, and equipment can. The amount that can be depreciated is limited to its cost less salvage value. If our $100,000 machine required a major overhaul costing $50,000 or so, a total of $150,000 could be depreciated.

There are a number of ways that depreciation can be calculated, but basically the difference in method relates to the speed with which an asset is depreciated. Some common approaches to depreciation follow.

Straight-line method.   Here, annual depreciation is constant in absolute terms and is determined by dividing the amount to be depreciated by the years of useful life. Thus, if the cost of an asset is $130,000, its estimated salvage value is $10,000 and its estimated useful life is 15 years, $8,000 in depreciation would be taken each year: ($130,000 - $10,000) ÷ 15 = $8,000.

This approach to depreciation considers that an asset decreases in value as a function of time only. It does not take into consideration the possible decline in utility of the asset caused by usage.

Depreciation based on production. The best measure of useful life of an asset might be production hours or units of production. In this case the amount to be depreciated is divided by production hours or production units. From the example given earlier, if $120,000 needed to be depreciated over 100,000 units of production, the depreciation would be $1.20 per unit of production. Thus, if in the first year 10,000 units are manufactured the depreciation to be charged would be $12,000.

Sum of the years' digits. This approach accelerates depreciation during the early years and charges less in the late years. If a machine had an estimated life of ten years, 10/55 of the total value to be depreciated would be charged the first year, 9/55 during the second, 8/55 during the third year, and so on. The sum of the digits one through ten is 55.

All that depreciation does is to allocate the depreciable value of an asset over a number of years or over a volume of production. Depreciation is not a process that puts a "current" value on an asset. The adjusting entry to record depreciation is

DEBIT   Depreciation expense   xxxx
CREDIT   Accumulated depreciation   xxxx

Accumulated depreciation is shown in the position statement as a deduction from the asset's involved such as

Machinery	$350,000
Less: Accumulated depreciation	250,000
Machinery, net	$100,000

Two additional observations are pertinent here. The relation between the cost of an asset and the accumulated depreciation may be an indicator of the useful life remaining for the asset. In the illustration given, less than 30 percent of the useful life of machinery remains—it may be getting old.

There are many instances where fully depreciated assets are of considerable value to the firm, yet they have a book value of zero. A precision lathe may have completed its useful life in the tool room yet may be a valuable machine for the maintenance department. Conceivably, a manufacturing organization could be operating at a profit with fixed assets that had no book value at all.

Impact of depreciation methods. Alternate depreciation methods have no impact on the total dollar value that will be depreciated over the life of an asset. Different methods will yield different annual depreciation amounts. Table 2-4 shows the difference in annual depreciation and book value under straight-line and sum of the years' digits methods. A machine cost $220,000 and has an estimated salvage value of $20,000. Its estimated useful life is five years.

Table 2-4 illustrates several things. First, the annual depreciation, which is an expense for the year, varies considerably, and consequently the net book value of the asset at the end of each of the first four years also varies. (Net book value of a fixed asset is its acquisition cost minus total accumulated depreciation.) At the end

TABLE   2-4

Impact of Depreciation Methods

Year	Percentage/ fraction	Annual depreciation	Accumulated depreciation	Net book value
		Straight-line depreciation		
1	20%	$40,000	$ 40,000	$160,000
2	20	40,000	80,000	120,000
3	20	40,000	120,000	80,000
4	20	40,000	160,000	40,000
5	20	40,000	200,000	0
		Sum of the years' digits		
1	5/15	$66,667	$ 66,667	$133,333
2	4/15	53,333	120,000	80,000
3	3/15	40,000	160,000	40,000
4	2/15	26,667	186,667	13,333
5	1/15	13,333	200,000	0

of five years the net book value of the asset is zero in each case, and no further depreciation can be taken. This does not mean that the asset has lost all its value. If for some reason the firm were able to sell a fully depreciated asset for $50,000, the buyer could depreciate the $50,000 minus any scrap value. However, the firm that sold a fully depreciated machine for $50,000 would have to report a gain on the sale of an asset and show it as "other revenue" in the income statement.

The process of adjusting a firm's books of account at the end of an accounting period is frequently much more involved than our illustrations imply. Our purpose has been to show that there is such a process and to give some indication of the bases on which adjustments are made.

SUMMARY

Managers are very concerned with the firm's profitability and financial condition because each throws light on the effectiveness of business operation. But the basic financial statements—the balance sheet and the income statement—probably will not tell management what it needs to know to evaluate the firm's performance. To fully appreciate what these statements mean, management must have an understanding of how these statements were developed and be provided benchmarks for comparison.

The income statement shows revenue, expenses, and profit (loss) when certain theories of revenue and expense measurement are applied. But other theories can produce different results. Many people think that the balance sheet shows the market value of a firm, but this is not the case. A balance sheet only describes the firm's financial position when certain accounting conventions were used. Because of this financial statements as currently prepared may be of limited value to management as sources of information. It is imperative that good communication exist between the accounting people and management.

KEY TERMS

accounting equation	current liability
accounts payable	depreciation
accounts receivable	income statement
accrual basis of accounting	long-term debt
current asset	owner equity

1. "In our society, accounting is a multi-purpose activitiy." Explain the significance of this statement.

2. Distinguish between an income statement and a statement of financial position.

3. Distinguish between a current asset and a long-term asset.

4. Why is the relationship between current assets and current liabilities important?

5. Why must the value of assets as shown on the statement of financial condition be taken "with a grain of salt"? Explain asset by asset.

6. Would the value of a liability need to be taken "with a grain of salt"? Explain.

7. What separate accounts comprise the owner equity section of the statement of financial position?

8. What are retained earnings?

9. If a financial statement shows owner equity to be $100,000, just what does this number mean?

10. What is the basic accounting equation?

11. How does the accountant determine the specific accounts that will be needed to record transactions?

12. Point out the major differences between the cash and accrual bases of accounting.

13. How is it that the cash basis for accounting provides some flexibility to the businessman in the matter of measuring income for an accounting period?

14. Every attempt should be made to match revenue and expense. Explain this statement and show the importance of this concept.

15. Might it be detrimental to a firm to strive for a zero credit loss position? Explain.

16. What two factors should be considered in an analysis of a firm's accounts receivable?

17. What is the purpose of the allowance for uncollectable accounts account?

18. When accounts receivable actually go bad, does this actually reduce the firm's current assets? Explain.

19. In a period of rising prices, what impact does first-in, first-out inventory valuation have on net income? Explain.

20. "The book value of a long-term assets tends to equal its market value at any point in time." Do you agree? Explain.

21. Why is prepaid insurance considered an asset?

PROBLEMS

1. Recording transactions

Indicate the account that should be debited and the account that should be credited to record the following (not necessarily related) transactions:

   a. Purchased a piece of land for $50,000 cash.
   b. Purchased merchandise inventory on account costing $20,000.
   c. Borrowed $25,000 from a bank giving the bank a 30-day note.
   d. Sold merchandise inventory on account for $25,000.
   e. Received $1,000 for rent of an office in the building.
   f. Paid the light bill amounting to $250.
   g. Invested an additional $10,000 cash in the business.
   h. Paid wages of $1,250.
   i. Sold merchandise inventory for $18,500 cash.
   j. Withdrew $1,000 for personal use.

2. Adjusting entries

Indicate the accounts to be debited and credited to record the following adjustments on December 31:

   a. Rent of the building for the month of December has not been recorded or paid.
   b. A portion of the accounts receivable are expected to be uncollectable.
   c. Only one-half of the insurance premium paid should be considered an expense for the year. The balance of the premium covers next year.
   d. Depreciation of the machinery must be recorded.
   e. Wages were earned by the workers during the last week of the month but have not been paid.
   f. The firm is holding an interest-bearing note from a customer which falls due next week.

3. Types of accounts

Identify, where applicable, the following items as (A) assets, (L) liabilities, (OE) owner equity, (R) revenue, and (E) expense.

   a. Land owned by the company.
   b. Cash sales
   c. Accounts receivable
   d. Capital stock
   e. Merchandise inventory
   f. Plant and equipment owned by the company
   g. Retained earnings
   h. Efficient management
   i. Cost of merchandise sold

j. Paid-in capital
k. Cost of heating the building
l. Accounts payable
m. Gross margin
n. Salaries paid
o. Salaries payable
p. Credit sales
q. Sales orders received but not yet shipped
r. Borrowing money from a bank
s. Purchases
t. Cost of goods sold

4.   Retained earnings

The Shakey Company started in business in 19X6. The annual net income (loss) for each year of operation is as follows. Assuming that no dividends have been paid, what is the balance of retained earnings at the end of 19X8?

	Net income (loss)
19X6	$(45,000)
19X7	5,000
19X8	50,000

5.   Cost of goods sold account

Given the following information, determine the year-end inventory balance.

Sales	$2,500
Inventory, beginning	200
Gross margin	600
Purchases for the year	2,200

6.   Financial statements

From the following information prepare in good form a balance sheet and an income statement.

Cash	$150
Sales and administrative expenses	100
Inventory, beginning	100
Accounts receivable	300

Retained earnings,	
beginning of the year	500
Property and plant, net	600
Sales	650
Accounts payable	200
Capital stock	250
Inventory, ending	450
Purchases	700
Notes payable	350

7. Financial statement relationships

For the following three independent cases fill in the missing information:

	Case A	Case B	Case C
Assets (ending balance)	$105	$150	$50
Liabilities (ending balance)	____	40	15
Capital stock (beginning balance)	40	30	20
Capital stock (ending balance)	60	30	25
Dividends paid during the year	11	11	____
Net income	____	15	____
Sales	____	115	50
Expenses	70	____	40
Retained earnings (beginning balance)	20	____	8
Retained earnings (ending balance)	18	____	____

8. Cost of goods sold accounts

Given the following information, what is the amount of ending inventory?

Gross margin	30%
Inventory, beginning	$ 750
Purchases	650
Sales	1,000

9. Depreciation methods

At the beginning of the year, Newport purchased an automatic turret lathe for $15,000. It is estimated that this lathe will be used for four years and will then be sold for $5,000.

Required:

a. Compute the annual depreciation for each of the four years using (1) straight-line depreciation and (2) sum of the years' digits depreciation.

b. What is the net book value of the machine for each of the four years under both methods?

10.   Inventory valuation

The Yankee Corporation wants to know its ending inventory and cost of goods sold. The firm's records for the year showed the following:

No beginning inventory	
Purchases	
March 15	1,000 units @ $10
June 22	2,000 units @ $ 9
July 8	500 units @ $11
October 3	300 units @ $ 8
December 24	500 units @ $12
Ending inventory	750 units

Required:

a. Using the first-in, first-out cost flow assumption, what is Yankee's cost of goods sold and ending inventory for the period?

b. Repeat the problem using the last-in, first-out cost flow assumption.

11.   Depreciation methods

Flower purchased a machine on January 2, 19X9 for $120,000. It was estimated that the useful life of the machine would be ten years and that it would have a salvage value of $10,000.

Required:

a. Calculate the first two years' depreciation expense for this machine using straight-line depreciation.

b. Repeat the calculations using the sum of the years' digits.

c. Repeat the requirement using the production method. It is estimated that the machine will produce 18,000 units the first year, 12,000 units the second year, and 10,000 units for each of the next eight years.

12.   Financial statements

The following is the trial balance of North Harwich Consolidated Industries, Inc.

North Harwich Consolidated Industries, Inc.
Trial Balance, December 31, 19XX

	Debits	Credits
Cash	$ 36,275	
Accounts receivable	124,845	
Merchandise inventory, beginning	219,615	
Marketable securities	12,500	
Land and buildings	175,000	
Equipment	84,500	
Accounts payable		$ 31,950
Notes payable		15,000
Taxes payable		48,950
Mortgage payable		75,000
Capital stock, common		250,000
Retained earnings		212,500
Sales		985,400
Purchases	485,900	
Salaries and wages	241,100	
Office expense	84,920	
Advertising	85,000	
Interest expense	6,000	
Building expense	57,580	
Insurance expense	5,565	
	$1,618,800	$1,618,800

The merchandise inventory on December 31 was $240,000.

Required:

a. Prepare an income statement.

b. Prepare a statement of financial position.

13. Impact of inventory valuation

Refer to Problem 12. If, for some reason, the value of the December 31 merchandise inventory had been stated as $225,000 instead of $240,000, what bearing would this have had on each financial statement? As before, if the value of the inventory had been stated as $250,000?

14. The accounting cycle

The following is the statement of financial position for the True Blue Corporation.

True Blue Corporation
Statement of Financial Position, December 31, 19X4

Assets

Current assets

Cash		$ 12,000	
Accounts receivable		48,000	
Inventory		82,000	
Total current assets			$142,000

Long-term assets

Land and building	$290,000		
Less accumulated depreciation	100,000	$190,000	
Machinery	$146,000		
Less accumulated depreciation	62,000	84,000	
Total long-term assets			$274,000
Total assets			$416,000

Liabilities and owner equity

Current liabilities

Accounts payable	$ 64,000		
Notes payable	40,000		
Taxes payable	18,000		
Total current liabilities		$122,000	

Long-term liabilities

Bonds payable (8%)		100,000	
Total liabilities			$222,000

Owner equity

Common stock		$150,000	
Retained earnings		44,000	
Total owner equity			$194,000
Total liabilities and owner equity			$416,000

During the year 19X5 the following summarized transactions took place:

1.	Sales on account	$850,000
2.	Purchases (added to inventory)	400,000
3.	Cost of goods sold	420,000
4.	Accounts receivable collections	860,000
5.	Accounts payable paid	440,000
6.	The interest on bonds and taxes payable were paid	
7.	Purchased machinery for cash	100,000
8.	Sold additional shares of stock	100,000
9.	Paid operating expenses	250,000
10.	Paid on note payable	5,000
11.	Depreciation of building	10,000
12.	Depreciation of machinery	22,000
13.	Paid administrative salaries	80,000
14.	Declared and paid a dividend	20,000

Forty percent of net income before taxes is set aside for income taxes.

Required:

a. Prepare a statement of financial position as of December 31, 19X5.

b. Prepare an income statement for the year 19X5.

15. Adjusting entries

Prepare journal entries indicating the accounts and the amount to be debited and credited to record the following adjustments on December 31:

a. A new truck was purchased on March 1 for $6,000. The truck has an estimated life of five years at which time it will have an expected trade-in value of $1,000. Assume (1) straight-line depreciation and (2) sum of the years' digits depreciation.

b. A 6 percent note for $4,000 was received from a customer on December 1 in payment of an account.

c. A premium of $3,000 was paid on July 1 for a three-year fire insurance policy. On July 1 prepaid insurance was debited $3,000.

d. As above, assume that insurance expense account was debited $3,000 on July 1.

e. Accounts receivable balance, $800,000; allowance for doubtful accounts should equal 2½ percent of accounts receivable. The present balance is $8,500.

f. There are five employees who are paid $300 per week each. This year December 31 falls on a Wednesday and the pay period ends on the following Friday.

16.   Adjusting entries and financial statements

The trial balance of the Pinedell Corporation for the year was

Pinedell Corporation
Trial Balance, December 31, 19XX

Cash	$ 45,000	
Accounts receivable	155,000	
Notes receivable	5,000	
Merchandise inventory, beginning	200,000	
Prepaid insurance	6,000	
Land	50,000	
Building	300,000	
Machinery	500,000	
Accounts payable		$ 40,000
Accrued taxes payable		12,000
Mortgage payable		250,000
Capital stock		600,000
Retained earnings		140,000
Sales		924,000
Sales salaries expense	165,000	
Merchandise purchases	400,000	
Advertising expense	50,000	
Administrative expenses	80,000	
Supplies expense	5,000	
Miscellaneous expenses	5,000	
	$1,966,000	$1,966,000

Additional information on December 31 is

    a. Merchandise inventory, $200,000
    b. Insurance expense, $2,000
    c. Interest earned on note receivable, $200
    d. Depreciation of building is 2½ percent per annum
    e. Depreciation of machinery is 10 percent per annum
    f. Sales salaries earned but not paid are $3,500
    g. It is expected that 2½ percent of accounts receivable will be uncollectable.

Required:

a. Prepare an income statement and a statement of financial position using Tables 2-1 and 2-2 as guides.

3 Financial Analysis

CHAPTER OVERVIEW

The purpose of this chapter is to explore the ways in which financial information can be used to learn more about the effectiveness of a firm's management. This chapter deals with the subject of financial analysis which, in part, involves a number of comparisons—either horizontal or vertical. Horizontal comparisons relate to changes in the same activity, for example, sales in 19X1 versus sales in 19X2. Vertical analysis involves, for example, the asset section of the balance sheet and considers such things as the relation between current assets and long-term assets or inventory as a percentage of current assets.

We also consider changes in the financial position of the firm by measuring changes in the firm's working capital. Finally, we explore the impact of inflation on the measurement of profit and in expressing the value of the firm.

QUESTIONS FOR CONSIDERATION

1. How can ratio analysis help managers to learn more about the effectiveness of their operating plan?
2. What weaknesses do financial statements have as a source of information?
3. Have the firm's assets been used as effectively this year as last?
4. Has the firm's financial position improved or deteriorated during the past year?
5. How does inflation make the measurement of profit and establishing the value of the company more difficult?

The financial information that concerns us in this chapter comes from the firm's basic financial statements. We want to learn as much as possible from a firm's income statement, statement of financial position (balance sheet), and any other reports to uncover strengths and weaknesses that must be considered in formulating plans for the period ahead. At the outset we must recognize that these statements are basically historic documents and hence may be of limited value in the planning process. The conditions that led to a particular net income and financial position may not, for a variety of reasons, prevail in the period ahead. However, documents that may have limited use are often better than no documents at all.

We must recognize too that several groups have need for financial information and that informational needs will vary. The bank loan officer who expects payment of a note in 30 days has different information needs than the bank loan officer who is considering the granting of a 5-year loan. One group of managers in the firm may be primarily concerned for the inflow and outflow of cash whereas another group of managers may be primarily concerned for setting and attaining budgeted profits. Thus all of the discussions in this chapter may not be relevant to the information needs of all managers in the firm.

BASES FOR COMPARISON

Financial statements such as those in Tables 2-1 and 2-2 are of limited value as sources of information because they simply summarize what has happened by using certain accounting conventions. A cash balance of $100,000 or a sales volume of $1,000,000 means little or nothing by itself. Actual happenings must be compared to some benchmark; comparisons are the heart of financial analysis. A benchmark could be the financial statements of a previous period, the financial statements of a competitor, or the firm's pro forma financial statements. Pro forma financial statements are a forecast of results if a particular budget or plan is followed.

Comparisons are made to evaluate past performance and to provide a basis for making decisions. Management seeks indicators of why goals were or were not achieved, and it seeks to identify trends that may be useful in the planning process. Thus financial analysis requires that comparisons be made over a period of years. This presents a number of problems because conditions do change over time. Management must consider the impact of inflation on the dollar values used. An increase of 15 percent in sales dollars from one year to the next will probably only reflect a 2 percent or 3 percent real increase due to the inflation factor. There may be changes in accounting methods which can obscure the significance of change such as a shift from FIFO (first-in, first-out) to LIFO (last-in, first-out) inventory valuation. Or the firm may have sold or added a division. Such events do not negate the value of financial analysis, they merely complicate the process.

Horizontal Analysis

Horizontal analysis is shown in Tables 3-1 and 3-2. The mechanics of the process are very simple. Year 19X1 is the base year which is compared to the latest year, 19X2. The dollar differences are identified and divided by the base year values to obtain the percentage difference. Thus the increase in accounts receivable in 19X2 is 24 percent ($90,000 ÷ $375,000) above 19X1 accounts receivable. But percentage changes are not the answers we need; they are merely attention getters or signals that investigation may be in order. The cash balance decreased 31 percent, but we cannot tell from this if the change is significant. If the decrease is the result of slower collections of accounts receivable, an investigation should be made to find out why. Are some of the customers in financial trouble? When, if ever, can we expect payment from them? If the decrease is the result of a management decision to purchase more materials than is normal to obtain a cost advantage, the reason for a lower cash balance may be self-evident. Thus the 31 percent decrease in cash merely signals that investigation is necessary.

Major changes in activity generally warrant special consideration as in the case of the 82 percent increase in inventory. Inasmuch as sales increased only 14 percent, this figure appears to be out of line. If the firm in question is a manufacturer who produces the inventory, $263,000 more of the current year's manufacturing cost is in inventory and classified as an asset than was the case a year ago. This, as is explained in Chapter 9, can impact on the firm's net income. It could be that the bulk of the net income shown is due to the increase in inventory level.

This example illustrates the impact of maintaining a larger

TABLE 3-1

Horizontal Corporation
Balance Sheets,
December 31, 19X1 and 19X2

	19X1	19X2	Change Dollar	%
Assets				
Current Assets:				
Cash	$ 124,000	$ 86,000	$ (38,000)	(31)%
Accounts receivable, net	375,000	465,000	90,000	24
Inventories	322,000	585,000	263,000	82
Prepaid expenses	29,000	24,000	(5,000)	(17)
Total Current Assets	850,000	1,160,000	310,000	25
Long-term Assets:				
Land	50,000	50,000	0	0
Buildings	340,000	320,000	(20,000)	(6)
Machinery and equipment	280,000	240,000	(40,000)	(14)
Furniture and fixtures	130,000	120,000	(10,000)	(8)
Total Long-term Assets	800,000	730,000	(70,000)	(9)
Total Assets	$1,650,000	$1,890,000	$240,000	15
Liabilities and owner equity				
Current Liabilities:				
Accounts payable	$ 260,000	$ 334,000	$ 74,000	28
Notes payable	80,000	60,000	(20,000)	(25)
Taxes payable	58,000	64,000	6,000	10
Total Current Liabilities	398,000	458,000	60,000	15
Long-term Liabilities:				
Bonds payable (9%)	400,000	400,000	0	0
Total Liabilities	798,000	858,000	60,000	8
Owner Equity:				
Common stock	600,000	600,000	0	0
Retained earnings	252,000	432,000	180,000	71
Total Owner Equity	852,000	1,032,000	180,000	21
Total Liabilities and Owner Equity	$1,650,000	$1,890,000	$240,000	15

TABLE   3-2

Horizontal Corporation
Income Statements
For the years 19X1 and 19X2

	19X1	19X2	Change Dollar	%
Sales	$2,200,000	$2,500,000	$300,000	14%
Less: Cost of goods sold	1,482,000	1,690,000	208,000	14
Gross Margin	$ 718,000	$ 810,000	$ 92,000	13
Operating Expenses:				
Selling	420,000	360,000	(60,000)	(14)
Administrative	250,000	150,000	(100,000)	(40)
Total Operating Expense	670,000	510,000	(160,000)	(24)
Net income before taxes	48,000	300,000	252,000	521
Income taxes (40%)	19,200	120,000	100,800	525
Net Income	$ 28,800	$ 180,000	$151,200	525

inventory, but it does not identify the reasons for it. A larger inventory can be justified if sales are expected to increase, if the firm expects labor trouble and a shutdown of facilities, or if costs of material, labor, and other manufacturing items are expected to increase significantly in the near future. But a larger inventory may not be justified if the production manager simply decided that the resulting lower unit production costs are more important than good inventory management.

One by one each item in the financial statements should be examined to determine the cause of the change. If this is not done, Tables 3-1 and 3-2 are not very valuable documents for the operating manager.

Vertical Analysis

Vertical analysis presents a different view of a firm's financial statements and signals different strengths and weaknesses. Vertical analysis is shown in Tables 3-3 and 3-4 which are common-size financial statements; that is, each item is expressed as a percentage of the total. Again, the mechanics of preparing common-size state-

TABLE 3-3

Vertical Corporation
Balance Sheets,
December 31, 19X1 and 19X2

	19X1	19X2	% of Total 19X1	19X2
Assets				
Current Assets:				
Cash	$ 124,000	$ 86,000	7.5%	4.6%
Accounts receivable, net	375,000	465,000	22.7	24.6
Inventories	322,000	585,000	19.5	31.0
Prepaid expenses	29,000	24,000	1.7	1.3
Total Current Assets	850,000	1,160,000	51.5	61.5
Long-term Assets:				
Land	50,000	50,000	3.0	2.6
Buildings	340,000	320,000	20.6	16.9
Machinery	280,000	240,000	17.0	12.7
Furniture and fixtures	130,000	120,000	7.9	6.3
Total Long-term Assets	800,000	730,000	48.5	38.5
Total Assets	$1,650,000	$1,890,000	100.0%	100.0%
Liabilities and owner equity:				
Current Liabilities:				
Accounts payable	$ 260,000	$ 334,000	15.8%	17.6%
Notes payable	80,000	60,000	4.8	3.2
Taxes payable	58,000	64,000	3.5	3.4
Total Current Liabilities	398,000	458,000	24.1	24.2
Long-term Liabilities:				
Bonds payable (9%)	400,000	400,000	24.2	21.2
Total Liabilities	798,000	858,000	48.3	45.4
Owner Equity:				
Common stock	600,000	600,000	36.4	31.7
Retained earnings	252,000	432,000	15.3	22.9
Total Owner Equity	852,000	1,032,000	51.7	54.6
Total Liabilities and Owner Equity	$1,650,000	$1,890,000	100.0%	100.0%

TABLE 3-4

Vertical Corporation
Income Statements
For the years 19X1 and 19X2

	19X1	19X2	% of Total 19X1	% of Total 19X2
Sales	$2,200,000	$2,500,000	100.0%	100.0%
Less: Cost of goods sold	1,482,000	1,690,000	67.4	67.6
Gross Margin	$ 718,000	$ 810,000	32.6	32.4
Operating Expenses:				
Selling	420,000	360,000	19.1	14.4
Administrative	250,000	150,000	11.4	6.0
Total Operating Expense	670,000	510,000	30.5	20.4
Net income before taxes	48,000	300,000	2.1	12.0
Income taxes (40%)	19,200	120,000	.8	4.8
Net Income	$ 28,800	$ 180,000	1.3	7.2

ments is simple. Every asset value is expressed as a percentage of total assets and every equity value is expressed as a percentage of total equities. In the income statement, every value is expressed as a percentage of sales.

A number of percentage of total changes stand out that perhaps warrant investigation. There has been a major shift in the balance between current assets and long-term assets that appears to be caused by an inventory-building decision and a decision not to replace long-term assets. There may be good answers for these decisions, but an outsider might wonder if the firm's management is more concerned with the present than with the future. On the surface an increase in net income of over 500 percent may look good, but an analyst may have reservations. Net income before taxes increased $252,000, whereas sales increased $300,000 and this is hardly a normal occurrence.

Further investigation reveals that operating expenses decreased from 30 percent to 20 percent of sales, and this is hardly normal. Such a drastic change could be a sign of strength or a sign of weakness. If the decrease resulted from the removal of "deadwood" in the organization and thus improved operating efficiency, so much the better. If the decrease resulted from a reduction in advertising and promotion efforts or if there are a number of management jobs that are not currently staffed, the firm may have to pay a price for that somewhere down the road.

RATIO ANALYSIS

A somewhat different view of a firm's financial position and financial performance can be obtained through ratio analysis. Ratios are another form of comparison that can be expressed as a percentage, a rate, or a quotient. The mechanics of ratio analysis are simple, but the effective use of ratios demands judgment. If a college has 1,000 students and 50 faculty members, the ratio of faculty to students is 1 to 20, and the ratio of students to faculty is 20 to 1. Whether this ratio is good or significant cannot be determined until the consequences of such a ratio is studied. Ratios have more meaning when compared with some benchmark. The benchmark could be the trend of a ratio over time, or it could be an industry average for firms of like size. Table 3-5 shows a number of typical ratios prepared and published by Dun & Bradstreet, Inc.

Ratio analysis is conducted to serve the purposes of several groups both within the firm and outside. Stockholders or potential investors are interested in such ratios as earnings per share, price-earnings ratio, net income to sales, and dividend payout. Operating managers are generally more concerned for ratios that measure the firm's ability to meet obligations and the effectiveness with which assets have been used. Our concern is for these two categories of ratios.

Ratios: Ability to Meet Obligations

Managers and creditors alike are interested in the firm's ability to meet obligations as they become due. The current ratio and the acid-test or quick ratio are commonly used for this purpose.

The current ratio.   This ratio compares a firm's current assets and current liabilities. It is expressed as follows:

$$\text{Current ratio} = \frac{\text{Current assets}}{\text{Current liabilities}}$$

TABLE   3-5

Some Typical Ratios

Business	Net profit to sales, times	Current ratio, times	Sales to inventory, times	Collection period, days
Manufacturing:				
Auto parts, etc.	4.55	2.52	5.8	40
Industrial chemicals	6.08	2.09	7.3	44
Drugs	5.93	2.94	6.5	44
Machine shops	2.08	4.28	11.7	43
Wholesalers:				
Auto parts, etc.	1.65	2.68	4.6	35
Drugs	1.64	2.58	6.7	34
Fruits and produce	0.90	2.72	50.5	15
Groceries	0.58	2.17	10.9	14
Hardware	1.48	2.98	4.6	41
Retailers:				
Department stores	2.18	3.37	5.4	*
Lumber and building	1.89	3.72	5.0	57
Women's specialty	1.91	2.45	6.7	*
Groceries, independent	1.30	1.97	16.6	*
Furniture	2.39	3.19	4.8	110

*Insufficient data.

Source: Adapted from *Key Business Ratios* prepared by Dun & Bradstreet, Inc., 1975.

Thus in the Horizontal Corporation (Table 3-1) the current ratio for 19X1 was 2.14 to 1, and in 19X2 it was 2.53 to 1. From a creditor's point of view this indicates a small improvement in the firm's ability to meet short-term obligations. From management's point of view having fewer dollars tied up in current assets may be more desirable. Current ratios vary considerably from industry to industry as shown in Table 3-5, and they may also vary significantly from season to season within the firm.

The acid-test ratio. This ratio compares the firm's most liquid assets and current liabilities. Generally the total of a firm's current assets minus inventories is compared with current liabilities. It is expressed as follows:

$$\text{Acid-test ratio} = \frac{\text{Current assets} - \text{inventories}}{\text{Current liabilities}}$$

Thus in the Horizontal Corporation (Table 3-1) the acid-test ratio for 19X1 was 1.25 to 1, and in 19X2 it was 1.20 to 1. The acid-test ratio is a more conservative measure than the current ratio because it removes inventory from consideration. The speed with which inventories are sold and converted into cash varies considerably; thus this ratio describes a firm's debt-paying ability over a shorter time span than the current ratio.

Ratios: Use of Assets

The purpose of these ratios is to measure the effectiveness with which a firm's resources are employed. More specifically, these ratios compare sales volume with a number of investments.

Plant-turnover ratio.   This ratio compares a firm's sales revenue with the dollar investment in plant and equipment required to generate that revenue. The plant-turnover ratio is expressed as follows:

$$\text{Plant-turnover ratio} = \frac{\text{Sales revenue}}{\text{Investment}}$$

The Horizontal Corporation had the following plant-turnover ratios:

In 19X1 it was $2,200,000 ÷ $800,000, or 2.75 times.

In 19X2 it was $2,500,000 ÷ $730,000, or 3.42 times.

Thus in 19X1 each dollar of investment generated $2.75 of sales revenue (investment turned over 2.75 times). In 19X2 each dollar of investment generated $3.42 in sales revenue. This appears to be an improvement—a 24 percent improvement—but, as noted earlier, the firm has not invested in new facilities during the past year, and this rate of "improvement" may not continue for long.

Plant turnover ratios vary drastically from firm to firm and from industry to industry. A firm that rents facilities will show a higher plant-turnover ratio than a firm that owns its facilities. Table 4-3 shows the assets employed and sales revenues for several large firms. Note that IBM in a recent year had $15 billion plus in investment and sales of $14 billion plus. Thus each dollar in assets generated less than one dollar of sales revenue. IBM is a technology-oriented company that must continue to invest in newer, better, and more adaptive equipment.

Return on investment.   A basic weakness of the plant-turnover ratio is that it emphasizes sales volume generated per dollar of investment and ignores profit. The return on investment ratio (ROI) compares net income and the total assets of the firm. The purpose of this comparison is to measure the profit earned per dollar of investment. The value of this ratio is that it provides a common denominator of the effectiveness with which assets are employed. It can be used to compare performance between divisions of the firm and to evaluate investment opportunities. The ROI ratio is expressed as follows:

$$\text{ROI} = \frac{\text{Net income}}{\text{Total assets}}$$

The ROI for the Horizontal Corporation for the year 19X2 is calculated as follows:

$$\text{ROI} = \frac{\$180,000}{(\$1,650,000 + \$1,890,000)/2} = \frac{\$180,000}{\$1,770,000} = 10.2\%$$

In other words, each dollar of assets generated 10.2 cents of profit in 19X2.

Inventory turnover.   Inventory turnover is important for a number of reasons. If inventory does not turn over at a satisfactory rate, it will decrease in value. A fruit and produce operation needs a turnover of about once a week (see Table 3-5) to protect inventory value. Style-related and fad items also should have a relatively high inventory turnover. Inventory is but one phase of a cycle that must take place in any manufacturing firm. Cash must be expended for material, labor, and other manufacturing costs to produce goods, goods must be sold to create receivables, and receivables must be collected to generate more cash so that the cycle can be repeated, perhaps at a higher level of activity. Thus, if inventories do not turn over at the desired rate, the cycle is slowed and growth may be impeded. Inventory turnover is expressed as follows:

$$\text{Inventory turnover} = \frac{\text{Cost of goods sold}}{\text{Average inventory}}$$

In our illustration, inventory turnover for 19X2 is 3.7 times per year computed as follows:

$$\text{Inventory turnover} = \frac{\$1{,}690{,}000}{(\$322{,}000 + \$585{,}000)/2} \quad \text{or 3.7 times per year}$$

It has been suggested that a high inventory turnover is preferred by management, but this must be qualified. We must consider how a high inventory turnover is obtained. A high inventory turnover can come from effective merchandising, and it can result from selling merchandise at giveaway prices.

Receivables turnover. As indicated, receivables are part of a cycle, and unless they are collected as planned the cycle slows down. The turnover of receivables compares credit sales and the average balance of accounts receivable. It is expressed as follows:

$$\text{Receivables turnover} = \frac{\text{Credit sales}}{\text{Average receivables}}$$

In our illustration the receivables turnover is 5.9 times per year (we have assumed that all sales are credit sales), computed as follows:

$$\text{Receivables turnover} = \frac{\$2{,}500{,}000}{(\$375{,}000 + \$465{,}000)/2} \quad \text{or 5.9 times per year}$$

Receivables have turned over an average of once every two months or approximately once every 60 days.

This data can be used to observe another characteristic of accounts receivable. If we divide average accounts receivable by credit sales, we will obtain the portion of the year's sales that are still unpaid. Multiplying this by 365 days tells us the average number of days that it takes to collect receivables. The following illustrates this concept.

$$\text{Average collection period} = \frac{\$420{,}000}{\$2{,}500{,}000} \quad \text{or .168 years}$$

The figure .168 years equals 61 days (.168 x 365). We can also approximate this figure in the following way. Turnover is approximately six times per year or once every 60 to 61 days. If the firm's credit terms are net/60 days, we can conclude that on an average collections are up to date. If credit terms are net/30 days we can conclude that the firm has a collection problem.

Other ratios. The use of ratios is not limited to financial statements. Sales, production, and personnel executives find ratios a convenient and reliable index to the status of their activities.

CHANGES IN FINANCIAL POSITION

Most students of business are not nearly as familiar with the statement of changes in financial position as they are with the balance sheet, income statement, or the statement of retained earnings. Prior to 1971 the inclusion of this statement with other financial statements was not mandatory, but since that date it is. The primary purpose of the statement of changes in financial position, which we will call the sources and uses of funds statement, is to identify changes in a firm's financial position that may not be apparent in the firm's balance sheet and income statement.

The funds statement focuses attention on the inflow and outflow of funds in an organization. It is more concerned with identifying liquidity than profitability. The funds statement is concerned with explaining why a firm's net working capital (current assets minus current liabilities) increased or decreased during an accounting period. It also identifies how a firm has financed its activities.

We will first identify the sources of (increases in) and the uses of (decreases in) working capital and then explain the preparation and use of a funds statement.

Funds come from

1. profitable operations
2. the sale of capital stock
3. the sale of noncurrent assets such as buildings, machinery, and patents
4. long-term borrowing

Funds are used to

1. offset unprofitable operations
2. repurchase capital stock
3. purchase long-term assets
4. pay cash dividends

Management is vitally concerned with its sources of funds. Ultimately, profitable operation is *the* source of funds because profit is necessary to stay in business.

Basic Data Needs

The basic data needs for preparation of a funds statement are

1. comparative balance sheets
2. an income statement for the current year
3. a statement of retained earnings
4. a statement of changes in net working capital

To simplify the process, the following statements are presented in somewhat abbreviated form (Tables 3-6, 3-7, 3-8, and 3-9).

TABLE   3-6

**Barbell Corporation
Comparative Balance Sheets,
December 31, 19X1 and 19X2**

	19X1	*19X2*	*Dollar change*
Assets			
Current assets	$11,800	$13,000	$1,200
Long-term assets	11,000	13,000	2,000
Total Assets	$22,800	$26,000	$3,200
Liabilities and owner equity			
Current liabilities	$ 4,000	$ 5,000	$1,000
Long-term liabilities	2,000	2,500	500
Owner Equity:			
Capital stock	13,000	14,000	1,000
Retained earnings	3,800	4,500	700
Total Liabilities and Owner Equity	$22,800	$26,000	$3,200

TABLE 3-7

Barbell Corporation
Income Statement,
For the year ended December 31, 19X2

Sales		$50,000
Less: Cost of goods sold		30,000
Gross Margin		$20,000
Expenses:		
Operating expenses	$18,500	
Depreciation	500	19,000
Net Income		$ 1,000

TABLE 3-8

Barbell Corporation
Statement of Retained Earnings,
For the year ended December 31, 19X2

Retained earnings, January 1	$3,800
Plus: Net income	1,000
Total	4,800
Less: Cash dividend paid	300
Retained Earnings, December 31	$4,500

TABLE 3-9

Statement of Changes in Net Working Capital,
For the year ended December 31, 19X2

	19X1	19X2	Dollar change
Current assets	$11,800	$13,000	$1,200
Current liabilities	4,000	5,000	1,000
Net Working Capital	$ 7,800	$ 8,000	$ 200

Comments:

1. $2,500 was paid for new equipment.
2. Long-term debt was increased by $500.
3. A cash dividend of $300 was paid.
4. Additional capital stock was issued for $1,000.
5. Depreciation of long-term assets was $500.

Preparing the Funds Statement

In the preparation of a funds statement we do not consider either current assets or current liabilities because we are looking for the reasons as to why net working capital increased by $200. Our concern must be for noncurrent items and their impact on the flow of funds.

First we look at long-term assets and notice a net increase of $2,000. But this does not reflect the impact that the purchase of long-term assets had on the flow of funds because $500 of depreciation was recorded in 19X2. Thus, as is shown under the comments, $2,500 of funds were used to acquire long-term assets.

Long-term liabilities increased by $500, and this is a source of funds for the firm. Similarly, $1,000 of funds was received from the sale of capital stock. Retained earnings increased by $700 because operations were profitable and this is a source of funds. Finally, funds were applied to pay a dividend of $300. All this is summarized in the funds statement in Table 3-10.

It appears from this statement that the Barbell Corporation enjoyed a reasonably good financial position on December 31, 19X2. The firm increased its long-term assets substantially without a corresponding increase in debt. Because long-term assets provide the means for generating revenue, there may be a good payoff in the years ahead because of this investment.

THE IMPACT OF INFLATION

Financial analysis begins with a comparison of numbers that appear on a firm's financial statements. The numbers generated in 19X2 are compared with numbers generated in 19X1. There is nothing wrong with this process provided that the dollar is a constant measure of value. But it is not. A dollar today is the same as a dollar

TABLE 3-10

Barbell Corporation
Statement of Changes in Financial Position,
For the year ended December 31, 19X2

Sources of funds		
From Operations:		
Net income	$1,000	
Plus: Expense not requiring current funds, depreciation	500	
Total from Operations		$1,500
From the sale of capital stock		1,000
From borrowing		500
Total Sources of Funds		$3,000
Uses of funds		
To purchase equipment		$2,500
To pay cash dividend		300
Total Uses		$2,800
Increase in Net Working Capital		$ 200

ten years ago, but the value one can obtain in exchange for a dollar has decreased markedly during this time period. Thus an increase of $200 in net working capital during 19X2 is not the same as an increase of $200 in net working capital during 19X1 because current dollars have less purchasing power. Similarly, a machine that was capable of producing $60,000 worth of goods per year ten years ago now can produce $100,000 worth of goods in a year with no increase in productivity. Because of unequal dollars it is difficult, often impossible, to make meaningful comparisons.

Financial statements are prepared in part to provide the reader with meaningful information concerning the profitability of operations and the financial position of the firm, but this is not always the case. During periods of inflation a dollar of sales revenue earned in January has more purchasing power than a dollar of sales revenue earned the following December, and a beginning inventory of

$25,000 represents more salable merchandise than an ending inventory of $25,000.

The balance sheet provides a list of assets that the firm owns, and some of these assets may be 5, 10, or 20 years old; their value, therefore, is based on dollars that are equally old. Thus, when we read "Plant and equipment, $1,000,000" on a balance sheet, we know very little about its current market value because of the different-size dollars used to identify its cost. A machine purchased ten years ago and having a current book value of $20,000 may be worth much more than a newly purchased machine costing $20,000. The changing value of the dollar makes it difficult to express the current value of assets.

To a great extent, therefore, horizontal analysis (as discussed earlier) involves comparing apples and oranges because of the change in the value of the dollar. What is needed is a means for converting old dollar values into current dollar values, but this is not an easy task. One approach that has been used with some success is to restate costs based on some published index number such as the Consumer Price Index. For example, an inventory item purchased for $600 when the index number was 100 would have its value restated as $690 when the index rose to 115. If all costs are based on the same measure of purchasing power, meaningful comparisons may be made.

The major problem is to find index numbers that can accurately reflect price changes of the costs involved. In some instances this is easy, but in most instances it is not. It is easy to compare the purchasing power of $100,000 in accounts receivable today with the purchasing power of $100,000 in accounts receivable five years ago as it relates to specific commodities such as steel, grain, or cement. But a firm's assets are a collection of perhaps thousands of items purchased over a number of years, and the prices of these items may change at different rates. The end result of restating cost could be a greater distortion than existed when historical costs were used.

The purpose of this section has been to look at another problem area that management must consider. We have described the problem and have suggested how it could be handled in specific instances. But, as long as inflation continues, management will have to contend with the disparity between stated historical values and some form of current market value.

Earlier in this chapter we discussed the flow of funds to see why there were changes in the firm's net working capital during the accounting period. Methods were suggested to measure changes in the age of accounts receivable and the speed with which inventories turn over and ultimately become cash. Here we are concerned only with activities that affect cash. Because cash balances can change rapidly, a statement of cash flow is frequently prepared on a weekly or monthly basis. This statement is similar to a cash budget but different in that the budget is a forecast of cash flow and the statement of cash flow is a recapitulation of what has happened.

We present in Tables 3-11 and 3-12 the information needed to prepare a cash flow statement.

TABLE   3-11

Balance Sheets,
January 1 and January 31, 19X5

	Jan. 1	Jan. 31
Assets		
Cash	$ 15,000	$ 20,000
Accounts receivable	30,000	25,000
Marketable securities	20,000	18,000
Inventory	40,000	50,000
Long-term assets, net	80,000	92,000
Total Assets	$185,000	$205,000
Liabilities and owner equity		
Accounts payable	$ 40,000	$ 50,000
Notes payable	25,000	20,000
Accrued liabilities	21,000	20,000
Capital stock	75,000	80,000
Retained earnings	24,000	35,000
Total Liabilities and Owner Equity	$185,000	$205,000

TABLE 3-12

Income Statement,
For the month of January 19X5

Sales		$150,000
Less: Cost of goods sold		90,000
Gross Margin		$ 60,000
Operating expenses	$ 37,000	
Depreciation	8,000	45,000
Net Income		$ 15,000

Other information:

1. A dividend of $4,000 was paid.
2. Securities were sold at cost for $2,000.
3. $5,000 of capital stock was issued.
4. A machine was purchased for $20,000 cash.
5. $5,000 was paid on the note payable.

The cash flow statement given in Table 3-13 provides some very important information. A number of things done during the month cost $45,000, and each of these could be viewed as an action that strengthened the firm. However, we need to consider the means used to finance them before reaching any conclusion. Only $23,000 came from operations and the balance from sources that the firm may not be able to use in the future. The firm may have speeded up pay-

TABLE 3-13

Cash Flow Statement

What was done (uses)		How it was financed (sources)	
Increased cash	$ 5,000	Reduced receivables	$ 5,000
Increased inventory	10,000	Sold securities	2,000
Purchased machine	20,000	Increased payables	10,000
Paid dividends	4,000	Issued stock	5,000
Paid on note	5,000	Contributed from	
Reduced accruals	1,000	operations	23,000
	$45,000		$45,000

ments of accounts receivable and postponed its accounts payable obligation. Over the long run, activities must be financed by profitable operations and cash.

SUMMARY

Management uses financial information to test the pulse of the business organization. The analysis of financial information always involves two steps. The first is mechanical and involves a number of comparisons such as current assets and current liabilities or sales revenue generated by each dollar of investment. The purpose of this step is to obtain indicators that things are moving satisfactorily or otherwise. If a particular ratio is abnormal, by management's standards, it can be a signal to investigate the causes of the deviation. The second step involves the investigation of areas that seem to be out of line. The purpose of the investigation should be to justify the causes of change or to prepare a basis for corrective action.

Profit is essential for the perpetuation of any business, but profit alone is not enough. Attention must be given to the flow of funds through the organization. Profit cannot be used to pay a firm's bills; payment of bills requires funds. Thus management must analyze its funds flow to test its liquidity. Finally, any analysis of a firm's financial position must consider the inflation factor. Financial analysis must be tempered by the fact that today's dollars may possess much less purchasing power than yesterday's dollars.

KEY TERMS

acid-test ratio

cash flow

current ratio

horizontal analysis

inventory turnover ratio

net working capital

plant-turnover ratio

ratio analysis

receivables turnover ratio

statement of changes in financial position

vertical analysis

QUESTIONS

1. Illustrate how the information needs of those business people concerned with financial analysis may vary.

2. Financial analysis requires that comparison be made over a period of years. What problems does this raise for those involved with financial analysis?

3. Distinguish between horizontal and vertical financial analysis.

4. A firm's cash balance decreased 30 percent during the past year. What does this decrease tell management?

5. Last year a firm's inventory increased in value by 82 percent. Is this a good signal or a poor signal? Explain.

6. An increase in profit from one year to the next is always a good sign of financial strength. Do you agree? Why or why not?

7. What benchmarks can be used to compare financial ratios?

8. How might a banker's interest in financial ratios differ from the interests of an operating manager?

9. Explain the current ratio.

10. Is a high current ratio better than a low current ratio? Explain.

11. What is the acid-test ratio? How does its purpose differ from the purpose of the current ratio?

12. Explain the plant-turnover ratio.

13. Do you agree with the idea that higher plant-turnover ratios are a sign of increased operating efficiency?

14. In what respects is a high inventory turnover rate desirable?

15. Explain the receivables turnover ratio.

16. Explain how a firm can determine the average number of days required to collect accounts receivable.

17. What is the purpose of the statement of changes in financial position?

18. What are the major sources of funds for a business firm?

19. What are the major uses that businesses have for funds?

20. What is an index number and how can index numbers be used to make financial analysis more meaningful?

PROBLEMS

1. Common-size statements

The following are the condensed income statements of the TOT Corporation for the past two years:

	19X1	19X2
Sales	$880,000	$960,000
Less: Cost of goods sold	545,600	624,000
Gross Margin	$334,400	$336,000

Selling expenses	132,000	98,000
Administrative expenses	106,000	192,000
Miscellaneous expenses	64,000	24,000
Total Expenses	$302,000	$314,000
Net Income	$ 32,400	$ 22,000

Required:

a. Express each of these income statements in common-size percentages.

b. Comment on any significant changes that have taken place.

2. Ratios

The following are the financial statements for the Excaliber Corporation for 19X5:

Income Statement for 19X5

Sales		$540,000
Less: Cost of goods sold		356,000
Gross Margin		$184,000
Operating Expenses:		
Selling	$55,000	
Administrative	88,000	
Other	21,000	
Total Operating Expenses		164,000
Net Income		$ 20,000

Balance Sheet, December 31, 19X5

Assets		Liabilities and owner equity	
Cash	$ 30,000	Accounts payable	$ 80,000
Accounts receivable	90,000	Taxes payable	30,000
Inventory	140,000	Accrues expenses	15,000
Marketable securities	12,000	Long-term debt	100,000
Plant and equipment	150,000	Capital stock	130,000
Depreciation	(40,000)	Retained earnings	27,000
Total Assets	$382,000	Total Liabilities and Owner Equity	$382,000

Required:

a. Calculate the following ratios:

(1) Current ratio

(2) Acid-test ratio

(3) Receivables turnover

(4) Inventory turnover

(5) Plant-turnover

(6) Return on investment

b. This is the second year of operation for Excaliber. Should the president be satisfied with the firm's financial position? Comment.

3.   Industry comparison

The Alpha Corporation and the Beta Corporation operate in tne same industry and use the same basic accounting methods. The following are the summarized financial statements of the two firms.

Balance Sheets, December 31, 19X2

	Alpha Corp.	*Beta Corp.*
Assets		
Cash	$ 148,000	$ 72,000
Accounts receivable	172,000	136,000
Inventory	272,000	176,000
Land and building, net	360,000	300,000
Machinery, net	320,000	348,000
Total Assets	$1,272,000	$1,032,000
Liabilities and owner equity		
Accounts payable	$ 120,000	$ 112,000
Taxes payable	23,000	21,000
Miscellaneous payables	41,000	51,000
Long-term debt	240,000	400,000
Capital stock	560,000	240,000
Retained earnings	288,000	208,000
Total Liabilities and Owner Equity	$1,272,000	$1,032,000

Income Statements, for the year ended December 31, 19X2

	Alpha Corp.	Beta Corp.
Sales	$2,440,000	$2,240,000
Less: Cost of goods sold	1,120,000	1,080,000
Gross Margin	$1,320,000	$1,160,000
Operating Expenses:		
Selling	412,000	330,000
Administrative	210,000	214,000
Salaries	200,000	161,000
Depreciation	224,000	192,000
Miscellaneous	10,000	15,000
Total Operating Expenses	$1,056,000	$ 912,000
Net income before taxes	264,000	252,000
Income taxes (40%)	106,000	100,000
Net Income	$ 158,000	$ 152,000

Required:

Apply every appropriate measure discussed in this chapter and any additional measures you can derive to answer the following:

a. On December 31 is the Alpha Corporation in better financial condition than the Beta Corporation? Discuss and show all calculations you have made.

b. To which firm would a banker prefer to grant a five-year loan for $100,000? Discuss.

c. Do these firms have the same or different philosophies regarding the financing of operations? Does either firm have an advantage over the other in this regard? Discuss.

d. In which firm would you invest your life savings of $50,000? Explain.

e. In practice are you likely to find a situation comparable to this? Explain.

4. The trend of ratios

The summarized financial statements of the Northeastern Corporation for the last four years are summarized as follows:

Northeastern Corporation
Income Statements,
For the years 19X1–19X4

	19X1	19X2	19X3	19X4
Sales	$100,800	$112,000	$126,000	$140,000
Less: Cost of goods sold	58,464	67,200	78,120	91,000
Gross Margin	$ 42,336	$ 44,800	$ 47,880	$ 49,000
Selling expenses	5,200	5,600	6,300	7,000
Administrative expenses	8,900	10,080	12,040	19,600
Total Expenses	$ 14,100	$ 15,680	$ 18,340	$ 26,600
Net income before taxes	28,236	29,120	29,540	22,400
Income taxes (40%)	11,294	11,648	11,816	8,960
Net Income	$ 16,942	$ 17,472	$ 17,724	$ 13,440

Northeastern Corporation
Balance Sheets,
December 31, 19X1–19X4

	19X1	19X2	19X3	19X4
Assets				
Current assets	$ 8,400	$10,500	$ 8,400	$ 7,000
Long-term assets	30,000	38,500	51,800	78,400
Total Assets	$38,400	$49,000	$60,200	$85,400
Liabilities and owner equity				
Current liabilities	$ 2,800	$ 3,500	$ 4,200	$ 5,600
Long-term liabilities	5,600	7,000	14,000	26,600
Capital stock	22,400	28,000	28,000	35,000
Retained earnings	7,600	10,500	14,000	18,200
Total Liabilities and Owner Equity	$38,400	$49,000	$60,200	$85,400

Required:

a. Compute the current ratio for each year. Have there been any significant changes in current ratios during these four years? Discuss.

b. Compute the net working capital for each year. Has there been any significant change in net working capital during these four years? Discuss.

c. Prepare common-size income statements for the four years and comment on any significant changes. What additional data would make your analysis more meaningful?

d. Prepare common-size balance sheets for each of the four years and comment on any significant changes.

5. Ratio analysis and related items

The following are the financial statements of the Barlow Corporation.

Barlow Corporation
Balance Sheet,
December 31, 19X4

Assets

Cash	$ 80,000
Receivables	160,000
Inventory	240,000
Prepaid expense	6,000
Land and buildings, net	40,000
Machinery, net	320,000
Total Assets	$846,000

Liabilities and owner equity

Accounts payable	$ 52,000
Notes payable	100,000
Accrued liabilities	10,000
Capital stock	500,000
Retained earnings	184,000
Total Liabilities and Owner Equity	$846,000

Income Statement,
For the year ended December 31, 19X4

Sales		$2,000,000
Less: Cost of Sales:		
Inventory, beginning	$ 200,000	
Purchases	1,580,000	

Cost of Goods Available for Sale	1,780,000	
Inventory, ending	240,000	1,540,000
Gross Margin		$ 460,000
Operating Expenses:		
Selling	180,000	
Administrative	160,000	340,000
Net Income		$ 120,000

Required:

a. Calculate the following ratios and relationships:

(1) Current ratio

(2) Acid-test ratio

(3) Receivables turnover

(4) Average collection period

(5) Return on investment

(6) Plant-turnover ratio

(7) Net income to sales

(8) Net income to total assets

b. What impact, if any, will the following transactions have on the current ratio?

(1) The sale of stock for $50,000

(2) A payment of $20,000 on accounts payable

(3) Purchase of equipment paid for with a 36-month note

(4) Acceptance of a note for $5,000 to extend for 90 days the time when an account must be paid

(5) Writing off as uncollectable an account receivable of $3,000. The allowance for bad accounts account has a balance of $5,000

(6) Collection of $50,000 from accounts receivables

(7) Purchase of a machine for $10,000 cash

6. Statement of financial position

The summarized financial statements of the Marygoround Corporation are as follows:

Comparative Balance Sheets,
December 31, 19X7 and 19X8

	19X7	19X8
Assets		
Current assets	$16,520	$18,200
Long-term assets	15,400	18,200
Total Assets	$31,920	$36,400
Liabilities and owner equity		
Current liabilities	$ 5,600	$ 7,000
Long-term liabilities	2,800	3,500
Capital stock	18,200	19,600
Retained earnings	5,320	6,300
Total Liabilities and Owner Equity	$31,920	$36,400

Income Statement,
For the year ended December 31, 19X8

Sales		$70,000
Less: Cost of goods sold		42,000
Gross Margin		$28,000
Operating Expenses:		
General	$25,900	
Depreciation	700	
Total Operating Expenses		26,600
Net Income		$ 1,400

Comments:

1. $3,500 was paid for new equipment.
2. Long-term debt was increased by $700.
3. A cash dividend of $420 was paid.
4. Additional capital stock was sold for $1,400.
5. Depreciation of long-term assets was $700.

Required:

a. A statement of retained earnings.

b. A statement of changes in net working capital.

c. A statement of changes in financial position.

7. Transactions impacting on working capital

The following is a portion of the Refill Corporation's balance sheet as of December 31, 19X8.

Assets	
Cash	$ 80,000
Securities	30,000
Accounts receivable, net	260,000
Notes receivable	40,000
Inventory	400,000
Prepaid expenses	10,000
Liabilities	
Accounts payable	$170,000
Notes payable	30,000
Accrued expenses	20,000
Long-term debt	150,000

During the year 19X9 the following activity took place:

a. Paid $10,000 on note payable.

b. Wrote off $30,000 of uncollectable accounts receivable.

c. Paid a cash dividend of $12,000.

d. Retired $40,000 of long-term debt.

e. Issued an additional $25,000 in capital stock.

f. $480,000 of accounts receivable were collected.

g. Sold $10,000 of marketable securities for $15,000.

h. Purchased inventory on account for $300,000.

i. Sold inventory costing $390,000 for $450,000 on account.

j. Paid $320,000 on accounts payable.

k. Purchased a machine for $20,000 cash.

l. $8,000 of the prepaid expenses expired.

m. The accrued expenses were paid.

n. The notes receivable were collected along with $3,000 in interest.

Required:

a. Calculate the following ratios as of December 31, 19X9:

   (1)   Current ratio

   (2)   Acid-test ratio

b. Prepare a statement of changes in net working capital for the year 19X9.

   8.   Sources and uses of cash

The Sharon Corporation's financial statements covering the first quarter of 19X1 are as follows:

**Balance Sheets,
January 1 and March 31, 19X1**

	Jan. 1	*Mar. 31*
Assets		
Cash	$ 24,000	$ 84,000
Accounts receivable	36,000	40,000
Inventory	60,000	80,000
Long-term assets	72,000	68,000
Total Assets	$192,000	$272,000
Liabilities and owner equity		
Accounts payable	$ 34,000	$ 46,000
Notes payable	20,000	25,000
Capital stock	100,000	130,000
Retained earnings	38,000	71,000
Total Liabilities and Owner Equity	$192,000	$272,000

**Income Statement,
First Quarter, 19X1**

Sales	$260,000
Less: Cost of goods sold	150,000
Gross Margin	$110,000

General expenses	$ 56,000	
Depreciation	4,000	60,000
Net Income		$ 50,000

A dividend of $17,000 was paid.

Required:

a. Prepare a statement for management that shows what was done with funds during the quarter and how these activities were financed.

9. Sources and uses of funds

The comparative balance sheets of the Frank Corporation as of December 31, 19X4 and 19X5 are as follows:

	19X4	19X5
Assets		
Current assets	$ 80,000	$125,000
Land	15,000	25,000
Buildings and equipment	180,000	222,500
Accumulated depreciation	(25,000)	(42,500)
Total Assets	$250,000	$330,000
Liabilities and owner equity		
Current liabilities	$ 45,000	$ 30,000
Long-term debt	50,000	100,000
Capital stock	60,000	85,000
Retained earnings	95,000	115,000
Total Liabilities and Owner Equity	$250,000	$330,000

Depreciation for the year was $17,500.

Required:

a. Prepare a statement of changes in net working capital for the year.

b. Prepare a statement of changes in financial position for the year.

10. Ratio comparisons

The following data has been taken from the records of the Tampa Corporation (000 omitted):

	19X3	19X4	19X5
Sales (all credit)	$237	$264	$288
Accounts receivable, December 31	19	29	38
Cost of goods sold	147	174	192
Inventory, December 31	23	26	30

Required:

a. Calculate the turnover of receivables for 19X4 and 19X5.

b. How many days of credit sales are outstanding at the end of 19X4 and 19X5?

c. Calculate the turnover of inventory for 19X4 and 19X5.

d. How many days' sales does the inventory represent on December 31, 19X4 and 19X5?

e. Do the answers obtained above suggest a more or less favorable trend?

11. Comparative balance sheets

Following are the balance sheets of the Apgar Corporation for the past two years. The values shown are in thousands.

	December 31	
	19X1	19X2
Assets		
Cash	$ 230	$ 200
Marketable securities	150	100
Accounts receivable, net	190	220
Inventory	900	860
Prepaid expenses	20	30
Long-term assets	2,000	2,400
Accumulated depreciation	(700)	(810)
Total Assets	$2,790	$3,000
Liabilities and owner equity		
Accounts payable	$ 170	$ 150
Accrued expenses	30	40
Long-term debt	200	400
Capital stock	2,000	2,000
Retained earnings	390	410
Total Liabilities and Owner Equity	$2,790	$3,000

Required:

a. Prepare comparative balance sheets showing dollar and percentage changes for each item.

b. Prepare comparative balance sheets showing percentages of totals.

c. Based on what you found in (a) and (b), can you detect any significant changes in the firm's financial picture? Explain.

12.   Inventory turnover

   In each of the past four years the Pilgrim Corporation has shown a profit, and there has been a steady increase in the firm's total assets. Management is disturbed because profits have stayed at about the same level. The following data, in thousands, has been given to you.

	Inventory, Dec. 31	Cost of goods sold
19X1	$535	$4,275
19X2	590	3,975
19X3	700	4,200
19X4	760	4,360

Required:

a. Can you suggest any reason why profits have not increased? Explain.

b. If the inventory turnover for each year were the same as in 19X1, what would the December 31 inventory have been for the three remaining years?

PART 2

Costs
and
Cost Behavior

4 Costs and Their Characteristics

The purpose of this chapter is to explore a number of cost categories and show how they are important to management. An understanding of cost is necessary to appraise past performance as well as to plan for future activities. But the term cost has so many meanings and applications that it is quite possible that two people discussing cost may have quite different things in mind. When a business-man says that it cost $456 to produce a product, this could be the exact cost, the average cost, or an estimate of what cost will be if things go according to plan.

Because cost is part of the planning process, managers need to know how costs will respond to changes in the volume of business activity. Some costs will not change, others will; some costs will change in direct proportion to changes in activity, others will change at a lower rate. Knowledge of cost behavior is essential to effective planning.

QUESTIONS FOR CONSIDERATION

1. Can a businessman measure costs with precision?
2. What can managers do to obtain greater control over cost?
3. Will growth result in lower unit costs of production?
4. What are the most meaningful measures of cost?
5. Should the firm rely more on machines or on manpower to get things done?

Before delving into a study of basic cost concepts, we need to understand the basic cost vocabulary. There are so many different types of costs and so many different meanings given to cost that the term "cost" per se has limited usefulness for our purposes. The term "cost" as we use it in general conversation has a rather universal meaning. Cost is determined by what we have to give up to acquire goods and services. When someone says that these groceries cost $35 or that a visit to a doctor cost $25, what is involved is perfectly clear. An amount—$35 or $25—was given to obtain specific goods and services. But cost is not always as obvious as in this illustration. Suppose, referring to an earlier illustration, that a person buys a new car for $3,300 plus a three-year-old car. Exactly how much did the new car cost the buyer? One person might reason that the old car was on its last legs and was worth only $1,500, making the cost of the new car $4,800. Another person might reason that old Betsey was worth $2,000, making the cost of the new car $5,300. Situations like this can be found in the business world. Suppose that a firm bought a new machine for $25,000 plus an old machine that had a book value of $5,000. Was the "true" cost of the new machine $30,000? Internal Revenue says that the cost of the new machine must be shown as $30,000, but, as you think about this, reflect on the meaning of book value.

To be meaningful, the cost of something must be expressed as so many dollars. But it is possible to acquire goods and services without paying cash dollars. The American Institute of Certified Public Accountants has defined cost as "the amount, measured in money, or cash expended, or other property transferred, capital stock issued, services performed, or a liability incurred, in consideration of goods and services received or to be received."[1] This definition serves to point out some of the difficulties involved in measuring the cost of something. If a corporation gave you 10 shares of stock having a par value of $50 per share for services rendered in organizing the business and setting up an accounting system, what did it "cost" the newly formed business for your services? Was the cost $500? Could the cost be zero? We want to make it clear at the outset that, even though costs may be expressed to five decimal places, they may still be subject to question.

[1]Committee on Terminology, American Institute of Certified Public Accountants, *Accounting Terminology Bulletin No. 4: Cost, Expense and Loss* (New York, 1957), p. 1.

SOME TYPES OF COST

We can begin to throw some light on "cost" by looking at some different types of cost. In the world of business, the term "cost" is seldom used without an expressed or implied modifier. It is the modifier that identifies how the term is being used, and it may provide a manager with an indication of whether he or she can do anything about it, or whether he or she should be at all concerned with the cost. If someone determines that the cost of an activity *was* $10,000, this is a historical cost and there is nothing that a manager can do about it. If, on the other hand, someone says that the cost of a project is expected to be $10,000, there are a number of things that can be done about it. Modifiers convey a very distinct and specific meaning for each cost.

Historical Costs

These are costs that have already been incurred, and, as noted, there is nothing that management can do about them. For good or bad, they are water over the dam. Historical costs should not be ignored simply because they are water over the dam, however. These costs can be analyzed and compared to provide valuable information as to why things turned out the way they did.

But there is a danger in relying too heavily on historical costs when planning for the future. History may not repeat itself. To illustrate, suppose that a firm purchased two acres of land for $25,000 back in 1960 and immediately constructed a building on it costing $1,200,000. The estimated useful life of the building was 30 years and no salvage value was anticipated. Each year, therefore, the firm charged $40,000 (straight-line depreciation) in depreciation as an expense. In view of the drastic increases in land and construction costs, however, how realistic is a charge of $40,000 against revenue for depreciation expense in, say, 1982? Does this historical cost provide a good basis for measuring future depreciation cost? Probably not.

Future Costs

These are costs that management plans to incur in the future. Businessmen are vitally concerned with future cost because these are the costs that they must live with and because future costs are costs over which some degree of control can be exercised. Managerial accounting is concerned primarily with future costs.

Direct and Indirect Costs

This is another important distinction among costs. All costs incurred by a firm must be assigned or attached to some cost object. A cost object could be a division of the firm, a production department, or a unit of production. The number and types of cost objects that the firm uses has a bearing on cost control and cost classification.

The terms "direct" and "indirect" have no meaning except as they relate to a particular cost object. The basic difference between these costs is their traceability. If a cost can be traced logically and practically to a cost object, it is a direct cost to that cost object; if not, it is an indirect cost. The salary of the personnel manager is a direct cost of the personnel department but it is not a direct cost of the stamping department which utilizes the services of the personnel department. Every cost incurred by your school is a direct cost to the school but not to the class in which you are enrolled.

Indirect costs, on the other hand, are quite different. In some respects, they are invisible costs to the manager who must absorb them. The $1.5 million paid in salary to General Motor's chairman of the board and president is a direct cost to General Motors' corporate headquarters, but part of this cost must be borne by every Chevrolet, Oldsmobile, A.C. spark plug, Frigidaire, and so on that is produced by the firm. In the final analysis, all costs must be borne by revenue-producing segments of the firm such as Chevrolet. The corporate headquarters does not produce any revenue, but it does enable other segments of the firm to do so. The problem is to determine how much of this indirect cost each unit of production should bear. In manufacturing, direct costs can be traced to specific units of production, and they are incurred only because there are units of production. Indirect costs must be allocated to units of production or to cost centers on some predetermined basis. The process for allocating indirect costs is discussed later in Chapter 10 under the heading manufacturing overhead.

Managers are concerned with the portion of total cost that is direct and the portion that is indirect. If the bulk of costs incurred are direct and traceable to a job or product, a manager has a much better basis for understanding why the cost was incurred and is in a better position to control it. Suppose that a given product is a cost center and that direct material and direct labor comprise the bulk of total costs. This allows the responsible manager to actually see what is going on as far as costs are concerned. He can see five tires, five wheels, and twenty lug nuts being applied to each car on the assembly line, no more, no less. He can see workmen performing their tasks within the allotted time. He can see mistakes, and he can correct them. But he may have no control at all over the portion of indirect costs his area of concern must bear.

Controllable and Noncontrollable Costs

There are some similarities between this category of costs and the previous category, but there are also significant differences. Businessmen are vitally concerned with costs having the attribute of uncontrollability and perhaps for obvious reasons. A controllable cost is one that can be regulated in whole or in part by the responsible manager. Note, that the rent that a particular A&P store must pay is a direct cost to the store—the cost center—but it is not controllable by the store manager. As we look at these costs, our vantage point must also be considered. All costs are controllable by someone in the organization. The rental for the A&P store was controllable by someone in the A&P organization, else there would not have been a lease to begin with.

If the costs incurred by a particular cost center cannot be controlled by the manager involved, there is little that he can do in the areas of cost control and cost reduction, which could be an undesirable position for the manager. If most of the costs incurred by a cost center are controllable by the manager involved, he is in a good position to exercise his expertise and take credit for any cost improvement. The managers of many food supermarkets, for example, are in a noncontrollable cost situation. They have no control over the cost of merchandise or its selling price, advertising cost, housing cost, maintenance cost, and many other areas of cost. About the only area of cost over which these managers can exercise some control is labor cost as it relates to the dollar volume of merchandise that goes through the checkout areas. Consequently, it is possible for a manager to work effectively and efficiently and still not show a good profit performance.

The previous discussions have pointed out, among other things, that certain costs are more easily measured and controlled than others. We might infer from this that there are costs that managers would like to have responsibility for and costs that they would prefer not to deal with. A logical question, therefore, would relate to whether a manager can exercise any control over the cost structure within which he must work, and if so, how.

One category of cost that is especially bothersome to a manager is indirect cost. Indirect costs are allocated to rather than being incurred by a particular department. It is possible to establish cost centers in such a manner as to reduce indirect costs. It would be too much to expect that all costs could be traced to cost centers. Because a basic purpose of cost accounting is to estimate the cost of a unit of production, it is logical to establish the product as a cost center whenever possible. When General Motors decided to produce the Chevy Vega, a decision was made not to produce it with the then existing facilities at Chevrolet. Had this not been done, it would have been difficult to isolate those costs attributable solely to the Vega. Instead, General Motors built a new facility at Lordstown, Ohio for the single purpose of producing this car. In a sense, then, all costs incurred at Lordstown were direct costs to Vega automobiles. This does not mean that all costs assigned to Vegas were direct costs. The support costs from both Chevrolet headquarters and General Motors headquarters will still be indirect costs, but the bulk of costs were direct.

If costs are direct, they are much easier to measure and control. For years, each automotive division of General Motors was responsible for the assembly of its cars. To a degree, therefore, the costs of assembling a Chevrolet were mixed with all the costs incurred by Chevrolet. In an effort to isolate and better control the cost of assembly, General Motors took this function away from the automobile divisions and assigned it to a newly formed assembly division. The result is much the same as with our Vega illustration; the bulk of the costs associated with the assembly function are direct costs.

Another classification of cost that is bothersome to any manager is uncontrollable costs—costs that may affect managerial performance over which the manager has no control. In a highly centralized organization, authority and decision making belong to high-level managers. These managers dictate both the type of cost that will be incurred and the amount of cost that must be absorbed at lower levels of organization. Quite often, the best information as to the type of cost and the amount of cost that should be incurred is in the hands of lower-level managers. A production supervisor may be the best informed person in the field of production, yet his knowledge may be ignored by top management.

Through decentralization, where decisions are made at the point at which they are applied, it is possible to increase the areas of cost that lower-level managers can control. The point is that if upper management only decides what costs will be incurred and for what purpose, it can lead to loss of control and lower-level management frustration.

Profit centers, an application of decentralization, are frequently employed to give responsible managers control over their cost structure. When profit centers are employed, an imaginary line is drawn around segments of an organization. The manager of each segment has a profit objective that he is expected to reach, and he is given considerable latitude over the costs involved in operating his domain. Dodge and Plymouth are each profit centers at Chrysler.

COST BEHAVIOR

An understanding of cost behavior—how costs respond to changes in the volume of activity—is a prerequisite in many decision-making areas. Costs come into being for two reasons: because of the passage of time and because activity is taking place. Time costs are referred to as *fixed* costs, and activity costs are referred to as *variable* costs. In the management of cost, all costs are classified as fixed or variable. In practice, however, we seldom see costs that are completely fixed or variable. Rather, certain costs tend to be fixed or tend to be variable. Also, there are some costs that contain an element of fixed cost and an element of variable cost in their total. Thus the $30 total cost to rent a car for a day could be expressed as $15 per day (time) plus 15 cents per mile for 100 miles (activity). Such costs are described as mixed or semivariable.

Fixed Costs

As implied above, a fixed cost is one that remains constant in total during a given time period regardless of the volume of activity that takes place. Using the car illustration, the $15-per-day charge would have been the same had 50, 150, or 300 miles been driven. For practical purposes we need to add a grain of salt to the notion that fixed costs remain constant in total regardless of activity. Within reasonable limits of time and changes in the volume of activity, we can expect the cost to remain constant. A given fixed cost, rent, for example, will change over time—when a new lease is written—and, if the firm needs 50 percent more area because of increased activity, the rent will probably increase. In practice, a fixed cost is likely to be put into a framework such as the following.

During the month of February, when production volume is expected to be between 8,000 and 10,000 units of X, the fixed cost will be $40,000. A fixed cost is fixed in total, but it is variable in relation to the volume of activity that takes place. The following illustrates this point:

Units produced	Depreciation	Depreciation per unit
8,000	$40,000	$5.00
8,500	40,000	4.71
9,000	40,000	4.44
9,500	40,000	4.21
10,000	40,000	4.00

What happens is that the total cost of $40,000 is spread over more units and the unit cost goes down. If zero units were produced, the fixed cost would still be $40,000. Note that the only meaningful expression of fixed cost is as a total. An expression of fixed cost as $4.44 is meaningless by itself. The $4.44 has meaning only if we know that production was 9,000 units.

This example illustrates another aspect of fixed cost. To the extent that a firm's costs are fixed, there is a direct unit cost advantage in increasing the level of activity. As the activity increases, the fixed cost per unit decreases.

A variable cost is one that increases in total in direct proportion to the level of activity. There is a linear relationship between total cost and the volume of activity. Again, we must add a grain of salt in terms of the time and activity dimensions. Direct labor might be a variable cost under normal conditions, but, if activity increased to the point that overtime were required, total labor costs would increase disproportionately to hours worked. In practice a variable cost is likely to be put in a framework such as that following.

During the month of February, when production volume is expected to be between 8,000 and 10,000 units of X, the variable cost of direct labor will be $1.00 per unit. A variable cost will change in total depending on the level of activity, but the unit cost will remain constant. The following illustrates this point:

Units produced	Direct labor cost	Unit labor cost
8,000	$ 8,000	$1.00
8,500	8,500	1.00
9,000	9,000	1.00
9,500	9,500	1.00
10,000	10,000	1.00

In this situation, if the volume of activity has been zero, the total direct labor cost will have been zero. Fixed costs are constant in total; variable costs are constant per unit. This is why we say that total fixed and unit variable are the meaningful measures of cost. An expression of total variable cost as $9,000 tells us little about variable costs unless the volume of activity is known.

The example illustrates another aspect of variable cost. To the extent that a firm's costs are variable, there is no unit cost advantage from increased production and no cost disadvantage if the level of production is reduced. Figure 4-1 shows fixed and variable costs expressed graphically.

What Costs are Fixed? Variable?

It is unwise to look at a cost and classify it as fixed or variable because of its title. Often direct labor is a variable cost, and often depreciation is a fixed cost. A cost is fixed because it remains the

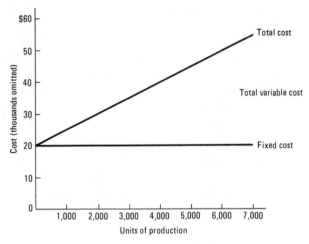

This is an application of the linear equation $y = a + bx$ where

y = total cost
a = total fixed cost ($20,000)
b = unit variable cost ($5)
x = units of activity

Total cost at 7,000 units = $20,000 + (7,000 × $5),   or $55,000

FIGURE   4-1.   Fixed and variable costs

same in total as activity changes. A cost is variable because it remains the same per unit as activity changes. Depreciation can be a variable cost; the basis for depreciation may be units of production or hours of operation. Direct labor can be a fixed cost. Many assembly-line workers in the automobile industry are guaranteed an annual wage regardless of the hours that they work.

Mixed Costs

Many costs change when the volume of activity changes but not in direct proportion. Such costs are called mixed or semivariable costs. Maintenance cost, for example, might drop only 5 percent as production drops 12 percent. Table 4-1 depicts the behavior of a mixed cost. A casual glance at the data reveals that there is some relationship between maintenance cost and units produced. This suggests the existence of a variable cost. But we can also see that the cost at the 20,000-unit level is less than double the cost at the 10,000-unit level. Therefore, we know that this cost is not completely variable. Also, we can see an element of inconsistency in these costs because the volume of activity for January and June is the same but the cost is different.

This cost is neither fixed or variable; it contains an element of each type of cost. Our task is to find that portion of this cost that seems to be variable and that portion that seems to be fixed. We will now look at some of the approaches used to isolate each element of cost.

TABLE 4-1

Maintenance Costs at Varying Outputs

Month	Production (units)	Cost
January	12,000	$40,000
February	16,000	54,000
March	14,000	43,000
April	18,000	60,000
May	22,000	66,000
June	12,000	38,000
July	15,000	50,000
August	10,000	36,000
September	14,000	44,000
October	17,000	58,000
November	21,000	63,000
December	20,000	62,000

The High-low Method

This method simply compares cost and volume changes between the lowest and highest level of activity. We will use the data in Table 4-1 to illustrate this method.

	Low level	High level	Change
Total cost	$36,000	$66,000	$30,000
Units produced	10,000	22,000	12,000

There was an increase of $30,000 in the cost of maintenance between the low and high levels. There was an increase of 12,000 units between the low and high levels. Therefore, we conclude that cost increased at the rate of $2.50 ($30,000 ÷ 12,000) per unit of production. This, then, is the unit variable cost of maintenance. We assume that the entire increase in cost is due to the increased production because fixed costs remain constant in total throughout the relevant range. We learned earlier that only variable costs increase in total as volume of activity increases.

Because the unit variable cost is $2.50, the total variable cost at the 10,000 unit level must be $25,000. Because total cost minus variable costs equals fixed cost, fixed cost must be $11,000 ($36,000 – $25,000). We now have a meaningful expression of maintenance cost that can be used for budgeting purposes or in other decision-making areas. If, for example, the level of activity for the following February were set at 16,250 units, the estimated cost for maintenance would be $51,625 (16,250 x $2.50 plus $11,000).

A cost approximated in this fashion might be a good ballpark figure but nothing more. This approach to extracting cost components has at least two defects. First, only two sets of values are used in the calculation and these are the extreme values. The ten in between values are ignored and wasted. Second, the estimate of total maintenance cost assumes that there is a linear relationship between cost and activity, even though we know that this may not be completely true. Thus we emphasize that this technique provides only an estimate of cost behavior.

Least-squares Regression Analysis

The first weakness in the high-low approach, including only two values, can be overcome by applying least-squares regression analysis. In Figure 4-2 the maintenance cost at varying levels of activity is plotted. If all points fell on a straight line, we would know that there is a perfect linear relation between cost and activity. Because they do not, the best that we can expect is to find a "line of best fit."

Least-squares regression analysis allows us to measure this line of best fit, that is, a line so placed that it minimizes the distance squared between all of the points and the line. Figure 4-2 shows that the high-low approximation does not provide as good a fit as least squares. The variable and fixed components of maintenance cost are found by solving the following equations:

$$b = \frac{n \, \Sigma XY - \Sigma X \, \Sigma Y}{n \, \Sigma X^2 - (\Sigma X)^2}$$

$$a = \frac{\Sigma Y}{n} - b\left(\frac{\Sigma X}{n}\right)$$

where

n = the number of observations used,

X = the value of the independent variable (units of production),

Y = the value of the dependent variable (cost),

a = total fixed cost

b = unit variable cost

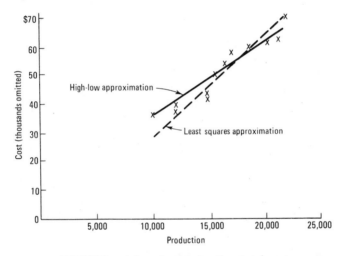

FIGURE 4-2. Approximating total cost

We have used the data in Table 4-1 and have computed the total fixed cost ($8,013) and unit variable cost ($2.706) as shown in Table 4-2. This approach to separating costs also assumes a linear relationship between total variable cost and the volume of activity. The estimated cost of maintenance to produce 16,250 units is found by using the following linear equation:

$$Y = a + bx \text{ (see Figure 4-1)}$$
$$= \$8,013 + (\$2.706 \times 16,250)$$
$$= \$51,986$$

The estimated cost of maintenance at a level of 16,250 units is about the same using either method. One should not conclude that the results of these two methods will be anywhere near the same. In our illustration, a significant amount of linearity was built into the cost-

TABLE 4-2

Separating Mixed Cost Using
Least-Squares Regression Analysis

Units produced[a] X	Maintenance cost[a] Y	XY	X^2
12	$ 40	480	144
16	54	864	256
14	43	602	196
18	60	1,080	324
22	65	1,430	484
12	38	456	144
15	50	750	225
10	36	360	100
14	44	616	196
17	58	986	289
21	63	1,323	441
20	62	1,240	400
$\Sigma X = 191$	$\Sigma Y = \$613$	$\Sigma XY = 10,187$	$\Sigma X^2 = 3,199$

(a) thousands omitted.

$n = 12$

$$b = \frac{n\,\Sigma XY - \Sigma X\,\Sigma Y}{n\,\Sigma X^2 - (\Sigma X)^2} = \frac{12(10,187) - (191)(613)}{12(3.199) - (191)^2} = 2.706$$

$$a = \frac{\Sigma Y}{n} - b\left(\frac{\Sigma X}{n}\right) = \frac{613}{12} - 2.706\left(\frac{191}{12}\right) = \$8,013$$

activity relationships. If the relationship between cost and activity is perfectly linear, there will be no difference in the results of the two methods, but, as linearity decreases, least squares ensures the best linear fit. There is no guarantee that any method can accurately identify the unit variable and total fixed portions of a mixed cost because factors other than activity, policy, for example, can cause costs to increase and decrease.

The Cost Balance Concept

Fixed and variable costs are present in most organizations, but there are significant differences in the importance of each type of cost from industry to industry, firm to firm, and from time to time.

In some industries whether costs will be predominately fixed or variable is conditioned by industry characteristics, but frequently there are opportunities for management to obtain a more favorable balance. Leasing as opposed to ownership is one way to change the balance, contracting work to other firms rather than buying equipment is another, and relying more on machines than manpower to get things done is still another.

In Table 4-3 we show the sales, assets, and number of employees for four selected firms. Some interesting comparisons can be made and several are shown in Table 4-4. First, we should note that the inputs required to produce products for sale are material, labor, and facilities. Table 4-3 shows that some firms rely more heavily on one factor than another to produce their products. In general, materials and labor are variable costs and facilities are fixed costs. One liberty taken in making the following comparisons is to call assets "facilities." This is not entirely true, but it does not unduely distort the comparisons that are made.

There are a number of extremes in Table 4-4. H. A. Hormel has nearly five times the sales per dollar of assets as IBM. But this does

TABLE   4-3

Comparison of Sales, Assets, and Employees, Selected Firms

Company	Sales (millions)	Assets (millions)	Employees
Ford Motor Co.	$24,009	$14,020	416,120
IBM	14,436	15,530	286,647
Beatrice Foods	4,191	1,658	64,000
H. A. Hormel	996	224	8,656

Source: Fortune, "500 Largest Industrial Corporations," May 1976.

TABLE   4-4

Sales Per Employee, Per $1 of Assets, and Assets Per Employee
Selected Companies

Company	Sales per employee	Assets per employee	Sales per $1 of assets
Ford Motor Co.	$ 57,700	$33,700	$1.71
IBM	50,000	53,800	0.93
Beatrice Foods	65,500	25,900	2.53
H. A. Hormel	115,000	26,000	4.45

Source: Table 4-3.

not mean that Hormel is any more efficient than IBM; rather, it shows the impact of a different cost balance. The reason for the difference is that Hormel's major cost is animals which are slaughtered and cut up into a variety of products. It does not take a great amount of manpower and equipment to generate a large sales volume. IBM has a very high amount of assets per employee. The reason for this is the vast investment in facilities that technology-oriented companies such as IBM must make. It would be difficult for Hormel to become fixed-cost oriented as long as it stays in the meat-packing business and it would be almost impossible for IBM to become variable-cost oriented.

Our basic concern over cost balance is this. If a firm's costs are predominately variable, there is a lesser unit cost advantage through increasing the volume of activity. Here, costs keep rising almost as fast as sales volume. But, to the extent that a firm's costs are fixed, there is a direct cost advantage through increasing the volume of activity. It would seem, therefore, that, where it is possible, businessmen should increase the percentage of their costs that are fixed and lower their variable costs. Almost every business function can be performed in a variety of ways. It is quite possible that different approaches to getting things done will produce a different cost balance.

As time passes, the technology available for performing tasks tends to improve. Processes tend to depend more on machine performance than on manual skills. Higher levels of technology generally involve a greater investment in facilities which are fixed costs and less labor which is generally a variable cost. A basic problem facing management is when to shift to a greater fixed-cost base. The following discussion explains the elements involved in solving this problem.

At the time of this writing, a major tire manufacturer in its TV tire commercials emphasized that the company's skilled craftsmen produce radial tires one at a time. It would seem that the level of technology available for producing radial tires is quite low and that the basic costs variable. Suppose that the company's radial-tire function now has the following cost balance: fixed costs are $15 million per year and variable costs are $33 for a particular size tire. The company is approached by a representative of a firm that specializes in tire-manufacturing equipment. He proposes that the company adopt a revolutionary process for making radial tires. The problem is that fixed costs will increase to $55 million per year, but it will reduce the variable cost component to $28 per tire. Should the company consider using the new process? The logic that we apply here is that any increase in fixed costs must be offset by a decrease in variable costs. In this case, fixed costs would be increased by $40 million per year, whereas variable costs would decrease by $5 per tire. Therefore, if more than 8 million radial tires are produced each year ($40 million ÷ $5) the new process will yield lower unit costs. All tires produced in excess of 8 million will cost $5 less to produce by the new process. The best cost balance, then, depends on the volume of activity that takes place. Problems at the end of this chapter describe situations where this concept applies.

THE RELEVANT RANGE

Costs can be expected to retain their fixed and variable characteristics only within a limited range of activity and over a limited period of time. We will limit our present discussion to activity implications. The relevant range of activity is that area in which costs behave as they should; that is, they are either fixed or variable in nature. It is that range of activity in which fixed costs remain fixed in total and variable costs remain fixed per unit of activity.

It would be little more than guesswork for a firm just beginning operations to pinpoint the relevant range of activity. In some instances where work methods and machine capacities are established and known, it could be possible to estimate the relevant range with some accuracy. This would be true in some segments of the garment industry, for example. But all firms are different, and it becomes necessary to observe cost behavior in a firm before nailing down the relevant range. We have already learned that the title given to a cost does not govern its behavior, and the fact that certain costs are fixed or variable in one situation does not mean that they will behave the same way in "our" firm. The greater the opportunity one has to observe the behavior of a firm's cost, the more certain one can be of their characteristics. Thus, in Figure 4-3, we assume that the costs shown at varying levels of activity are costs that have been observed for some time. Note that the cost curve begins at $5,000 for zero production. Then the cost curve rises sharply, and, at about the 2,000-unit level, it begins to rise in a somewhat linear fashion to about 7,000 units. We attribute the rapid rise of cost between zero

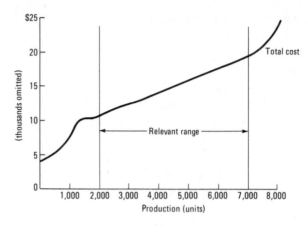

FIGURE 4-3. The Relevant Range

and 2,000 units to the fact that there are inefficiencies that accompany a limited use of facilities. Similarly, costs begin to rise sharply as the maximum-capacity level of 8,000 is approached.

Between the 2,000-unit and 7,000-unit levels, costs appear to be acting as they should; that is, they are increasing in total in a linear fashion as the level of activity increases. Such a cost curve implies that there is a level of fixed costs and a unit variable cost. Below the 2,000-unit level and above the 7,000-unit level, costs behave in an erratic and unpredictable manner, and these areas of activity are considered to be outside the relevant range of activity. That is, unit variable costs and total fixed costs will not remain constant.

THE RELEVANT RANGE—A SECOND LOOK

Another way to estimate the relevant range of activity is to examine costs as levels of activity change to see if there is a range of activity where unit variable costs remain about the same. Table 4-5 gives the total cost of operating at various levels of activity. Then the increase in cost from one level to another is shown. This increase in cost is divided by the increase in units from one level to another to arrive at a unit variable cost. Between the 2,000-unit level and the 7,000-unit level, the unit variable cost and the total fixed cost remains about the same. Therefore we conclude that this is the relevant range.

TABLE 4-5

Estimating the Relevant Range

Production	Total cost	Increase	Unit variable cost	Total fixed cost
0	$ 3,000			$3,000
1,000	4,600	$1,600	$1.60	3,000
2,000	5,700	1,100	1.10	3,500
3,000	6,820	1,120	1.12	3,460
4,000	7,930	1,110	1.11	3,490
5,000	9,050	1,120	1.12	3,450
6,000	10,160	1,110	1.11	3,500
7,000	11,250	1,100	1.10	3,550
8,000	12,550	1,300	1.30	2,150
9,000	14,000	1,450	1.45	950

There have been times when costs were stable for extended periods. There have been times when cost behavior was quite predictable. Today, cost levels and cost behavior are changing at very rapid rates due to such factors as inflation, increased levels of technology, and labor union demands. Consequently historical data has less value for decision making. The fact that the relevant range *was* between 2,000 units and 7,000 units of activity is no guarantee that this will be the case in the future. The time frame for making cost-behavior decisions gets shorter and shorter.

SUMMARY

In this chapter we have described a number of costs and how management can use them. Historical costs are a thing of the past and cannot be changed; yet they may provide a basis for predicting future costs. Since planning always involves future costs, a study of historical costs may prove valuable. If costs are direct and managers can see them flow into production, it is relatively easy to determine whether they are necessary. These same managers may have no control over the indirect costs they must absorb. Similarly, some costs are controllable by a department manager and others are not. Organization structures frequently can be altered to make more costs direct or controllable by department managers.

Costs are also classified according to their behavior when volumes of activity change. Fixed costs remain the same in total when activity changes, but unit fixed costs depend directly on the volume of activity. Variable costs are fixed per unit of activity but vary in total depending on the volume of activity. Thus, if the bulk of a firm's costs are fixed, there is a direct cost advantage when levels of activity are increased and a direct cost disadvantage when they are decreased. The description of most costs needs to be modified because every cost incurred by a firm is a direct cost to the firm and every cost incurred by a firm is controllable by someone in the firm. Similarly, variable and fixed costs will retain their characteristics only over a limited period of time and when there are limited changes in the volume of activity.

KEY TERMS

centralization	future cost
controllable cost	high-low method
cost	historical cost
cost balance	indirect cost
cost behavior	least-squares regression analysis
cost center	mixed cost
decentralization	profit center
direct cost	relevant range
fixed cost	variable cost

QUESTIONS

1. Can the cost of something always be measured scientifically? Explain.
2. What are the main elements of the AICPA definition of cost?
3. Of what value are historical costs to a manager?
4. Is there a danger in relying on historical costs? Explain.
5. What is a direct cost? In what respects are all of a firm's costs considered direct?
6. Would an operating manager be more concerned if he or she had more indirect costs than direct costs to manage? Explain.
7. "The distinction between controllable and uncontrollable costs is meaningless because all costs are actually controllable." Discuss.
8. a. Define fixed cost.
    b. Define variable cost.
9. Fixed costs are variable and variable costs are fixed. Explain this crazy statement.

10. For what two basic reasons do costs exist?

11. Which firm will benefit more from growth, one whose costs are basically variable or one whose costs are basically fixed? Explain.

12. "It is a dangerous practice to look at a cost and because of its title classify it as fixed, variable, or mixed." Do you agree? Explain.

13. How can management reduce the percentage of total cost that is indirect?

14. How can the percentage of total cost classified as noncontrollable be reduced?

15. Reference Questions 13 and 14. Is it sound practice to do what these two questions suggest?

16. What weaknesses are inherent to the high-low method?

17. What does the term "cost balance" imply? Why is this concept important to management?

18. What are the basic considerations entering into the decision to increase fixed costs?

19. Explain the phrase "costs behave as they should."

20. How can management estimate the relevant range of activity?

PROBLEMS _____

1. Cost curves

   Each of the graphs in Figure 4-4 on the following page depicts the behavior of a cost. You may need to use certain graphs more than once.

Required:

Which of these cost curves depicts

a. unit variable cost?   d. total variable cost?

b. unit fixed cost?   e. total fixed cost?

c. average unit cost?   f. total cost?

2. High-low method

   The following is indicative of the behavior of indirect labor cost at the Apex Corporation:

Units produced	Indirect labor cost
20,000	$40,000
32,000	46,000

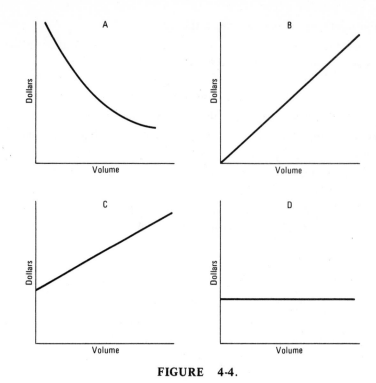

FIGURE 4-4.

Required:

a. Apply the high-low concept and estimate the unit variable and total fixed cost of indirect labor.

b. How valid are your estimates? Discuss.

c. Estimate the cost of indirect labor if 24,800 units are produced.

d. Estimate the cost of indirect labor if 50,000 units are produced.

3. Cost balance

The Ace Vending Machine Company supplies soft drinks at selected locations using coin-operated machines. Currently there is a machine in the student center that dispenses five flavors of drink in 12-ounce cans. It costs $1,200 per year to operate the machine, and the variable cost per drink is 18 cents. Drinks sell for 30 cents each. The firm's cost accountant has suggested that this machine be replaced with a new model that mixes syrup and soda water when the machine is activated. A machine that dispenses five flavors costs $3,300 per year to operate, and, because it is so much more efficient, has a variable cost of 11 cents per drink.

Required:

a. Evaluate the cost accountant's suggestion.

4. Cost balance

Spillway Sporting Goods Company takes pride in the fact that its golf clubs are hand crafted. The current method for producing a driver involves three steps as follows:

Step 1: 20 minutes of labor costing $6.00 per hour

Step 2: 15 minutes of labor costing $5.20 per hour

Step 3: 30 minutes of labor costing $6.00 per hour

Raw materials per club cost $7.70 and fixed costs total $5,000 per month.

The ABF Company has developed a computer-controlled machine that will produce a driver of similar quality in 5 minutes. This process involves the same raw material cost and requires the services of one machine operator who is paid $6.00 per hour. The fixed costs of this machine total $29,000 per month.

Required:

a. On a cost basis only, should Spillway consider buying this machine? Explain.

b. What other factors should be considered in this case?

5. High-low analysis

During the past six month Marcy's Retail Outlet recorded the following:

	Sales	*Supply cost*
January	$31,000	$2,600
February	42,000	3,000
March	58,000	3,700
April	72,000	4,600
May	64,000	4,000
June	60,000	3,800

Required:

a. Estimate the unit variable and total fixed cost of supplies.

b. Sales for the following September have been estimated at $100,000. Estimate the cost of supplies for September.

c. Would you expect this estimate to be accurate? Explain.

6.   High-low analysis

Two years ago the Grogan Company lost $20,000 on sales of 20,000 blurffs at $10 each. Last year the firm earned a profit of $50,000 on the sale of 40,000 blurffs at the same price. Fixed costs were the same for both years.

Required:

a. Determine the fixed cost for the firm.

b. What is the lowest price that 40,000 blurffs could be sold without losing money?

7.   High-low and the relevant range

The following are the costs incurred for maintenance during the past six months:

	Jan.	Feb.	Mar.	Apr.	May	June
Units produced	2,000	2,200	2,100	2,150	3,000	5,000
Cost incurred	$4,000	$4,200	$4,120	$4,140	$6,800	$11,500

Required:

a. Estimate the unit variable cost of maintenance.

b. Estimate the total fixed cost of maintenance.

c. If 2,195 units were produced in July, what would the estimated maintenance cost be?

8.   High-low analysis and income statements

The following are the income statements for the Marglow Corporation for the past two quarters:

	Q-I	Q-II
Sales	$250,000	$200,000
Less: Cost of goods sold	150,000	130,000
Gross Margin	$100,000	$ 70,000
Selling and administrative expenses	75,000	65,000
Net Income	$ 25,000	$ 5,000

Required:

a. During the second quarter sales were 80 percent of first quarter sales yet net income was only 20 percent of first quarter net income. Explain the reason for this drop in net income.

b. Prepare an estimated income statement for the third quarter when sales are expected to be $240,000.

9. Cost balance

The Pritt Company has been using a casting and machining process to produce a component part. The raw material cost is $3.00 per unit, the casting operation costs $6.00 per unit, and the machining operation costs $8.00 per unit. Fixed costs associated with this process amount to $50,000 per year.

The component part can also be made by a die casting machine which has annual fixed costs of $125,000. This machine uses materials which cost $2.00 per unit and other variable costs amount to $3.00 per unit.

Required:

a. At what production volume will the cost by each process be the same?

b. If 7,000 units are produced per year, which process will have the lower total cost? How much lower?

10. Cost balance

The treasurer of Flatz Brewery is conducting a study of the costs to bottle its beer. The process now used involves unloading bottles from the delivery truck, placing them individually on a conveyor, filling and capping each bottle, sending the bottles by conveyor to the packing area where they become six-packs, and finally putting four six-packs together to make a case. Each bottling line produces 12,000 filled bottles per 8-hour shift.

The Conway Glass Works, the bottle supplier, has suggested that Flatz use its facilities to six-pack bottles and ship them to the brewery by the case. Thus Flatz would unload cases of bottles and move them by conveyor to the filling area where 24 bottles would be filled at a time and 24 bottles would be capped at a time. Each bottling line could handle 30,000 bottles of beer per 8-hour shift. The filling, capping, and conveying machines would have to be modified if the change is made. The following cost estimates have been made:

	Present	Proposed
Materials per case	$2.16	$2.40
Labor per shift	$136	$48
Fixed cost per shift	$320	$500

Required:

a. Should the treasurer consider the Conway suggestion? Substantiate your answer with calculations.

11. High-low method

The following are the income statements for the Webster Company for the first two quarters of this year:

	Q-I	Q-II
Sales	$300,000	$350,000
Less: Cost of goods sold	180,000	196,000
Gross Margin	$120,000	$154,000
Operating Expenses:		
Sales and promotion	54,000	60,000
Administrative	60,000	62,000
Total Expenses	$114,000	$122,000
Net Income	$ 6,000	$ 32,000

Required:

a. Use the high-low method and estimate the unit variable and total fixed cost components of the three expense categories.

b. Explain why net income increases as rapidly as it did.

c. If sales for the third quarter are $380,000, estimate what the net income will be.

12. Least squares

For many years the Plympton Company has used the high-low technique to estimate the portion of mixed costs that were fixed and variable. The new plant manager has suggested that the more refined least-squares regression analysis be used. He noted that if the relationship between activity and cost is quite linear, there will be little difference in the results of the two techniques, but, as linearity decreases, differences may increase. You have been given the following data (in thousands) to work with:

Units of production (X)	Indirect labor cost (Y)	XY	X^2
10	$40	400	100
14	50	700	196
9	40	360	81
20	65	1,300	400
16	58	928	256
15	54	810	225
11	42	462	121
12	43	516	144
18	64	1,152	324
17	60	1,020	289
$\Sigma X = 142$	$\Sigma Y = 516$	$\Sigma XY = 7,648$	$\Sigma X^2 = 2,136$

Required:

a. Determine the unit variable cost and total fixed cost of indirect labor using least-squares regression analysis.

b. Repeat the requirements in (a) using the high-low technique.

c. Comment on any differences that you found.

5 Cost-Volume-Profit Relations

CHAPTER OVERVIEW _____

The purpose of this chapter is to show how cost concepts can be used in the profit-planning process. Profit should be planned because every firm has a variety of profit needs. But profit cannot be planned unless revenues and expenses can be planned. Thus in this chapter we are concerned with the behavior of cost; that is, the total of costs at various levels of activity. We are concerned with measuring the volume of activity needed to break even, to support new programs, or to earn a given target profit. We will also see the differences in the profit-planning process in retail and manufacturing organizations.

QUESTIONS FOR CONSIDERATION _____

1. What is a break-even point and how can it be determined?
2. Why might it be advantageous for a firm to have more of its costs fixed than variable?
3. What impact will lower selling prices have on break even and profit?
4. What additional sales volume will be needed to increase profit by 20 percent?
5. Can universities, hospitals, and other not-for-profit organizations use cost-volume-profit analysis the same as business organizations?

In this chapter we will apply a number of concepts developed in previous chapters to several decision areas. The goal of this chapter is to explain how management can use accounting data in the profit-planning process. It is common practice for business firms to have target profits because every business has a variety of profit needs such as expansion, the payment of dividends, or the retirement of long-term debt. Basically management needs to know the volume of activity that must be generated to yield a given target profit.

The amount of sales revenue needed to realize a net income of, say, $100,000 will vary from industry to industry and from firm to firm. In food retailing, a very small portion of each sales dollar—perhaps 3 percent—remains in the firm as profit. It would require $3.33 million of sales to yield a target profit of $100,000. In a job-order machine shop a much larger portion of each sales dollar—perhaps 20 percent—may remain in the firm as profit. Here a sales volume of $500,000 would generate $100,000 of profits.

Cost-volume-profit relations considers the impact on total cost when volumes of activity change. Cost-volume-profit analysis provides management with a technique that can be used to answer such questions as

What sales volume is needed to reach the break-even point?

What sales volume is needed to earn a particular target profit?

If selling price is lowered, what additional sales volume will be needed to increase net income by 10 percent?

What additional sales volume will be needed to support an advertising campaign costing $50,000?

CONTRIBUTION MARGIN CONCEPT

If a firm is to earn a target profit of $100,000, it must have a sales revenue that will cover all costs with $100,000 to spare. Management, therefore, needs the means for estimating total cost at various levels of activity. This, in turn, requires that every cost be expressed as unit variable or total fixed. We learned earlier that if costs are expressed in these terms total cost can be estimated for any level of activity within the relevant range. If management does not know how costs will behave when activity changes, profit planning will be a hit-or-miss proposition.

An income statement such as that shown in Table 2-2 is adequate for measuring the net income that was earned, but it is of little value in the profit-planning process. To be useful in this regard, costs must be separated to show the variable and fixed components. A profit planner would reconstruct the income statement along the lines of Table 5-1. (*Note:* This illustration is merely descriptive. We cannot determine which costs are variable or fixed from Table 2-2.)

TABLE   5-1

Income Statement

Sales		$2,000,000
Less: Variable Costs:		
Cost of merchandise sold	$1,160,000	
Sales commissions	200,000	
Other variable costs	140,000	1,500,000
Contribution Margin		$ 500,000
Less: Fixed Costs:		
Salaries	$ 300,000	
Advertising	90,000	
Other fixed costs	60,000	$ 450,000
Net income before taxes		$ 50,000
Income tax		17,500
Net Income		$ 32,500

Contribution is the difference between selling price and variable cost. It can be expressed in total as shown in Table 5-1, it can be expressed as a percentage of sales, or it can be expressed on a per unit basis. If an electric motor sells for $50 and has a variable cost of $30, the unit contribution is $20 and the contribution margin ratio is 40 percent ($20 ÷ $50). Unit contribution and contribution margin ratio are the two expressions of contribution that we will be using.

There is an advantage in expressing costs as fixed and variable. Our income statement shows that 75 cents or 75 percent ($1,500,000 ÷ $2,000,000) of every sales dollar is consumed by variable cost, leaving 25 cents to cover fixed cost and profit. If sales should increase or decrease variable cost will remain a constant 75 percent of sales and contribution will remain a constant 25 percent of sales.

In our electric motor illustration, the $20 contribution contributes first to covering fixed cost. When the total contribution equals total fixed cost, total revenue equals total cost and the firm is at the break-even point. Suppose that fixed cost is $10,000 per month. Sales revenue will equal total cost when 500 motors are sold per month ($10,000 ÷ $20) as shown below.

Sales (500 x $50)	$25,000
Variable cost (500 x $30)	(15,000)
Contribution margin	$10,000
Fixed cost	(10,000)
Net Income	0

If more than 500 units are sold per month, profit will equal the unit contribution times sales in excess of 500 units. Thus, if 550 motors are sold during a month, profit will be $1,000 (50 x $20). Let's prove it.

Sales (550 x $50)	$27,500
Variable cost (550 x $30)	(16,500)
Contribution margin	$11,000
Fixed cost	(10,000)
Net Income	$ 1,000

BREAK-EVEN ANALYSIS

When we consider break-even, we are concerned for that volume of activity where total revenue equals total cost. The activity can be expressed in units or in sales dollars. Graphically this is shown as the point at which the total cost curve intersects the total revenue curve

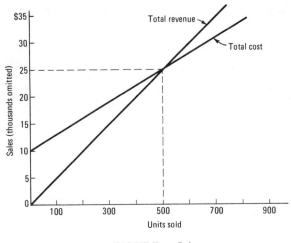

FIGURE   5-1

as in Figure 5-1. Thus if we drop a straight line from the break-even point to the units sold axis we can read break-even as 500 units. A line drawn from the break-even point to the sales axis and perpendicular to this axis shows break-even at $25,000 of sales (500 units x $50 per unit).

Breaking even is seldom a basic objective of a firm over the long haul. However, for a firm that has been experiencing losses, breaking even can be a valid interim objective. Knowing the break-even point provides management with a basis for making a number of important decisions. For example, a firm may be a consistent profit maker, but management still needs to know the impact on profit that would result from any changes in the volume of activity. In some instances a 10 percent reduction in activity could eliminate profit completely; in others, such a reduction may have only a minor impact on profit. Similarly, increases in the volume of activity have varying impacts on profit depending on the firm's cost structure.

Break-even Points

Break-even points can be located in a number of ways. We will be concerned only with two. First, break-even can be calculated, and, second, it can be observed from a graphic presentation as in the illustration given above. There are three values that are necessary for the determination of a break-even point. They are

1. the selling price of the unit
2. the unit variable cost
3. the total of fixed costs

The following illustration shows how these values are used to determine the break-even point. An item sells for $25 and has variable costs of $15 per unit. The fixed costs associated with this item are $50,000 for the time period involved. The break-even point is 5,000 units, and it is calculated as follows:

Selling price per unit	$25
Variable cost per unit	(15)
Unit contribution	$10

Each unit sold contributes $10 over variable cost. Again, this contribution does two things. First, the contribution must cover the balance of costs—the fixed cost—and, after this is done, contribution becomes profit. The break-even point is determined by dividing the total fixed cost by the unit contribution. Hence break-even is 5,000 units for the time period involved ($50,000 ÷ $10).

Using the contribution margin approach, we can come to the same conclusion. The contribution margin ratio is 40 percent ($10 ÷ $25). If we divide fixed cost by the contribution margin ratio, we obtain the break-even sales volume of $125,000 which is the equivalent of 5,000 units at $25 each. Let's make sure that we have found the break-even point.

Revenue from 5,000 units at $25	$125,000
Variable cost of 5,000 units at $15	(75,000)
Contribution margin	$ 50,000
Fixed cost	(50,000)
Net Income	0

If the level of activity realized is less than 5,000 units, a loss will result. If the level of activity realized is more than 5,000 units, a

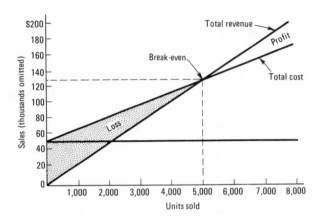

FIGURE 5-2. The Break-even Chart

profit will result (see Figure 5-2). Again, the profit per unit will be the unit contribution because at the 5,000-unit level all costs have been covered. Thus at the 8,000-unit level there is a profit of $30,000 (3,000 units above break-even × $10). You can also determine this by looking at Figure 5-2. At the 8,000-unit level revenue is $200,000, and total costs are $170,000.

Cost Balance and Break-even

In the previous chapter reference was made to the cost balance concept, the relation of fixed costs and variable costs to total cost. If a firm's variable costs are a high percentage of total cost, the unit contribution will be lower than with the reverse combination of cost. The lower variable costs are as a percentage of total costs, the higher the contribution will be with a given selling price. Because contribution equals profit above break-even volume, the balance of costs plays an important part in the speed with which profits are accumulated and losses pile up.

Suppose that a firm is producing a product that sells for $5 per unit. This product can be made by two different processes which the firm has the capacity to use. The first process (Figure 5-3A) involves a fixed cost of $5,000 and a unit variable cost of $4. The break-even point with this process is 5,000 units. A second process (Figure 5-3B) involves a fixed cost of $24,000 and a variable cost of $1 per unit. This process will have a break-even point of 6,000 units. The process with the lower fixed cost, A, has the lower break-

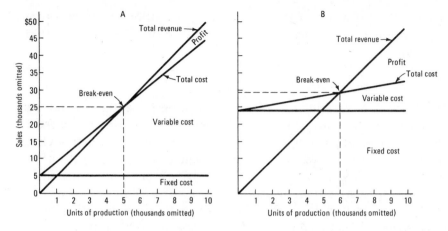

FIGURE 5-3. Break-even with Different Cost Balances

even point, but the important consideration is the angle of the profit wedge. B's profit wedge is much wider. At 6,333 units of activity each process yields the same profit, but at 10,000 units, B shows a profit of $16,000 versus a profit of only $5,000 for A. It would require the sale of 21,000 units made by process A to yield a $16,000 profit.

Profit Planning

The previous section is part and parcel of the profit-planning process, but there are other considerations. A product sells for $30 per unit and variable costs are $20 per unit. Fixed costs for the period are $20,000, and the firm has a target profit of $15,000. The problem is to determine the sales volume needed to earn the target profit. There are at least two ways to obtain the answer. The logic of the first approach is that the entire contribution above break-even is profit. In this illustration, break-even is 2,000 units (fixed cost of $20,000 ÷ unit contribution of $10). Therefore an additional 1,500 units ($15,000 ÷ $10) must be sold to obtain a target profit of $15,000.

The logic of the second approach is that contribution must now cover fixed cost plus profit, or $35,000. The volume needed to cover this amount is 3,500 units ($35,000 ÷ $10).

The contribution margin can be used to solve problems such as this. In this illustration the contribution margin is 33 1/3 percent

($10 ÷ $30). Dividing $35,000 by the contribution margin gives the sales volume needed to achieve the target profit. This is $105,000, or 3,500 units.

Profit-volume Chart

The data presented in Figure 5-2 can be presented in a number of ways to show different things. Figure 5-4 is a profit-volume chart. Rather than emphasizing the break-even point as such, this chart identifies the profit or loss that will result from operating at various levels of activity. At zero volume of activity there is no contribution or variable cost, but there is a fixed cost of $50,000. Thus at zero activity there is a loss of $50,000. The total contribution curve meets the zero net income (break-even) line at 5,000 units. The value of this chart is that it permits a quick reading of profit or loss at any level of activity between zero and 8,000 units. At a level of 3,000 units we can read that the loss will be $20,000, and at a level of 7,000 units we can read that the profit will be $20,000.

This chart also permits a direct reading of break-even and profit or loss at any level of activity when the selling price is changed. The dotted line in Figure 5-4 indicates that a selling price of $27.50 per unit will reduce the break-even point to 4,000 units and increase profit at the 7,000-unit level to $37,500.

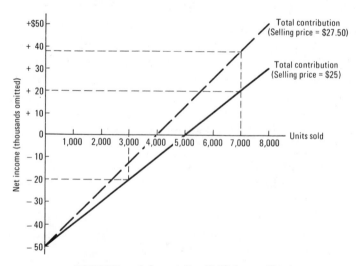

FIGURE   5-4.   A Profit-Volume Chart

Break-even in Retailing

In retailing it may not be possible to use data on unit selling price and unit variable cost to measure break-even. The reason for this is that a variety of products is sold and that each product may generate a different amount of contribution. Here we must use total sales dollars, total variable costs, and total fixed costs and apply the contribution margin approach. Here, contribution margin is actually the average contribution margin. The following illustration should clarify this.

Last year, a retailer earned a profit of $2,000,000 on sales of $10,000,000. The retailer knows that the fixed costs were $2,000,000 and is concerned with that point in sales volume that profit began to accumulate. We will show the break-even point in two steps. First, we will put down the facts as given.

Sales revenue	$10,000,000
Variable costs	—
Contribution margin	—
Fixed costs	2,000,000
Net Income	$ 2,000,000

There are three values given, but we need two additional values to complete the picture. The two additional values are easily determined because, if profit is $2,000,000, total cost must have been $8,000,000. Because fixed costs are $2,000,000, then total variable cost must have been $6,000,000 as shown below.

Sales revenue	$10,000,000
Variable costs	(6,000,000) 60%
Contribution margin	$ 4,000,000 40%
Fixed costs	(2,000,000)
Net Income	$ 2,000,000

This second illustration is given so that we can see the next step in our analysis. Variable costs are fixed per unit of activity *or* as a percentage of sales dollars. Variable costs are 60 percent of sales in this illustration. Thus contribution must be 40 percent of sales. Break-even occurred at a sales volume of $5,000,000 (fixed cost of $2,000,000 ÷ contribution of .40). A simple income statement at this volume of sales follows:

Sales revenue	$5,000,000
Variable costs	(3,000,000)
Contribution margin	$2,000,000
Fixed costs	(2,000,000)
Net Income	0

The retailer can conclude that all of his profit was earned on the last $5,000,000 of sales at the rate of 40 cents on the sales dollar.

This concept can also be used in profit planning. Earlier, we said that a given number of units had to be sold to break even. Here, we express the activity needed to achieve a profit objective as so many sales dollars. Suppose that the retailer desired a profit of $2,500,000. What increase in sales volume is needed to achieve this objective? Again, we can apply two approaches. First, we can reason that, because 40 cents of each sales dollar above break-even is profit, it will require an additional $1,250,000 in sales to increase profit by $500,000 ($500,000 ÷ .40). Earning a profit of $2,500,000 would require a sales volume of $11,250,000. A second approach considers that contribution must now cover fixed costs of $2,000,000 and profit of $2,500,000. Thus it would require $4,500,000 ÷ .40 or $11,250,000 of sales volume to achieve this objective.

Increased Fixed Cost and Break-even

There are times when management may wish to increase the total of fixed costs to improve operations. The increase could be to obtain more management talent, to increase the advertising budget, to purchase new equipment, or to obtain the services of an athletic superstar. Suppose, using the previous illustration, that management is studying the possibility of an advertising campaign that will cost $400,000 over a one-month period. Such an expenditure must be justified by increased sales volume. The question facing management is the amount by which sales volume must be increased to justify the expenditure. The computation is simple and involves the same concept as in the previous illustration. Sales must increase by $1,000,000 ($400,000 ÷ .40) just to break even on the additional expenditure.

The decision to embark on the advertising campaign depends on whether or not the firm has the capacity to increase sales volume in excess of $1,000,000. To illustrate, at one time the Boston Bruins hockey team had a superstar defenseman, Bobby Orr. Bobby's contract expired, and he asked for an astronomical—to us—salary increase which the Bruin's management refused to meet. At the same time the Chicago Black Hawks were "happy" to meet Bobby's demands. How come? For years, the Bruins had played to capacity crowds at home, while the Black Hawks had not. Thus the Black Hawks thought they could justify the increased fixed costs on the grounds that revenue would increase with the addition of a superstar. In theory, and only in theory, the Bruins could not increase the gate by Bobby's presence. Therefore, an increase in fixed cost seemed unjustified by Bruin's management.[1]

Price Changes and Break-even

A basic economic principle states that, when the price of a good or service decreases, the demand increases. The amount by which demand will increase if the selling price is decreased depends on the magnitude of the reduction and whether the demand for the good or service in question is elastic or inelastic.[2]

Obviously, if the selling price of a good or service is reduced and costs do not change, the unit contribution to fixed cost and profit is also reduced. This will result in a higher break-even point. However, as the volume of activity increases within the relevant range, the average unit cost decreases. Refer to Figure 5-2 and you

---

[1] By the same token, the average attendance at Black Hawk games would need to increase by only 1,000 spectators to cover additional fixed costs of $300,000 (1,000 fans x 40 home games x $7.50 contribution per fan).

[2] Demand is said to be elastic when a "small" movement in price results in a "large" change in demand. Demand is inelastic when changes in price have little effect on demand.

can see that at the 5,000-unit level total costs are $125,000 and the average cost is $25.00 which, at break-even is the same as the unit selling price. Move over to the 8,000-unit level and you can see that total costs are $170,000, making the average unit cost $21.25.

Continuing with this illustration, suppose that management decided to reduce the selling price of this item from $25.00 to $22.50. The first concern is the impact of this change on break-even point. This is shown below.

Unit selling price	$22.50
Unit variable cost	(15.00)
Unit Contribution	$ 7.50

The break-even point with a $22.50 selling price is 6,667 units ($50,000 ÷ $7.50). Thus sales would have to increase by one-third to break-even at the new price. The second concern is whether the demand for this item is sufficiently elastic to result in such a sales increase. This we cannot determine without more information.

A Review Illustration

The following illustration adds another dimension to the impact of a price change on break-even and profit. The following is a simple income statement for last year, and the same cost experience is expected during the coming year.

Sales (6,500 units at $25)	$162,500
Variable costs (6,500 units at $15)	(97,500)
Contribution margin	$ 65,000
Fixed costs	(50,000)
Net Income	$ 15,000

Management would like to utilize more of its capacity with the hope that profits will increase. It seems likely that a 5 percent reduction in selling price will result in a 15 percent increase in unit sales volume.

The basic question is whether the firm would be better off selling at the lower price. The following calculations will provide the answer.

Sales (7,475 units at $23.75)	$177,531
Variable costs (7,475 units at $15)	(112,125)
Contribution margin	$ 65,406
Fixed costs	(50,000)
Net Income	$ 15,406

The moral of this illustration is that it may require a very substantial increase in sales volume to compensate for a relatively small reduction in selling price.

Our second illustration emphasizes the unit contribution approach. Each of these situations should be considered separately unless reference is made to a previous situation. A product has a selling price of $50 and a unit variable cost of $30. Fixed cost for the accounting period is $100,000.

Question: What is the break-even point for this product in units?

Answer: Break-even is $100,000 ÷ ($50 − $30) = 5,000 units.

Question: What is the break-even point for this product in dollars of sales?

Answer: Break-even comes at 5,000 units x $50 = $250,000, or $100,000 ÷ ($20 ÷ $50) = $250,000.

Question: What sales volume in units is needed to earn a target profit of $50,000?

Answer: Sales volume must now cover $150,000 to achieve this objective (fixed cost of $100,000 plus profit of $50,000). Sales volume needed is $150,000 ÷ $20 = 7,500 units.

Question: What dollar sales volume is needed to achieve the objective stated above?

Answer: Sales volume in dollars needed is 7,500 x $50 = $375,000, or $150,000 ÷ ($20 ÷ $50) = $375,000.

Question: Management would like to earn a target profit of $50,000 but also increase the advertising budget by $60,000 to stimulate sales. What sales volume in units and dollars is needed to achieve this objective?

Answer: Sales volume needed to cover fixed cost ($100,000), profit ($50,000), and advertising ($60,000) is $210,000 ÷ $20 = 10,500 units, or $525,000.

Question: Suppose that management expected the advertising campaign to increase profit to $70,000. What sales volume would be needed to achieve this objective?

Answer: Sales volume needed must cover

Original fixed cost	$100,000
Additional advertising	60,000
Profit	70,000
Total	$230,000

Sales volume needed to cover $230,000 more than variable costs is $230,000 ÷ $20 = 11,500 units, or $575,000.

Question: If the unit selling price is reduced $5, what sales volume in units would be needed to break even?

Answer: Contribution is now $15, or $45 - $30; therefore break-even is 6,667 units ($100,000 ÷ $15).

Question: If the unit selling price is reduced by $5 and variable cost per unit is reduced by $5, what impact will this have on the unit break-even point?

Answer: Break even will be 5,000 units because unit contribution will be $20 as in the first question.

Question: If fixed costs, variable costs, and selling price are each reduced by 20 percent, what sales volume in units and dollars will be needed to earn a target profit of $40,000?

Answer: Selling price ($40) minus variable cost ($24) provides a unit contribution of $16. Contribution must cover fixed cost of $80,000 plus profit of $40,000, or $120,000. Sales volume needed is 7,500 units ($120,000 ÷ $16) or $300,000 (7,500 x $40).

NOT-FOR-PROFIT ENTERPRISE

The use of cost-volume-profit analysis is not limited to profit-making organizations; it can be applied in many other institutions. The principal difference between business enterprise and not-for-profit enterprise is that the former has owners and the latter does not. State laws allow certain organizations such as private universities,

Blue Cross-Blue Shield, the Red Cross, Care, and the Ford Foundation to acquire property, borrow money, and engage in business-type
activities even though no one owns the organization.

Many not-for-profit organizations operate in direct competition
with business enterprises; others, such as the Ford Foundation, do
not. Blue Cross-Blue Shield competes with private insurance companies in the health care field, privately owned magazine publishers
compete with *Reader's Digest,* and the Y.W.C.A. or the Y.M.C.A.
competes with motels and health spas for the same customers.
Those not-for-profit organizations that operate in direct competition
with private business often operate like a profit-oriented business,
and often the techniques that facilitate better business management
also facilitate better not-for-profit management.

Not-for-profit enterprise cannot show a profit in the same sense
as business enterprise, but all organizations except governments must
have an excess of revenues over costs if they are to grow or survive.
It is quite possible that many not-for-profit organizations plan a
specific excess of revenue over cost—a "target profit". The question
is not one of "profits" but where the profits go. In business enterprise part of profit may go to the owners in dividends, but in the
not-for-profit organization "profit" must stay in the organization.

Whether an organization can apply cost-volume-profit analysis
hinges not on the matter of ownership but on the organization's
cost structure. A private not-for-profit university can measure break-
even, or the "profit" that will result from the admission of 100
more students, provided that it can express its costs as unit variable
or total fixed. This is difficult to do with a total university, but it
can be applied to special programs. For example, the dean of a
college of business was contemplating the operation of an executive
master of business administration program. Rather than running the
program on campus the dean decided to rent space at a local hotel
and use its facilities. In the feasibility study the following costs were
estimated:

Rent of hotel facilities	$10,000
Faculty salaries	9,000
Texts and supplies, per student	300
Meals, per student	400
Promotion of the program	1,000
Guest speakers	1,000

This summarized data was used for a number of purposes. It was used first to check on the feasibility of running the program. The dean felt that through effective promotion a class of 25 students willing to pay $2,000 in fees could be attracted. Thus he drew up the following:

Revenue from 25 students		$50,000
Variable Costs:		
Texts and supplies		
(25 x $300)	$ 7,500	
Meals (25 x $400)	10,000	17,500
Contribution margin		$32,500
Fixed Costs:		
Rental	$10,000	
Faculty	9,000	
Promotion	1,000	
Guest speakers	1,000	21,000
Excess of Revenue Over Cost		$11,500

Thus it appears that the program could be a financial success if 25 students enrolled in the program. The dean was also interested in the number of students needed to make the program yield $10,000 over costs and made the following analysis.

Revenue per student	$2,000
Variable cost per student	(700)
Contribution Per Student	$1,300

The number of students needed to achieve this objective is 24 ($31,000 ÷ $1,300).

Cost-volume-profit analysis is used in some phases of government and in many segments of not-for-profit enterprise. Without such analysis institutions cannot tell which segments of the organization are pulling their weight and which are not. To repeat, if any organization can express its cost as unit variable and total fixed, it can utilize this analysis.

SUMMARY

Breaking even may not be the goal of most businesses, but every business needs to know the level of activity needed to break even because, until this point is reached, no profit can be earned. If a firm has high fixed cost in relation to variable cost, it will need a higher sales volume before profit is earned than will a firm having the reverse combination of cost. But the firm having higher fixed cost will show a greater profit per dollar of sales above the break-even point. The reason for this is that the firm with high fixed cost will have a greater contribution margin than the firm having high variable cost. Above the break-even point, contribution is profit.

Any organization, be it business, government, a hospital, or a university, can measure break-even and establish target "profit" provided its costs can be expressed in unit variable and total fixed terms.

KEY TERMS

break-even analysis

break-even chart

break-even point

contribution

contribution margin

not-for-profit enterprise

profit-volume chart

QUESTIONS

1. Why must some firms have a greater volume of sales revenue to earn a given target profit than others?
2. What is contribution and why is it important to management?
3. What is the difference between unit contribution and contribution margin? In what types of situations would each be used?
4. Breaking even is seldom a goal of business. Why is it that businessmen are so interested in determining break-even points?
5. "It is better to have high variable costs than high fixed costs because break-even comes at a lower level of activity." Do you agree? Explain.
6. Any organization, business or otherwise, can use cost-volume-profit analysis. Do you agree? Explain.

7. An increase in fixed cost will always increase the break-even point. Do you agree? Why?

8. What are some of the assumptions that underlie the use of break-even analysis?

9. If the selling price of Glop is $2.00 per gallon, the variable cost to manufacture is $1.95, and the variable selling cost is $.10 per gallon, the only way Glop can be profitable is if tremendous quantities are sold. Comment.

10. A salesman guarantees that your company's sales will increase $50,000 if you hire him. If these sales do not materialize you will not have to pay him $35,000 a year in commissions. Would you get involved with this "no risk" proposition?

PROBLEMS _____

1. Cost-revenue relationships

Figure 5-5 shows the cost-revenue relationships in the generator division of the Apex Electrical Products Corp.:

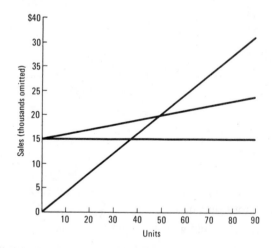

FIGURE   5-5

Required:

a. The unit selling price of a generator is $_____ .

b. The break-even point is $_____ .

c. The break-even point is _____ units.

d. The unit variable cost is $_____ .

e. Total fixed costs are $_____ .

f. At capacity of 90 units profit is $_____.

g. If 80 rather than 90 units are sold, profit will decrease by $_____.

2. Break-even analysis

The Farewell Razor Company produces a custom razor that sells for $20. Variable costs are $12 per razor and fixed costs are $56,000 per month.

Required:

a. Construct a break-even chart to show these cost-revenue relationships.

b. The break-even point in units is _____.

c. The break-even point in dollars is $_____.

d. How many razors must be sold to earn a profit of $10,000 per month?

e. What profit will be earned if 8,000 razors are produced and sold in one month?

f. If variable costs increase by $2.00 per unit, what impact will this have on the break-even volume?

g. Plant capacity is 15,000 razors per month. At this level of activity what selling price per razor is needed to earn a profit of $30,000 per month?

3. Profit

Sue Smith bought a plastic engraving machine and a table saw for $1,550. She made a large sign for a hospital which earned her $125. The materials for this sign cost $7.50.

Required:

a. What profit did Sue make on this sign? Explain.

4. Break-even analysis

The selling price of an item is $40 and the unit variable cost is $28. Fixed costs amount to $192,000 per year.

Required:

a. What is the break-even point in units?

b. What is the break-even point in dollars?

c. Calculate the break-even point in dollars using a different approach than the one used above.

d. How many units must be sold to earn a profit of $72,000?

e. Management has decided to increase the advertising budget by $60,000 per year. How many additional units must be sold to make this expenditure worthwhile?

5. Cost-volume-profit relationships

The following data came from the records of the Twibold Corporation.

	Alphas	Betas	Iotas	Omegas
Sales price (unit)	$_____	$50	$ 100	$ 80
Variable cost (unit)	40	25	60	——
Contribution margin (unit)	20	——	——	40
Fixed cost (total)	$20,000	——	$200,000	$100,000
Break even (units)	1,000	5,000	——	——

Required:

Fill in the blanks.

6. Profit-volume chart

The manager of the generator department wants to have a ready reference to show the impact on profit when volumes of activity change. One product is produced in the department and it sells for $60. Variable costs are $40 per unit and fixed costs total $160,000. The relevant range of activity is 4,000 - 14,000 units.

Required:

a. Prepare a profit-volume chart.

b. What profit or loss would you estimate at the 6,000 unit level? Pinpoint the profit on the profit-volume chart.

7. Break even in retailing

The income statement for Marshall Sales Co. is shown below.

Marshall Sales Co.

Income Statement, For the year ended 19X5

Sales		$1,500,000
Cost of goods sold (variable)		950,000
Gross Margin		$ 550,000
Sales commissions	$220,000	
Annual salaries	125,000	
Other fixed costs	100,000	445,000
Net Income		$ 105,000

Required:

a. On what sales volume did Marshall break even?

b. On what volume of sales was profit earned? At what rate per dollar of sales?

c. Management is very unhappy with this profit figure. What sales volume is needed to increase profit by 50 percent?

8. Pricing

The Skidmore Skate Company is certain that it can sell 50,000 pairs of skates during the coming season. The following data relating to costs has been made available.

Materials	$ 18.40 per pair
Labor	$ 4.60 per pair
Fixed costs	$360,000.00 per year

Required:

a. What price must be charged per pair of skates just to break even?

b. If management wants to earn a profit of $10.00 per pair of skates, what selling price must be charged?

9. Profit-volume measurement

The Bay State Bombers, a professional football team, is concerned with their profit-volume picture for the coming year. Early forecasts of costs showed the following:

Fixed Costs:	
Salaries	$4,000,000
Rent, etc.	$1,390,000

The average price of a ticket is $8.00 but each fan spends enough money for "goodies" while at the stadium to increase the club's take by 50 cents per fan. Variable costs are 80 cents per fan.

Required:

a. What attendance will be required just to break even?

b. If 800,000 fans attend the Bomber games during the season, what profit will be earned?

On July 1, the veteran Bomber players went on strike, and the team was forced to start the season with free agents and rookies making up the team. The strike reduced salary costs by $2,000,000, but attendance is expected to drop to 500,000 fans for the 16-game schedule.

c. How will the Bombers fare financially if the strike continues?

d. If there had been no player strike, attendance for the 16 games was estimated at 880,000 fans. How much will the strike cost the owners of the Bombers?

10.   Break-even and pricing

Fred Barker is a traveling salesman for the Massapoag Industrial Packing Corp. The firm pays Fred 16 cents per mile for the use of his car. Fred is on the road 200 days a year and averages 150 miles of travel each day. Fred's car cost $8,500, and it is expected that it will have a trade-in value of $2,500 at the end of three years. The car gets 18 miles to a gallon of gasoline. Additional costs are

Oil change every 6,000 miles	$ 24.00
Tune-up every 20,000 miles	140.00
Gasoline per gallon	1.08
Insurance and taxes per year	1,000.00
Tires every 30,000 miles	240.00

Fred uses straight-line depreciation.

Required:

a. How many miles per year would Fred have to drive just to break even on a 16 cents per mile allowance?

b. Fred maintains that he should get at least 18 cents per mile for the use of his car. Do you agree? Explain.

11.   Pricing

The We Haul Trailer Company is engaged in the trailer rental business. Depreciation, insurance, and other fixed costs average $600 per trailer per year. Variable costs are negligible and are not considered in the development of a pricing policy.

Required:

a. Explain how the We Haul management can determine the amount it should charge for the use of a trailer. Your answer can be per day or per mile, whichever you think is better.

b. In a situation such as this should depreciation be a fixed or variable cost? Explain.

12. Cost-volume-profit analysis

Last year the Pueblo Corporation earned a profit of $300,000 on the sale of 80,000 specialty butane lighters. The break-even sales volume was 50,000 units and the contribution margin ratio was 40 percent.

Required:

a. Determine the contribution per unit sold.

b. What was the total of fixed costs?

c. What was the unit selling price of a lighter?

d. What was the variable cost of a lighter?

e. Prepare an income statement for the year.

13. Cost-volume-profit relations

Meyers Industries manufacturers and distributes a special valve used to control the flow of chemicals under pressure. The following data was taken from the firm's records for last year:

Sales (20,000 units)	$10,000,000
Direct materials used	2,200,000
Direct labor used	1,600,000
Variable overhead	800,000
Fixed overhead	1,000,000
Variable selling and administrative costs	1,200,000
Fixed selling and administrative costs	1,800,000

Required:

a. Calculate the unit selling price.

b. Calculate the unit variable cost.

c. Calculate the unit contribution.

d. Calculate the break-even point in units and in dollars.

e. Calculate the net income earned.

14. Pricing

The Capricon Company has developed a new consumer product called Fix-All. The market research division of the firm estimates that sales of the product during the next year will be 200,000 units. The variable cost associated with this product is $2.50 per unit, and fixed cost is estimated at $300,000 for the year.

Required:

a. What selling price should be established for Fix-All if the firm has a first-year goal of breaking even?

b. If the firm desires a return equal to 20 percent of its fixed investment, what selling price should be established?

15. Pricing

Harbour Cruises, Inc. operates a sight-seeing boat out of Hamilton, Bermuda. Fixed costs for the boat are $80,000 per year and this includes the skipper's salary. Variable costs average $400 per trip. The boat makes two runs per day and operates 360 days per year. Patronage averages 100 fares per trip.

Required:

a. The company has a target profit of $100,000 per year. How much should be charged per fare to cover costs and earn the target profit?

b. With this fare, how many trips would the boat have to make a year just to break even?

c. When asked, the president of Harbour Cruises said that the business really did not have any variable costs. Could this be possible? Explain.

16. Break-even analysis

The Moor Machine Company's income statement for last year is as follows:

Moor Machine Company
Income Statement, For the year ended 19XX

Sales (20,000 units)		$1,200,000
Materials ($24 per unit)	$480,000	
Labor ($8 per unit)	160,000	
Variable overhead	100,000	
Fixed overhead	60,000	800,000
Gross margin		$ 400,000
General expenses, variable	$ 40,000	
General expenses, fixed	260,000	300,000
Net Income		$ 100,000

Required:

a. At what volume of sales did the company break even? In dollars $_____, in units _____.

b. On what volume of sales dollars was the profit earned and at what rate per dollar?

c. Mr. Moore was advised that an advertising campaign costing $60,000 would increase sales by 10 percent. Would you advise Mr. Moore to invest the $60,000? Explain.

17. Cost balance

The following are the income statements for the Varley Corporation and the Farley Corporation for last year. The two firms produce and sell an identical product and their sales volume and selling prices are identical.

	Farley	Varley
Sales (20,000 units)	$500,000	$500,000
Variable costs	100,000	300,000
Contribution margin	$400,000	$200,000
Fixed costs	350,000	100,000
Net Income	$ 50,000	$100,000

The president of the Farley Corporation is concerned that his competitor earned twice the net income on the same volume of sales and is studying the situation.

Required:

a. At what volume of sales did each firm break even?

b. What sales volume would the Farley Corporation need to earn a net income of $100,000?

c. If the demand for the product increases so that each firm will sell 30,000 units next year, which firm will have the greater net income? Assume no changes in cost behavior.

18. Cost-volume-profit analysis in retailing

Last year the Dixon Furniture Outlet earned a profit of $70,000 on sales of $800,000. Mr. Dixon knows that his fixed costs for the year were $210,000 but wants to know more about the year's operations.

Required:

a. What was the break-even point in sales dollars?

b. On what sales volume was profit earned and at what rate per sales dollar?

c. What percentage decrease in profit would Mr. Dixon experience if sales decreased by 10 percent?

d. What percentage increase in profit would Mr. Dixon experience if sales increased by 10 percent?

e. Explain the increase and decrease in profit calculated above.

19.   Cost-volume relations

Rose Budd has been working as a salesperson in a profitable company for several years. Her manager, however, feels that she is not working as effectively as possible and therefore is not worth the $17,800 in annual salary. The company has a variable cost ratio of 75 percent. It is estimated that, if the manager fires Rose Budd, the firm will lose $50,000 a year in sales.

Required:

a. Ignoring qualitative factors, should Rose Budd be fired?

b. What impact would the manager's decision have on net income next year?

c. What sales volume is needed to support Rose Budd's salary?

20.   Cost-volume-profit analysis

Syncon Industries of Cambridge, Massachusetts has been in the flocking business for more than 20 years and has experienced a steady rate of growth. Mr. Humbert, the owner of Syncon, wants to add another flocking unit because of anticipated demand but does not have the space in the rented Cambridge facility.

A building available in a near-by town can be purchased for $700,000 excluding land. If purchased, the building would need $300,000 in alterations to make it ideal for flocking operations. The estimated life of the remodeled facility is 25 years, and Mr. Humbert feels that he could recover $200,000 from the sale of the building when it is fully depreciated. Syncon uses straight-line depreciation.

If the move is made, out-of-pocket fixed costs have been estimated at $148,000 for the first year. Variable costs per yard of flocked material average as follows:

Flocking material	$0.40
Adhesives	0.28
Labor	0.12
Other variable costs	0.10

On an average, Syncon receives $1.10 per yard of material processed.

Required:

a. How many yards of material must be processed the first year just to break even in the new facility?

b. If 1,100,000 yards of material are processed the first year, what profit should be earned?

c. Capacity at the new plant is 1,500,000 yards per year. If the plant operates at capacity, what profit can be anticipated?

6 Cost-Volume-Profit Relations –A Further Look

CHAPTER OVERVIEW ⎯⎯⎯⎯⎯⎯⎯⎯⎯⎯⎯⎯⎯⎯⎯⎯⎯⎯⎯⎯⎯⎯⎯⎯

The purpose of this chapter is to put additional dimensions on the concepts developed in the previous chapter. The impact of income taxes on target profit is considered first. We note next that ownership form may have a bearing on break-even volumes because certain items that are expenses for a corporation may not apply to proprietorships and partnerships. In addition, we use this chapter to identify certain assumptions that were made earlier and show how they impact on cost-volume-profit analysis.

Because most business firms sell goods that have varying contribution margin ratios we need to consider the impact of changing sales mixes on break-even and profit. The amount of profit that a firm will earn depends both on how much is sold and what is sold.

QUESTIONS FOR CONSIDERATION ⎯⎯⎯⎯⎯⎯⎯⎯⎯⎯⎯⎯⎯⎯⎯⎯⎯

1. How much before-tax profit must be earned to yield a given after-tax target profit?
2. Why might proprietorships appear to be more profitable and have lower break-even points than comparable corporations?
3. Are total cost and total revenue curves likely to be linear in the world of business?
4. Can a business have more than one break-even point?
5. What impact will shifting sales mixes have on break-even and profit?

In the previous chapter we presented a conceptual picture of cost-volume-profit relationships. The purpose of this theoretical presentation was to identify the basic ideas and processes involved in this type of analysis. A number of assumptions were made, and a number of problem areas were intentionally omitted. In this chapter we will apply the basic concepts to other problem areas.

TAX IMPLICATIONS

In our illustrations we have referred to net income and target profit without identifying the inescapable impact of income taxes. Profit planning must include after-tax profit as well as before-tax profit because only after-tax profit remains with the firm. To achieve a target profit after taxes of, say, $100,000 requires a larger before-tax profit.

The impact of taxes on after-tax profit depends on the magnitude of the profit and the tax rate. The tax rate in turn depends on the magnitude of the profit and the form of business ownership. At law, corporations are considered legal entities and must pay a corporate income tax.

Proprietorships and partnerships do not pay any income tax at the federal level. These ownership forms are common-law institutions wherein the business and the owners' are one and the same. A proprietor's personal income is the proprietorship profit. A proprietor's profit is taxed at the same rates as our income from salaries and wages.

The process for determining the amount of before-tax profit needed to yield a particular target profit is simple. The logic is this: If, say, 40 percent of profit goes to Uncle Sam, then 60 percent remains with the firm. Thus, if a firm had a target profit of $60,000 after taxes, a before-tax profit of $100,000 would be needed ($60,000 ÷ .60). Earlier we mentioned that contribution had to cover fixed costs plus profit. Now we add another consideration; it must also cover income taxes, or before-tax income.

To illustrate, a retailer has fixed costs of $600,000. Variable costs are 60 percent of sales; therefore, the contribution margin must be 40 percent. The retailer is aiming for an after-tax profit of $120,000. Taxes are expected to be 40 percent of before-tax profit. What sales volume is needed to achieve the target profit of $120,000?

The before-tax profit that must be earned is $200,000 ($120,000 ÷ .60). Contribution must now cover fixed costs ($600,000) plus target profit ($120,000) plus taxes ($80,000). The sales volume needed to cover $800,000 more than variable cost is $2,000,000 ($800,000 ÷ .40). The income statement looks like this:

Sales	$2,000,000
Variable costs (60%)	(1,200,000)
Contribution margin	$ 800,000
Fixed costs	600,000
Net income before taxes	$ 200,000
Income tax (40%)	80,000
Net Income After Taxes	$ 120,000

Break-even and Ownership Form

The "profit" or net income of a business can depend in part on the form of ownership. Two firms can show the same net income on a given volume of sales, yet one firm can return more dollars to the owner(s) than the other.

We will point out how this is possible and how break-even can also differ through an illustration. Frank Briles has been operating a haberdashery for a number of years as a sole proprietor and has been quite successful. The business has no debt, and Mr. Briles owns the block in which his store is located. Mr. Briles feels that a person with his know-how could command a salary of $30,000 a year working for someone else. The estimated rental value of the store is $12,000 per year.

Because Mr. Briles is a proprietorship, the business cannot pay him a salary nor can it pay him rent for the use of the building. The reason for this, as pointed out earlier, is that the business and the owner are one and the same. You cannot pay yourself a salary. An owner can draw money out of the business for personal use, but this would result in a reduction of capital; it would not be a business expense. If the business was incorporated, it could pay Mr. Briles, who could be the sole owner, a salary of $30,000 and $12,000 rent for the use of the building. We use income statements to show how both net income and break-even are affected by ownership form.

TABLE   6-1

Profitability of a Proprietorship versus a Corporation

	As a proprietorship	*As a corporation*
Sales	$400,000	$400,000
Variable costs	240,000	240,000
Contribution margin	$160,000	$160,000
Fixed Costs:		
Manager's salary		30,000
Rent		12,000
Insurance	5,000	5,000
Employee salaries	45,000	45,000
Advertising	50,000	50,000
Total fixed costs	$100,000	$142,000
Net Income Before Taxes	$ 60,000	$ 18,000

This illustration shows that a bottom-line figure of $60,000 in one situation is the same as $18,000 in another. In each instance the number of dollars involved is the same, but the classifications are different. As a proprietor, Mr. Briles pays an income tax on gross income of $60,000. As a manager of a corporation, Mr. Briles pays a tax on his salary of $30,000 plus the profit realized from renting the property, and the corporation pays a tax on the $18,000 net income. However, if Mr. Briles had hired someone to manage the corporate business and had paid a landlord rent of $12,000 for the year, the same net income would be shown for each ownership form. Thus this illustration shows what the impact of ownership form could be rather than what will be.

The possible impact of ownership form on break-even should now be apparent. Proprietorships tend to show a higher net income and lower fixed costs than a corporation, all factors being equal. As a proprietorship, Briles breaks even at $250,000 of sales ($100,000 ÷ .40); as a corporation, Briles breaks even at $355,000 of sales

($142,000 ÷ .40). Comparisons of business firms must take owner-ship form into consideration.

Some Basic Assumptions

Our discussions of cost-volume-profit relations to this point are based on a number of assumptions. Cost-volume-profit analysis can be a valid and useful tool for management only if these assumptions hold true or if management recognizes that these assumptions are no longer valid and makes the appropriate adjustments.

Constant Dollars

In our illustrations we have assumed that there was no change in the value of the dollar. It would be foolhardy to compare today's dollar values with those of only a few years ago. Before comparing current values with past or future values, each should be based on the same price level. Of major concern here are the values given to long-term assets such as buildings and machinery. Suppose a firm constructed a building in 1965 and took out a 25-year mortgage. Depreciation and interest for the next 25 years is set at $100,000 per year. Assume these to be the only fixed cost. Additional information is as follows:

	1965	*Today*
Selling price	$10.00	$20.00
Variable cost	(6.00)	(12.00)
Unit Contribution	$ 4.00	$ 8.00

In 1965, break-even came at a volume of 25,000 units. Today the break-even comes at a volume of 12,500 units. This "improve-ment" in break-even can be misleading because eventually these long-term assets will have to be replaced at current prices, and break-even could skyrocket over night. Because profit depends on the volume of activity in excess of break-even, profit potentials could easily be exaggerated if constant dollars are not used.

Revenue a Function of Volume

We have shown revenue curves as linear—a function of volume. This may or may not occur in practice. In some instances as volume

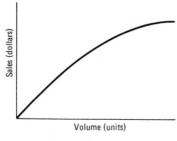

FIGURE   6-1

of activity increases the unit selling price decreases and the revenue curve could be as shown in Figure 6-1.

Or, for some reason, management may learn that after a given volume of activity selling prices will have to be increased. If so, the revenue curve could be as shown in Figure 6-2.

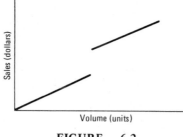

FIGURE   6-2

These are but two variations that can happen to revenue curves. The important consideration is that the revenue curve has a bearing on the break-even volume. Thus management must be able to approximate the course of the revenue curve if it is to approximate the point of break-even.

Costs Behave as They Should

We have assumed that total variable costs are a function of the volume of activity and that the total of fixed costs remains constant. This probably will not be true in practice. This in itself will not negate the usefulness of break-even analysis provided management does know the behavior of costs. For example, as volumes of production increase, the volume of direct material that must be purchased will also increase. The consequence could be lower unit costs for

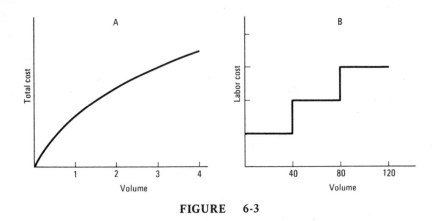

FIGURE   6-3

material and thus a total variable cost curve such as in Figure 6-3A. Direct labor could be a pure variable cost if workers were paid by piece rate; that is, a specific amount of money is paid for each operation completed regardless of volume. More likely, the cost curve for direct labor will increase in steps such as in Figure 6-3B. The reason for this is the impossibility of equating numbers of workers to numbers of units produced.

Suppose that a firm has a standard output per hour of 40 units for each production worker who is paid $8 for each hour worked. Two production workers will be needed whether the production level is 41 or 80 units per hour. Whether 1 or 40 units are produced per hour, the total labor cost per hour is $8. Thus within specific ranges of activity labor costs are fixed. Management should try to operate at volumes of 40, 80, or 120 units per hour to minimize the unit cost of labor.

The Combination Effect

Because of the many variations that can take place in cost and revenue behavior, the break-even chart of a firm could be quite unlike the charts we have used in our illustrations. In fact, it is possible for a firm to have several break-even points depending on the characteristics of the firm's costs. Figure 6-4 is an illustration of what could happen in practice.

This illustration also points out that there can be "right way" and "wrong way" break-even points. Break-even points A and B are "right way" break-even points because volumes in excess of break even produce profit. Break-even point C is a "wrong way" break-

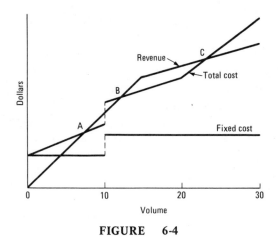

FIGURE   6-4

even point because volumes in excess of this break even will result in losses. Because of multiple break-even points, management must decide which level of activity should be established.

SALES MIX

Break-even, as we have learned, is a function of fixed costs and contribution margin. When a firm deals with a single product or a group of products each of which has the same contribution margin ratio sales mix presents no problem in measuring break-even. Problems arise when a firm deals with a variety of products each of which has a different contribution margin ratio.

In an earlier illustration, a retailer had fixed costs of $2,000,000 and an average contribution margin ratio of 40 percent. We determined the break-even point to be $5,000,000 of sales. However, we cannot conclude that the retailer will always break even at this volume of sales even though fixed costs remain the same. The reason for this is that the retailer may sell a different combination of products in the future having an average contribution margin ratio greater than or less than 40 percent.

Greater sales volumes will not necessarily lead to greater profits even though fixed costs do not change. It is quite possible that greater sales volumes will lead to lower overall profits. The deciding factor is contribution. Profit planning requires consideration of both sales volume and contribution margin. One General Electric sales engineer, at least, had his sales forecast rejected even though it was

25 percent higher than the forecast for the previous year. The reason for the rejection was that the forecast included too large a portion of low-margin items. Few, if any, Ford dealers, for example, can earn a satisfactory profit if the only cars they sell are stripped model Pintos. A dealer would probably rather sell one LTD model for $8,500 than two stripped Pintos for $4,250 each.

We will approach the sales-mix problem through a number of illustrations. Last year's income statement for Highway Motors is as follows:

	Standards	Deluxe	Used	Total
Sales	$800,000	$800,000	$400,000	$2,000,000
Variable costs	640,000	560,000	300,000	1,500,000
Contribution margin	$160,000	$240,000	$100,000	$ 500,000
Fixed cost	120,000	120,000	60,000	300,000
Net Income	$ 40,000	$120,000	$ 40,000	$ 200,000

Note that the same net income was earned on used cars as on standard models, although sales volume of used cars was only one-half as much as for standards. And three times as much profit was earned on deluxe models as on standards with the same sales volume. Again, the important factor is contribution.

Determining Break-even

Because the average contribution is .25 ($500,000 ÷ $2,000,000), break-even for this dealer came at a sales volume of $1,200,000 ($300,000 ÷ .25) but this is not an adequate expression of break-even. Sales mix must be considered. In this situation the dealer broke even on the following sales:

Standards (40% x $1,200,000)	$ 480,000
Deluxe (40% x $1,200,000)	480,000
Used (20% x $1,200,000)	240,000
	$1,200,000

To emphasize the importance of sales mix, let us assume that the sales manager brought the owner a sales plan for next year calling for the following sales:

Standards	$1,000,000
Deluxe	600,000
Used	400,000
	$2,000,000

Would the owner be pleased with this forecast which has the same total sales as the previous year? Contribution margins will remain the same as a percentage of sales for each product, and fixed costs will remain the same in total. It is the policy of the dealer to allocate fixed costs to products based on sales volume. Here is what the dealer can expect from this sales forecast:

	Standards	Deluxe	Used	Total
Sales	$1,000,000	$600,000	$400,000	$2,000,000
Variable costs	800,000	420,000	300,000	1,520,000
Contribution margin	$ 200,000	$180,000	$100,000	$ 480,000
Fixed cost	150,000	90,000	60,000	300,000
Net Income	$ 50,000	$ 90,000	$ 40,000	$ 180,000

This mix of products will yield $20,000 less profit because more of the low-margin items and fewer of the high-margin items are involved.

Forecasting Break-even

We can use the concepts contained in the previous illustration to forecast break even and to plan profit. For example, a retailer sells three products called standards, deluxe, and used. Thirty percent of sales are standards, 50 percent are deluxe, and 20 percent are used. The contribution margins are 20 percent, 30 percent, and 25 percent respectively. Fixed costs are $320,000 and the retailer has a target

profit of $200,000 before taxes. What sales volume must be achieved?
The process for answering this question follows:

Item	Percent of total		Contribution margin		Total cont. margin
Standard	30%	x	.20	=	.06
Deluxe	50	x	.30	=	.15
Used	20	x	.25	=	.05
		Total Contribution Margin		=	.26

The needed sales volume is fixed cost ($320,000) plus profit
($200,000) divided by the contribution margin (.26), or $2,000,000.
Again, the retailer will not necessarily cover his fixed cost and earn
a profit of $200,000 on sales of $2,000,000. The $2,000,000 must
have the expected sales mix. Thus break-even sales are expressed as

Standard (30%)	$ 600,000
Deluxe (50%)	1,000,000
Used (20%)	400,000
Total	$2,000,000

Another Sales-mix Illustration

Contribution margin equals selling price minus variable costs
but the cost of merchandise purchased is only one of several variable
costs that are incurred. In this illustration we will explain how other
variable costs impact on the measurement of break-even points.

The Cornwall Company sells power boats, sailboats, and rowboats. Variable-cost data relating to the three classes of boats follows.
Each variable cost is expressed as a percentage of selling price.

	Power	Sail	Row
Cost of purchases	52	62	72
Commissions	12	10	8
Other variable costs	6	5	5
Total	70	77	85

The company estimates that power and sailboats will each contribute 40 percent of sales volume and rowboats 20 percent. Total fixed costs are estimated to be $101,500. Management needs to know the sales volume by class of boat needed to earn a profit of $80,000, before taxes.

The analysis.

	Power	*Sail*	*Row*	*Total*
Selling price	1.00	1.00	1.00	
Variable cost	.70	.77	.85	
Contribution margin	.30	.23	.15	
X % of total	40	40	20	
Total Contribution	.12	.092	.03	.242

The solution.   The sales volume needed to achieve the objective is $181,500 ÷ .242, or $750,000, distributed as follows:

Power	$300,000
Sail	$300,000
Row	$150,000

If a larger-than-planned percentage of sales is powerboats, the break-even point will be less; if rowboats are a higher percentage of sales than planned, the break-even sales volume will be higher.

Contribution Margin and Unit Volume

On the surface it might appear that a sales mix having a large percentage of high contribution items is better than a sales mix that emphasizes low contribution items but this is not always the case. More important than unit contribution margin or contribution margin ratio is the total dollars of contribution that can be generated with a given level of fixed cost. The best sales mix therefore depends on the firm's merchandising abilities.

Planning the sales mix and the sales volume needed to obtain a target contribution is a relatively easy process but adhering to the plan may not be easy. Competitive pressures may force selling prices down or it may be impossible to raise selling prices when costs rise. Thus it is essential that progress toward the contribution goal be closely monitored.

SUMMARY

In this chapter we have gone beyond the basics of cost-volume-profit analysis to consider the more practical aspects of the concept.

The only profit that management can use is after-tax profit, but the profit that must be earned is before-tax profit. Management, therefore, is concerned with the volume of activity required to yield a given after-tax profit.

Because owner-managers of proprietorships and partnerships cannot receive salary and certain other payments from the business and owner-managers of corporations can, comparable corporations may show lower profit and higher break-even points than their proprietorship-partnership counterparts.

Over time, break-even points may change due to inflation. If fixed costs do not increase as fast as variable costs and selling prices, and this is a likely situation, break-even points may fall simply because the contribution per unit of product sold has risen.

Profit will not necessarily increase when sales volumes increase; in fact, higher sales could result in lower profit. Attention must be given to what is sold as well as to how much is sold. The reason for this is that different classes of goods may have different contribution margins. If additional low-contribution-margin goods are sold at the expense of high-contribution items, profit will go down and the break-even point will rise.

KEY TERMS

after-tax profit   sales mix

constant dollars   step variable cost

QUESTIONS

1. Are proprietorships and partnerships taxed the same as corporations? Explain.

2. An owner-managed proprietorship will probably have a lower break-even point than an identical business formed as a corporation. Why is this so?

3. If the income tax rate is 40 percent, what before-tax net income is needed to yield an after-tax profit of $75,000?

4. Fixed costs are $100,000 and the contribution margin ratio is 40 percent. Taxes are 40 percent, and the firm has an after-tax target profit of $60,000. What sales volume is needed to earn the target profit?

5. Can inflation lower break-even points when break-even is stated in units sold?

6. Is it reasonable to expect that total cost and total revenue curves will be linear? Explain.

7. Can a firm have more than one break-even point? Explain.

8. Why is sales mix an important factor in profit planning?

9. Is it possible to forecast a break-even point if the product mix is unknown? Explain.

10. Can a firm show a lower profit on an increased volume of sales even though total fixed costs remain the same? Explain.

11. "A firm should carry as many high-contribution-margin items as possible and forget low-contribution items." Do you agree? Explain.

12. A retailer had sales of $300,000, variable costs of $200,000, and a contribution margin of $100,000. Why do we describe the contribution margin ratio of 33 1/3 percent as an average contribution margin ratio?

PROBLEMS

1. Total contribution

The Village Variety Store has a fixed amount of shelf space to devote to bread. If a new brand is added, space must be taken from other brands to make room for it. The sales manager of Pepper Valley Farms, a baker of specialized bakery products, is trying to get shelf space in the variety store for its bread products. His breads have an average selling price of 70 cents per loaf and cost the retailer 48 cents. The brand that this bread would replace sells for 62 cents a loaf and costs the retailer 50 cents.

Required:

a. Would the variety store owner be at all interested in carrying the new brand? Identify the factors that would be considered in reaching a decision.

2. Sales mix

The Rubberride Tire Company produces and markets two lines of automobile tires, bias belted and radial. Typical cost-price relationships per tire are as follows:

	Bias belted	Radial
Sales price	$40	$70
Variable cost	30	45
Contribution Margin	$10	$25

Sales for the tires average 200,000 units for bias belted and 100,000 for radials per month. The sales manager has recommended a plan to stimulate radial tire sales. It involves a 10 percent decrease in the price of radial tires and an advertising campaign costing $50,000 per month. The sales manager feels that his plan would result in a 20 percent increase in radial tire sales which have the higher contribution margin and a corresponding decrease in bias-belted tire sales which have a lower contribution margin.

Required:

a. Should the sales manager's plan be adopted? Explain.

3. Sales mix

An abbreviated income statement for the Monumental Sales Outlet for last year follows:

	Dry Goods	Furniture	Hardware	Total
Sales	$5,000,000	$3,000,000	$2,000,000	$10,000,000
Variable costs	3,000,000	1,200,000	1,000,000	5,200,000
Contribution margin	$2,000,000	$1,800,000	$1,000,000	$ 4,800,000
Fixed costs				3,000,000
Net Income				$ 1,800,000

Required:

a. On what total sales volume did the firm break even?

b. Prepare an abbreviated income statement by product line that proves that your answer to (a) is the break-even point.

c. What net income was earned on each line of goods?

d. Suppose that sales were as follows:

Dry goods	$6,000,000
Furniture	2,000,000
Hardware	2,000,000

What impact would this product mix have on break-even and net income?

4. Impact of taxes

If the contribution margin is 40 percent, fixed costs are $250,000, and target profit after taxes is $90,000, what sales volume must be generated to obtain the desired after-tax profit? Taxes are 40 percent of before-tax income.

5. Pricing

Amalgamated Airlines is considering a new fare structure to increase patronage between Metropolis and Disney World during periods when planes fly with only 60 percent of the seats occupied. A typical trip has 100 adult passengers paying a full fare of $150 one way and 50 youngsters paying half fare.

A survey indicates that reducing the adult fare by 20 percent would result in a 20 percent increase in adult fares and a 60 percent increase in half-fare patrons. Variable costs are $10 per fare regardless of the type of passenger.

Required:

a. Would it be wise to revise the fare structure? Comment.

6. Sales mix

The Ardmore Company sells three products. Last year's income statement is as follows:

	Alphas	Betas	Omegas	Total
Sales	$400,000	$600,000	$1,000,000	$2,000,000
Variable costs	160,000	420,000	600,000	1,180,000
Contribution margin	$240,000	$180,000	$ 400,000	$ 820,000
Fixed costs	115,000	172,000	287,000	574,000
Net Income	$125,000	$ 8,000	$ 113,000	$ 246,000

Required:

a. Compute the break-even point for overall operations.

b. Compute the break-even point by product line.

c. Next year's sales forecast calls for a 20 percent reduction in the sales of alphas and a 30 percent increase in the sales of betas. The sale of omegas is not expected to change. What effect will this shift in product mix have on the firm's break-even point and profit?

7. Sales mix

The management of the Glow and Glitter Jewelry Outlet is preparing a sales and profit plan for the coming year. The store carries a wide variety of items ranging in value from less than a dollar to many thousands of dollars. For purposes of control the firm's merchandise is put into one of four categories based on contribution margin. The categories and contribution margin are as follows:

Class	Contribution margin
Costume jewelry	50%
Sterling silver	45
Unset stones	35
Rings and watches	40

Of the total, 10 percent of sales are expected to be for unset stones and the balance equally distributed over the other three categories of merchandise.

Required:

a. If fixed costs are $198,000 per year, what sales volume in each category will be needed to break even?

b. Suppose that sales are spread evenly over each category of merchandise, what impact will this have on break-even?

8. Sales mix and profit planning

The Caswell Liquor Store has been located in downtown Berwick for more than 25 years. The store occupies 1,800 square feet of area and is located just one block from the Wellington Liquor Store which is approximately the same size. The commercial area in Berwick has been deteriorating for many years, and at the present time there are ten vacant stores in the quarter-mile-long commercial center. Last year Mr. Caswell earned just over $10,000 on sales of $140,000.

Mr. Caswell, prodded by his energetic son, is contemplating a move to a newly opened shopping mall about 1½ miles west of the present location. The shopping mall is located at a major intersection and it abuts the towns of Wiley and Post. Post is a dry town and has no liquor stores. Mr. Caswell is concerned for the level of sales necessary to afford locating in a shopping mall. His present rent is $2,400 per year and the location in question has 8,000 square feet of space and the annual rental is $30,000.

Additional fixed costs, if the move is made, are expected to run $6,000 per month. Variable costs other than the cost of merchandise are expected to be quite low, averaging 4 percent of sales volume. Mr. Caswell expects that his sales will be made up of 40 percent hard liquors, 30 percent wines and cordials, and 30 percent beer and ale. The margin on these items varies considerably, and a significant shift in the product mix could be critical. Hard liquors carry a margin of 30 percent, wines and cordials, 20 percent, and beer and ale, 15 percent.

Mr. Caswell said that he would not take on the additional headaches of a larger-scale operation unless it earned him an after-tax profit of at least $30,000 annually. Taxes are expected to be 40 percent of before-tax profit. What sales volume must be maintained to make the move pay off for Mr. Caswell?

9.   Sales mix

The income statement for the Conglomerate Company last year was

	Dis	*Dat*	*Dother*	*Total*
Sales	$60,000	$140,000	$200,000	$400,000
Variable costs	42,000	84,000	80,000	206,000
Contribution margin	$18,000	$ 56,000	$120,000	$194,000
Fixed costs	21,825	50,925	72,750	145,500
Net Income (loss)	$ (3,825)	$ 5,075	$ 47,250	$ 48,500

Required:

a. What was the break-even sales volume for the firm? What was the break-even sales volume by product?

b. If sales of dis increase by $20,000, sales of dat remain the same, and sales of dother decrease by $20,000, what impact will this have on break-even and net income? Fixed cost is allocated based on sales volume.

c. If variable costs remain the same as a percentage of sales and fixed cost remains the same in total, what sales volume will be needed to break even if sales are distributed as follows:

Dis	10%
Dat	45%
Dother	45%

10. Sales mix

Hooterville Ford is engaged in profit planning for the next model year. Ford cars come in four categories as far as cost to the dealer is concerned:

A group cost: 70% of selling price

B group cost: 72% of selling price

C group cost: 74% of selling price

D group cost: 76% of selling price

Sam Hooter, the owner, expects that the sales mix will be 35 percent, 30 percent, 10 percent, and 25 percent, respectively. Fixed costs for the year have been estimated at $337,500. The only additional budgeted cost is salesmen's commissions which average 5 percent of sales.

Required:

a. What sales volume by category must Sam have to break even?

b. Target after-tax profit is $67,200. What sales volume is needed to reach this goal? Taxes are 40 percent.

11. Break-even comparisons

The income statement for the X Manufacturing Company for last year follows:

Sales (8,000 units)		$80,000
Less: Cost of Goods Sold:		
Beginning inventory	0	
Production Costs:		
Variable costs (10,000 units)	$40,000	
Fixed costs	20,000	
Total production costs	$60,000	
Ending inventory	12,000	$48,000
Gross Margin and Net Income		$32,000

Required:

a. Suppose that this firm is a retailer dealing in a single product. The retailer purchased 10,000 units for resale paying $40,000. The retailer's fixed costs are $20,000. What difference, if any, will there be in net income? Explain using numbers.

12. Planning sales mix

The income statement for the TruVal Supermarket for last year follows:

	Meats	Grocery	Dairy	Total
Sales	$200,000	$100,000	$100,000	$400,000
Variable costs	130,000	80,000	82,000	292,000
Contribution margin	$ 70,000	$ 20,000	$ 18,000	$108,000
Fixed costs				65,000
Net Income				$ 43,000

The company is contemplating increasing the size of the store. If it does, rent will be $40,400 per year and other fixed costs will be $7,000 per month. Variable costs will remain the same percentage of sales. The store owner will not enlarge the store unless he can earn an after-tax profit of $42,000 (taxes are 40 percent). If the product mix stays the same, what sales volume by product line is needed to achieve this target profit?

13. Break-even and sales mix

The following information relates to the three products sold by the Bacon Company. Bacon's fixed costs were $224,000.

	A	B	C
Selling price per unit	$10	$12	$8
Variable cost per unit	6	9	6
Units sold	20,000	40,000	40,000

Required:

a. What was Bacon's break-even point in dollars?
b. At break-even how many units of B were sold?
c. An additional investment of $61,000 in fixed costs will result in a $1.00 re-

duction in unit variable cost for each product. What impact would the additional investment have on break even? Assume the same sales mix.

d. A reduction of $1.00 in the unit selling price of each product would still provide the original unit contribution but should cause sales of A to increase 10 percent and the sales of B and C to each increase by 20 percent. Should the selling prices be reduced $1.00 per unit? Explain with calculations.

14.   Changing products

The Cosmos Corporation produces and sells three products. Abbreviated income statements for last year's activity follow:

	A	B	C
Sales	$100,000	$200,000	$300,000
Variable costs	70,000	120,000	120,000
Contribution margin	$ 30,000	$ 80,000	$180,000
Fixed costs	40,000	80,000	120,000
Net Income (loss)	$(10,000)	0	$ 60,000

Required:

a. At what sales volume did the firm break even?

b. Would the firm be better off to drop product A and keep products B and C? Explain.

c. A new product X having a contribution margin ratio of 40 percent can be added to the product line in place of the money-losing A product. X would generate a sales volume of $150,000 per year, but carrying product X would cause the sales of product C to drop by 20 percent. Sales of B will be unchanged. Fixed costs are allocated to products based on sales volume.

Should product X be substituted for product A?

15.   Break-even with two segments

Bruce Scott purchased a motel-restaurant combination in Downeast, Maine. The motel has 12 units, and a restaurant seating 36 people is attached to the north end of the motel unit. From June to October Mr. Scott's main problem is being polite to the many patrons he must turn away from both the motel and the restaurant. During the winter months Mr. Scott does not have this problem because travel in this section of New England slows to a snail's pace. Mr. Scott does not know whether to close down the motel and/or restaurant during the winter months or stay open. It is very important that he knows the break-even volume in both segments of the establishment.

Required:

a. Explain to Mr. Scott how he can determine the break-even point for the motel in rooms rented.

b. Explain to Mr. Scott how he can determine the break-even sales volume for the restaurant. Can the same analytical approach be applied in both situations?

c. Can variable costs in the restaurant be a function of the chef's appetite or lack thereof? Explain.

16.   The impact of pilfering

A major problem facing supermarkets is pilfering by employees and customers.

Required:

a. What impact does pilfering have on a supermarket's break-even sales volume? Be specific.

b. Explain how a retailer can calculate the increased sales volume needed to compensate for the pilfering of a 35-cent coke and a 50-cent bag of chips by an employee.

PART 3

Budgeting

7 Budgets and Budgeting

CHAPTER OVERVIEW

Profit planning is a basic management function. A central part of the profit-planning process is budgeting and budgets. A budget is a document that emerges from the budgeting process, and it specifies the events that must take place if objectives are to be achieved. The end result of the budgeting process is a forecast of the income statement and balance sheet at the close of the period. The logic of the process is this: Start with the present financial statements, do what the budget suggests, and this is what the financial statements will look like at the end of the period.

In this chapter we describe the process used in budget preparation. We show the relationship between the various subbudgets. We show how a sales budget is used to develop a production budget and how material, labor, and overhead budgets evolve from the production budget. Throughout this chapter we show how the budgeting process enables managers to coordinate their activities with other segments of the firm.

QUESTIONS FOR CONSIDERATION

1. Why is budgeting considered a management function and not an accounting function?
2. Why is the sales budget the key to the entire budgeting process?
3. What is inventory policy and how does it affect budgets?
4. Should managers be allowed to exceed budget allocations?
5. How can budgeting improve the management of a firm?

Budgets and budgeting are terms that have a variety of meanings. To a student who must live on $50 per week, budgeting may simply involve the setting of priorities and regulating the flow of cash. To a university, a budget is a plan that identifies the nature and volume of expenditures and the expected sources of revenue for a period of time. In business, a budget is a comprehensive plan of what the firm seeks to achieve and what must be done to carry out the plan. A budget is a document, a quantifiable plan; budgeting is a process through which the document is developed and administered.

THE NATURE OF OBJECTIVES

In business, budgeting is a part of the overall profit-planning and control process. Although it requires accounting information, it is basically a management function. Every business should have a profit objective because every business has specific profit needs which can be measured. Most firms need profit for such purposes as the payment of dividends, providing resources for the future, and paying off long-term debt. These are needs that should not be ignored.

But profit is not the primary objective of a business. The simple equation revenue – expenses = net income shows that profit is the end result of achieving a number of more basic objectives including

1. a market objective that will provide the necessary revenue
2. a production objective that will ensure the economic manufacture of the goods which the market demands
3. a research and engineering objective that will ensure a flow of new and better products or services (Polaroid, IBM, Kodak, Gillette, and Xerox are good examples of firms having a strong research and engineering emphasis)
4. a financial objective that will ensure that the funds needed to achieve other objectives are available
5. a manpower objective to ensure that the required human resources will be available

Thus through budgeting, management specifies the events that must transpire in a number of areas of activity to ensure that target profit and other objectives will be achieved.

THE NEED FOR BUDGETING

On the surface it would seem that all organizations, business and otherwise, would engage in budgeting and operate on a budget because it identifies where the firm intends to go and what must be done to get there. The hard fact is that most businesses in our society are small and do not engage in a formal budgeting process. (It also follows that most businesses have little idea of where they are headed.) Budgeting involves a lot of hard work, it can be expensive, and there is no guarantee that it will result in improved operations. If done improperly, chaos can be the result of budgeting.

The fact that many organizations either by law or corporate bylaw are required to prepare and operate on a budget suggests that budgeting can make sense. Some of the positive aspects of budgeting follow:

1. It forces managers to establish goals, to indicate what they intend to do, to determine how much this activity will cost, and to justify the expenditures that must be made. Once established, a budget can become a benchmark against which managerial performance can be evaluated.

2. It can force the coordination of activity. The purchasing manager, for example, must consider production requirements, inventory policy, and the firm's ability to make payments on specific dates before establishing specific plans and objectives. Budgeting therefore facilitates goal congruence.

3. It forces managers to give early consideration to what they plan to do in the upcoming period. Often budgets are finalized weeks or months before the budget period begins. This early planning can bring a number of benefits:

   a. it identifies both the types and number of employees that will be needed within the various segments of the firm and when they will be needed. Thus the impact of layoffs, transfers, accessions, or retraining can be ameliorated.

   b. it provides a basis for making long-term agreements relating to purchasing, leasing, borrowing, and the like. This facilitates having what is needed, when it is needed, and at a reasonable cost.

   c. it facilitates the economic use of money. A cash budget will show when the firm will have an excess or deficiency of cash. This has two advantages. First, it allows time to plan for the effective utilization of excess funds, and, second, lending institutions look most favorably on those organizations that can show why they will have future cash needs and when they will have the ability to repay loans.

4. It can lead to better organization. In theory, at least, everything that needs to be done to achieve objectives has been identified and made the responsibility of some manager. In theory, provision has been made in the budget so that everything that needs to be done can be done. If, in fact, it is found that things needing to be done were not funded, the organizational weakness can be quickly identified.

BUDGETS HAVE LIMITATIONS TOO

A budget is merely a document, and documents do not have the capacity to do anything; they merely express something. In this case the document is a plan, a plan that may be good or bad depending on the efficacy of those who developed it and whether the planning premises held. As the budget is being used, management should have a number of considerations in mind.

1. Budgets are only an estimate, and deviations from it should be expected. Too often superior managers will praise subordinate managers when they spend less than their budget allocations and criticize them when they go over budget. Spending more than or less than budgeted amounts might well be the better course of action depending on circumstances. The regional sales manager of a large publisher told his sales representatives in mid-December one year to stay home for the rest of the month, do not travel, make no phone calls—do nothing that would incur an expense—because he was already over the budget. The fact that this action might have resulted in lost textbook sales and profit was not important; the budget was. And the home office was none the wiser.

2. Budgets must be adapted to new conditions. As we have seen, changes in the volume of activity impact on cost. In addition there are many outside forces that can cause the costs of operation to change. If the Environmental Protection Agency says "Clean up or close up," there may be no alternative to exceeding the budget.

3. The execution of a budget is not automatic. Managers must be educated in this area of activity before budgets can become effective tools of managers. The behavioral side of budgeting is discussed below.

4. Budgets and budgeting cannot take the place of management. They are merely tools that can make management more effective.

THE BEHAVIORAL SIDE OF BUDGETING

We should expect that the reaction of people in organizations to budgets and budgeting will vary because it does not impact uniformly on all people. Most people will view budgeting as an absolutely necessary function on a macro basis—"of course the university needs a budget; it provides a measure of insurance that I will get paid." But on a micro—the individual manager—basis, the view might be different. There are a number of reasons for this.

1. Budgeting demands the involvement of every manager to some degree. In a decentralized organization, managers at all levels may be required to develop their entire operating budget. As mentioned earlier, managers may be forced to think out a plan for their area of activity and indicate how they intend to implement it. Some managers view this task as an opportunity and welcome it, whereas others would prefer to have no part in the process.

2. It is a control device—it forces compliance. Budgets can limit the amount of money that can be spent in every expense category such as salaries, supplies, travel, and entertainment. Managers may not like this degree of control over how their budget will be spent, arguing that it is the overall results that count, not the amount spent for paper clips and travel.

3. Similarly, budgets can be an excuse for making unnecessary expenditures. "If you do not spend your budget allotment this year, you will get less next year." This, of course, is not an indictment of budgeting; rather, it is an indictment of managerial behavior.

4. It may cause conflicts. The goal of the production manager might be to produce a minimum variety of products at a uniform annual rate. The goal of the marketing manager might be to have a

wide variety of products and a large enough inventory so that customer needs can be satisfied immediately. The financial manager wants inventories as low as possible, and the purchasing manager may want to take advantage of large-scale purchasing economies.

None of the areas of conflict should be blamed on the budgeting process. With or without budgeting they can exist. The point is that through budgeting attention is focused on these shortcomings and they become topics for discussion. Each of the negative remarks made above can be erased by a competent management team.

BASES FOR BUDGETING

The easiest budgets to prepare are those that involve the production of a standardized product. The reason for this is that the amount of material, labor, and other resources required per unit of production has been established. Much of the budget can be a function of units to be produced.

In a service segment of a firm such as a personnel department it is far more difficult to justify a budget request because so many degrees of service are adequate or possible. Similarly, the number of dollars needed to operate a college of business administration having 3,000 students is also variable. In these situations the reputation and negotiating ability of the manager or dean are decisive factors in budget determination. In other situations budgets may reflect the philosophical and political views of those in power.

Text book discussions tend to show budgeting as a mechanical process and to some degree this is true. But the reason for this is that it is impossible to describe the impact of different personalities on those who participate in the budgeting process. The only way that we can understand what is involved in the preparation of a given budget is to actively participate in the entire process. Our model for explaining the budgeting process is a production environment because here personality and other variables are minimized.

BUDGETARY PROCEDURES

There are at least two approaches to budgeting. One is to use the existing budget as the starting point for developing the next budget. This may be the easier approach, but not necessarily the wiser. As a generalization, with this approach budgets tend to get larger and larger and often fatter and fatter over the years. This approach to budgeting may place a premium on spending. Governments use this approach to budgeting, and this alone is a major reason for governments' spending more year after year.

Another approach is called zero-base budgeting. This approach—the clean-slate approach—puts much less emphasis on what was budgeted in the past and focuses on what must be done to achieve objectives. Because certain amounts were spent last year for certain activities is no reason to continue such spending. Zero-base budgeting starts from scratch each year and therefore is a more time-consuming process. But it can be a better approach because it can weed out the unnecessary activities that budgeting often perpetuates.

In its final form a budget is a collection of figures showing such things as planned sales, production costs, marketing costs, and asset changes. This plan may be set up week by week, month by month, year by year, or for longer periods of time. Short-term budgets tend to be quite specific, whereas long-range budgets are more of a conceptual nature. Many firms operate on a continuous budget. As each month passes, an additional month is added.

There are two kinds of budgets—operating budgets and financial budgets. These are shown in Figure 7-1, a budget schematic. The components of an operating budget are the sales, production, materials, labor, and overhead budgets. Financial budgets include the all-important cash budget, pro forma financial statements, and other financial information. The keys to successful budgeting are accurate sales forecasts and the ability to predict cost behavior as volumes of activity change. Each of the major budgets is described in the following paragraphs.

THE SALES BUDGET

The budget schematic (Figure 7-1) shows in part the importance of the sales budget. The unit sales budget impacts on several subbudgets with a chain reaction effect. Sales dictates production volumes, and production volumes dictate material, labor and overhead requirements which, in turn, impact on cash requirements. The dollar sales budget is important because it shows the timing and quantity of expected cash receipts. This chain reaction effect exists only in

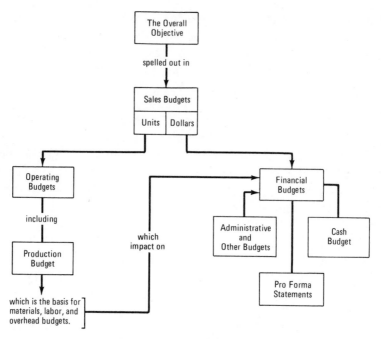

FIGURE 7-1. A Budget Schematic

manufacturing firms; in retail stores sales are usually budgeted in dollars only, as explained in the next section.

The sales budget is the end result of a number of activities. A sales budget may be viewed as the share of the total market for a product that the firm hopes to capture during the budget period. Thus the starting point for developing a sales plan is to make a sales forecast or a projection of consumer demand for the time horizon of the budget. At times making a sales forecast is difficult and at other times it is fairly easy. Estimating total customer demand for automobile tires is relatively easy because there are basically only two types of customers for tires: auto manufacturers and the replacement market. The number of tires that will be purchased by automobile manufacturers is known with reasonable accuracy because these people have production goals of their own. The tire replacement market is also relatively certain because tire use and replacement frequencies are well known in the industry. A forecast of customer demand considers a number of factors such as

1. past sales performance
2. economic conditions in the market
3. the impact of technology on the quality and price of products
4. the impact of technology on the life of a product
5. the impact of technology on the need for a product
6. general statistical indicators such as measures of consumer optimism

Once the forecast is completed, management must measure the portion of the market that it is likely to obtain. This cannot be done until the firm's strategy has been developed. A firm's strategy comprises the actions—the policies—it plans to implement to achieve objectives. A firm can attempt to obtain the desired market share in many ways such as

1. additional outlets for its products
2. introduction of new models
3. advertising and promotion
4. pricing policies
5. extended warranties

There is no certainty that a firm's target sales will be realized. It is more likely that planned sales will be overstated or understated. Thus revisions of sales budgets may be necessary as each month passes and new information is gathered.

The Sales Budget—Retailing

Retailers, to a degree, do not care what they sell; dollar sales volume and contribution margin ratio are the important considerations. This is especially true of independent retailers and less the case with chain retailers such as Sears. Thus top management may charge each department manager with the responsibility for generating so many dollars of contribution margin and leave it to the manager to figure out how the goal will be reached. The manager of a camera department may buy high-priced, high-markup merchandise and earn the required contribution margin on a relatively low volume of sales, whereas the manager of a toy department may stress a high sales volume of low-contribution items.

THE PRODUCTION BUDGET

A production budget for the budget period depends on three factors:
(1) the number of units that the sales budget indicates will be sold
during the period, (2) the number of units that management wants in
inventory at the end of the period, and (3) the anticipated inventory
at the start of the budget period. The relationship between these
three factors is shown as follows:

Ending inventory requirements (units) + Required for sales (units)

= Total requirements (units) – Beginning inventory (units)

= Units that must be produced

A very important consideration in preparing a production budget is
the firm's inventory policy. Inventory policy establishes the relationship between inventory on hand at the beginning of a period, such as
a month, and the expected sales for that period.

A firm's inventory policy should be based on a cost-benefit
analysis that compares the cost of carrying larger inventories with
the benefit that comes from customer satisfaction when stock-outs
are avoided. Most firms do not attempt to avoid stock-outs because
it is too costly to carry inventories that will satisfy the needs of any
customer at any point in time. Rather, firms try to strike a balance
between inventory investment cost and the cost of customer dissatisfaction when the firm cannot deliver. This topic is discussed at length
in Chapter 15.

The following illustration explains the process of preparing a
production budget and the impact of inventory policy. The Cabot
Corporation produces and sells a single product. The budgeted sales
in units for the first six months of next year are as follows:

January	3,000	April	4,400
February	3,200	May	5,000
March	4,000	June	4,800

The company has a policy of keeping an inventory of finished goods
at the start of each month equal to two times the sales for the
month. We will assume that the inventory at the beginning of January
reflects this policy. The production budget follows:

	Jan.	Feb.	Mar.	Apr.	May	Summary
Ending inventory	6,400	8,000	8,800	10,000	9,600	9,600
Plus: Sales for month	3,000	3,200	4,000	4,400	5,000	19,600
Total requirements	9,400	11,200	12,800	14,400	14,600	29,200
Less: Beginning inventory	6,000	6,400	8,000	8,800	10,000	6,000
To be produced	3,400	4,800	4,800	5,600	4,600	23,200

Explanation

We will take time to analyze the process used in the preceding discussion because the same concept is used in other budgets. There are several steps involved in creating this budget. First, the estimated sales for each month are recorded. Second, inventory policy is applied to the sales figures to obtain the beginning inventory requirement. Notice that in this budget the beginning inventory for each month is two times the sales for that month. Third, since the beginning inventory for one month must be the same as the ending inventory for the previous month, we record the ending inventory values as the arrows show. Finally, we add and subtract to determine the amount that should be produced. In this illustration we cannot include June production requirements because July sales are not available.

Production budgets are developed on a unit basis rather than on a dollar basis. The reason for this is that the total budgeted production cost is the sum of the materials budget, the labor budget, and the manufacturing expense budget. These budgets are prepared separately as described in the next section.

Materials and Purchase Budgets

Material requirements planning is a function of production. A bill of materials, which accompanies each production order, specifies the types and quantities of material needed per unit of production. To simplify this discussion we will assume that a unit of production requires only one type of raw material. In practice, if a firm carries

300 material items, 300 material use and purchase budgets must be prepared. Let us assume that each unit of production in our illustration requires 2 lb. of Glob. Continuing our previous illustration, the material requirements for the five months are:

January	3,400 units x 2 lb = 6,800 lb
February	4,800 units x 2 lb = 9,600 lb
March	4,800 units x 2 lb = 9,600 lb
April	5,600 units x 2 lb = 11,200 lb
May	4,600 units x 2 lb = 9,200 lb

In addition to the material requirements for production we again need to know the firm's policy with regard to inventory of raw materials. The purchases budget that follows has applied a policy of having a beginning inventory for any month equal to 150 percent of that month's material requirements.

Purchases Budget

	Jan.	*Feb.*	*Mar.*	*Apr.*	*Summary*
Ending inventory	14,400	14,400	16,800	13,800	13,800
Plus: For production	6,800	9,600	9,600	11,200	37,200
Total requirements	21,200	24,000	26,400	25,000	51,000
Less: Beginning inventory	10,200	14,400	14,400	16,800	10,200
To be purchased	11,000	9,600	12,000	8,200	40,800
Dollar purchases	$22,000	$19,200	$24,000	$16,400	$81,600

The process used to develop this budget is the same as the one used to develop the production budget. Unlike the production budget, the purchases budget must be expressed in dollars as well as in units because the timing of purchases impacts on cash requirements. All that is needed to convert a unit budget into a dollar budget is the unit cost of material. We have assumed in our illustration that a pound of Glob costs $2.00.

Purchases Budget—Retailing

The purchases budget in retailing is generally expressed in dollars rather than in specific units of merchandise. Retailers may have considerable freedom in deciding what merchandise will be purchased to generate the desired sales volume and contribution margin.

To develop a purchases budget in retailing, we need to know the planned sales for the period and the cost of the goods to be sold expressed as a percentage of sales. In addition, the firm's inventory policy must be known. The following illustrates the development of a purchases budget in retailing. Planned sales are as follows:

	At retail	At cost
January	$100,000	$60,000
February	80,000	48,000
March	120,000	72,000
April	110,000	66,000

The cost of sales is 60 percent of sales. The firm's inventory policy requires an ending inventory for a given month to be twice the budgeted sales for the following month. We will assume that the beginning inventory for January reflects this policy. The first quarter purchases budget is shown as follows:

Purchases Budget—Retailing

	Jan.	Feb.	Mar.	Summary
Ending inventory	$ 96,000	$144,000	$132,000	$132,000
Plus: For sales	60,000	48,000	72,000	180,000
Total requirements	$156,000	$192,000	$204,000	$312,000
Beginning inventory	120,000	96,000	144,000	120,000
To be purchased	$ 36,000	$ 96,000	$ 60,000	$192,000

Retailers buy at wholesale prices, and, as a result, sales figures must be expressed at cost for purchasing purposes.

DIRECT LABOR BUDGET

For each unit of production, there is a bill of materials that identifies the types and amounts of materials needed. Similarly, for each unit of production, there is an indication of the types of labor needed to complete the job together with an indication of the labor-hours it should take to complete the job. In manufacturing it is common practice to establish allotted times for the completion of tasks.

Through time and motion study the "best way" to get a task done is established. Often this results in a standard operating procedure which requires every worker involved with the task to complete it in the same manner. This standardization of work methods enables management to establish time standards for the completion of tasks. This, in turn, provides a basis for establishing a standard output per hour. If a time standard allows 60 seconds for the completion of a task, the standard output per hour is 60 units per worker. Time standards serve a number of useful purposes:

1. They facilitate the determination of labor requirements.

2. They facilitate the production scheduling process. Time standards are an absolute necessity where assembly lines are used. They are used to determine the speed with which the line moves given the manpower available.

3. They facilitate the prediction of labor costs.

4. They enable a higher degree of control over labor cost. In many firms workers are not paid by the hour. Rather, they are paid based on the quantity of work that they produce. A piece rate, for example, is nothing more than a time standard that has been given a dollar value. For example, a firm establishes a time standard of 60 seconds to complete a task and a standard output per hour of 60 units. If the base rate for the job is $6 per hour, the piece rate is $0.10. Under piece rate, workers earn $0.10 per unit whether their output is 40 or 70 units per hour. The labor cost per unit is fixed, but hourly earnings vary.

We will not illustrate a direct labor budget because it is a simple routine once the necessary values are obtained. For example,

Units to be produced per week	120,000
Standard output per hour	60 units
Labor-hour requirements	2,000 hours
Labor cost at $7 per hour	$14,000
Workers required (40-hr week)	50

MANUFACTURING EXPENSE BUDGETS

Production costs fall into one of three categories: direct material, direct labor, and manufacturing overhead. Overhead by definition includes all production costs except direct material and direct labor.

Direct costs as a rule are easy to budget, because, as we have seen, they may be a function of production volume. In theory, at least, the only reason for total direct costs to be more or less than budgeted direct costs is that actual production was more than or less than the amount budgeted. This assumes, of course, that there have been no changes in the unit cost of inputs. Indirect costs are not as easy to manage.

Fixed Budgets

Manufacturing expense budgets take two forms. Where fixed or static budgets are used, allotments are designated for each expense category, and these allotments are allowed to stand regardless of the actual level of activity that is attained. Ideally, a fixed budget would be used in situations in which the bulk of expenses are of a fixed nature, but they may have to be applied in other situations. Governments, universities, churches, and certain businesses operate on fixed budgets. The basic problem with a fixed budget is that the actual level of activity and dollars spent may differ from the budget, and it is difficult, if not impossible, to identify the causes of overspending or underspending.

Suppose that a firm had a fixed overhead budget of $100,000 for a year and actual overhead costs for the period totaled $120,000. Does this difference of $20,000 automatically characterize budget performance as good or bad? We cannot tell because this difference could be the result of uncontrolled spending (possibly bad) or the result of a higher level of activity than planned for—more units were produced than were expected (possibly good).

Flexible Budgets

The second form of budgeting uses a flexible budget. Here budgets are attuned to the actual volume of activity attained. One way of describing flexible budgets is to say that there is a budget for every level of activity within the relevant range. Thus actual costs can be compared with what they should have been for the level of activity attained. [With flexible budgets variances between budgeted and actual are strictly spending variances because each reflects cost for the same volume of activity.] This, of course, facilitates the control process.

Flexible Budgets Illustrated

The basic cost information needed to develop a flexible budget is shown in columns A and B of Table 7-1. In this illustration the firm planned to operate at a level of 30,000 units and budgeted the costs shown in column C. These budgeted amounts were obtained as shown in Table 7-1.

If the cost is fixed, the amount shown in column B is budgeted for all levels of activity within the relevant range. If the cost is treated as variable, the budget allocation is obtained by multiplying the budgeted volume by the unit variable cost (30,000 x $0.35 = $10,500). If there are two elements of cost, as in indirect labor, the total variable cost is added to the total fixed cost to obtain the budget allowance. Indirect labor is made up of $139,500 variable cost (30,000 x $4.65) plus $20,000 of fixed cost. An easy way to check the total budget allowance of $470,000 is to multiply 30,000 times the total of unit variable costs and add the total of fixed cost.

Column D shows that actual costs were $473,350, or $3,350 more than budgeted. We cannot conclude whether this is good or bad by looking only at total cost. We need to know the volume of activity that led to these costs. Because actual activity was 35,000 units, it is futile to compare mixed or variable costs in columns C and D. Therefore we prepare a budget based on the actual level of activity attained (column E) and compare this with actual costs. Because each set of costs is based on the same volume of activity, any difference is a spending or efficiency variance (column F). Variances with a U suffix are called unfavorable variances because actual cost is greater than budget. The letter F after a variance signifies a favorable variance because actual cost is less than budgeted

TABLE 7-1
Flexible Budgeting

Expense	A Unit variable	B Total fixed	C Budget 30,000 units	D Act. cost 35,000 units	E Budgeted 35,000 units	F Spending variance(a)
Indirect material	$0.35		$ 10,500	$ 13,000	$ 12,250	$ 750 U
Indirect labor	4.65	$ 20,000	159,500	185,000	182,750	2,250 U
Supervision		45,000	45,000	48,000	45,000	3,000 U
Power/light	0.15	6,000	10,500	13,350	11,250	2,100 U
Depreciation		65,000	65,000	45,000	65,000	20,000 F
Maintenance	3.85	64,000	179,500	169,000	198,750	29,750 F
	$9.00	$200,000	$470,000	$473,350	$515,000	$49,750 F
						8,100 U
				$41,650		$41,650 F

F - Favorable variance.

U - Unfavorable variance.

(a)Spending variances can result from changes in the level of prices, or they can be the result of efficiencies or inefficiencies.

cost. The difference between these plus and minus variances should equal the difference between total budgeted costs for 35,000 units and the actual costs incurred.

This simple illustration of flexible budgeting also points out the danger of simply looking at the "bottom line." In this instance there is a favorable variance of $41,650 but we should not conclude that this is necessarily good or the result of efficient and effective operations. Spending $29,750 less than budget for maintenance could turn out to be a very expensive "saving".

This illustration is also incomplete. In practice, management should be dissatisfied having a mixed cost such as indirect labor expressed only in total. Attempts should be made to determine whether the variable or fixed component, or both, led to the spending variance of $2,250.

Before a firm can develop a flexible budget, conditions must be such that manufacturing expenses—overhead—can be expressed in terms of the unit variable and total fixed cost components. Manufacturing expenses are either fixed or mixed in nature even though some may be treated as variable. It is quite unlikely, for example, that indirect material cost shown in Table 7-1 is purely variable. In an earlier chapter we learned that mixed costs could be divided into a unit variable and total fixed component by using such techniques as the high-low method or least-squares regression analysis. We also learned that these techniques were imperfect because they are based on the assumption that the only reason that total cost changes is because the volume of activity has changed.

Measures of Activity

Costs are charged to production (to jobs or to production lots) based on some measure of activity. Direct materials and direct labor are charged to production based on the number of units produced in process production. In job-order production these costs are charged to production based on actual quantities used. In Table 7-1 overhead was also charged to production based on the number of units produced. But there are a number of costs whose total bears little relationship to the volume of units produced or any other measure of activity. Purchasing and inventory costs could be more a function of purchasing and inventory policy than the number of units produced or hours worked during a particular period of time. Unless there is a reasonably good relationship between some measure of activity, or

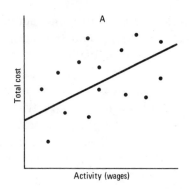 

FIGURE 7-2. Scattergrams

a combination of activities, and total cost, flexible budgeting will be ineffective at best.

To determine whether there is a reasonable relationship between total cost and a measure of activity, we can use scattergrams (see Figure 7-2). Here, the measure of activity (the independent variable) is identified on the horizontal axis, and total cost (the dependent variable) is identified on the vertical axis. In Figure 7-2B there is a reasonably good relationship between direct labor hours and the total of this cost. We use the term "reasonably good" because this is what the eye tells us. Charging this cost to production based on the number of direct labor-hours worked seems logical.

If the best relationship that can be established between the two variables is as shown in Figure 7-2A, the use of a flexible budget should be questioned. Thus we see the reason that so many firms, business and otherwise, are forced to operate on fixed or static budgets. A university has no objective means for charging the costs of library operation to the various colleges because total library costs do not increase or decrease in proportion to any measure of activity. The consequence is that costs are allocated on some arbitrary basis such as the number of students in each college.

STATIC AND FLEXIBLE BUDGETS

The concepts of static and flexible manufacturing expense budgets can be applied on a much broader basis than we have implied. We have said that with a given forecast of sales and given inventory policies, the production, purchases, and other budgets will evolve in the manner shown. These are static budgets based on a predetermined volume of activity. There is always a high probability that actual sales activity will be different from planned activity and that actual production and costs will be different from the budgeted amounts. This can create a situation such as we have in Table 7-2.

This report has very little value as a control mechanism. Total variable costs increased by $41,200, but we do not know why nor do we know if the increase is justified. One very important bit of information has been omitted on purpose, and that is the budgeted and actual volumes of activity. It could be that actual activity was

TABLE   7-2

Static Budget Report

	Budget	Actual	Variance
Sales	$600,000	$720,000	$120,000 F
Variable Costs:			
Material	$ 80,000	$ 93,600	$ 13,600 U
Labor	60,000	73,200	13,200 U
Overhead	30,000	37,200	7,200 U
Indirect labor	20,000	25,200	5,200 U
Selling	70,000	72,000	2,000 U
Total	$260,000	$301,200	$ 41,200 U
Contribution margin	$340,000	$418,800	$ 78,800 F
Fixed Costs:			
Depreciation	50,000	40,000	10,000 F
Insurance	10,000	12,000	2,000 U
Property taxes	30,000	35,000	5,000 U
Factory			
administration	70,000	71,000	1,000 U
Selling	60,000	70,000	10,000 U
Administrative			
salaries	90,000	100,000	10,000 U
Total	$310,000	$328,000	$ 18,000 U
Net Income	$ 30,000	$ 90,800	$ 60,800 F

F - Favorable variance.

U - Unfavorable variance.

greater than budgeted activity, and thus these variances could be the result of two factors. Part of the variance could be the result of overspending, and part could be due to operating at a level of activity above budget. But we have no basis for attributing the variances to either cause. We do not face this problem with fixed costs because they should remain the same in total at any level of activity within the relevant range. Thus any variance between budgeted and actual fixed costs is a spending variance.

What we need is an expression of what costs should have been for the actual volume of activity. In Table 7-2 budgeted volume was 10,000 units and actual volume was 12,000 units. Now we will compare actual costs with budgeted costs at a 12,000-unit level. Table 7-3 makes this comparison.

Note the completely different picture of operations that Table 7-3 presents. Here, every variance is a spending variance because actual costs are compared with the budgeted allowance for the actual level of activity and actual contribution margin and net income are compared with what they should have been at the 12,000-unit level.

TABLE   7-3

Flexible Budget Report

	Budgeted: 12,000 units	Actual: 12,000 units	Spending variances
Sales	$720,000	$720,000	0
Variable Costs:			
Material ($8)	$ 96,000	$ 93,600	$ 2,400 F
Labor ($6)	72,000	73,200	1,200 U
Overhead ($3)	36,000	37,200	1,200 U
Indirect labor ($2)	24,000	25,200	1,200 U
Selling ($7)	84,000	72,000	12,200 F
Total	$312,000	$301,200	$10,800 F
Contribution margin	$408,000	$418,800	$10,800 F
Total fixed cost	$310,000	$328,000	$18,000 U
Net Income	$ 98,000	$ 90,800	$ 7,200 U

F - Favorable variance.

U - Unfavorable variance.

Rather than a favorable net income variance of $60,800 as shown in Table 7-2, we find an unfavorable net income variance of $7,200. The managers responsible for controlling variable costs were able to keep total variable cost below the budgeted amounts by $10,800, but the managers responsible for fixed cost overspent their budgets by $18,000. When we consider that there was a favorable variance of $10,000 in the depreciation account, the actual spending variance in this class of cost was $28,000. Clearly, management knows far more about managerial performance from an examination of the flexible budget report than it could obtain from a static budget report.

JOB-ORDER AND PROCESS PRODUCTION

The previous discussions of budgets and budgeting apply only to process production where specific products having specific material, labor, and overhead requirements are produced and sold. Job shops do not manufacture products as such; rather, they provide a specialized service generally for other manufacturers. The specific jobs that the shop will work on during the budget period may be unknown at the time the budget is being developed.

Budgets are developed based on a forecast of direct labor or machine hours that will be worked rather than on specific units of production. Variable costs, break-even, and contribution margin are each measured on a per hour basis.

SUMMARY

Through budgeting management can determine whether a particular operating plan is likely to achieve the desired results. A basic advantage of budgeting is that it forces management to express in specific terms what it intends to do, how much these actions will cost, and the benefits that will accrue to the firm if these actions are taken.

The sales budget is central to the development of operating budgets because the amount of material, labor, and other resources needed depends to a great degree on the overall volume of activity that takes place.

Some firms, due to their cost structure, are forced to operate on fixed budgets. It is difficult to measure managerial performance when fixed budgets are used because overspending or underspending could be caused by managerial performance or because the actual volume of activity attained differed from the plan and there is no way to separate the two. Flexible budgeting provides a budget for every volume of activity within the relevant range. Thus, when budgeted costs are compared with actual costs, there are no volume variances, and all variances can be attributed to spending practices.

KEY TERMS

budget

budgeting

fixed budget

flexible budget

inventory policy

variance

zero-base budgeting

QUESTIONS

1. Should profit be the basic objective of a business? Explain.

2. What advantages accrue when management gives early consideration to what it plans to do?

3. How can budgeting lead to better organization?

4. Under what circumstances can spending in excess of the budget allotment be justified?

5. How can a firm's approach to organization impact on budgets and the budgeting process?

6. It has been said that budgeting can lead to unnecessary spending. Do you agree? Explain.

7. "The ideal starting point for developing next year's budget is our current budget." Do you agree? Explain.

8. What is zero-base budgeting and how does it differ from other approaches to budgeting?

9. What factors decide the production budget for a period? Express these factors as a formula.

10. What impact does inventory policy have on a production budget or a purchases budget?

11. Should a production budget be expressed both in units and in dollars? Explain.

12. How does a retailer's purchases budget differ from a manufacturer's purchases budget?

13. What is a time standard and of what value is it to management?

14. What basic information is needed to prepare a flexible budget?

15. Can all organizations use flexible budgets? Explain.

16. Costs are charged to production based on some measure of activity. How can management determine if it is using the "right" measure of activity?

PROBLEMS

1. Retail purchases budget

The cost of merchandise sold at the Sampson Retail Outlet averages 45 percent of sales. The sales forecast for the first five months of 19X5 is

January	$120,000	March	$140,000
February	$100,000	April	$150,000
		May	$110,000

The company has a policy of maintaining an inventory at the end of each month of sufficient amount to provide for sales during the following two months. Thus the inventory on December 31 must be large enough to cover January and February sales.

Required:

a. Prepare a purchases budget for the first quarter of 19X5.

b. Additional variable costs are 10 percent of sales, and fixed costs are $30,000 per month. Prepare income statements for the first three months of 19X5 and for the quarter as a whole.

2. Production budget

Maxim Products Corporation which produces a single product called Max 9 has budgeted the following sales in units:

January	8,000	March	12,000
February	10,000	April	9,000
		May	11,000

Maxim has a policy of maintaining a finished goods inventory at the end of each month equal to twice the estimated sales for the following month. The December 31 inventory reflects this policy.

Required:

a. Prepare a production budget for the first quarter.

3. Purchases budget-manufacturing

Refer to Problem 2. Each unit of Max 9 requires 2 lb. of a chemical called Bromax and 1½ lb of a chemical called Dyhard. Maxim maintains raw material inventory at the end of each month equal to 150 percent of the following month's production requirements.

Required:

a. Prepare purchases budgets for the first quarter.

4. Budget variances

The following activity report was presented to the plant manager of the Paranoid Corporation:

	Budget	*Actual*	*Variance*
Variable cost	$56,000	$ 61,000	$5,000 U
Fixed cost	40,000	41,000	1,000 U
Total	$96,000	$102,000	$6,000 U
Production (units)	40,000	44,000	4,000 F

Required:

a. The plant manager was quite concerned with the $6,000 unfavorable variance and asks you to dig into the matter and report back to him. What will you report? Explain.

5. Flexible budgets

The Pothro Corporation has a normal operating level of 80,000 direct labor-hours and has established the following estimates of overhead costs:

Item	*Unit variable*	*Total fixed*
Indirect material	$1.50	$ 1,000
Indirect labor	4.50	15,000
Supervision		30,000
Power and light	0.50	6,000
Depreciation		38,000
Maintenance	2.50	10,000
Total	$9.00	$100,000

During the past month the company operated 90,000 direct labor-hours and incurred the following costs:

Indirect material	$137,500
Indirect labor	380,000
Supervision	32,000
Power and light	55,900
Depreciation	30,000
Maintenance	190,000
Total	$825,400

Required:

a. Prepare an expense report for management that provides a basis for evaluating the month's performance.

b. Are you satisfied with the bottom-line results? Explain.

6. Activity measures

Historically the Complex Rubber Corporation has charged overhead to production based on the budgeted production of tires. Using this basis—measure of activity—has resulted in extremes in charging overhead to production. During some months overhead is significantly overapplied, whereas during other periods it is significantly underapplied, even though the production volumes have varied only slightly. Management attributes this to the variations in the tire-size mix which cannot be accurately predicted. Management must find some measure of activity that will provide a better basis for assigning overhead costs to production, that is, a better predictor of overhead costs. The following are maintenance costs for a typical year together with three measures of activity:

	Maintenance cost	Direct labor-hours	Machine hours	Prime cost[a]
January	$14,000	19,600	7,000	$18,200
February	18,000	32,400	12,600	22,500
March	16,000	17,600	6,400	20,400
April	24,000	36,000	14,400	30,000
May	20,000	28,000	6,000	25,000
June	17,000	34,000	6,000	20,000
July	22,000	22,000	15,000	27,500
August	28,000	36,400	14,000	35,000

September	18,000	27,000	10,000	22,000
October	20,000	34,000	8,000	25,000
November	18,000	32,000	9,000	22,500
December	16,000	19,200	7,500	19,000

(a)Prime cost is the total of direct material and direct labor costs.

Required:

a. Prepare scattergrams to show the relationships between maintenance cost and each measure of activity.

b. Which measure of activity appears to have the best relationship to maintenance cost?

c. Could you reach the same conclusion using some other approach? Explain.

7. Impact of inventory policy

Planned sales for the first four month of 19X2 at the Bygone Sales Corp. are

January	$ 80,000	March	$120,000
February	100,000	April	90,000

The cost of goods purchased averages 60 percent of the selling price, and Bygone plans to have an inventory at the beginning of each month equal to one and a half times the requirements for that month.

Required:

a. Prepare a purchases budget for the first quarter of 19X2.

b. The company controller feels that the firm's inventory policy results in excessive inventory levels. He suggests that a beginning inventory equal to the monthly requirements is enough. If this policy is adopted, what impact will it have on the size of the firm's average inventory?

8. Development and use of flexible budgets

The Dixon Company has six major overhead cost categories. The following total costs are averages for the volumes shown:

	Production level (units)	
	20,000	25,000
Indirect material	$ 16,000	$ 19,750
Indirect labor	85,000	105,000
Supervision	40,000	40,000

Power	13,000	13,750
Depreciation	30,000	30,000
Maintenance	122,000	152,000

Required:

a. Prepare a flexible budget formula by determining the total unit variable cost and total fixed cost as shown in Problem 5. (*Note:* This requires the use of high-low analysis.)

b. Dixon plans to produce 22,000 units in the month of August. How many dollars will be budgeted for each cost category?

c. Actual production for August was 23,500 units and actual costs were as follows:

Indirect material	$ 19,095
Indirect labor	101,350
Supervision	46,000
Power	13,760
Depreciation	25,000
Maintenance	148,750

Prepare a report that shows each spending variance.

9. Production budget—sales exceed plan

Sales in units for the X-Pert Company for the first four months of 19X4 were budgeted as follows:

January	5,000	March	9,000
February	8,000	April	6,000

The firm's inventory policy requires an inventory of finished goods at the beginning of each month equal to one and a half times the sales for that month.

Required:

a. Prepare a production budget for the first quarter of 19X4.

b. Sales for January were 7,000 units, and management has revised February, March, and April sales to 9,000, 11,000 and 8,000 units, respectively. Prepare a revised production budget for February and March.

10. Impact of inventory policy on average inventories

The Ramco Company has a policy that requires an inventory of finished goods at the beginning of each month equal to the sales for that month plus the sales for the following month. Raw material inventory at the beginning of each month must be twice the production requirements for that month. Sales in units for the first six months of 19X8 are estimated as follows:

January	7,000	April	6,000
February	5,000	May	9,000
March	8,000	June	8,000

Required:

a. Prepare a production budget for the first quarter of 19X8.

b. Each unit of production uses 4 lb. of cast iron. Prepare a purchases budget for the first quarter of 19X8.

c. Management feels that its investment in inventories is much too high. It has decided to reduce all inventory requirements to one and a half times monthly sales or production. What impact will this change in policy have on the average inventory of finished goods and raw materials? Your answer must show the exact change in units involved.

11. Inventory policy and inventory investment

The sales manager and the production manager at the Armko Company have a disagreement regarding inventory policy. The sales manager wants an inventory of finished goods at the beginning of each month large enough to cover sales for the current month plus the following month. This, he argues, will keep the number of stock-outs and possible customer dissatisfaction at a low level. The production manager, who is responsible for finished goods inventory, argues that the sales manager's policy is too costly and wants finished goods inventory to be one and a half times the current monthly requirement. Sales in units for the first five months of 19X7 are as follows:

January	20,000	March	22,000
February	18,000	April	19,000
		May	17,000

Required:

a. Prepare a production budget based on the sales manager's inventory policy.

b. Prepare a production budget based on the production manager's inventory policy.

c. The cost of each unit produced is $10.00. How many dollars less will the average inventory of finished goods be if the production manager's policy is adopted?

12. Adjusted purchases budget—retailing

The merchandise manager at Calgor Sales, Inc. has a policy of maintaining a merchandise inventory at the beginning of each month equal to 150 percent of the sales for that month. On average, the cost of merchandise is 60 percent of its selling price. Planned sales for the next six months are

July	$180,000	October	$180,000
August	200,000	November	280,000
September	220,000	December	350,000

Required:

a. Prepare a purchases budget for the third quarter.

b. What contribution margin did Calgor plan to earn in the third quarter?

Early in July it became apparent that Calgor would have to reduce its selling prices because of competition. Sales, therefore, would have to increase or the planned contribution margin could not be earned. The merchandise manager reduced prices so that, on the average, cost of merchandise was 70 percent of selling price.

c. Revise the planned sales for August, September, and October to the nearest thousands of dollars so that the planned contribution margin can be earned.

d. Prepare a purchases budget for August, September, and October. Sales and selling prices for November and December will not be changed.

13.   Budget variances

The following activity report has been given to you, the general manager of the Apsco Company:

	Budget	*Actual*
Sales ($5.00 per unit)	$100,000	$120,000
Variable costs	48,000	60,000
Contribution margin	$ 52,000	$ 60,000
Fixed costs	40,000	45,000
Net Income	$ 12,000	$ 15,000

Required:

a. Actual net income earned was 25 percent above budget. Are you pleased with the performance of your subordinates? Explain.

14.   Budget variances

Kasko Products Corp. manufactures and sells a single product. The sales forecast for the first six months of 19X3 was for 22,000 units, but actual sales were only 20,000. Here are the budgeted and actual income statements for this period:

	Budgeted	*Actual*	*Variance*
Sales	$440,000	$400,000	$40,000 U
Variable Costs:			
Material	$ 66,000	$ 62,000	4,000 F
Labor	44,000	42,000	2,000 F
Overhead	22,000	20,000	2,000 F
Selling	44,000	44,000	0
Total	$176,000	$168,000	$88,000 F
Contribution margin	$264,000	$232,000	$32,000 U
Fixed Costs:			
Depreciation	30,000	25,000	5,000 F
Insurance	8,000	9,000	1,000 U
Supervision	60,000	58,000	2,000 F
Salaries	80,000	84,000	4,000 U
Other	22,000	20,000	2,000 F
Total	$200,000	$196,000	$ 4,000 F
Net Income	$ 64,000	$ 36,000	$28,000 U

    F - Favorable variance.

    U - Unfavorable variance.

Required:

a. Comment on the favorable and unfavorable variances.
b. Prepare a report that provides a more realistic basis for evaluating managerial performance.

8 Financial Budgeting

CHAPTER OVERVIEW

The purpose of this chapter is to show how the information contained in the operating budgets can be used to prepare a cash budget and pro forma financial statements. The sales budget is important because it provides an indication of when cash will be received and also the amounts of cash that will be received during a given period of time. The other operating budgets are important because they identify the principal cash requirements of the firm.

Two major objectives of any firm should be to earn a target profit and to maintain a sound financial position. In this chapter we will see how operating budgets are extended to estimate net income and the financial position that will result if budgets are followed.

QUESTIONS FOR CONSIDERATION

1. What is a cash budget and how is it developed?
2. Why do businesses accept credit-card customers?
3. What is the relationship between a production budget and a cash disbursements budget?
4. What are pro forma financial statements?
5. What is the purpose of preparing pro forma financial statements?

The topics covered in this chapter may appear to have little or no relationship to the materials covered in the previous chapter, but this is not the case. The cash budget and pro forma financial statements discussed in this chapter cannot be developed until the operating budgets are finalized. The sales forecast is needed before a forecast of cash receipts can be made and the other operating budgets are needed before a forecast of cash requirements can be made. Thus the material covered in this chapter is an extension of material presented in Chapter 7.

THE CASH BUDGET

Business transactions generate a flow of cash into and out of the firm. The cash budget shows the net effect of budgeted transactions on cash balances. Over a period of time it is expected that an amount of cash accumulations will result which can be used to pay dividends to the stockholders. Typically, the flow of cash is such that at times there may be an excess available, while at other times there may be shortages. A measure of a company's success in managing its cash is its ability to keep idle cash—which is a sterile asset—to a minimum.

The cash budget is the device that enables management to gain a preview of the cash position. There are two basic elements to a cash budget. One deals with the inflow (receipts) of cash, and the other deals with the outflow (disbursements) of cash. The principal inflow of cash for the going concern comes from the sale of goods and services. If all sales are for cash, budgeting cash receipts is simplified. If credit sales are involved, budgeting cash receipts is more involved. The terms of sale such as net/30 days will provide some indication of cash inflow, but customers frequently do not pay their bills on time. However, if management knows the debt-paying habits of its customers, even though they pay late, it is possible to get a good estimate of the inflow of cash. The writer recalls a very good customer of his shop that always paid bills 90 days from the date of the invoice even though the terms of sale required payment within 30 days. Today many firms simplify the cash flow problem associated with credit sales by accepting credit cards. Although banks may charge 3 percent to 7 percent of credit sales for this service, the certainty of an immediate cash inflow may justify the use of credit cards.

Whether management has any leeway in preparing its cash payments or disbursements budget depends on the nature of the payment. Payment of wages and taxes and the repayment of loans must be made when due to avoid possible penalties. In making payments to trade creditors businesses behave much the same as individuals do at bill-paying time. In their efforts to postpone the need for short-term borrowing to cover cash requirements, they sometimes stagger payments to creditors on the basis of who squawks the loudest. They write checks on Friday and hope to have the cash to cover them deposited before they clear. Boston-based firms have their checking accounts in a bank located in Boondocks, Montoming hoping to gain a few days before they have to come up with the cash. A basic justification for one business resorting to such practices is that other businesses do the same thing. A byword of those who manage cash is to speed up receipts and slow down disbursements. However, it is impossible to forecast cash receipts and cash payments unless specific guidelines are established. These guidelines are discussed in the paragraphs that follow.

Cash Receipts Budget

The sales forecast itself does not show when cash will flow into the firm. If sales are for cash or by credit card, the inflow will be immediate, but, to the extent that credit sales will be made—and this is the rule for most manufacturing firms—an element of uncertainty enters the picture. If credit sales are made to established customers the firm may have evidence of their paying habits which can be used when estimating cash inflow. It may be more difficult to estimate cash inflow from new credit customers. The firm's credit department plays a very important role regarding the inflow of cash from credit customers. An aggressive collection program that is consistent with credit policy can provide a great amount of control over this source of cash receipts.

Cash receipts budget illustrated. The balance of accounts receivable on January 1 is estimated to be $45,000. The sales forecast for the first quarter of the year is

January	$50,000
February	80,000
March	60,000

It is expected that 40 percent of sales will be for cash and that 60 percent will be on account. It is also expected that credit sales will be paid in the month following the sale. A cash receipts budget for the quarter follows:

	Jan.	Feb.	Mar.	Total
From cash sales	$20,000	$32,000	$24,000	$ 76,000
From previous months sales	45,000	30,000	48,000	123,000
Total Cash Receipts	$65,000	$62,000	$72,000	$199,000

Jan. sales $50,000

Feb. sales $80,000

Accounts receivable on March 31 should be $36,000 which is 60 percent of March sales.

A more involved illustration. The accounts receivable on January 1, 19X3 were

Balance from November sales	$20,000
Balance from December sales	60,000

Sales for the first six months of 19X3 are forecast as follows:

January	$100,000	April	$110,000
February	140,000	May	90,000
March	120,000	June	100,000

It is estimated that 20 percent of each month's sales will be for cash and that the balance sold on account. Of credit sales 50 percent will be collected in the month following sale, and the balance will be collected in the second month following sale.

The fact that the collections from sales for any month are spread over three months can complicate the preparation of a cash receipts budget. We can clarify and simplify the measurement of cash inflow by stating the specific sources of cash inflow for each month. The following shows how this can be done.

January receipts	*February receipts*
All November receivables	50% December receivables
50% December receivables	40% January receivables
20% January sales	20% February sales

March receipts	*April receipts*
40% January sales	40% February sales
40% February sales	40% March sales
20% March sales	20% April sales

May receipts	*June receipts*
40% March sales	40% April sales
40% April sales	40% May sales
20% May sales	20% June sales

Having this before us it is a simple task to fill in the numbers as shown in Table 8-1.

Two additional factors can also affect the inflow of cash. It is common practice to offer a sales discount to customers who pay cash or who pay amounts due within, say, 10 days of the billing date. If a 2 percent sales discount is taken, cash inflow would be only 98 percent of the gross amount. A second factor that can affect cash inflow is bad accounts which must be written off. Most bad accounts have long passed the normal collection period, but on occasion accounts go bad shortly after they have been opened. Once identified, these accounts should be deducted from potential sources of cash.

Cash Disbursements Budget

The cash disbursements that must be budgeted for a period include liabilities carried over from the previous period plus current period costs and less those costs that can be postponed until some future period. As a generalization, the major payments of cash in a manufacturing firm are for items included in the current budgets.

We will explain the development of a cash disbursements budget by an illustration which is an extension of that illustrated in Table 8-1. The additional information needed to complete this budget is given as follows:

1. The production budget in units for the first six months of 19X3 is

January	16,000	April	9,000
February	11,000	May	8,000
March	10,000	June	12,000

TABLE 8-1

Cash Receipts Budget, January - June 19X3

Source	Jan.	Feb.	Mar.	Apr.	May	June	Total
Second previous month	$20,000	$30,000	$ 40,000	$ 56,000	$ 48,000	$ 44,000	$238,000
Previous month	30,000	40,000	56,000	48,000	44,000	36,000	254,000
Current month	20,000	28,000	24,000	22,000	18,000	20,000	132,000
Total receipts	$70,000	$98,000	$120,000	$126,000	$110,000	$100,000	$624,000

Budgeted accounts receivable, June 30, 19X3 are $116,000 calculated as follows:

Accounts receivable January 1		$ 80,000
Sales for the six months		660,000
Total		$740,000
Cash receipts		624,000
Accounts receivable, June 30		$116,000

Verification of accounts receivable:

May sales	$ 90,000	
Collected on May sales	54,000	
Balance due		$ 36,000
June sales	100,000	
Collected on June sales	20,000	
Balance due		80,000
Total		$116,000

2. The purchases budget in units for the first six months of 19X3 is

January	13,000	April	6,000
February	5,000	May	14,000
March	10,000	June	12,000

3. Material per unit of production, 1 lb of X costing $2.00

4. Labor per unit, $4.00

5. Variable overhead per unit, $1.00

6. Annual fixed overhead is $64,000 of which $16,000 is depreciation (a noncash expense)

7. Administrative salaries are $10,000 per month

8. Selling price is $10.00 per unit

9. Selling expenses are 10 percent of sales

10. All costs except purchases are paid in the month incurred. Purchases (accounts payable) are paid in the month following purchase. The January 1 accounts payable balance is $20,000

We will use this information to prepare the cash disbursements budget (Table 8-2). Remember, the production budget, not the sales budget is the basis for estimating variable production costs.

THE CASH BUDGET—A SUMMARY

The cash budget is easy to prepare once the cash receipts and cash disbursements budgets are completed. Cash receipts for each month are added to the beginning cash balance, and total cash disbursements are subtracted from this total to obtain the cash balance at the end of the month. The cash balance at the end of January is the beginning cash balance for February, and so on. In our illustration the beginning cash balance for January is $80,000.

Cash balances are not always on the plus side, and borrowing may be required to meet cash requirements. If this is done, the amount borrowed is a cash receipt when received and a cash disbursement when paid. One advantage of a cash budget is that it indicates to a potential lender when the firm should be able to pay off the loan. The cash budget appears in Table 8-3.

TABLE 8-2

Cash Disbursements Budget,
January - June 19X3

Account	Jan.	Feb.	Mar.	Apr.	May	June	Total
Labor	$ 64,000	$ 44,000	$40,000	$36,000	$32,000	$ 48,000	$264,000
Variable overhead	16,000	11,000	10,000	9,000	8,000	12,000	66,000
Fixed overhead	4,000	4,000	4,000	4,000	4,000	4,000	24,000
Admin. salaries	10,000	10,000	10,000	10,000	10,000	10,000	60,000
Selling expense	10,000	14,000	12,000	11,000	9,000	10,000	66,000
Purchases	20,000	26,000	10,000	20,000	12,000	28,000	116,000
Total Payments	$124,000	$109,000	$86,000	$90,000	$75,000	$112,000	$596,000

TABLE 8-3

Cash Budget,
January - June 19X3

	Jan.	Feb.	Mar.	Apr.	May	June	Total
Beginning cash balance	$ 80,000	$ 26,000	$ 15,000	$ 49,000	$ 85,000	$120,000	$ 80,000
Cash receipts	70,000	98,000	120,000	126,000	110,000	100,000	624,000
Total cash available	$150,000	$124,000	$135,000	$175,000	$195,000	$220,000	$704,000
Cash disbursements	124,000	109,000	86,000	90,000	75,000	112,000	596,000
Closing Cash Balance	$ 26,000	$ 15,000	$ 49,000	$ 85,000	$120,000	$108,000	$108,000

The types of budgeted data that we have presented in this and in the previous chapter provide the basic ingredients for preparing a pro forma income statement. A pro forma income statement is the same as the income statements you have seen and prepared except that the values used are estimates of revenues and expense rather than actual values. The purpose of this statement is to see if the overall budget plan will yield the desired target profit. Quite often, budgets must be revised over and over before the right combination of revenue and expense is obtained. This might be the case if management was dissatisfied with a projected profit of $40,000 on sales of $660,000 as shown in the pro forma income statement of Table 8-4. This statement is based on data used in our continuing illustration.

TABLE   8-4

Pro Forma Income Statement,
First six months of 19X3

Sales		$660,000
Less: Cost of Goods Sold:		
Material (66,000 units at $2.00)	$132,000	
Labor (66,000 units at $4.00)	264,000	
Variable overhead (66,000 units at $1.00)	66,000	
Fixed overhead	32,000	494,000
Gross margin		$166,000
Operating Expenses:		
Administrative salaries	60,000	
Selling expense	66,000	126,000
Net Income		$ 40,000

Pro forma balance sheet.   Part of the information needed to prepare a pro forma balance sheet is contained in our budget illustrations. The cash, accounts receivable, inventory, and accounts payable balances on June 30 have been established. We could also determine taxes payable and notes payable if they were factors in our illustration. Thus most current assets and current liability balances can be obtained through the budgets we have discussed. What we have not considered are long-term assets and liabilities. These values do not evolve from the normal budgeting process; rather, they are the result of specific management decisions. Activity regarding these accounts does not follow a single pattern; it depends to a great extent on the long-term objectives of the firm. For this reason we will not attempt to illustrate a pro forma balance sheet.

SUMMARY

Top management is probably more interested in the cash budget and the pro forma financial statements than in the basic operating budgets. From management's point of view a budget is acceptable only if it achieves objectives, and objectives are more likely to be expressed in terms of net income and asset position than in sales volume and production costs.

The cash budget is of primary importance because it presents a picture of the firm's future liquidity. More specifically, it indicates when the firm can anticipate a surplus of cash or the need for short-term financing. This is essential for effective cash management.

Pro forma financial statements are a forecast of earnings and financial position if the budget plan is achieved. If actual activity tends to follow the budget, management has a firm basis for planning future programs.

KEY TERMS

cash budget

pro forma financial statements

QUESTIONS

1. What are the two basic elements of a cash budget?
2. Customers who do not pay their bills on time are not good customers. Do you agree? Explain.
3. How can management justify the use of credit cards that can reduce cash inflow by 3 percent to 7 percent of sales?
4. What information is needed for the preparation of a cash budget?

5. What information is needed for the preparation of a cash disbursements budget?

6. What is a pro forma income statement? How does it differ from other income statements?

PROBLEMS

1. Cash receipts budget

The sales forecast for the Glasco Corp. for the fourth quarter of 19X1 is October, $160,000; November, $240,000; December, $400,000. Of total sales 20 percent are for cash, and the balance is made on open account. It is expected that credit sales will be paid for during the month following the sale. Accounts receivable on September 30 are expected to be $80,000.

Required:

a. Prepare a budget of cash receipts for the fourth quarter.

b. What were September sales?

c. What is the estimated balance of accounts receivable on December 31?

2. Cash receipts budget

The sales forecast (in thousands) for the Merrill Company for the first six months of 19X3 follows:

January	$200	April	$260
February	240	May	280
March	210	June	300

Cash sales are 20 percent of total sales, and the balance is credit sales. Collections on credit sales are planned as follows:

Month following sale, 70 percent

Second month following sale, 30 percent

The firm gives a 2 percent discount on all cash sales, and the accounts receivable balance on January 1 will be $300. Of this balance $250 is for December sales, and $50 is for November sales.

Required:

a. A cash receipts budget for the first six months of 19X3.

b. Estimate the balance of accounts receivable on June 30.

3. Cash receipts budget

Sales at the Clayborn Company were $40,000 in May and $50,000 in June. The sales forecast for the third quarter of 19X8 is July, $30,000; August, $60,000; September, $70,000. Collections of cash from sales follows the following pattern:

Cash sales, 10 percent of total sales

Month following sale, 60 percent of total sales

Second month following sale, 30 percent of total sales

Required:

a. What was the accounts receivable balance on June 30?

b. Prepare a budget of cash receipts for the quarter.

c. What accounts receivable balance can be expected on September 30?

4. Production, purchases, and cash disbursements budgets

The sales forecast in units for the Acme Corporation for the first five months of 19X6 follows:

January	3,000	April	7,000
February	4,000	May	5,000
March	6,000		

The firm's finished goods inventory policy requires an inventory at the beginning of each month equal to 150 percent of that month's sales and raw material inventory at the beginning of each month equal to twice the monthly requirements.

Additional information:

a. Each unit produced requires 3 Klaxons costing $4.00 each.

b. Labor cost per unit is $16.00.

c. Variable overhead is $10.00 per unit.

d. Fixed overhead is $12,000 per month.

e. Accounts payable on January 1 are $90,000.

f. All costs are paid in the month incurred except purchases (accounts payable) which are paid in the month following purchase.

Required:

a. A production budget for the first quarter.

b. A purchases budget for the first quarter.

c. A cash disbursements budget for the first quarter.

d. What will be the balance of accounts payable at the end of the quarter?

5. Production, purchases, and cash disbursements budget

The Fast-Flow Corporation has budgeted unit sales for the first five months of 19X1 as follows:

January	12,000	March	18,000
February	16,000	April	14,000
		May	13,000

Because of the short production cycle at Fast-Flow, finished goods inventory at the beginning of each month is only 50 percent of the monthly requirements.

Required:

a. Prepare a production budget for the first quarter of 19X1.

Each unit of production requires 3 lb of Chemco costing $3 per lb. Raw material inventory at the beginning of any month must cover production requirements for that month.

b. Prepare a purchases budget in units and in dollars for the first quarter of 19X1.

Labor cost is $8.00 per unit; variable production costs are $5.00 per unit; factory overhead is $15,000 per month. Each of these costs is paid during the month incurred. Purchases are paid for in the month following purchase. December purchases were 49,000 lb.

c. Prepare a cash disbursements budget for the first quarter of 19X1.

d. What will the accounts payable be on March 31?

6. Comprehensive budget

The sales forecast for the Bygone Sales Corp. for the first four months of 19X2 follows:

January	$ 80,000	March	$120,000
February	100,000	April	90,000

Collections on sales are expected to follow past performance which is

50 percent during the month of sale

50 percent during the month following sale

The firm gives a 2 percent cash discount on all payments made during the month of sale. The balance of accounts receivable on December 31, 19X1 is expected to be $50,000.

Required:

a. Prepare a budget of cash receipts for the quarter.

The cost of purchases is 60 percent of selling price, and the firm has a policy that requires an inventory at the beginning of each month equal to twice the sales requirements for that month.

b. Prepare a purchases budget for the quarter.

Additional variable costs are 10 percent of sales. Fixed costs are $4,000 per month, and $1,000 of this is depreciation. Variable and fixed costs are paid during the month incurred. Purchases are paid for in the month following purchases. Additional information as of December 31, 19X1 follows:

Cash balance	$25,000
Accounts payable	60,000

c. Prepare a budget of cash disbursements for the quarter.

d. Prepare a cash budget for the quarter.

e. Prepare a pro forma income statement for the quarter.

7. Production, purchases and cash budgets

The Creston Manufacturing Company produces and sells a single product. Estimated sales in units for the first six months of 19X8 are

January	3,000	April	4,000
February	2,500	May	4,500
March	3,500	June	5,000

The firm has a policy of maintaining an inventory of finished goods at the beginning of each month equal to the sales for that month plus the sales for the following month.

Required:

a. Prepare a production budget for the first quarter.

Each unit produced requires 3 lb of Zack costing $2.00 per lb. Material inventory at the beginning of each month must be twice the material requirements for that month.

b. Prepare a purchases budget for the first quarter in units and in dollars.

Each unit sells for $20. It is expected that 40 percent of sales will be paid for during the month that the sale is made and the balance in the month following sale. Accounts receivable on January 1 are expected to be $48,000.

c. Prepare a budget of cash receipts for the first quarter.

d. How many units were sold during the previous December?

The labor cost is $4.00 per unit and other variable costs are $3.00 per unit. These costs are paid in the month incurred, but purchases are paid for in the month following purchase. Fixed costs amount to $10,000 per month of which $3,000 is depreciation. These costs are paid for in the month incurred. Accounts payable on January 1 will be $28,000, and the cash balance will be $40,000.

e. Prepare a budget of cash disbursements for the first quarter.

f. Prepare a cash budget for the first quarter.

8. Comprehensive budgets

Clipper Novelty Sales has made the following forecast for the period ahead:

July	$80,000	September	$ 90,000
August	60,000	October	100,000

The cost of merchandise sold averages 40 percent of sales. Additional variable costs amount to 20 percent of sales, and fixed costs are $20,000 per month. The firm has a policy of maintaining beginning inventory at twice the monthly sales requirement.

Additional information:

- a. Merchandise purchases are paid for during the month following purchase. June purchases were $24,000.
- b. Additional variable costs are paid during the month incurred.
- c. Of the $20,000 monthly fixed costs, $5,000 is depreciation of building and equipment. Fixed costs are paid during the month incurred.
- d. Sales are one-half cash and one-half on account. The firm's experience has been that 75 percent of accounts are paid during the month following sale and 25 percent during the second month following sale. The accounts receivable balance on June 30 will be composed of the following:

Balance of May receivables	$20,000
June receivables	70,000

e. The cash balance on June 30 is expected to be $35,000.

Required:

a. Prepare a purchases budget for the next quarter.

b. Prepare a cash budget for the quarter.

c. Prepare pro forma income statements for each month and for the quarter.

PART 4

Product
Costing

9 The Flow of Cost

CHAPTER OVERVIEW

In this chapter we will explain how the basic elements of manufacturing cost, direct material, direct labor, and overhead flow to the production areas and become associated with the goods and services the firm produces. Management needs to know the cost of work performed, because cost is frequently a basic input to the selling price decision.

The flow of cost in any manufacturing firm depends on the type of production involved. In process production where batches of identical products roll off the line, management assumes that each unit of production should share equally the total cost of production. Where job-order production is used, every job or product can be different and therefore could involve different amounts of cost.

The assignment of direct costs such as material and labor should not be difficult because production is the reason that these costs are incurred. Ascertaining the "right" amount of indirect cost that should be allocated to a product is difficult because the total of these costs will not be known until after the accounting period has ended.

QUESTIONS FOR CONSIDERATION

1. What is the difference between a direct and indirect cost?
2. What is the difference between process production and job-order production?
3. How are indirect costs applied to production?
4. What price should be charged for materials as they move from inventory into production?
5. How does income measurement differ between retailers and manufacturers?

In Chapter 4 we identified and described the various types of cost which occur in business operations and provided some indication of their importance. Frequently in these discussions we have simply stated that the cost of a unit of production was $10, $15, or some such figure without explaining the process whereby costs are determined. This is an extremely important area of activity because cost accumulation and costing is a prerequisite for price and profit determination.

We know that there are costs involved in creating any good or service, but we need to understand how the costs incurred by a firm become assigned to units of goods and services that are created. It is a simple matter to establish that the cost for rent will be $50,000 for the year or that the payroll for the month of July was $45,000, but it is quite another matter to ascertain how much of these costs should be charged to a particular job or to a particular unit of production. When a firm produces a single product, it is less difficult to measure what the unit cost of production was and to predict what future costs will be. But, when a variety of products is involved, there is the problem of cost allocations, and this is far from being a routine task.

THE BASIC PROBLEM

To understand the purpose of this discussion, you must first visualize a two-step process. In the first step, costs are incurred by the firm and recorded in the books of account (journals). For example, the bill for light and power is received by the firm, and the treasurer makes out a check to pay the bill. This is the cost incurring step which involves the following journal entry:

DEBIT	Light and power expense	xxxx	
CREDIT	Cash		xxxxx

This step gets the cost of light and power on the books, but that is all. In the second step, a portion of this cost must be allocated to the goods and services produced.

If a firm is to earn a profit, all costs incurred such as rent, materials, payroll, and taxes must be recouped and more. This recouping of costs also involves a two-step process. First, a portion of these costs must be assigned to each job that is done or to each unit of production that is completed. Second, the goods or services must be sold at a price that is greater than the total of cost. In the final analysis costs can only be recouped through the sale of goods and services.

The charging of direct costs such as direct labor and direct material is not a difficult task provided that the proper records are kept because these costs are incurred only because specific units of goods and services are produced. The major problem in costing involves the assignment of indirect costs—overhead—to units of production. This problem is complicated by the fact that the sum total of indirect costs for an accounting period probably will not be known until the end of the period. Yet a portion of this "unknown" cost must be assigned to every unit of production beginning with day one.

Our concern in this chapter is to examine and evaluate the traditional process by which costs flow into and out of production and to identify the basic philosophy of this process.

Income Statements

We begin this section with a brief review of income statements for a retail firm and a manufacturing firm. The purpose of this discussion is to point out differences between the two and to identify the types of activity involved in the cost flow process. Table 9-1 is a simplified income statement for a retail firm.

TABLE   9-1

Simplified Income Statement—Retailing

Sales, net		$5,000,000
Less: Cost of Goods Sold:		
Inventory, beginning	$ 850,000	
Purchases	2,500,000	
Cost of goods available		
for sale	$3,350,000	
Inventory, ending	(750,000)	2,600,000
Gross margin		$2,400,000
Less: Selling expense	900,000	
Administrative expense	500,000	
Miscellaneous expense	300,000	1,700,000
Net Income		$ 700,000

TABLE   9-2

Income Statement—Manufacturing

Sales income		$5,000,000
Less: Cost of goods sold		3,500,000
Gross margin		$1,500,000
Less: Operating Expenses:		
Selling	$440,000	
Administrative	550,000	
Depreciation of office equipment	50,000	
Miscellaneous	60,000	1,100,000
Net Income		$ 400,000

Attention should be focused on the cost of goods sold section. Note that the cost of goods sold is simply the total value of merchandise on hand at the beginning of the accounting period plus the net cost of merchandise purchased, less the cost of merchandise on hand at the end of the accounting period.

In a manufacturing firm the income statement (see Table 9-2) seems to be simpler than that in our retail illustration. The reason for this is that the cost of goods sold is presented in summary form. In retailing, goods sold are generally in the same form as when they were purchased; not so in manufacturing. In manufacturing, the cost of goods sold is generally shown via a separate statement such as in Table 9-3 because much more information must be shown. There are two main sections in this statement. The first shows the cost of the goods that were manufactured during the period—the total of all costs incurred in production for the period—plus or minus any change in the work-in-process inventory. An increase in the cost of an ending inventory over the cost of a beginning inventory has the effect of reducing the cost of goods manufactured. This is due to the fact that more of the costs incurred during the period are still in inventory and will not become expenses until sold.

The first section of this statement summarizes the three basic classifications of manufacturing cost which are direct material, direct labor, and manufacturing overhead. Manufacturing overhead by definition includes all costs reasonably associated with getting the

TABLE   9-3

Cost of Goods Sold Statement

Direct Materials Used:		
Inventory, beginning	$ 80,000	
Material purchases	800,000	
Cost of material available		
for use	$880,000	
Inventory, ending	(200,000)	$ 680,000
Direct labor		2,000,000
Overhead: Variable	$700,000	
Fixed	420,000	1,120,000
Total production cost for		
the period		$3,800,000
Less: Increase In Work In		
Process:		
Work in process, ending	$400,000	
Work in process, beginning	(200,000)	200,000
Cost of goods manufactured		$3,600,000
Less: Increase In Finished Goods:		
Finished goods inventory,		
ending	$400,000	
Finished goods inventory,		
beginning	(300,000)	100,000
Cost of goods sold		$3,500,000

product ready for sale except direct material and direct labor. In effect, the cost of work in process at the beginning of the period is added to the manufacturing costs incurred during the period, and this total is reduced by the value of work in process at the end of the period.

The second part of this statement shows the cost of goods that were sold. In effect, the cost of the finished goods inventory at the beginning of the period is added to the cost of goods manufactured, and this total is reduced by the cost of the finished goods inventory remaining at the end of the period.

In summary, our concern in this chapter is to see how and why these manufacturing costs flow into production and become attached to jobs or units of production. More specifically we are concerned with the process that will ensure insofar as is possible that $3,800,000 (see Table 9-3) will be charged to the goods that were worked on during the period.

THE FLOW OF COST

The flow of cost in a manufacturing organization is governed by the flow of products through the production process. If there are ten steps in a production process, there may be ten costs centers where costs are accumulated and applied to the products in process. Thus there must be a system that allows the appropriate costs to be assigned to each step in the overall process. In addition, there must be a system that permits assigning costs to each job or unit of production as it moves through each stage of production.

In a macro sense, the flow of cost is the same in all manufacturing firms because in all firms material, labor, and overhead are combined to produce a good (see Figure 9-1).

Here we can see how material, labor, and overhead become an asset (work in process) and become an expense (expired cost) when sold and charged to the cost of good sold account.

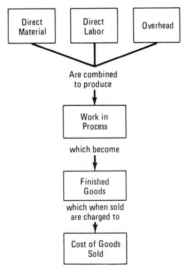

FIGURE   9-1.   Flow of Manufacturing Costs

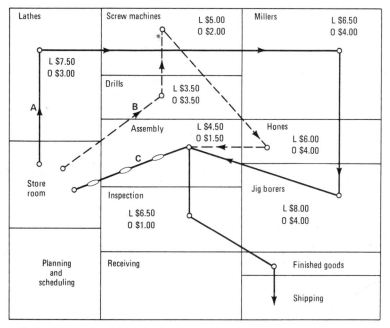

FIGURE   9-2   Job-order Shop Layout

L - Direct labor cost per hour
O - Overhead per direct labor hour

In a micro sense, the flow of cost differs significantly based on the nature of the manufacturing process. Costing in a job-order shop is quite different from costing in process production. Figure 9-2 illustrates the movement of a job in a job shop. The job illustrated requires the production of two parts A and B which are then combined with part C in the assembly section. The amount of cost that this job picks up, in addition to materials, depends on the departments where work is performed and the number of hours of labor and overhead the job requires. Thus, if part A was worked on five hours in the milling department, it would pick up $32.50 in labor cost and $20.00 in overhead cost. Every job worked on could go through a different sequence of operations and spend varying amounts of time in each department.

In process production every unit in the production lot goes through the same sequence of operations and picks up an identical amount of cost in each department. Figure 9-3 shows that material, labor, and overhead costs are assigned to each department. The amount of labor cost that a unit of product will pick up in, say, the

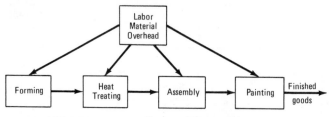

FIGURE 9-3 Process Production Layout

forming department depends on the total labor cost assigned to this department during a time span and the number of units that were worked on in this department. Thus, if total direct labor cost in February was $8,000 and 10,000 units were completed that month, each unit should pick up 80 cents in labor cost.

Our concern now is for a method that will result in charging the appropriate amount of direct material, direct labor, and overhead to each department. In Chapter 11 we will show how departmental costs are charged to jobs or to units of production. We will deal with each cost separately.

Direct Material Cost

Direct material is material that can be traced logically and practically to a job or a unit of production. Spark plugs, wheels, and tires are each a direct material in the manufacture of automobiles. This does not mean that the cost of spark plugs is always a direct material cost at an auto assembly plant. The cost of spark plugs used in a fork-lift conveyor by the maintenance department would be treated as manufacturing overhead. A given material is classified as direct or indirect based on the use to which it is put.

The flow of material cost is described via the T-account:

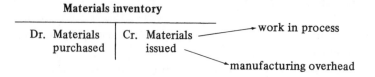

The journal entry to record the addition of materials to inventory by purchase is

DEBIT   Materials inventory   **xxxxx**
CREDIT   Accounts payable or cash   **xxxxx**

When materials are issued for production the journal entry is

DEBIT   Work in process   **xxxxx**
CREDIT   Materials inventory   **xxxxx**

When materials are issued for nonproduction use such as maintenance, the journal entry is

DEBIT   Manufacturing overhead   **xxxxx**
CREDIT   Materials inventory   **xxxxx**

Materials flow into inventory primarily as a result of purchases, and they flow out of inventory because they have been requisitioned (see Figure 9-4). Material, whether direct or indirect, should not be allowed to move from inventory unless there is formal authorization. This is essential for a number of reasons. First, a record of material leaving inventory is necessary to ascertain quantities on hand without taking a physical count. It is common practice in many firms to reorder a material when the "on hand" balance falls to a predetermined level. Inventory control systems depend on complete, current,

E.S. Stockwell Co.				
Material Requisition				
Charge to:			Date _____	
Job number _____				
Prod. lot number _____				
Account number _____				
Quantity	Item	Code	Unit price	Total price
Authorized by _____				

FIGURE   9-4.   Material Requisition

and accurate information. Without this, the danger of overstocking or stock-outs is greatly increased. Second, every piece of material leaving inventory must be charged somewhere—to a job, to a batch of production, or to overhead—and the material requisition identifies the account to be charged (see Figure 9-4). We mentioned earlier that the only way for a firm to recoup its costs is to charge them to production and then sell the units.

Direct materials should not be released from inventory except in anticipation of production. Production planners must decide the specific jobs (job-order production) or the number of units (process production) that will start in production in a given department at a given point in time. The authorization to produce should carry with it the authorization to requisition those materials that the production order specifies. For every production order, there should be a bill of materials that indicates the part name, the part number, and usage of each component. This process provides a good measure of assurance that only the materials that should be issued will leave the inventory area.

To this point we have emphasized only the physical flow of materials from inventory to production. We have not identified how material costs flow into production. At this point some of the basic problems in inventory costing will be identified, but we will reserve until later the detailed discussion of inventory management.

The unit cost of materials charged to a given production order depends initially on the composition of inventory at the time the material requisition is filled. Let us suppose that the job in question calls for 1,000 toggle switches to be issued on December 12. The inventory card for this item shows the following:

Date	Description	Units	Unit price	Total
11-5	Purchase	12,000	$1.10	$13,200

Because each switch in inventory cost $1.10, there is no question as to the cost to be charged to production. Suppose, however, that on the morning of December 12, the inventory card showed the following:

Date	Description	Units	Unit price	Extension	Total
12-01	Balance	3,000	$1.10	$3,300	$ 3,300
12-04	Purchase	5,000	1.20	6,000	9,300
12-10	Purchase	4,000	1.30	5,200	14,500

Total inventory consists of three batches of material, each having a different unit cost. The question is, which price should be charged for the 1,000 toggle switches that are issued on December 12? The fact that the oldest switches are issued first does not mean that they will be charged to production at $1.10. The cost charged to production depends on the firm's costing policy. For example,

1. A policy of average cost would result in a unit cost of $1.2083 ($14,500 ÷ 12,000).

2. A first-in, first-out policy would result in a unit cost of $1.10.

3. A last-in, first-out policy would result in a unit cost of $1.30.

Thus the direct material cost charged to production may or may not be the actual cost incurred for the materials issued.

Direct Labor Cost

In many respects the flow of direct labor cost is similar to the flow of direct material cost because each is a direct cost. When a production order is generated, it is common practice to identify the types and amounts of direct labor required. Frequently workers are expected to punch a time clock when they begin work on a job and again when they complete their work on a job. Time sheets may be used to account for 480 minutes of each direct laborer's time for each 8-hour day.

There may be a difference between the amount of money earned by direct laborers and the amount of direct labor cost that is charged to production. From time to time workers will be idle for a variety of reasons, and they are paid for this idle time. There may be a poor flow of work, or machines may need to be stopped for adjustment or similar-type interruptions. The pay that workers receive for such periods of idleness is not directly associated with specific batches of production and therefore should not be charged to production as a direct labor cost. Such labor costs should be treated as overhead and be charged to production accordingly (see Chapter 10).

Frequently direct laborers receive wage premiums such as shift differentials and overtime. These premiums add to the cost of operations, but, if they are charged directly to production, distortions in cost will result. We can see this distortion in the following illustration. Here we assume that identical products are being produced during normal (straight) time and during a period involving overtime (time and a half). If overtime is included as a part of direct labor, the cost of units produced during overtime periods increases by $5.00. This is, of course, true, but it also indicates that these overtime units are of greater value than straight-time units which is nonsense.

	Normal time	*Over- time*
Direct material	$12	$12
Direct labor	10	15
Overhead	15	15
Total Cost	$37	$42

In manufacturing, all manufacturing costs—material, labor and overhead—become assets when charged to production. First, these costs comprise the cost of the work-in-process inventory, and later they comprise the cost of the finished goods inventory (see Figure 9-1). Manufacturing costs do not become expenses until the time that the goods and services are sold. To the extent that ending inventories, either in process or finished goods, contain "overtime" units, their cost is inflated. Therefore, such "extra" wages should be treated as overhead and be absorbed by all units produced during the accounting period.

There may be instances where this line of reasoning is faulty. The normal work week of a firm may include overtime. Management may reason that certain economies accrue by working 10 people 44 hours per week rather than working 11 people 40 hours per week. For example, there is a maximum amount that an employer must pay per employee for Social Security (F.I.C.A.), unemployment compensation, life insurance, health insurance, and the like. Fewer employees means less cost. If overtime is the normal state of affairs for a firm, the inclusion of overtime as a direct labor cost is justified, at least from a management point of view.

Including overtime in direct labor costs may also be justified in the following-type circumstances. A customer calls a job-order machine shop late on Friday requesting that it make a replacement part for a much-needed machine. The customer must have the part by 8 o'clock on Monday morning. The customer is told that the part can be made Saturday morning and that overtime will be charged to the job. When overtime is specifically contracted for, it may be considered a direct labor cost.

Fringe benefit costs such as company-paid insurance, retirement, and medical benefits arise in part because there are direct laborers, but they are considered labor-related costs and are added to overhead. Generally, such benefits are accorded all full-time employees, not just those involved in direct labor activity. They are costs of having employees.

Overhead Costs

Manufacturing overhead includes all manufacturing costs except direct materials and direct labor. When a job or a batch of production is completed, it is possible, if not probable, that management can determine the exact direct material and direct labor costs that should be attached to it. But there is no practical way to ascertain the exact amount of overhead that a particular job should absorb. For example, a foreman was out ill for a week and was paid his salary of $300. How much of this $300 should be charged to job X? Job X was started and completed during the foreman's absence, and no replacement foreman was engaged.

Overhead, or indirect costs, have another characteristic that makes their assignment to production difficult. Let us assume that production job number 4567 is completed, shipped, and billed on May 14. At this point in time, all the direct material and direct labor that the job should bear has been charged to it. However, overhead costs continue to accumulate from the first day of the accounting period to the last, and it will not be until some time after the accounting period is over that management will know the total of its overhead costs. The problem is that on May 14 job number 4567 must be charged its "fair share" of the annual overhead costs; otherwise the gross margin earned on the job cannot be determined.

Consequently, businessmen must make two very important judgments prior to the start of every accounting period. First, an estimate must be made of the total overhead costs that are likely to be incurred during the upcoming period. Second, an estimate must be made of the volume of activity that is expected for the same period. Activity can be expressed in such measures as direct labor-hours, direct labor cost, units of production, or machine hours. Whatever measure of activity is used, it should, hopefully, be related to overhead costs. These two estimates are used to obtain an estimated overhead rate per unit of activity. Thus, if the estimate of overhead costs is $500,000 and the expected volume of activity is 100,000 direct labor-hours, the estimated overhead rate is $5.00 per direct labor-hour. Referring back to job number 4567, if this job used a total of 56 direct labor-hours, $280 in overhead costs would have been applied (charged) to the job when transferred to finished goods. An unanswered question is whether $280 is the proper portion of indirect costs that should be charged to the job. On May 14 we do not know.

In practice relatively few firms operate with a single overhead rate. More likely, every production department will have its own estimated rate. Overhead costs in some production departments may constitute a large portion of total manufacturing cost and in others, a small portion. Having separate overhead rates for each department increases the possibility that the "right" amount of overhead will be charged to each unit of work.

In Chapter 4 reference was made to the fact that indirect costs (overhead) are harder to manage than direct costs. We have pointed out another reason why this is true. If the actual total of indirect costs for a period turns out to be $500,000 and the actual direct labor-hours worked are 100,000 then just the right amount of overhead will be applied to production. But the odds of this happening are very remote, and the more likely situation is that too much or too little overhead will be applied to production.

Suppose at year's end it was determined that the total of indirect (overhead) costs incurred was $512,000 and that 110,000 direct labor-hours were worked. Because applied overhead equals the actual amount of activity times the estimated overhead rate, a total of $550,000 would be applied to production. This is $38,000 more than actual cost, but, at the time this is known, nothing can be done about it. Most of the work in process probably has been finished and perhaps sold. When applied overhead is greater than actual overhead, we have overapplied overhead. The overhead T-account would appear as follows:

Manufacturing overhead

$512,000	$550,000
Actual cost	Applied

   During the period each job or production lot was charged for its "appropriate" portion of overhead, and the total of these charges to work in process was $550,000. Unless some adjustment is made, total manufacturing costs for the period will be overstated, and this causes inventory and cost of goods sold to be overstated. Consequently, manufacturing overhead must be debited for $38,000 to close out the account, and, expediently, the cost of goods sold account can be credited for $38,000. Crediting cost of goods sold has the effect of reducing the charges to revenue from applied to actual cost. A probably explanation for overapplying overhead is that 10,000 more direct labor-hours were worked than planned for.

   When the overhead applied to production is less than the actual overhead costs incurred, overhead has been underapplied. The overhead T-account would appear as follows:

Manufacturing overhead

$600,000	$575,000
Actual cost	Applied

Here we have assumed values wherein overhead is underapplied by $25,000. Thus $25,000 of cost incurred was not charged to the goods produced. Again, we cannot at this time charge an additional $25,000 to production because the work in process may have been finished and sold. Because too little manufacturing overhead has been charged to production, $25,000 must now be charged (debited) to the cost of goods sold account.

   Overapplied overhead increases net income and underapplied overhead decreases net income. This underscores the need to properly plan both overhead costs and the expected volume of activity.

Fixed and Variable Overhead

The process of charging overhead to production can be made simpler and perhaps more accurate if total overhead is separated into its fixed- and variable-cost components. The methods for isolating unit variable and total fixed cost were discussed in Chapter 4—the high-low method and the least-squares regression analysis. Thus overhead could be expressed as, for example, $250,000 per year plus $5.00 per direct labor-hour. The advantage of separating overhead as indicated is that variable overhead is a function of activity and the fact that actual activity was 90,000, 100,000, or 110,000 direct labor-hours makes little difference. The amount of variable overhead applied to production should approximate the variable overhead incurred. Applying fixed overhead to production will always be a problem. A variable overhead rate remains constant per unit of activity throughout the relevant range of activity, but a fixed overhead rate is based on a specific estimated volume of activity. Overhead will be treated in greater detail in Chapter 10.

Summarizing Cost Flow

The following is a summary of activity at the Monarch Company last year. We assume that there were no inventories at the start of the period.

Raw material purchased	$280,000
Raw materials used in production	250,000
Direct labor cost incurred	320,000
Direct labor cost applied to production	320,000
Variable overhead incurred	220,000
Fixed overhead incurred	300,000
Estimated variable overhead	240,000
Estimated fixed overhead	280,000
Cost of products completed	800,000
Cost of products sold	700,000
Estimated direct labor-hours	80,000
Actual direct labor-hours worked	70,000

The flow of cost is as follows. Costs are incurred such as raw materials purchased or variable overhead incurred. (In this illustration we do not show the offsetting credit—assume it to be cash.) Then as activity takes place costs are assigned to work in process. When goods are completed they are charged to finished goods, and when sold they are charged to the cost of goods sold account.

1. Materials inventory is debited for $280,000 to record the purchase.
2. Materials inventory is credited for $250,000 and work in process is charged $250,000. The source of this data is the material requisitions.
3. Direct labor is debited for $320,000 to record the applicable direct labor cost.
4. Direct labor is charged to work in process.

Materials inventory

(1) 280,000	(2) 250,000
Bal 30,000	

Direct labor

(3) 320,000	(4) 320,000

Work in process

(2) 250,000	(9) 800,000
(4) 320,000	
(7) 210,000	
(8) 245,000	
Bal 225,000	

Finished goods

(9) 800,000	(10) 700,000
Bal 100,000	

Variable overhead

(5) 220,000	(7) 210,000
	(12) 10,000

Fixed overhead

(6) 300,000	(8) 245,000
	(11) 55,000

Cost of goods sold

(10) 700,000	
(11) 55,000	
(12) 10,000	

5. Variable overhead is charged for costs incurred.
6. Fixed overhead is charged for costs incurred.
7. Estimated variable overhead is $240,000; estimated activity is 80,000 direct labor-hours. Therefore the estimated variable overhead rate is $3.00 per hour. Because 70,000 direct labor-hours were worked, $210,000 of variable overhead is charged to work in process.

8. Estimated fixed overhead is $280,000; estimated activity is 80,000 direct labor-hours. Therefore the estimated fixed overhead rate is $3.50 per direct labor-hour. Because a total of 70,000 direct labor-hours were worked, $245,000 of fixed overhead was applied to production.

9. Charge finished goods for the work completed, $800,000, and credit work in process for the same amount.

10. The cost of products sold, $700,000, is charged to the cost of goods sold account and finished goods is credited for a like amount.

At this point several of the T-accounts have balances. Materials inventory, work in process, and finished goods normally do have balances. The balance in these accounts shows the cost of inventory at the end of the period. Each of these accounts identifies an asset that can be used in the following period. The two overhead accounts cannot have balances in the final analysis. Balances in these accounts represent costs incurred that were not applied to production or excess amounts that were charged to production. In this illustration, the balances in these two accounts represents costs incurred but not charged to production. Any balance in these accounts is transferred to the cost of goods sold account.

11. Debit cost of goods sold for $55,000 and credit fixed overhead for a like amount.

12. Debit cost of goods sold for $10,000 and credit variable overhead for a like amount.

Thus $65,000 of cost was incurred that did not become attached to the goods produced. One reason for this is that 10,000 fewer direct labor-hours were worked than planned. The consequence of this planning error could be a reduction of $65,000 in net income.

Accumulating Overhead Costs

At this point we will back up a bit and examine the process whereby overhead costs are accumulated. Many approaches can be used so the following is merely descriptive of what might take place. First, as costs are incurred they are assigned to the appropriate account as in the following:

Maintenance		Power and light	
$50,000	$10,000 F	$30,000	$ 5,000 F
	40,000 V		25,000 V

Indirect labor		Supervision	
$25,000	$20,000 F	$40,000	$40,000 F
	5,000 V		

The second step is to break each cost into its fixed and variable components, where appropriate, and charge these amounts to the fixed or variable overhead account. The amounts shown as fixed (F) or variable (V) are only illustrative.

Fixed overhead		Variable overhead	
$10,000		$40,000	
5,000		25,000	
20,000		5,000	
40,000			
$75,000		$70,000	
Actual	Applied	Actual	Applied

Thus the two overhead accounts are debited for the actual cost incurred. These accounts are credited periodically as work is performed and the offsetting debit is to work in process. Overhead is applied to production based on the estimated overhead rate and the actual volume of activity as in the previous illustration.

ABSORPTION AND VARIABLE COSTING

It is common practice to charge costs to production in the manner described earlier. It is a reasonably logical process, but as we have seen this process does not provide management with all the information it needs about cost.

Absorption Costing

Absorption costing is generally accepted by the accounting community as *the* way in which to handle manufacturing costs. The previous discussions of cost flow applied the absorption costing concept. This method, also called full costing, attempts to charge all manufacturing overhead costs to work in process regardless of whether they are variable or fixed.

This method of costing permits the inventorying of both variable costs and fixed costs. We are not concerned with the inventorying of variable costs because they are directly attributable to the units of production in inventory. Regardless of when units of production are made and sold, variable costs must be incurred. However, fixed costs are to a great extent time or period costs, and this method of costing allows a portion of one year's costs—rent, interest, depreciation, taxes, and the like, to be expensed—charged against revenue—in a future period. That is, a portion of last year's depreciation becomes an expense in a following period when the goods are sold. This raises the question of whether or not it is sound management policy to expense fixed costs in any period other than that in which they were incurred.

It is interesting to note that these same types of cost—rent, taxes, depreciation, and the like—are not treated the same way in other situations. Fixed costs that are of a nonproduction nature are treated differently. More specifically, generally accepted accounting principles allow fixed costs to be inventoried in the production division but not in the administrative division. Note in Table 9-2 that the entire amount of depreciation on office equipment of $50,000 is charged against the current year's revenue. The same practice is followed in retail and service businesses.

This inventorying of fixed costs has an interesting impact on profit. If the values of inventories (in process and finished goods) at the end of an accounting period is greater than it was at the start of the period, the effect is to increase profit or decrease the loss regardless of sales volume. The reason for this is that with a larger inventory value at the end of the period, more of the current period's fixed cost is carried over to the next accounting period as inventory.

The reverse is also true. If an ending inventory is less than a beginning inventory, the previous period's fixed costs are expensed along with the current period's fixed cost. The result is a depressing of profit for the current period. Under absorption costing, profit is a function of production rather than of sales. Tables 9-4 and 9-5 show why this is true.

Last year a firm produced 10,000 units of X but sold only 8,000 units. Variable costs were $50 per unit and fixed costs totaled $200,000. There was no inventory at the beginning of the year. The income statement follows in Table 9-4.

During the current year 6,000 units of X were produced and 8,000 units were sold at the same price. Unit variable and total fixed costs remained the same. The income statement follows in Table 9-5.

TABLE 9-4

Income Statement, 19X1

Sales (8,000 x $100)		$800,000
Less: Cost of Goods Sold:		
Inventory, beginning	0	
Production Costs:		
Variable cost		
(10,000 x $50)	$500,000	
Fixed cost	200,000	
Total	$700,000	
Inventory, ending	140,000	560,000
Gross margin and net income		$240,000
Variable cost (2,000 x $50)	$100,000	
20 percent of fixed cost	40,000	
Total	$140,000	

TABLE 9-5
Income Statement, 19X2

Sales (8,000 x $100)		$800,000
Less: Cost of Goods Sold:		
Inventory, beginning	$140,000	
Production Costs:		
Variable cost		
(6,000 x $50)	300,000	
Fixed cost	200,000	
Total costs	$640,000	
Inventory, ending	0	$640,000
Gross Margin and Net Income		$160,000

Even though sales were the same for each year and the cost structure remained the same, net income for the current year decreased by $80,000. The reason for this is that $40,000 of the previous year's fixed costs plus all of the current year's fixed costs was charged to revenue during the current year.

Variable Costing

Variable costing, also called direct costing, is of relatively recent origin. The term "variable" better describes this approach to costing albeit "direct" is the term more widely used. This approach to costing only inventories variable manufacturing cost.

Absorption costing treats all manufacturing costs as product costs. We observed earlier that all costs required to complete a unit of production are charged to work in process under absorption costing. Under variable costing, only direct material, direct labor, and variable manufacturing overhead are charged to work in process. Fixed overhead is treated as a period cost (expense) and is charged in total against current revenue as shown in Figure 9-5.

Under variable costing, no fixed overhead is charged to production, and consequently inventory cost does not include any fixed overhead. Thus a given inventory of goods would have a lower cost under variable costing than under absorption costing. In certain situations this could have a major impact on the net income for a period.

ABSORPTION AND VARIABLE-COST FLOW

Figure 9-5 compares the flow of cost under these two costing techniques. The cost flow under absorption costing is the same as in previous illustrations. Note that, to the extent there is an inventory of work in process or finished goods at the end of any accounting period, the costs associated with these inventories stay behind and are not expensed until sold in a future period. Thus the period's revenue may not bear all of the period's cost.

Under variable costing, only variable product costs get into inventory and fixed costs are charged to the cost of goods sold and consequently to revenue for the period. Cost flow in retailing follows the variable costing concept.

Profit Shown versus Profit Earned

We learned earlier that profit can be a function of the units produced—units sold relationship. Producing more units than are sold during a period has the effect of stimulating profit. Look at

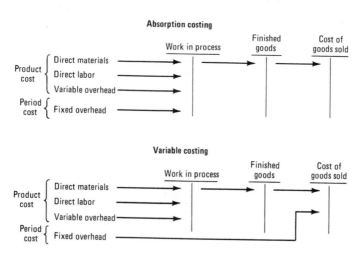

FIGURE   9-5.   Absorption and Variable Costing Compared

Table 9-6 where the firm (an actual case) showed a profit of $163,000 after five years of losses. Does the firm have reason to celebrate? Not at all, because profit resulted from producing $279,000 more goods than were sold. If the inventory is sold at favorable prices, profit may result. Profit is earned only after goods are sold. Under variable

TABLE   9-6

Comparative Balance Sheets

Assets	Latest	Year Ago
Cash	$ 62,000	$ 51,000
Receivables	400,000	152,000
Inventory	623,000	344,000
Prepaid expenses	14,000	18,000
Property, plant & equipment	119,000	132,000
	$1,218,000	$697,000
Liabilities and Owner Equity		
Current liabilities	852,000	494,000
Long-term liabilities	0	0
Common stock	411,000	411,000
Retained earnings	(45,000)	(208,000)
	$1,218,000	$697,000

costing, any profit shown is earned; not so with absorption costing. In this case the inventory did not move, and the owner was forced to liquidate the business at a substantial loss.

Variable Costing—an Assessment

Variable costing exponents cite a number of advantages to management through the variable costing process. Arguments in favor of using variable costing include the following:

1. It forces management to express costs in both fixed and variable components. Because most costs are neither completely fixed nor variable, this breakdown provides a better basis for understanding cost behavior and for making cost projections.

2. It provides the means for continuously measuring break-even. Table 9-7 is an income statement reflecting the variable-cost approach. After five months the firm shows a loss of $100,000. Management needs to know how much additional sales revenue is needed to break even. Sales minus variable cost equals contribution margin. The contribution is 35 percent of each sales dollar ($350,000 ÷ $1,000,000); therefore a total of $1,285,714 in sales is necessary to break even ($450,000 ÷ .35).

3. We have been trained to expect that income is a function of sales, not production. In Table 9-7, the key intermediate value is

TABLE   9-7

Income Statement,
First five months of 19XX

Sales revenue		$1,000,000
Less: Variable Costs:		
Variable manufacturing costs	$400,000	
Other variable costs	250,000	650,000
Contribution margin		$ 350,000
Less: Fixed Expenses:		
Fixed manufacturing costs	$300,000	
Other fixed costs	150,000	450,000
Net Income (loss)		$ (100,000)

contribution margin. By definition, total variable costs are a function of activity (sales). Therefore the amount of contribution margin shown is a function of sales. In Table 9-2, the key intermediate value is gross margin. There is no such relationship between sales and gross margin because absorption costing allows fixed costs to be inventoried.

4. It eliminates the need for fixed overhead rates. Under variable costing, actual fixed overhead costs are charged as a period cost, not to work in process. Obviously there can be no over- or under-applied fixed manufacturing overhead.

Variable costing can be a useful management tool, but its use is restricted to internal reporting only. The accounting profession has not put its stamp of approval on variable costing. If a firm wishes to apply variable costing, it must keep two sets of costing records. Reporting to Internal Revenue and other outside groups must be based on absorption costing. The additional work involved in keeping two sets of records may be well worth the effort because of the additional information available to management.

SUMMARY

The price at which a firm sells its goods and services must cover cost before a profit can be earned. Frequently prices are based on cost, and it follows that costs must be known before selling prices that will yield the desired target profit can be established. Ascertaining the direct costs associated with a job or batch of production is not difficult provided the firm has an adequate system of records. The reason for this is that direct costs—material and labor—can be precisely measured. Overhead, or indirect costs, present a problem because the actual total of overhead costs is not known until after the accounting period has ended. The amount of overhead charged to a job or batch of production is only an estimate.

The problem of assigning overhead to production can be simplified if overhead can be categorized as variable and fixed. Because variable overhead is fixed per unit of activity, the appropriate amount should be charged to each unit produced even though the actual volume of activity is more or less than planned. Fixed overhead is fixed in total amount but variable per unit as activity levels change. Thus, if there is a difference between the actual and planned volume of activity, too much or too little cost is charged to production.

Some firms avoid the problems of assigning fixed overhead to production by applying the variable costing technique. Here only variable manufacturing costs are applied to work in process, and all fixed costs are charged directly as expense. This approach to costing assures that all current costs will be charged against current revenue, and it also allows management to determine at any point in time how close activity is to the break-even point.

KEY TERMS ──

absorption costing	period cost
bill of materials	product cost
cost flow	production order
finished goods	profit earned
fixed overhead	profit shown
material requisition	underapplied overhead
overapplied overhead	variable costing
overhead	variable overhead
overhead rate	

QUESTIONS ──

1. Why is charging direct costs to goods produced a relatively easy process, whereas the allocation of overhead costs presents several problems?

2. How does the cost of goods sold section of an income statement differ among retail and manufacturing firms?

3. Materials should not be allowed to move from inventory unless there is formal authorization. For what reasons is this so?

4. How can a firm ascertain that only the "right" materials leave inventory?

5. At 8:00 A.M. a material was charged to production at $2.00 per unit. Later in the same day the same type of material was charged to production at $2.20 per unit. Does this make sense? Explain.

6. When materials are charged to production, will they be charged at the cost actually paid for them? Explain.

7. There may be a difference between the amount of money earned by direct laborers and the amount of direct labor cost charged to production. Explain why this is true.

8. Why is it questionable policy to charge overtime pay to work in process?

9. Describe two situations where charging overtime as a direct labor cost can be justified.

10. Why are fringe-benefit costs excluded from the direct labor cost charged to work in process?

11. Define overhead.

12. Why is it difficult to charge the "right" amount of overhead to a particular lot of production?

13. Define estimated overhead rate.

14. Describe the process whereby overhead costs are charged to work in process.

15. Why might overhead rates differ from department to department?

16. a. Define overapplied overhead.
    b. Define underapplied overhead.

17.

| Estimated overhead | $600,000 | Estimated activity (units) | 120,000 |
| Actual overhead | $700,000 | Actual activity (units) | 140,000 |

Was overhead overapplied or underapplied? Explain.

18. The variable overhead account has a debit balance of $42,000. What does this mean?

19. What is the principal difference between absorption costing and variable costing?

20. Under what circumstances can profit shown exceed profit earned?

21. Whether one uses absorption or direct costing has no impact on profit when there is no change in inventory levels. Do you agree? Explain.

22. Why might a firm want to keep two sets of books—one for absorption costing and one for direct costing? Why not report net income based on direct costing?

PROBLEMS

1. Overapplied and underapplied overhead

Planned fixed overhead for the year at the Jason Company was $400,000; planned variable overhead was $1.40 per unit of production. Planned production was 100,000 units; actual production was 110,000 units. Actual fixed overhead was $430,000; actual variable overhead was $149,000.

Required:

a. Compute the over- or underapplied fixed and variable overhead for the year.

b. What impact does this have on the cost of goods sold account?

2. Overapplied and underapplied overhead

The following was taken from the records of the Malden Company:

Planned fixed overhead	$250,000
Planned variable overhead	$100,000
Planned production (units)	50,000
Actual fixed overhead	$265,000
Actual variable overhead	$110,000
Actual production (units)	52,000

Required:

a. Was fixed and variable overhead overapplied or underapplied during this period?

b. What impact, if any, will the results of requirement **(a)** have on the cost of goods sold account?

3. Cost flow—absorption costing

The following data was taken from the records of the Raymon Corporation for last year. There were no inventories at the beginning of that year.

Estimated fixed overhead	$ 50,000
Estimated variable overhead	42,000
Materials purchased	82,000
Direct materials used	60,000
Direct labor used	40,000
Actual fixed overhead	50,000
Actual variable overhead	45,000
Cost of goods completed	180,000
Sales revenue	320,000
Ending inventory of finished goods	10,000
Variable selling expenses	85,000
Fixed administrative expenses	60,000

Estimated production for the year was 10,000 units, but actual production was 11,000 units.

Required:

a. Set up the appropriate T-accounts and make all relevant entries.

b. Comment on the accuracy of the work-in-process inventory balance.

c. What was the net income for the period before taxes?

4. Cost flow—variable costing

Complete requirements (a) and (b) in Problem 3 applying variable costing. Assume the cost of goods completed to be $125,000.

5. Cost flow—absorption costing

The following data was taken from the records of the Blackwell Corporation for the year ended December 31, 19X5:

Inventories, January 1, 19X5:	
Raw materials	$ 16,000
Work in process	20,000
Finished goods	36,000
Raw material purchases	192,000
Direct materials used	160,000
Direct labor used	120,000
Variable overhead incurred	44,000
Fixed overhead incurred	96,000
Cost of goods finished	384,000
Cost of products sold	400,000

The normal fixed overhead rate is $3.60 per unit of production, and the normal variable overhead rate is $1.60 per unit of production. The normal level of production is 27,500 units; actual production was 26,000 units.

Required:

a. Determine the balances of the three inventory accounts at the end of the year.

b. What was the amount of over- or underapplied overhead for the year?

6. Costing inventory

The inventory card for material X is as follows:

Date	Description	Units	Unit price	Extension	Total
1-01	Balance	5,000	$2.00	$10,000	$10,000
1-12	Purchase	6,000	2.10	12,600	22,600
1-28	Purchase	4,000	2.20	8,800	31,400

On January 29, 8,000 units of material X were issued for Job 1234.

Required:

a. At what cost should materials be charged to production if inventories are valued on (1) a first-in, first-out basis, (2) a last-in, first-out basis, or (3) an average-cost basis.

b. What value would this inventory item have on January 31 if inventories are valued on each of the above bases?

7. Cost flow—absorption costing

The following data relates to manufacturing operations at Murphy Mills for the year 19X4:

Raw materials purchased	$200,000
Raw materials used in production	150,000
Direct labor cost incurred	300,000
Fixed overhead incurred	120,000
Estimated fixed overhead	100,000
Variable overhead incurred	180,000
Estimated variable overhead	160,000
Estimated production (units)	40,000
Actual production (units)	45,000

Required:

a. Set up the appropriate T-accounts and make all relevant entries.

b. Determine whether overhead was over- or underapplied.

8. Cost flow and inventory valuation

Two firms have identical cost structures; that is, each has the same unit variable cost and total fixed cost. One is a retailer whose variable cost is for merchandise purchased, and the other is a manufacturer whose variable cost is a production cost. The retailer charges fixed cost to current revenue, the manufacturer considers fixed cost as another cost of production. Activity figures for the past three years for each firm are

	19X1	19X2	19X3
Units sold (at $40)	4,000	5,000	6,000
Units purchased (retailer)	5,000	5,000	5,000
Units produced (manufacturer)	5,000	5,000	5,000

Neither firm had an inventory at the beginning of 19X1. Variable costs are $25 per unit, and fixed cost totals $45,000 for each firm.

Required:

a. Prepare income statements for each firm for each of the three years.

b. Explain with calculations why the net income is not the same for each firm for every year.

c. Comment on the net income shown for each firm in 19X2.

d. Comment on the net income shown for each firm for the three-year period.

9. Cost flow—absorption and variable costing

The following data comes from the records of the Rickie Company for last year:

Raw material purchases	$240,000
Direct material used	200,000
Direct labor used	180,000
Variable overhead cost incurred	70,000
Fixed overhead cost incurred	120,000
Estimated variable overhead	80,000
Estimated fixed overhead	130,000
Cost of products completed	520,000
Cost of products sold	480,000
Estimated production (units)	40,000
Actual production (units)	37,000

Required:

a. Use T-accounts to show the flow of cost into work in process, finished goods, and the cost of goods sold accounts using absorption costing. There was no inventory at the start of the period.

b. Show the flow of cost using variable costing. Note that certain of the values given above are not appropriate for variable costing. Both the cost of products completed and the cost of products sold will be less. Why? Assume them to be $420,000 and $390,000, respectively.

10. Valuation of work in process

The Agar Machine Shop is a job-order operation. It has a policy of buying materials after each production order is received and consequently has no raw material inventory. Jobs are delivered and billed immediately after completion and the firm therefore has no inventory of finished goods. Their only inventory is work in process. The following is Agar's income statement for last year:

Sales		$250,000
Less: Cost of Goods Sold:		
Materials	$ 10,000	
Direct labor	160,000	
Overhead	40,000	
Total	$210,000	
Less: Work in process, December 31	30,000	$180,000
Gross margin		$ 70,000
Administrative expenses		50,000
Net Income		$ 20,000

On December 31, Agar had one job in process. It was an electronic echo chamber which would sell for $40,000 when completed. The chamber was 99 percent completed—one simple operation remained. This one job had utilized all shop facilities for the month of December.

Required:

a. Comment on the net income of $20,000. Has it been earned?
   On January 2 of the next year Ed Allthumbs was assigned the final operation of drilling and threading a mounting hole on one end of the chamber. Ed put the hole in the wrong end of the chamber rendering it worthless.
b. Comment again. (*Note:* This is a true-life venture.)

11. Cost flow and inventory valuation—absorption costing

The following are the inventory account balances as of December 31, 19X5 and December 31, 19X6:

	19X5	*19X6*
Raw materials	$58,000	$65,000
Work in process	85,000	97,000
Finished goods	71,000	86,000

The following was taken from the income statement at the end of 19X6:

Raw material purchases	$131,000
Direct labor	247,000
Variable overhead	38,000
Fixed overhead	92,000

Required:

a. How much raw material was used in 19X6?

b. What was the cost of goods manufactured in 19X6?

c. What was the cost of goods sold in 19X6?

12. Cost flow and cost of goods sold—absorption costing

The following data relates to the Pritt Corporation for the year just ended:

Work in process, January 1	40,000
Finished goods inventory, January 1	60,000
Raw materials inventory, January 1	70,000
Direct labor	510,000
Material purchases	200,000
Factory overhead	180,000
Work in process inventory, December 31	80,000
Finished goods inventory, December 31	80,000
Raw materials inventory, December 31	50,000

Required:

a. Prepare T-accounts and record the data given.

b. What was the cost of goods sold for the year?

13. Cost flow—absorption costing

The following data was taken from the records of Carter, Inc. for last year:

Estimated variable overhead	$120,000
Estimated fixed overhead	90,000

Actual variable overhead	135,000
Actual fixed overhead	95,000
Estimated direct labor-hours	60,000
Actual direct labor-hours	65,000

Required:

a. How much variable overhead was charged to production during the year?

b. How much fixed overhead was charged to production during the year?

c. Were the overhead accounts over- or underapplied? By how much?

14. Income measurement—retailing and manufacturing

The income statement for the X Manufacturing Company, which uses absorption costing, follows:

Sales		$80,000
Less: Cost of Goods Sold:		
Beginning inventory		0
Production Costs:		
Variable costs		
(10,000 units)	$40,000	
Fixed costs	20,000	
Total production cost	60,000	
Ending inventory	12,000	$48,000
Gross Margin and Net Income		$32,000

Required:

a. Suppose that this firm is a retailer dealing in a single product. The retailer purchased 10,000 units for resale paying $40,000. The retailer's fixed costs are $20,000. What difference, if any, will there be in net income? Be specific.

b. Respond to the previous question assuming that the manufacturer applied variable costing.

15. Impact of inventory on net income

A firm was plagued with sagging sales and high costs of production for several years. Finally, the operating vice president resigned and a new operating vice president was brought in from a competing firm. As part of the financial package, the new operating vice president was offered 10 percent of the before-tax profit for the next five years. The directors of the firm thought that this was a good arrangement inasmuch as the firm had not shown a profit for any of the past five years.

After reviewing the firm's operating records, the new vice president concluded that the high cost of production was caused by extreme peaks and valleys in the firm's production schedule. Consequently he determined the most economic level of production for the firm and insisted that production be pegged at that level for the next fiscal year. At year's end, the firm's accountant reported a before-tax profit of $1,630,000 as follows:

Sales		$10,000,000
Less: Cost of Goods Sold:		
Inventories, January 1	$ 3,440,000	
Cost of goods manufactured	10,060,000	
Cost of goods stocked	$13,500,000	
Inventories, December 31	7,270,000	6,230,000
Gross margin		$ 3,770,000
Less: Selling expense	$ 1,110,000	
Administrative expense	1,030,000	2,140,000
Net Income Before Taxes		$ 1,630,000

Shortly after the year's profit was announced, the operating vice president picked up his $163,000 and left for parts unknown. Neither the firm's auditors nor the Internal Revenue Service could find anything wrong with the firm's records. As chairman of the board, how would you respond to this whole affair?

10 Cost Allocation

for

Product Costing

It is of paramount importance that management know what it costs to complete a job or produce a unit of product. Measuring the direct costs of production is relatively easy and certain as was explained in Chapter 9. Measuring indirect costs, we observed, is neither easy nor certain. In this chapter we will describe indirect or overhead costs in greater detail and show how these costs are allocated to units of production.

The cost-allocating process as we describe and illustrate is not difficult to follow once the basic data are established. The basic data needed are the total of a cost such as rent and the basis on which allocations are to be made. The basic problem is to find a measure that accurately reflects the benefits each segment of the firm receives from an expenditure. Often this is not possible, and the consequence is that some products may bear more or less cost than they should. The process that we describe must be tested and retested before the right combinations are found.

QUESTIONS FOR CONSIDERATION

1. Why must costs be allocated?
2. How are cost allocation bases established?
3. What are the different categories of overhead cost?
4. What are normalized overhead rates and how are they established?
5. How are transfer prices determined?

The costs of operating a segment of a firm generally are of two types. There are costs that are incurred by and for a single department such as the salary of a departmental foreman, and there are costs incurred for the benefit of more than one segment of the firm such as the cost of operating a building. Costs such as this must be allocated.

Cost allocation involves the spreading of a cost over the segments of a firm that benefit from it. The portion of a cost that a segment bears should reflect the benefit received from the cost. The cost of operating a building, for example, may be allocated to the several departments that occupy the building based on the square feet of floor space assigned to each department.

Cost allocations are made for two purposes. They must be made to ascertain the cost of goods and services produced. This aspect of cost allocation is the theme of this chapter. In addition, cost allocations should be made as a part of an overall management evaluation program. Allocations are necessary to determine the cost that each segment should bear. This aspect of cost allocation is discussed in Chapter 16.

In manufacturing, cost allocation applies to certain indirect costs that are incurred to serve more than one segment of the firm or more than one product. Cost allocations may be made at several levels of organization. The vice president (see Figure 1-1) may allocate costs to the plant manager who in turn may allocate costs to each department in the production area. Department managers may then allocate costs to each section of their department. The objective of the cost allocation process is not simply to divide and subdivide but to obtain optimal control over costs. The manner in which costs are allocated impacts on several areas of activity that we have discussed such as cost flow and overhead rates.

COST ALLOCATION AND ORGANIZATION

In organizations there are two distinct types of functions. Line functions, concerned with production and distribution, are revenue producing functions and therefore can bear cost. Service functions, concerned with providing specialized services for other segments of the organization are non-revenue producing activities and cannot bear cost. Nor should they bear cost because the only logical reason for their existence is that they make the work of the line functions more productive.

The purchasing department, for example, exists only because it can perform services for other segments of the firm better than the segments can perform them individually. Thus the only reason there is a purchasing department cost is that other segments of the firm have no purchasing cost. Through cost allocation, each segment of the firm that benefits from the purchasing function is required to bear a portion of the cost of this department.

Since the only segments of an organization that can bear cost are those that come in contact with the goods and services produced, all costs in the factory must come to rest in the production departments. If you will, every production department is charged a "fee" for such things as personnel, purchasing, methods engineering, internal auditing, inventory management, and the like. Whether the managers of production departments have any control over the amount they are charged is explored later in this chapter.

BASES FOR COST ALLOCATION

Sound cost allocation requires an allocation base which reflects, as accurately as possible, the benefits that the several segments of the firm will receive because the cost was incurred. If the service segments are set up as profit centers and the profit center bills its "customers" for services rendered, cost allocation may take care of itself. The computer division of a large insurance company bills its "customers" monthly. This is a sure way to allocate costs, but it may not be a sure way to please "customers."

More likely, central administration will establish the bases for allocating costs. The following illustrates bases that may be used to allocate certain costs:

Cost	*Basis for allocation*
University library operation	Number of students
Personnel department	Number of hires
Purchasing department	Number of purchase orders
Tool room	Number of requisitions
Maintenance	Number of labor hours
Building maintenance	Square feet of floor space
Maintenance of grounds	Square feet of floor space

Cost	Basis for allocation
Receiving	Number of deliveries
Cost accounting	Number of transactions
Dispensary	Number of employees

This list was prepared with a number of objectives in mind. First, take a critical look at each basis and see if you can challenge it. Should the cost of the library be allocated to each college based on the number of students in each college? "Our students seldom use the library." "Liberal Arts students have to use the library twice as much as our students." Each of these bases can be challenged because there is no direct relation between cost and activity. If any of these costs could be traced logically and practically to a cost center, they would be direct costs and we would not be concerned for allocation.

Second, a particular basis for allocation may be used because the data needed for a better one simply is not available. The cost of operating the receiving department is allocated based on the number of deliveries. Weight, volume, special handling, and the number of items received perhaps should also be considered in establishing a basis for allocation, but, if this data is not available, it obviously cannot be used—perhaps it would cost more to obtain this data than it is worth. Also, businessmen generally prefer simple rather than complicated allocation bases.

However, simplicity should not be the objective in selecting a basis for allocation because a simple base could work against effective management. In retailing, the simplest basis for allocating costs is sales dollars because both planned and actual sales figures are readily available. If this basis is used, the department manager who really hustles and significantly increases sales volume would be required to absorb more cost while the less productive manager would absorb less.

It is quite probable that, regardless of the allocation basis used, certain managers will be unhappy because it forces them to absorb more cost than they think is justified. Allocated costs are imposed costs, and frequently department managers argue that they do not need many of the services that they are required to support. In this regard they act as you and I do, the payers of property taxes; they do not like the assessment and therefore negotiate for an abatement.

The end result.   The end result of the cost allocation process is assigning the appropriate amount of indirect cost to every job or unit of production. The process involves several steps. First, costs must be allocated to all departments that use the services provided by the expenditure. Second, the costs of service departments must be allocated to the production departments. And, finally, costs are charged to products as they move through the production area.

Categorizing Overhead Costs

Before describing the process for determining overhead rates we will examine the three categories of overhead cost. One purpose of this discussion is to show the extent to which a production department manager can control the costs for which he is responsible.

1. Costs incurred by a department because of actions taken in the department. A maintenance department, for example, employs labor, purchases supplies, or rents equipment. As a rule, department managers are expected to estimate—budget—these costs in advance of the accounting period. A department manager may have some control over the type and amount of cost that he budgets. Costs on line 1 of Table 10-2 fall in this category.

2. Costs that are factory-wide but must be allocated to the several departments in the factory. The factory may have a single bill for power and light, heat, or real estate taxes that must be absorbed by the departments. It is up to management to decide the "best basis" for dividing the total bill among the several departments. A department manager probably will have little voice in deciding the portion of the bill that must be absorbed. Costs on line 2 of Table 10-2 fall in this category.

3. Costs of service departments that must be borne, in the final analysis, by production departments. The toolroom (see Table 10-2) exists to serve the production departments. Therefore the cost of this function should be distributed over the departments it serves. The basis for allocation is bound to be somewhat arbitrary because there is no production department activity that bears a direct relationship to the cost of running a toolroom. Costs on lines 3, 4 and 5 of Table 10-2 illustrate this category of cost.

TABLE 10-1

An Allocation Plan

Item	Prod A	Prod B	Prod C	Toolroom	Maintenance	Gen'l factory
Costs budgeted by departments	$42,000	$58,000	$64,000	$20,000	$24,000	$40,000
Light/power allocation*	22%	20%	18%	15%	10%	15%
Square feet occupied	20,000	25,000	35,000	15,000	5,000	
Labor-hours of maintenance	3,300	3,000	3,600	100		
Toolroom requisitions	1,300	1,200	1,500			
Direct labor-hours	25,000	26,000	27,000			

*Estimated light and power cost is $32,000.

The Byron Machine Works has six departments in its shop. They are designated as production A, production B, production C, toolroom, maintenance, and general factory. The data needed to establish overhead rates follows in Table 10-1.

We are concerned here with the process through which these estimated costs can be "properly" allocated to the three production departments. Our goal is to establish hourly overhead rates for each of these departments as shown in the bottom line of Table 10-2. The first step is to record the costs budgeted by each department. These are shown on line 1 of this figure. The next step is to allocate the cost of light and power. The plant manager has decided that the allocation should be based on the percentages shown in Table 10-1.

These percentages point out a basic problem in dealing with indirect costs. There is probably no way that the plant manager can prove that light and power will be consumed on this basis. This can create a problem because the head of the maintenance department, knowing that he has to absorb only 10 percent of the cost may be less frugal in his use of light and power than the manager who must absorb a much higher percentage. One way to get around this problem might be to install "meters" in each department and make this cost a direct cost to the department—a line 1 cost. Line 2 of Table 10-2 shows the distribution of light and power cost. In practice there may be several costs which, like light and power, must be distributed over the departments concerned on some predetermined basis.

Thus the total estimated overhead cost for the shop is $280,000. This is the total of the costs that the departments have budgeted plus the cost of light and power. The next step in the process is to allocate all the service department costs in a logical manner so that they come to rest in the three production departments.

One by one the service departments are "closed out" to the departments that use the service. In some instances the sequence in which service departments are closed out is based on solid evidence, in others it is not. For example, in our illustration let us assume that it is a known fact that general factory serves all other departments but, in turn, is serviced by no other department. This, then, would be the logical department to close out first. The next step is to determine the "logical" basis for allocating the $44,800. We cannot tell

TABLE 10-2

Determination of Overhead Rates

Cost allocation basis	Production departments			Service departments			Total
	A	B	C	Toolrm	Gen'l. Fac.	Maint.	
1. Budgeted by dept.	$42,000	$58,000	$ 64,000	$20,000	$40,000	$24,000	$248,000
2. Distribution of power/light	7,040	6,400	5,760	4,800	4,800	3,200	32,000
3. Distribution of gen'l factory	8,960	11,200	15,680	6,720	$44,800	2,240	$280,000
4. Distribution of maintenance	9,715	8,832	10,599	294		$29,440	
5. Distribution of toolroom	10,340	9,544	11,930	$31,814			
6. Total department cost	$78,056	$93,976	$107,969				$280,000
7. Overhead rate/hr	$3.122	$3.614	$4.00				

from the information given. Again, let us assume that most of the costs accumulated in this department relate to the building and other occupancy costs. Because we are dealing with area costs, the square footage assigned to each department might be the most logical basis for allocating the general factory cost. The total square footage occupied by the departments is 100,000. Therefore the general factory cost is distributed to the five departments at the rate of $.448 ($44,800 ÷ 100,000) per square foot. The distribution is shown on line 3 of Table 10-2.

Applying the same logic, we next close out the cost of the maintenance department. This department serves all remaining departments, and we will assume that it is not served by any other departments. Whether or not a sound basis exists for distributing maintenance cost depends on the records that are available. If the only records of maintenance department activity are the number of work orders completed or the labor-hours worked in each department, one or the other must be used as a measure of activity even though it may not be a precise measure. Let us assume that labor-hours worked is the better basis for allocating this cost.

Because maintenance expects to work 10,000 hours, the cost of maintenance is allocated to each department concerned at the rate of $2.944 per labor-hour ($29,440 ÷ 10,000). Thus production C must absorb $10,599 ($2.944 x 3,600) of maintenance cost. At this point we do not know that the cost of operating maintenance will be $29,440, nor do we know that production C will require 3,600 labor-hours of maintenance. In this process we make use of the best estimates we can find.

We are now down to our last service department. Let us assume that the best basis available for allocating toolroom cost is the number of tool requisitions. Because the estimated number of tool requisitions is 4,000, the estimated cost is allocated at the rate of $7.9535 per tool requisition ($31,814 ÷ 4,000). This allocation is shown on line 5 of Table 10-2.

At this point the entire $280,000 of estimated factory overhead has come to rest in the three production departments. The final step in this process is to determine the appropriate measure(s) of activity that will be used to allocate overhead to production. The measure of activity could be machine hours, direct labor-hours, direct labor cost, or prime cost, for example. We will use direct labor-hours because there does not appear to be a better basis given. By dividing the total department overhead cost by the estimated direct labor-hours, we arrive at the hourly overhead rate for each department (line 7 of Table 10-2).

Thus we have accomplished our objective of developing a process that will allocate or charge indirect costs to production. If a job or batch of production requires 80 hours of direct labor in department A, 110 hours in department B, and 130 hours in department C, overhead would be charged to production as follows:

Department	Direct labor-hours	Overhead rate	Total overhead
A	80	$3.122	$250
B	110	3.614	398
C	130	4.00	520

If the total direct labor-hours actually worked equals the estimate, a total of $280,000 in overhead will be charged to production.

The process described here is carried out prior to the start of the accounting period, and the rates used to charge indirect costs to production are based on estimates. We should expect some difference between costs incurred and the costs applied to production. At the end of the accounting period, the allocation process is repeated using actual data. Estimated overhead rates can be compared to what rates should have been and this should provide a basis for refining the cost allocation process.

NORMALIZED OVERHEAD RATES

Normalizing overhead rates involves the establishment of the appropriate time span of activity to serve as the basis in determining the estimated overhead rate for fixed manufacturing expenses. The objective of normalized overhead rates is to stabilize, within reason, the unit fixed overhead cost. There are two reasons as to why normalizing is needed to provide a meaningful indication of cost flow.

The rate at which fixed costs are incurred can vary significantly from period to period. The shorter the time frame, the greater is the possibility for major variations in expense. For example,

	Jan.	Feb.	Mar.	Total
Fixed overhead	$10,000	$40,000	$55,000	$105,000
Direct labor hours	10,000	10,000	10,000	30,000
Overhead per direct labor-hour	$1.00	$4.00	$5.50	$3.50

Thus with no change in the level of activity, the overhead rate varies significantly as does the cost of a unit of production. Suggesting monthly overhead rates borders on the absurd; this illustration is aimed at the concept involved.

Overhead rates vary with the volume of activity. This is because fixed costs are variable per unit of activity. For example,

	Year 1	Year 2	Year 3	Total
Fixed overhead	$50,000	$50,000	$50,000	$150,000
Direct labor hours	10,000	20,000	30,000	60,000
Overhead per direct labor-hour	$5.00	$2.50	$1.67	$2.50

Normalizing overhead rates requires that management estimate the level of expense and the level of activity that can be expected over some time frame. If $150,000 in expense and 60,000 direct labor-hours could normally be expected during the coming three-year time frame, then $2.50 per direct labor-hour is the normalized rate. With normalized overhead rates, the difference between costs incurred and costs applied to production can vary significantly in the short run, giving rise to large amounts of overapplied or underapplied overhead. This in turn impacts on net income.

Refer to the first illustration in this section where January fixed cost is $10,000. If the normalized overhead rate of $3.50 per direct labor-hour is used, $35,000 in overhead will be applied to production, and $25,000 in overapplied overhead will be shown. Conversely, in March when fixed costs are $55,000, only $35,000 in overhead will be applied and overhead will be underapplied by $20,000. These situations defeat the purpose of normalized rates. Consequently, management frequently will "set aside" short-term variances and compare actual and applied costs at the end of the time period used to develop the normalized rates.

We cannot expect that the exact number of dollars spent for overhead will be charged to products as they are produced. It is imperative that management refine the estimating process so that it will approximate the actual experience. There are two reasons as to why this is important—one obvious and one less obvious.

Return to the T-accounts on page 233. Because of an estimating error, $10,000 of variable overhead was not charged to production; therefore it could not be charged to finished goods. It is quite possible that this $10,000 of cost was not recaptured in the selling price of goods sold. Yet this cost had to be absorbed during the current accounting period, and profit is consequently reduced by $10,000. The same is true in this illustration of fixed overhead, making the total impact on profit $65,000.

Now, let us look at the work-in-process account. It shows a balance of $225,000 at year's end, but is this an accurate picture of what the difference between the debits and credits should be? The total of the charges to work in process is $1,025,000, but the total of manufacturing costs consumed during the period is $1,090,000. Thus the balance shown does not reflect what should have taken place. Similarly, the $800,000 credit to work in process is less than it would have been if all costs had been absorbed in production.

TRANSFER PRICING

In any business in which a number of divisions or departments serve as sources of supply for other divisions, a question arises regarding the price, if any, that one division should charge another for goods provided or services rendered, or what portion of the supplying department's cost should be allocated to the receiving department. It is generally agreed that some form of transfer pricing is better than none. If divisions of General Motors were to give component parts to Chevrolet at no cost, it would be difficult, if not impossible, to determine what it costs to produce a car. If Chevrolet must buy component parts from supplying divisions, a better picture of cost can be obtained. The problem that we face is, simply stated, determining the cost that one division should be allowed, or required, to charge another for work done.

This problem varies from firm to firm, but in many businesses a basic source of raw materials and component parts for one division of a firm is another division of the same firm. A basic source of component parts for General Motor's car-producing divisions are such semiautonomous divisions as AC Spark Plug, Delco, Harrison Radiator, and Rochester Carburetor. In many instances the only source of supply for one division is another division of the parent corporation. It is doubtful that General Motors' management would permit Ford-made spark plugs to be used in their cars even though they may be lower in cost and higher in quality.

Transfer Pricing and Organization

The approach that a firm uses to organize its resources can have a bearing on transfer pricing. If the component parts division of a firm are set up as profit centers and the managers of these divisions are charged with a specific target profit, this can impact on the prices that one division would like to charge another. A basic question that we cannot answer here is whether one division of a firm should be allowed to earn a profit from another division. If division X earns a profit of $10 in one transaction with division Y, and later division Y earns a profit of $10 in a transaction with division X, how much profit was earned? Profit must come from external, not internal, sources. However, including something called profit in transfer prices may have certain advantages. We will explore these later. If we agree that a division should earn a profit on all sales transactions, there still remain two questions. Should the same pricing policy be applied to both internal and external customers? If not, one group of customers might be preferred over the other by the supplying division. This could create supply problems for the buying division. Also, if we agree that AC Spark Plug should make a profit on every fuel pump, oil filter, and spark plug that it sells to Buick, there still remains the question of an appropriate level of profit. This is especially important where supplying divisions have a captive market.

In an attempt to mitigate the transfer pricing problem, some firms give divisional managers the freedom to utilize external sources of supply if internal sources are noncompetitive. A large electronics firm established a machine shop to serve a number of its research and development divisions. Because of a number of dissatisfactions with the machine shop operation, a policy was initiated that required all jobs estimated to cost more than $500 to go out for competitive bids. If the firm's machine shop could underbid competition, it got the job; otherwise it did not. The consequence of this policy was a reduction in the cost of machine shop work and an improvement in service. Such a policy tends to legitimatize the transfer price.

Approaches to Transfer Pricing

A variety of approaches to transfer pricing are in use today and each has certain advantages. Often a firm may be forced to use an approach that is less than desirable simply because management lacks the information necessary to utilize a more desirable approach.

Cost

This is a relatively simple way to establish a transfer price because the basic information needed to establish a price is already in existence. The job-order cost sheet in the next chapter (Figure 11-2) shows that *the* cost of the job was $209. The cost of production report in the next chapter (Figure 11-4) shows that *the* unit cost was $1.

Several observations will help to evaluate this approach to transfer pricing. This approach suggests that the firm may be using cost centers, not profit centers; that is, it is concerned with recovering all costs incurred in a division. If inefficiency prevails and the cost of inefficiency can be passed on from one division to another, this approach is suspect. It could well be that the total of costs using this approach is greater than the final selling price of the product being made. If the firm operates with a standard cost system and if actual costs approximate standard costs, the cost approach to transfer pricing could be reasonable.

Using cost as a transfer price may prevent management from determining the contribution that each division is making to the firm's overall effort. One division might produce a component part costing $10 that adds $20 in value to the unit being produced, whereas another division might produce a component part costing $10 that adds only $12 of value.

A basic component of digital watches, hand calculators, and countless electronic devices is a silicone chip. One division in a company was producing a chip for, say, $3 which was competitive with industry pricing. Because of a technological breakthrough which drastically increased the yield from a given input, the cost of the chip in question was reduced to less than $2. The dollar value of the department's products decreased by one-third on a unit cost basis. Some unknowing person might infer that the department is now contributing less rather than more to the firm's objectives.

Cost Plus Markup

The purpose of this approach is to bring the transfer price in line with the "market" price. There may be goods transferred between divisions that are one-of-a-kind or truly unique. Thus they cannot be obtained in any market. The uniqueness could be the result of a patent or the application of a new level of technology. The purpose of adding a markup to the cost is to approximate what the market price would be if a market existed. For example, the market price for a particular class of good might generally be 25 percent above cost.

Market Price

On the surface, at least, this might appear to be the best basis for establishing a transfer price. If an item costs $50 in the open market, this is what it is worth, and this should be the transfer price. However, before this approach can be used, a market must truly exist. In the previous section we mentioned that a market may not exist for some products because of their uniqueness. Even when a market does exist for something, market price may not be a good transfer price. There are a number of reasons why the transfer price should not be $50 when the market price is $50. For example, the inside supplier

1. has no selling expense to absorb
2. has no collection expense or bad account losses
3. has full knowledge of his customer's requirements

Each of these factors has an impact on the appropriate transfer price. How much? This will have to be negotiated.

We cannot judge from these comments on approaches to transfer pricing which one is "best." In fact, a firm may utilize a variety of approaches depending on circumstances. We need to know the objectives that the firm seeks to achieve. If an objective is to provide division managers with a high degree of autonomy, there probably will be considerable negotiating between divisional managers over transfer prices. If an objective is to stimulate divisional performance, some modification of market price might be used.

SUMMARY

Management studies the flow of cost and cost allocations for at least two reasons. First, management wants a high degree of certainty that the costs incurred in business operations are assigned to the goods produced and paid for through sale. Second, management wants a system whereby the "appropriate" amount of cost is allocated to each unit of production. If actual events conform to planned events, there is a good chance that management will recapture its cost and more when goods are sold. Whether each unit of production bears the "appropriate" amount of cost depends on the cost allocation process that is applied. Because there are so many ways that costs can be allocated, the probability of poor allocations is always present.

The major problem in product costing is in the area of indirect costs. Direct costs are not a problem here because one can see the amount that is required for a unit of production. Thus, if management can increase the percentage of total costs that are direct, it can develop a clearer picture of actual product cost.

KEY TERMS

allocation bases

cost allocation

line functions

market price

overhead rate

service functions

transfer price

QUESTIONS

1. What purpose is served through cost allocation?
2. Is it true that only indirect costs must be allocated? Explain.
3. Every segment of a firm incurs cost, but only certain segments can bear cost. Do you agree? Explain.
4. Explain the role of a service function. Should a service function bear cost? Explain.
5. Is it true that there is no perfect basis for allocating any indirect cost? Explain.

6. Refer to page 254. Comment on each allocation basis listed. Can you suggest a better basis for allocating each cost shown?

7. In retailing the easiest and best basis for cost allocation is the sales volume of each segment. Do you agree? Explain.

8. What end result does management seek through cost allocation?

9. Describe the three categories of overhead cost.

10. Describe the process used to determine departmental overhead rates.

11. How does management determine the specific amount of indirect cost that a given job should bear?

12. What is a normalized overhead rate? What are the advantages of using such a rate?

13. In the short run, overhead variances are minimized when normalized overhead rates are used. Do you agree? Explain.

14. What is a transfer price and what purposes does it serve?

15. Evaluate cost as a basis for determining a transfer price.

16. Market price is clearly the best transfer price. Do you agree? Explain.

PROBLEMS

1. The need for cost allocation

The planned indirect cost of the Gilmore Foundry next year is $160,000. The foundry has five production departments and four service departments. The production departments plan to work a total of 50,000 direct labor-hours during the year. Management has decided to allocate—charge—indirect costs to production at the rate of $3.20 per direct labor-hour worked.

Required:

a. Comment on this approach to the allocation of indirect cost.

b. What suggestions do you have to improve the allocation process?

2. The need for cost allocation

Figure 10-1 presents a floor plan of Apex Discount House.

The company records sales on a departmental basis and, after deducting the variable costs of each department, arrives at a contribution margin for each department. It then subtracts the total of fixed costs from the total contribution margin to determine the net income for the store. Each department manager receives an annual bonus when actual contribution margin is greater than planned contribution margin.

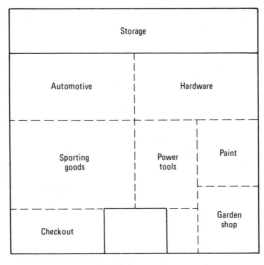

FIGURE   10-1

Required:

a. What weaknesses do you see in this operating plan?

b. Draw up a plan that will eliminate these weaknesses and provide management with greater control over operations.

3. Cost allocation—overhead rate determination

The Calloway and Sons plant is divided into four departments. Fabrication and assembly are production departments; maintenance and production administration are service departments. The following estimates for 19X2 have been made:

	Fabrication	Assembly	Production adminis- tration	Maintenance
Budgeted by department	$130,000	$118,000	$42,000	$38,000
Allocated costs	31,000	26,000	12,000	10,000
Maintenance hours	3,000	2,800	200	
Direct labor	$220,000	$180,000		
Direct labor-hours	33,850	38,000		

Required:

a. Determine the hourly overhead rates to be applied in 19X2. Explain any assumptions that you make.

The following data which was taken from the company records at the end of the year shows what actually happened.

	Fabrication	Assembly	Production adminis- tration	Maintenance
Departmental costs	$134,000	$121,000	$45,000	$40,000
Allocated costs	33,000	29,000	15,000	12,500
Maintenance hours	3,500	3,200	300	
Direct labor	$224,000	$191,000		
Direct labor-hours	34,500	31,000		

b. Using the same format as in (a), determine whether overhead in each production department was over- or underapplied and by how much.

4. Cost allocation—overhead rate determination

The manufacturing division of Key Ways, Inc. is divided into three production divisions and three service divisions. The following estimates have been made for the year ahead: (See page 271.)

Other information:

Building maintenance costs are included in building division costs.

Plantwide costs include insurance, $25,000; power and light, $60,000; and heating, $15,000.

Required:

a. Determine the hourly overhead rates for each division that should have a rate. You will have to select the "best" basis for allocating costs and explain why you selected the particular base.

b. What additional information would you like to have to meet the requirements of this problem?

5. Normalized overhead rates

The Atlas Company developed a new product that required considerable tool and die work by an outside machine shop. To make certain that new tooling would be available when needed, Atlas contracted with the machine shop in the following amounts:

19X1	$125,000	19X3	$80,000
19X2	60,000	19X4	75,000

Planned and actual production figures in units for the four years are:

	Casting	Machining	Assembly	Engineering	Maintenance	Building
Costs budgeted	$ 80,000	$150,000	$100,000	$25,000	$135,000	$100,000
Plantwide costs distribution base	20%	25%	22%	7%	7%	20%
Square feet occupied	20,000	18,000	15,000	2,000	5,000	
Maintenance work orders	350	400	600	50		
Maintenance hours	6,000	8,000	5,500	500		
Direct labor-hours	40,000	70,000	60,000			
Direct labor payroll	$200,000	$490,000	$310,000			

	19X1	19X2	19X3	19X4
Planned production	50,000	52,000	48,000	,50,000
Actual production	47,000	55,000	46,000	52,000

Required:

a. Determine the over- and underapplied overhead for tool and die work for each year and in total using a nonnormalized overhead rate. Contracted costs are also actual cost.

b. Complete (a) using a normalized overhead rate for the four years.

c. Why does each approach show a different total amount of applied overhead?

6. Transfer pricing

Maxim Electric Company has been producing a line of small-horsepower electric motors for many years and has an excellent reputation for quality at a fair price. Last year Maxim bought out a small manufacturer of washing machines. At present motors for washing machines are being purchased from the Major Electric Company, but Maxim has the capacity to produce these motors. The standard cost sheet for the motor in question shows the following unit costs:

Material	$11
Labor	8
Variable overhead	6
Fixed overhead	5
Unit Costs	$30

Management has decided that in the near future motors for washing machines will be provided by Maxim. The market price for an equivalent motor is $55.

Required:

a. Prepare a report to management wherein you evaluate the different approaches to transfer pricing. What price do you suggest Maxim charge its subsidiary?

b. Would your answer be the same if supplying these motors required the firm to work overtime?

7. Transfer pricing

The bookstore buys a typewriter ribbon for $1.20 and sells it in the store for $1.95. The management department requisitions ten ribbons from the bookstore for use in office typewriters. What price should the bookstore charge the management department for these ribbons?

8. Transfer pricing

Casco Bay Motors is a large automobile dealership that sells new and used cars. The used-car inventory consists primarily of cars traded in for new models. The company is organized as three profit centers: new cars, used cars, and parts and repairs.

Required:

a. What price should the new car division charge the used car division for transferred cars?

b. Almost all cars require some parts and repair work. What price should the used-car division pay for parts and repair work? List price? book rate? Discuss.

11 Cost Accounting
Systems

CHAPTER OVERVIEW

The purpose of this chapter is to describe the processes used to determine the cost of a product. More specifically, we are concerned with the amount of labor, material, and overhead dollars that should be charged—allocated—to a job or a unit of production. The manner in which costs are charged depends on the type of production involved.

In this chapter we will first show how costs are allocated to jobs in job-order production. Here, every job worked on can be different, and we therefore need a system that is flexible enough to handle a variety of situations ranging from simple to complex and short-term to long-term jobs. In process production where every unit in a production lot is assumed to be identical, we need another approach to costing.

Both approaches to costing have inherent weaknesses, but they do provide the means for determining, with reasonable accuracy, how much it costs to produce a given amount of work.

QUESTIONS FOR CONSIDERATION

1. What is the difference between job-order and process production?
2. What are the basic differences between job-order and process costing?
3. How is the value of work-in-process inventory determined?
4. Can a job-order producer determine the profit earned on each job completed?
5. Why are job-order and process cost systems deficient in providing cost control?

In previous chapters we have seen how costs incurred flow into work in process, finished goods, and the cost of goods sold. We have also seen how costs are allocated to different segments of the firm. In this chapter we are concerned with product costs. More specifically, we are concerned with measuring the cost of completing a job or producing a unit of product. We will examine job-order and process cost systems with a twofold purpose in mind. First, we will look at the mechanics of these systems to see what they report and how they report, and, second, we will look at these systems as they relate to the cost flow process.

Different approaches to the production of goods require different costing methods. The two most common approaches to production are job-order, or custom, production and process production. A look into the activity that takes place in these two situations will help to explain why costs are accumulated as they are.

A job shop, as a rule, does not have a line of homogeneous products. A true job shop will not engage in production until it has a specific job to do. Most job shops have the capacity to provide a wide range of related services. Figure 11-1A depicts a job-order machine shop which provides five types of services. The machinery and equipment in a job shop tends to be of a general-purpose nature; that is, it can perform a wide range of operations in a wide variety of situations. A milling machine could be used to cut a key way in a motor shaft or, with little adaptation, square the face of a casting. In a job shop there is little certainty as to the specific work that will be done; this depends on the jobs that the shop can obtain. A particular job may involve work in only one department or it could involve all departments; it may require a few hours to complete or

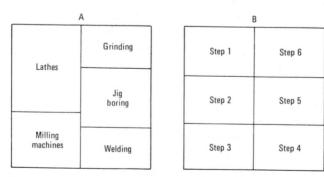

FIGURE   11-1   Job-order and Process Production Layouts

many months. The purpose of a job-order cost system is to determine the cost involved in completing a specific job.

In process production, the focal point for cost accumulation is the product—a unit of production. Figure 11-1B depicts process or homogeneous production in which every unit produced goes through the same sequence of steps. Thus we can assume that the cost of every unit of production in a particular production run is the same. It is assumed that the same amount of direct material, direct labor, and overhead goes into every copy of this text that is printed. This is quite unlike job-order production in which every job worked on could involve different amounts of direct material, direct labor, and overhead.

We should not infer from the previous description that every product produced by a process production facility goes through the same set of steps. It is quite possible that a product requires only steps 1, 2, and 6 or 1, 4, and 5, for example. The point is that each of the units we are costing goes through the same series of steps in the manufacturing process.

JOB-ORDER COST ACCUMULATION

The specific activity involved in job-order cost accumulation depends on the characteristics of each job. Some jobs are simple and can be completed in minutes or a few hours, whereas other jobs are complex and may be in process for many weeks. Some jobs can be completed in the shop, and others may need to be sent out for such special services as heat treating, lapping, or plating. The number of units that the order calls for also has a bearing on the activity that will be involved. The same production process probably would not be used to make 50 gear blanks as would be used to make a single gear blank. An inexpensive drill press might be the ideal tool for making six holes in a single gear blank, whereas a much more expensive multispindle drill press that makes six holes in a single operation might be ideal if a lot of 50 gear blanks is being processed.

Even though every job may be different in job-order production, every job goes through the same sequence of steps as shown in the following schematic.

Job-order Schematic

The sales order	Blueprints, specifications, quantities
↓	
Production planning	Design of production process, steps involved, machines to be used, labor skills required
↓	
The production order	Material requirements, machine-hour requirements, labor-hour requirements, overhead requirements, outside services

Jobs are identified by blueprints. A production planner must examine the blueprints and ascertain how the job will be done. The planner must identify the nature and number of operations needed to complete the job. Failure to include all operations or failure to detect the complexity of operations could lead to a selling price that would not allow the firm to recapture its costs.

It is also important to select the right sequence of operations to minimize the number of machine set-ups that must be made and to reduce the chances of error in the manufacturing process. Also, the operations that are selected must be consistent with machine and labor capabilities. Once the operations are defined, an estimate of the time required to complete them must be made. The level of labor skill that each operation demands must be carefully identified because this will impact on the time required to complete the job and the total labor cost. Planners frequently use standard times in the estimating process. Thus they have a good idea of how long it will take to set up an automatic screw machine, drill a ½-inch hole in a particular grade of aluminum, or turn a thread on a stainless steel rod.

In a job shop, overhead is commonly charged to production based on the direct labor-hours consumed. Another task which confronts the planner is to prepare a bill of materials for the job. Material specifications are usually provided by the customer and may be an adjunct to the blueprints.

Thus in job-order production estimates of material, labor, and overhead costs are made for each job, and the customer may be quoted a selling price and delivery date before the job goes into production. Because of this arrangement, job shops frequently have little or no finished goods inventory at any point in time.

Job-order Cost Sheet

The job-order cost sheet provides the means for assembling the costs associated with each job. The cost sheet is a simple device; the important part of job-order costing is a system that guarantees, insofar as is feasible, that the cost information will flow to the cost sheets. There is a great amount of detail in job-order costing that must be performed such as assuring that every item of direct material issued from inventory is charged to the appropriate job. There must be a mechanism whereby material requisitions numbers 2056, 2120, and 2220 (see Figure 11-2) find their way to the Job No. 268 Cost Sheet.

Similarly, there must be a mechanism for assigning the appropriate direct labor cost to each job. If there are 25 direct laborers in the shop each working an 8-hour day, 200 hours of direct labor must be assigned to the jobs being worked on, or to overhead if conditions warrant. Frequently time cards are prepared for each job or worker, and workers record the time spent on each job by punching the time clock when work begins and when work is finished.

Each production department has an overhead rate. The determination of overhead rates was discussed earlier. The hours worked in each department multiplied by the overhead rate determines the overhead that will be assigned to a job. In summary, the cost of materials used in Job No. 268 could be exactly $32, and the direct labor consumed by this job could be exactly $102, but the overhead of $75 is an estimate. Thus we refer to the gross margin as estimated.

Additional Job-order Cost Considerations

A job-order shop may on occasion obtain work without first establishing the selling price of the job. The customer's need may be so urgent that cost is no object, or the job may be too risky to guarantee a fixed price.

As a rule, job shops must bid for the jobs they receive. Bidding can be a costly function, and there is no guarantee that a given bid will be successful. In other words, management will incur costs that will bring no return to the firm. To control the bidding cost, manage-

Apex Machine Shop

Job Cost Sheet

Job No. ___268___

Customer: Buswell Corp.
289 Atlantic Avenue
City, State

Started ___6/14/19–___
Completed ___6/20/19–___

Materials

Date	Req. #	Description	Cost
6/14	2056	Steel plate	$28.00
6/18	2120	Bushings	3.00
6/20	2200	Allen screws	1.00
			$32.00

Direct Labor

Date	Oper.	Hrs	Rate	Total
6/14	268-1	6	$4.00	$ 24.00
6/14	268-2	2	5.00	10.00
6/15	268-3	8	5.50	44.00
6/18	268-4	3	5.00	15.00
6/20	268-5	2	4.50	9.00
				$102.00

Overhead

Date	Hrs.	Rate	Total
6/14	6	$4.00	$24.00
6/14	2	3.50	7.00
6/15	8	3.00	24.00
6/18	3	5.00	15.00
6/20	2	2.50	5.00
			$75.00

Summary
Bid price	$290.00
Material	$ 32.00
Labor	102.00
Overhead	75.00
	209.00
Estimated gross margin	$ 81.00

FIGURE 11-2 Job-order Cost Sheet

ment should screen each "request for quotation" before it gets to the planning department. This screening should take the form of a cost-benefit analysis where in the risks involved in accepting a particular job are weighed against the gains that would come from successful completion of the job. Generally jobs that are easy to perform and carry little risk will yield a smaller gross margin than complex jobs that are risky. The problem is to match jobs to the firm's abilities so that the risk inherent in complex work can be reduced.

Finally, how does a job shop know whether it is earning a profit on the jobs it completes? The $81 estimated gross margin shown in Figure 11-2 is 28 percent of the bid price, and this may be well above expectations, but this is no guarantee that profit is being earned. In fact a firm can show exceptional gross margins on every job completed and still lose money. The reason for this is that the overhead rate is based on a particular level of activity and actual activity could be above or below this estimate.

Work-in-process Inventory

In our earlier illustrations of cost flow, the cost of work-in-process at the end of the accounting period was determined by subtracting the credits from the debits in the work-in-process T-account (see page 233). But this summary figure tells us no more about the status of this inventory than the summary accounts receivable figure of $300,000 (see Table 2-1) tells us about the status of individual accounts receivable. A subsidiary ledger is needed to identify individual account balances.

Similarly, we need a subsidiary account of work-in-process inventories. Suppose, to illustrate, that a firm closed its books on June 15. Referring to Figure 11-2 we see that the work-in-process inventory, as far as Job No. 268 is concerned, is $161 on June 15 (material, $28; labor, $78; and overhead, $55). The total of material, labor, and overhead in each job at a given point in time should equal the summary figure.

But this could raise some serious questions. Suppose, for example, that due to a number of errors or mistakes the cost of material, labor, and overhead already applied to Job No. 268 on June 15 was $300 and that the job still had a way to go before completion. Because the job will bring in only $290, is it reasonable to give this job a $300 inventory value? We will not discuss this issue now; this situation points out again that sound cost management requires much more than following a system.

Journal Entries

The job-order cost sheet (see Figure 11-2) provides the information for charging costs to work in process. During the period that Job No. 268 is in process, work in process is charged $209 for direct material, direct labor, and overhead. On completion of this job, finished goods will be charged $209 and work-in-process inventory credited for the same amount.

JOB-ORDER COST ILLUSTRATED

On January 1, 19X8, Pilgrim Machine Company had the following jobs in process:

Job no.	Material	Labor	Overhead	Total
818	$ 48	$140	$110	$298
820	110	230	200	540
824	27	80	53	160
Total	$185	$450	$363	$998

During the month the following costs were incurred for the jobs shown:

Job no.	Material	Labor	Overhead	Total
818	$ 12	$ 12	$ 28	$ 80
820	120	250	200	570
824	140	300	240	680
825	70	280	210	560
826	60	260	200	520
827	90	300	240	630
Total	$492	$1,430	$1,118	$3,040

Jobs 818, 820, 824, and 826 were completed and delivered to the customers; the remaining jobs were still in process. The following T-accounts are used to show activity as it relates to each job.

818			820			824		
1-01	298		1-01	540		1-01	160	
1-31	80	378	1-31	570	1,110	1-31	680	840

825			826			827		
	560			520	520		630	

During January a total of $3,040 of costs was charged to work in process. This is the total of all charges to the jobs in production during the month. Four jobs whose cost totalled $2,848 were completed and transferred to finished goods and then to the cost of goods sold. The work-in-process account shows a balance of $1,190 on January 31, which is also the total of costs charged to the two jobs still in process at that time. This activity is shown in the following T-accounts:

Work in process			Finished goods		Cost of goods sold	
1-01	998	378	378	2,848	2,848	
1-31	3,040	1,110	1,110			
		840	840			
		520	520			
		1,190				
		bal.				
	4,038	4,038	2,848	2,848		

PROCESS COST ACCUMULATION

This approach to costing is used in process production. Here, a quantity of products assumed to be homogeneous is manufactured by a predetermined sequence of operations. Process production is applied to the manufacture of petroleum products, automobiles and automobile tires, food products, paper products, textbooks, and the like. Because each unit emerging from the production process is assumed to be identical, each unit is expected to bear the same portion of the total costs incurred. Process costing accumulates the costs of operating a department or a process for a period of time and divides this cost by the equivalent number of units produced in that period. Through process costing the average unit cost of production is determined. The basic concepts of process costing will be developed through a series of illustrations beginning with a very simple situation and proceeding to more complex situations. The reader should understand that process costing involves much more than is presented here. (See Appendix for this chapter).

Illustration 1

One department of the Whatway Compass Company produces a compass used in automobiles. During the week of August 12, 100,000 compasses were started in production, and all of these were completed during the week and transferred to finished goods. The following costs were assigned to the department for the week: direct material, $60,000; direct labor, $20,000; and overhead, $40,000. Our goal is to determine the average cost of producing a compass. We will use an approach which will be carried through all of our illustrations.

	Total cost	*Cost per compass*
Direct material	$ 60,000	$0.60
Direct labor	20,000	0.20
Overhead	40,000	0.40
Total	$120,000	$1.20

The reader may wonder why we go through all of this formality to determine that the average cost to produce a compass was $1.20. There are two reasons for this. First, it is a good idea to identify unit costs item by item as we have done so that comparisons can be made and trends noted. Second, when work-in-process inventories are involved, as in later illustrations, this approach is necessary.

Illustration 2

During the week of August 19, 150,000 compasses were started in production. At week's end 120,000 had been completed and transferred to finished goods. The balance was still in process. It was estimated that the units in process had all the necessary material applied to them but only half of the labor and overhead. The following costs were incurred by or assigned to the department for the week: direct material, $91,500; direct labor, $25,650; and overhead, $55,350.

The Equivalent Unit Concept

In our first illustration each total cost was divided by 100,000 units to obtain the cost per unit. The reason we did this is because every unit that went into process was finished and therefore should bear the same portion of total cost.

When there is work in process at the end of a period, someone must estimate how much direct material, direct labor, and overhead, on an average, has been applied to production. This is not an exact process, but it must be done to obtain a reasonable estimate of average production costs. Thus, as mentioned, it was estimated that the 30,000 units in process at week's end are complete as far as direct materials are concerned but only half completed as far as labor and overhead are concerned. The balance of the labor and overhead needed to complete these units will be applied in the next period. The entire 150,000 units, therefore, must bear the cost of direct materials. In the case of direct labor and overhead the total cost must be borne by 135,000 units (120,000 completed plus one-half the 30,000 units in process).

The logic of the equivalent unit concept is

30,000 units, 50% completed, is equivalent to 15,000 completed units.

20,000 units, 40% completed, is equivalent to 8,000 completed units.

50,000 units, 25% completed, is equivalent to 12,500 completed units.

The determination of the cost to produce a compass during the week of August 19 follows:

	Total cost	Equivalent units	Cost per compass
Direct material	$ 91,500	150,000	$0.61
Direct labor	25,650	135,000	0.19
Overhead	55,350	135,000	0.41
Total	$172,500		$1.21

COST OF PRODUCTION REPORT

In our first illustration, all units started in production during the week were completed and transferred to finished goods. Therefore, all costs of production for the week can be charged out of work in process and into finished goods. In this illustration we need to separate the total cost of $172,500 into the amount that should be charged to finished goods and the amount that should remain in process. Here is how this is done:

Transferred to finished goods	
(120,000 units x $1.21)	$145,200
In Process:	
Direct material (30,000 x $0.61)	18,300
Direct labor (30,000 x 50% x $0.19)	2,850
Overhead (30,000 x 50% x $0.41)	6,150
Total	$172,500

The 120,000 compasses completed were charged to finished goods at the unit price of $1.21. Because the units in process have all of the material applied, 30,000 x $0.61 is the value of material in process. These same 30,000 units have only half the labor and overhead applied and are considered the equivalent of 15,000 units. Of course, the 30,000 units in process could be multiplied by one-half the unit cost for labor and overhead to obtain the same result. The purpose of this illustration is summarized in Table 11-1.

Illustration 3

In this illustration we will add two more ingredients of process cost accumulation. First, in process production it is quite possible and probable that some of the units started in production will be lost or spoiled for a variety of reasons. Lost units, of course, cannot bear cost, and they increase the cost of remaining units. Second, we will see how process cost accumulation operates when a series of departments is involved in the production process.

Apex Corporation manufactures a washing detergent called Stainset in three successive departments called mixing, blending, and packaging. During the month of March 90,000 lb of the product were started in the mixing department. Of this total, 60,000 lb were

TABLE 11-1

Cost of Production Report
Week of August 19, 19X5

Expense	Total Cost	Unit Cost
Direct material	$ 91,500	$0.61
Direct labor	25,650	0.19
Overhead	55,350	0.41
Total	$172,500	$1.21
Summary:		
Completed and transferred	$145,200	
In Process:		
Direct material	18,300	
Direct labor	2,850	
Overhead	6,150	
Total	$172,500	

Equivalent Units:	
Direct material	150,000
Direct labor ($120,000 + 50\% \times 30,000$)	135,000
Overhead ($120,000 + 50\% \times 30,000$)	135,000

completed and transferred to the blending department and 28,000 lb were still in process at the end of the month with all the material and half the labor and overhead applied. The balance of 2,000 lb cannot be accounted for and is presumed lost. The blending department completed and transferred 50,000 lb to the packaging department, and the balance was in process with half the labor and overhead applied. There is no direct material cost in this department. The packaging department completed and transferred 45,000 lb of product to finished goods. The balance was in process with no material and 20 percent of the labor and overhead applied.

This data can be summarized as follows:

	Mixing	Blending	Packaging
Started or received	90,000 lb	60,000 lb	50,000 lb
Completed and transferred	60,000 lb	50,000 lb	45,000 lb

In process	28,000 lb		10,000 lb		5,000 lb
Lost	2,000 lb				
Total	90,000 lb		60,000 lb		50,000 lb

We will now use this data along with the cost data which is shown in Table 11-2 to determine the cost of a unit of production during the month of March. To understand this process, direct your attention first to the equivalent unit section at the bottom of Table 11-2. In the mixing department there were 60,000 lb of product completed and transferred to the next department and 28,000 lb

TABLE   11-2

The Apex Corporation
Cost of Production Report,
March 19XX

	Mixing		Blending		Packaging	
	Total	Unit	Total	Unit	Total	Unit
Cost transferred in			$21,000	$0.35	$35,000	$0.70
Direct material	$12,320	$0.14			4,500	0.10
Direct labor	8,880	0.12	8,800	0.16	4,140	0.09
Overhead	6,660	0.09	10,450	0.19	5,060	0.11
	$27,860	$0.35	$40,250	$0.70	$48,700	$1.00
Summary:						
Cost transferred out	$21,000		$35,000		$45,000	
Work in process						
Direct material	3,920					
Direct labor	1,680		800		90	
Overhead	1,260		950		110	
Value transferred in			3,500		3,500	
	$27,860		$40,250		$48,700	
Equivalent Units:						
Material	88,000				45,000	
Direct labor	74,000		55,000		46,000	
Overhead	74,000		55,000		46,000	

were still in process having all of the material cost applied. Therefore there is the equivalent of 88,000 lb of product that must bear the direct material cost of $12,320. The direct labor and overhead cost must be borne by the 60,000 lb of product completed and transferred plus the equivalent of 14,000 lb (50% x 28,000 lb) that are in process, or 74,000 lb. The units that were lost cannot bear any cost.

Similarly, we determine the equivalent units in the remaining departments. Because there is no material cost in the blending department, there are no equivalent units shown for materials.

The next step in this process is to divide each cost by the appropriate equivalent units to obtain the average cost:

	Total cost	*Units*	*Unit cost*
Mixing:			
Direct material	$12,320	88,000	$0.14
Direct labor	8,880	74,000	0.12
Overhead	6,660	74,000	0.09
Blending:			
Direct labor	8,800	55,000	0.16
Overhead	10,450	55,000	0.19
Packaging:			
Direct material	4,500	45,000	0.10
Direct labor	4,140	46,000	0.09
Overhead	5,060	46,000	0.11

The unit costs calculated are the unit costs shown in Table 11-2.

Now direct your attention to the summary section of Table 11-2. In the mixing department we must account for a total of $27,860 in cost that was incurred during the month. Of this total $21,000 (60,000 units x $0.35) was transferred to the blending department and the balance must still be in process. Note that the $21,000 transferred to the blending department becomes an added cost for this department. The values shown for the work-in-process inventory in mixing were obtained as follows:

Direct material (28,000 x $0.14)	$3,920
Direct labor (28,000 x 50% x $0.12)	1,680
Overhead (28,000 x 50% x $0.09)	1,260

In the blending department, the cost of work transferred in is added to the departmental costs to make the cost to account for $40,250. The unit cost for direct labor and overhead was calculated, as before, by dividing total cost by the equivalent units. $35,000 of cost (50,000 x $0.70) was transferred to the packaging department, and $5,250 is the cost of the inventory in process. Direct labor and overhead in process were calculated by multiplying the equivalent units in process (5,000) by the unit costs. At the bottom of the summary there is something new—value transferred in. The reason for including this is that each of the 10,000 units in process had a cost of $0.35 before being processed in the blending department. The $800 and $950 represent the cost added to the units in process in the blending department only. The costs in the packaging department were calculated just as they were in the blending department.

Thus the average cost of processing a pound of Stainset during March was $1.00. Whether this reflects good or poor performance we cannot tell. We know that the unit cost would have been lower if 2,000 units had not been lost in the mixing department, but we do not know how much lower. This depends on their degree of completion in the department when lost.

Process costing does not allow for effective cost control because costs are automatically transferred from department to department based on units transferred and the unit cost. Managers of receiving departments have no control over the cost of goods transferred to them. Thus process costing indicates what unit cost was rather than what it should have been. This is one reason why standard cost systems have been developed.

SUMMARY

Product costing is a very important management function because frequently unit cost is the basis for establishing a selling price. The manner in which product costs are determined depends on the type of production involved. With job-order production, costs are determine for each job because each job can be different. In process production, where every unit in a production lot is considered the same, product cost is average cost. Thus the total cost of material, labor, and overhead is divided by the number of units produced to obtain a unit cost. As a rule, the number of units that must bear cost consists of completed units plus those that are still in process. To determine the amount of cost that a unit in process should bear, management must judge the degree to which units in process are completed.

Both job-order and process cost systems measure what costs were rather than what they should have been. Thus these systems are not capable of providing effective cost control.

KEY TERMS

bill of materials   process production

job-order production

APPENDIX: ADDITIONAL PRODUCT COST CONSIDERATION

The purpose of this section is to identify some product cost considerations not included in previous discussions. We include this material to answer a number of questions that may have occurred to the reader.

Lost Units—Process Costing

We mentioned lost units in our discussion of product costing, but we limited the topic to the original producing department. Units can be lost in any department whether job-order or process production is used. We will first explore the impact of lost units in departments other than the first department when process production is used.

Suppose that 50,000 units were transferred from department A to department B at a unit cost of $4.50. Let us also assume that 1,300 units were lost in department B. Now there remains only 48,700 units (50,000 - 1,300) to bear the total transfer cost of $225,000. Each remaining unit must therefore bear $4.62 of cost ($225,000 ÷ 48,700), and this causes the transfer price to rise $0.12 as shown in the following descriptive illustration.

	Total	Department B Unit	X
Cost transferred in	$225,000	$4.50	$4.50
Material	102,270	2.10	2.05
Labor	48,700	1.00	0.97
Overhead	38,960	0.80	0.78
Lost unit adjustment		0.12	
Total	$414,930	$8.52	$8.30

The $0.12 lost unit adjustment does not identify the total impact of lost units on unit cost. In column X we show what the unit cost would be if no units were lost in department B and all units were completed and transferred to finished goods. Because all units were completed and transferred to finished goods, a total of $414,930 was also transferred. But look at these comparisons:

No lost units: 50,000 units x $8.30 = $414,930

With lost units: 48,700 units x $8.52 = $414,930

The cost of lost units can be calculated as follows:

48,700 units x $8.52 = $414,930

48,700 units x $8.30 = $404,210

Cost of lost units = $ 10,720

Lost Units—Job-order Costing

We did not discuss lost units in job-order production but will use the following illustration to demonstrate their impact. If a firm had an order to deliver 50 gear blanks on September 21, the odds are that more than 50 units would be put in process to obtain the desired quantity of units that will meet specifications. Suppose that material, labor, and overhead costs are $10.00 per gear blank and that 58 units are processed. Whether 50 or 58 gear blanks are completed to specification is of no significance because only 50 blanks can be sold. Thus, because of the possibility of lost units, the unit production cost rises to $11.60 ($580 ÷ 50). Lost units are almost always a certainty when large quantities are produced because of the inherent variability in things and human performance.

QUESTIONS

1. What is a general-purpose machine?
2. Distinguish between job-order production and process production.
3. Distinguish between the purpose of job-order costing and process costing.
4. Is the management of finished goods inventory generally a problem for the job-order firm? Explain why or why not.
5. In job-order production a certain amount of precosting may be required. What does this mean and what does it involve?

6. When job-order costing is used, how can management determine the value of the work-in-process inventory at any point in time?

7. Referring to Question 6, is there any danger in measuring inventory value in this fashion?

8. When process costing is used, how can management determine the value of the work-in-process inventory at any point in time?

9. Referring to Question 8, should this inventory value be subject to question? Explain.

10. Explain the flow of cost when job-order costing is used.

11. Explain in general terms how process costing works.

12. Explain how, in process costing, the number of units that should bear cost is determined.

13. In process production units are often lost. Is it possible to determine the cost to the firm when units are lost? Explain.

14. Discuss the basic weaknesses in job-order and process costing from management's point of view.

PROBLEMS

1. Overhead application in job-order costing

The following data was taken from the records of the Easton Company:

Estimated overhead	$120,000
Actual overhead	127,000
Estimated direct labor-hours	40,000

Direct labor-hours for the jobs completed were

Job no.	Direct Labor-hours
123	7,200
124	8,000
125	8,300
126	11,000
127	9,500

There were no work-in-process inventories at either the beginning or the end of the period.

Required:

a. At what rate was overhead charged to production?

b. How much overhead was charged to each job?

c. Was overhead over- or underapplied? Explain.

2. Job-order costing

Bay State Industries uses a job-order cost system. On October 1 the firm had one job, No. 567, in process. The cost sheet shows that $800 in material, $1,600 in labor, and $2,400 in overhead has been charged to this job. Overhead is charged to production at 100 percent of prime cost.

During October the following costs were incurred for jobs as shown:

Job no.	Material	Labor
567	$ 200	$ 700
568	1,400	1,600
569	1,600	2,000
570	1,000	1,400

Job nos. 567 and 568 were completed and sold for $8,000 and $7,500, respectively. The remaining jobs are still in process.

Required:

a. What gross margin was earned on the jobs completed and sold?

b. What was the value of work in process on October 31?

3. Unit cost computation

The Compost Company produces a single product. Management estimated that its variable overhead would be $2.00 per unit of production and that its fixed overhead would be $240,000 for the year. The following is a summary of activity for the year:

	Q-I	Q-II	Q-III	Q-IV
Direct materials	$ 45,000	$ 15,000	$ 60,000	$ 90,000
Direct labor	30,000	10,000	40,000	60,000
Variable overhead	60,000	20,000	80,000	120,000
Fixed overhead	60,000	60,000	60,000	60,000
Total manu- facturing cost	$195,000	$105,000	$240,000	$330,000
Units produced	30,000	10,000	40,000	60,000
Unit cost	$6.50	$10.50	$6.00	$5.50

The problem facing management is the variation in unit cost from quarter to quarter. We are to assume that the firm operated with the same degree of efficiency during each quarter.

Required:

a. Suggest a better way to compute unit costs.

b. What would unit costs have been during each quarter if your suggestion had been applied? Explain.

4. Job-order costing

The Marathon Company specializes in the manufacture of materials-handling equipment used in the packaging of dry cereals. Every unit is made to customer specifications, and the firm ships each job as soon as possible after completion. On June 30, 19X1 there were three jobs in process having the following costs charged to them:

Job no.	Material	Labor	Overhead	Total
137	$ 850	$1,640	$ 820	$ 3,310
138	1,090	2,170	1,085	4,345
139	960	1,090	545	2,595
Total	$2,900	$4,900	$2,450	$10,250

During July the following costs were incurred:

Job no.	Material	Labor
137	$ 410	$1,060
138	840	1,730
139	2,180	2,810
140	3,240	3,420
141	2,600	4,160

Overhead was applied to production on the same basis as was used in June. Job Nos. 137, 138, 139 were completed and delivered. The other jobs were in process at the end of July.

Required:

a. Determine the cost of each job completed.

b. How much cost was still in process on July 31?

5. Product costing—job order

Custom Van, Inc. customizes panel trucks and vans to customer order. The firm plans to operate 10,000 direct labor-hours this year and expects that variable overhead will be $3.00 per direct labor hour. Fixed overhead is estimated at $40,000 for the year. During January, the first month of operation, four jobs were started and completed. There was no work in process at month's end. The following relates to these jobs:

	Job 77-1	Job 77-2	Job 77-3	Job 77-4
Direct material	$ 380	$ 440	$ 655	$ 520
Direct labor	1,370	1,400	1,500	1,400
Direct labor-				
hours	180	210	220	200
Bid price	4,000	4,750	5,000	4,750

The company adds 40 percent to production cost to arrive at a selling price. Of this, 25 percent covers selling and administrative costs and 15 percent covers the planned profit.

Required:

a. Explain to management whether a profit was made on each of these jobs. Be specific.

6. Job-order costing

Action Industries specializes in producing indexing heads that are used on a variety of machine tools. Each job is produced to customer specifications. Selected data for January 19X5 follows.

Inventories:	
Materials	$16,500
Work-in-process (Job No. 1115,	
1118, 1120)	9,695
Finished goods (Job No. 1111)	8,000

Work in process, January 1:

Job no.	Materials	Direct labor	Overhead
1115	$1,325	400 hr $2,400	$ 640
1118	810	250 hr 1,375	400
1120	765	300 hr 1,500	480
Total	$2,900	$5,275	$1,520

Material requisitions during January:

Req. no.	Job no.	Cost
56	1118	$515
57	1120	665
58	1121	910
59	1122	720

Labor cards for January:

Job no.	Hours	Cost
1115	50	$ 290
1118	120	720
1120	85	510
1121	65	455
1122	30	180
Total direct labor	350	$2,155
Indirect labor	24	115
Total labor costs		$2,270

a. Materials purchased during January cost $3,890.

b. Materials of $100 and $50 were returned to the storeroom on material requisitions 56 and 58, respectively. These returns have not been recorded.

c. Supplies and depreciation amounted to $120 and $400, respectively.

d. After careful consideration, Action Industries' cost accountant decided to apply overhead to production at the rate and manner used last month.

e. Job nos. 1115, 1118, and 1121 were completed during January. Job nos. 1111, 1115, and 1118 were sold for $9,800, $4,000, and $3,000, respectively.

Required:

a. Prepare T-accounts for the preceding information.

b. Prepare a simple cost sheet for each job.

c. Give the ending balance for materials, work in process, and finished goods.

d. Was overhead over- or underapplied?

7. Process costing—equivalent units

Production of 100,000 units was started in department A. Of these, 70,000 were completed and transferred to department B. 28,000 units were in process with three-fourths of the material applied and one-half the labor and overhead.

Required:

a. Prepare a simple statement showing the equivalent units for each cost.

8. Process costing—equivalent units

Production of 150,000 units was started in department A. Of this, 110,000 units were completed and transferred to department B, and 10,000 units were completed but not yet transferred at month's end. The balance was in process with all material and 60 percent of the labor and overhead applied.

Required:

a. Prepare a simple statement showing the equivalent units for each cost.

9. Simple process costing

The Sub-Par Golf Cart Corp. assembles both electric and gasoline-powered golf carts. Last month 1,000 electric golf carts were started in production. Of these, 700 were completed and transferred to the sales division. The balance was in process having two-thirds of the material cost applied and one-third of the labor and overhead costs. The costs for the month were:

Direct material	$294,300
Direct labor	86,400
Overhead	99,200

Required:

a. A simple statement showing the equivalent units that must bear cost.

b. A cost of production report showing the cost of a unit completed and the value of the work-in-process inventory.

10. Cost of production report—process costing

One production line at Babco Electronics produces CB radios. For costing purposes the production line has one segment called assembly where component parts are brought together to make the radio chassis and a second segment where the chassis is installed into the radio case and tested.

During April 100,000 chassis assemblies were started in production. Of these, 79,000 were completed and transferred to the casing department; 20,000 units remained in process at month's end having all of the material cost and one-half the labor and overhead cost applied. The casing department completed and transferred 50,000 units to finished goods. The balance was in process having one-half of the material cost and 40 percent of the labor and overhead cost applied.

The material, labor, and overhead costs charged to each department during the month is shown in Table 11-3.

TABLE 11-3

Cost of Production Report
for April 19XX

	Assembly Total	Unit	Casing Total	Unit
Cost transferred in				
Material	$1,188,000		$206,400	
Labor	712,000		129,360	
Overhead	445,000		86,240	
Total cost	$2,345,000			
Summary:				
Cost transferred out				
Work in process:				
Material				
Labor				
Overhead				
Transfer cost				
Total cost				

Required:

a. A statement showing the number of units that must bear each cost.

b. Complete the cost of production report.

c. What is the value of work in process on April 30?

11. Process costing

One department of the Finewood Furniture Company produces kitchen chairs. A process cost system is used to compute unit costs because each chair must go through two departments called assembly and finishing. Last week's production involved model 941-K chairs. The plan was to start and complete 2,400 chairs during the week, but due to a power outage each department had work in process at week's end. Assembly completed 1,990 chairs, 400 chairs were still in process with all material and one-half the labor and overhead applied. The balance was lost due either to defective materials or to workmanship.

The finishing department completed 1,600 chairs, and the balance was in process having one-half the material and two-thirds of the labor and overhead applied.

Production costs for the week were

	Assembly	Finishing
Direct material	$26,768	$1,795
Direct labor	10,731	4,464
Overhead	6,351	2,790

Required:

a. A cost of production report showing the cost of a unit completed and the work-in-process inventories.

12. Process costing

The Albemarle Corporation manufactures a product that requires three separate processes. Component parts are first punched out or formed in the sheet metal department and are then transferred to the fabrication department where they are assembled into a completed unit. The product is then transferred to the packaging department and from there goes into the finished goods inventory.

In January, 42,000 units were scheduled for production in the sheet metal department. Of the total, 30,000 units were completed and transferred to the fabrication department and 10,000 units were still in process with all material and an estimated 60 percent of the labor and overhead applied. The balance was lost.

The fabrication department completed 25,000 units which were sent to the packaging department. 5,000 units were in process with 40 percent of the labor and overhead applied.

The packaging department completed and transferred 22,000 units to finished goods. The balance was in process with 50 percent of the material, labor, and overhead applied. Costs were

	Sheet metal	Fabrication	Packaging
Direct material	$32,000		$8,695
Direct labor	22,320	$29,700	5,170
Overhead	10,080	16,200	9,400

Required:

a. A cost of production report showing the cost of a unit completed and the work-in-process inventories.

12 Control
Through Standards
and
Standard Costs

CHAPTER OVERVIEW

In this chapter we will explain how management can overcome the basic weakness of job-order and process costing systems through the use of standard costs. Standard costs provide a benchmark of what costs should be for a unit of production and when actual costs are compared to the standard management can determine whether resources were wasted or saved.

We will explain how material, labor, and overhead standards are developed to serve as benchmarks. These standards contain two elements, a quantity element and a price element. Thus a labor standard can be expressed as 4 hours of labor at $8 per hour, or $32. If actual results show more or less hours used per unit of output or an hourly rate more or less than $8, management can then determine the reasons for the difference.

Thus after standards are established, management focuses its attention not on total costs but on the differences—the variances—between what happened and what should have happened. Standard costing, therefore, facilitates the management by exception concept.

QUESTIONS FOR CONSIDERATION

1. What must be done to control activity?
2. How can management determine the amount of control it should exercise over an activity?
3. How are standards established?
4. How do standards facilitate cost control?
5. How does the use of standard costs simplify the accounting process?

Both job-order and process costing as described in Chapter 11 report historical events—they report what costs were for a particular job or batch of production. The basic purpose of standards and standard cost programs is to provide a basis for more effective control over cost. In some respects the budget, discussed earlier, develops a standard and provides a basis for cost control. A standard cost system goes beyond the budgeting process in facilitating control by identifying the reasons for over- or underspending.

Virtually all aspects of business operation should be subjected to some type of control, although the nature and degree of control should vary from one situation to another. The reason that control must be exercised is the inherent variability in processes and the output of human beings and machines.

THE CONTROL PROCESS

Control is a basic management function and the control process involves a number of specific steps no matter where control is being exercised. Cost control involves the same steps as quality control, inventory control, or sales control. These steps are

1. The development of standards to provide an indication of what should be. The cost of materials needed to produce one unit of X should be 3 lb of Groz at $4 per lb, or $12.

2. The measurement of what actually happened. The actual cost of materials used to produce one unit of X was $13.

3. The identification and analysis of any variances. (The difference between what should be (standard) and what is (actual) is called a variance.) Was the $1.00 variance in unit material cost due to (a) the quantity of material used? (b) the price paid for a unit of material? or (c) both?

4. Taking corrective action. Based on the results obtained in step 3, management should be able to prescribe a course of action that will help guard against future variances if they are unfavorable.

An effective control process requires that the standards established be realistic, and it requires a reporting process that can provide an indication of what actually happened within a short period of time. If it takes a month to determine what actually happened, and frequently it does, the opportunity to exercise effective control has been lost for at least a month.

How Much Control?

In business, and elsewhere, control is a relative rather than absolute concept. Seldom will management attempt to maintain absolute control (whatever this means) over everything—we see this in the quality of goods and services we buy—because of the cost involved. Control is justified only to the extent that it produces values that are in excess of the costs involved. Thus in some instances exercising little control may be the best policy. Some classroom instructors use a seating plan and note absences at each class session to control attendance. Others will merely look around the room and observe the general level of attendance to achieve what they feel is the same end.

It frequently happens that, as more and more control is exercised over an activity, the cost of control increases at an accelerated rate. And, as more and more control is exercised, its value tends to level off and at times decline. The cost of adding a ninth coat of paint to an automobile body to ensure quality will probably cost more than a consumer would be willing to pay. Somewhere along the continuum between no control and "absolute" control there is a point (see Figure 12-1) where the spread between cost and value is maximized—between 5 and 6 degrees in the diagram. This indicates the optimum degree of control.

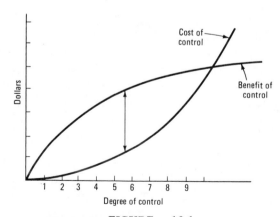

FIGURE　12-1

Two elements are involved in establishing standards—a quantity element and a price element. Each is a benchmark against which actual performance can be compared. Thus the standard cost of labor for a batch of production may be expressed as 2,000 hours of direct labor at $7 per hour, or $14,000. If the actual quantity of direct labor used in this batch of production is "about" 2,000 hours and the actual rate per hour is "about" $7 per hour, management would conclude that labor cost is under control and drop the matter. If the actual hours required to do the job, or the hourly rate, varied "significantly" from the standard, management would ferret out the reasons and take the necessary steps to remedy the situation. The terms "about" and "significantly" are discussed later in this chapter. A standard cost system, therefore, permits management by exception.

TYPES OF STANDARDS

Standards can be based strictly on empirical data, and standards can contain an element of management philosophy. If a nut holding part of an assembly must be tightened with 84 lb of torque to properly seat against a lock washer, 84 lb of torque can be a standard based on empirical data. Often such standards cannot be challenged. Standards based in part on one's philosophy are discussed in the following paragraphs.

Ideal Standards

An ideal standard is established on the premise that nothing should go wrong. Workers should produce at the standard rates, there should be no defective materials, and there should be no unplanned work stoppages. The probability that actual performance will measure up to an ideal standard may be very remote, yet there are managers who insist that such standards be established—this is their philosophy. Advocates of ideal standards reason that

1. They reveal how near or far actual performance is from what it might be—theoretical perfection.

2. They will probably continue to show that there is room for improvement, and this could have a positive motivational impact. (Others will argue that unattainable standards stifle motivation.)

3.   Any other standard is an expression of the amount of waste that management will tolerate. For example, the quantity of spark plugs needed for 1,000 V-8 engines is 8,000. This is an ideal standard. If the standard is set at 8,205 spark plugs it means that management is willing to accept 2½ percent defects.

Ideal standards do not have widespread use in business, but the basic concept underlying ideal standards is worth mentioning. Perhaps it would be worthwhile to have ideal standards as a point of reference rather than to use them to establish standard costs.

Currently Attainable Standards

A currently attainable standard is one that can be reached if the firm operates with a "high" degree of efficiency and effectiveness. These standards recognize that breakdowns, delays, and imperfections are a fact of life. Because they will probably be achieved, they are helpful in planning production, expenses, cash flow, and the like. These standards can be an integral part of the budgeting process. Ideal standards cannot be used effectively for these purposes because actual performance is likely to fall far short of the standard.

Standard Costs and Budgets

Standard costs and budgets can be essentially the same thing, provided that the standard is currently attainable. The only difference is that a standard cost is a budget for one unit of production. Budgets include the total costs for a given span of time and are based on a predetermined volume of activity.

STANDARD COSTS

A standard cost should be established for every variable cost item. Standard costs contain two elements: the quantity standard expressed in hours, pounds, board feet, and the like, and the price per quantity unit. Thus a variable overhead standard can be expressed as 4 direct labor-hours at $6 per hour for a unit of production. Because fixed costs bear no relation to volume (within the relevant range), we do not consider fixed-cost standards.

Standard cost programs are very costly to install and operate, and the following discussions could be misleading without a word of explanation. We speak of a standard cost for material, labor, and variable overhead. Actually there can be hundreds or thousands of material standards in a manufacturing plant. If there are 10,000 material items in an automobile, there can be 10,000 material standards. Similarly, there may be a standard labor cost for each production operation and a variable overhead standard cost in each production department. The following discussion of standard costs describes a process that may have to be repeated thousands of times.

Material Standards

"If everything goes right," determining the quantity of material that should be used in a unit of production is a simple process. 8,000 spark plugs are needed for 1,000 V-8 engines. As a rule, management reasons that it cannot afford to control to the degree necessary to ensure that "everything goes right."

The bill of materials discussed earlier is just the starting point for establishing materials standards. There are a number of factors that must be considered and we will use the spark plug illustration to identify them. 8,000 spark plugs is a reasonable standard provided that

1. every spark plug meets specifications.
2. the process for making engine blocks is refined to the point that every block is threaded properly to accept the plug.
3. the process for installing plugs is so refined that no plugs will be damaged or lost during installation.

The odds that these conditions will always prevail are very remote—this degree of control is generally too costly. However, if management can determine the likelihood of failure in each of these areas, it is possible to establish a reasonable standard. This should be the case because reliability is a key element in process design. In dealing with suppliers, management may require that at least 98, or some other, percent of all spark plugs meet specifications. This is done to obtain the "best" price. The process for making engine blocks is designed to have a specific degree of reliability as is the installation process. By knowing the reliability of each element involved, management can determine how many more than 8,000 spark plugs will be needed.

Once established, a materials quantity standard can be used as long as there are no changes in the variables. Material price standards, however, are subject to constant change and require frequent revision in today's economy. A material price standard should be the price paid under the most favorable conditions. What constitutes the most favorable conditions depends on a number of factors. Acceptable inventory levels, purchase lot size, lead time, method of delivery, each are factors affecting the standard price.

A material standard cost per unit of production can be expressed as follows:

5 yd of A at $2.00 per yd

4 pieces of B at $0.80 per piece

Labor Standards

As with materials, there are two parts to a labor standard cost— the quantity of labor (hours) and the price of labor (wage rate). Labor standards were used in industry long before the advent of standard cost systems. Early practitioners of scientific management developed time standards and piece-rate systems of wage payment in an effort to control cost and provide an incentive for increased production. Reference was made to labor standards earlier in Chapter 7. A quick review of this section will provide an introduction to this discussion.

Labor standards are frequently described as engineered standards. That is, management determines the method that will be applied to complete a job and designs tools and equipment consistent with the needs of the method. In many instances there is only one approved way that the job can be done—a standardized way. By observing workers as they perform their jobs, management, through time study, can determine the time it takes a worker to complete a job cycle. As the time-study engineer observes the worker, he rates the skill and effort that the worker exhibits. If the engineer rates the worker at 10 percent below average, he rates the worker as .90. Thus, if a worker's average time to complete a job was 70 seconds, the time would be adjusted downward to 63 seconds. In theory, 63 seconds is the time that an average worker should take to complete a job. Allowances, say, 20 percent, are added to the 63 seconds to cover such things as machine adjustments and personal needs. Thus the time standard is 75.6 seconds per unit (1.2 x 63). This will result in a standard output per hour of 47.6 units (3,600 ÷ 75.6). If the prevailing wage rate is $6.60 per hour, the standard labor cost per unit is $0.139. Another way to express the standard is 1.26 minutes at $0.11 per minute, or $.139.

A labor standard cost per unit of production can be expressed as follows:

5 hours of direct labor at $7 per hour

4 hours of direct labor at $5 per hour

Variable Overhead Standards

Variable overhead standards require little explanation. If the measure of activity used to charge variable overhead to production is direct labor-hours, the quantity standard for variable overhead per unit of production is provided by the labor standard. The process for determining the variable overhead rate per direct labor-hour, or per unit of production, was described in Chapter 7 (see column A in Table 7-1). If variable overhead accumulates at the rate of $9 per direct labor-hour and 9 hours of direct labor are required per unit, variable overhead standard is $81.

Dealing with Variances

A variance is nothing more than the difference between standard and actual, be it hours, dollars, or some other attribute. If actual costs are less than standard, the variance is considered favorable (F). If actual costs are more than standard, the variance is considered unfavorable (U). Dealing with variances involves two steps. First, the overall quantity and price variances are identified, and, second, the monetary amounts involved are calculated.

The following illustration identifies the basic concepts involved in the treatment of variances. The material standard for a unit of production is 6 lb of Zerbol at $2 per lb, or $12. Last month 5,000 units were produced and 31,000 lb of Zerbol costing $60,450 were used. The analysis of variances follows:

Step 1.

Standard for 5,000 units: 30,000 lb   x $2.00   or $60,000
Actual for 5,000 units: 31,000 lb   x $1.95   or $60,450

Variances   1,000 lb (U) $0.05 (F) $ 450 (U)

The total variance is unfavorable by $450 because the actual cost for materials is greater than the standard. Note that the quantity of material used is greater than the standard and the unit price paid is less than the standard. Because $450 is the net difference between a favorable and unfavorable variance, the individual deviations from standard can be much greater than $450. The reason for this is given below.

Step 2. To determine the magnitude of the deviation from standard, we must measure both the price variance and the quantity or usage variance. The price variance by definition equals the actual quantity of material used times the unit price variance. The quantity or usage variance equals the unit variance times the standard price. Thus,

Price variance =   31,000 lb × $0.05   or $1,550 (F)
Usage variance =   1,000 lb × $2.00   or $2,000 (U)

Net variance $ 450 (U)

Thus we have accounted for the overall variance of $450 (U) mentioned earlier. $1,550 was saved because of a favorable unit price, and $2,000 was lost because of the number of units consumed. Note that the magnitude of the variance is $3,550. This suggests that even a very small variance should be examined. For example, a material standard for a unit of production is 2 ft of electric cable at $0.60 per ft. During the past month 20,000 units were produced, and they consumed 37,500 ft of cable costing $24,000. A comparison of total material cost with the standard shows no variance. Should management be satisfied with actual performance or should it look further? We will follow the procedure just used to obtain the answer.

Step 1.

Standard for 20,000 units: 40,000 ft × $0.60   or $24,000
Actual for 20,000 units: 37,500 ft × $0.64   or $24,000

Variances   2,500 ft $0.04   0

Step 2.

Price variance =   37,500 × $0.04   or $1,500 (U)
Usage variance =   2,500 × $0.60   or $1,500 (F)

Net variance   0

Although the net variance is zero, the magnitude of the variance is $3,000 and probably well worth investigation.

Material Price Variances in Practice

In practice material price variances probably will not be handled as we have shown. Rather, price variances are recorded when purchased materials are received. The result is that all materials are charged into and out of inventory at the standard price. To illustrate, suppose that the standard price for a material is $1.50 per lb and that an order for 20,000 lb is received costing $30,600. There is an unfavorable price variance of $600 which is then charged to the cost of goods sold account. This approach eliminates the need to calculate material price variances each time materials are issued from inventory. We did not use this approach in our illustrations because we wanted to follow the same steps for analyzing each variable cost.

Direct Labor Variances

The identification and analysis of labor variances is handled the same way as material variances. Different terms are used to describe these variances. The quantity variance is called an efficiency variance, and the price variance is called a rate variance. The following illustrates how labor variances are identified and analyzed. The standard labor cost per unit of production is 6 hours of labor at $7 per hour, or $42. Last month 2,500 units were produced and 14,750 hours of labor costing $106,200 were used.

Step 1.

Standard for 2,500 units:	15,000 hr × $7.00	or $105,000
Actual for 2,500 units:	14,750 hr × $7.20	or $106,200
Variances	250 hr $0.20	$ 1,200 (U)

Step 2.

Rate variance	=	14,750 × $0.20	or $2,950 (U)
Efficiency variance =		250 hr × $7	or $1,750 (F)
Net variance			$1,200 (U)

Here the magnitude of the variance is $4,700.

Variable Overhead Variances

The process for identifying and analyzing variable overhead variances is the same as that used in the preceding discussion. However, the price portion of this variance is called a spending variance, and the quantity portion is called an efficiency variance. The following illustrates the identification and analysis of variable overhead variances, and it is based on the labor standard illustration presented earlier. The variable overhead rate is $5 per direct labor-hour, but last month $72,275 was spent on variable overhead.

Step 1.

Standard for 2,500 units:	15,000 hr × $5.00	or $75,000
Actual for 2,500 units:	14,750 hr × $4.90	or $72,275
Variances	250 $0.10	$ 2,275 (F)

Step 2.

Spending variance =	14,750 × $0.10	or $1,475 (F)
Efficiency variance =	250 × $5.00	or $1,250 (F)
Total variance		$2,725 (F)

Control Through Variance Analysis

The process of identifying and analyzing variances is not an end in itself. This is merely an output of the standard cost system that is given to the responsible manager. It is up to the responsible manager to answer two important questions regarding every variance whether it is favorable or unfavorable.

1. *Is the variance significant?* Variances should be considered the rule rather than the exception. The odds that actual quantities and prices will be the same as the standard are very remote. In fact, management should be concerned if this condition existed with any degree of consistency because maintaining this condition may signal manipulation or a forcing of actual to agree with standard.

The basic problem facing management is deciding when a particular variance should be investigated or, put another way, deciding when variances should be ignored. The management by exception principle states that managerial control efforts should be concentrated on the exception, not on activities that are adhering to the plan. To apply this principle, management must first define "exception" and "adhering." Defining these terms is not easy, but a number of criteria can assist in this process.

The first criterion is the magnitude of the variance. When is a variance large enough to warrant investigation? A variance can be considered an exception if it deviates, for example, plus or minus 10 percent from the standard. Variances under 10 percent would be considered adhering to the standard and would not be investigated. This measure of magnitude may need to be modified because in certain instances a 5 percent variation could involve thousands of dollars whereas a 20 percent variation could involve a very small amount. Thus management might say that all variances exceeding 10 percent of standard and involving $1,000 or more will be investigated.

A second criterion relates to the consistency of occurrence. A once-in-a-decade variance of $5,000 may not be as significant as a $900 variation that recurs frequently. A third criterion relates to management's ability to control the variance. To a degree management can control the quantity of electric power consumed and the number of telephone calls made, but the rates that must be paid per kilowatt-hour or per call to New Orleans are beyond management control. In some instances, therefore, usage or quantity variances may warrant investigation, whereas price or rate variances may not. "If you cannot do anything about it, forget it" is a phrase frequently heard in management circles.

Another criterion is the specific cost involved. Some costs yield an immediate and measurable return, whereas other costs yield a longer-range benefit. Overspending for direct labor during a particular month probably will not yield any long-run gain. Other costs such as advertising, sales promotion, and systems development may improve long-run profitability to such a degree that spending in excess of the plan is justified.

In the final analysis variances should be investigated when the probable saving through investigation appears to be greater than the probable costs of making the investigation.

2. *What action should be taken?* All too often variances are used to praise and belittle managers. This is not the purpose of a control system. Management should get to the root causes of variances before any praising or belittling of managers takes place. If variances are favorable, the causes should be found. Was the cause a loose standard, something beyond the manager's control, a one-shot condition, or truly effective management? Similarly, unfavorable variances should be investigated. Should purchasing be blamed for unfavorable price variances? Not necessarily, because there are so many variables to consider, and many of these may be beyond the

control of purchasing. There may have been unexpected price increases, quantity discounts may have been lost due to smaller purchases, or there may have been a large number of rush orders.

In summary, all variances should be looked at, and all significant variances should be investigated. Corrective action, if any, depends on the conditions surrounding the variance. Managers should remember that overcontrol can be as dysfunctional as undercontrol.

Standard Cost Accounting

In job-order and process cost systems, direct material and direct labor are charged to work in process based on actual amounts consumed. Variable overhead is charged to work in process based on the estimated overhead rate and the actual amount of activity (direct labor hours, units of production, etc.). With standard costing, all costs are charged to work in process at the standard cost. Thus work-in-process and finished goods inventories are valued based on the standard cost. This simplifies the accounting process. Any differences (variances) between actual and standard cost are treated separately.

Suppose that the following standards have been set for a unit of production:

Direct material, 6 lb at $2 per lb
Direct labor, 4 hr at $6 per hr
Variable overhead, $3 per direct labor-hour

During the month 3,000 units were produced (there were no inventories of work in process) with the following results:

Direct material, 18,200 lb costing $37,310
Direct labor, 11,700 hr costing $71,370
Variable overhead costing $39,200

We will use this data to show how costs flow with a standard cost system. To do this, we first must determine what the costs should have been for the volume of production attained:

Direct materials,	18,000 lb at $2	or $36,000
Direct labor,	12,000 hr at $6	or $72,000
Variable overhead,	12,000 hr at $3	or $36,000

Next we will set up the necessary T-accounts to show the actual flow of cost. The sum of $37,310 was paid for material that left inventory, but only $36,000 is charged to work in process. The balance is charged directly to the cost of goods sold account. Because the actual cost of direct labor is less than standard, the difference, a favorable variance, is credited to the cost of goods sold account. The actual cost of variable overhead was greater than the standard and the difference is charged to the cost of goods sold account. The effect of this process is to charge all costs against revenue. Standard amounts are charged to work in process, and unfavorable variances are debited to the cost of goods sold account and favorable variances are credited to this account.

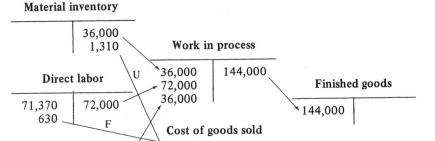

Standard Cost and the Income Statement

We will use a standard cost income statement (Table 12-1) to further illustrate the flow of cost. The values used in this statement are hypothetical and bear no relation to previous illustrations. Note that gross margin is first determined based on standard cost and then increased by favorable variances and decreased by unfavorable variances. The net effect of this as indicated below is to ascertain that actual costs are charged to revenue.

TABLE 12-1

Income Statement

Sales (10,000 units at $50)		$500,000
Cost of Goods Sold at Standard:		
Direct material (20,000 lb at $4)	$ 80,000	
Direct labor (30,000 hr at $6)	180,000	
Variable overhead (30,000 hr at $2)	60,000	
Fixed overhead	40,000	360,000
Standard gross margin		$140,000
Variances:		
Direct material	$ 7,000 (F)	
Direct labor	8,000 (U)	
Variable overhead	3,000 (F)	
Net		2,000 (F)
Gross profit		$142,000
Selling and administrative expenses		100,000
Net Income		$ 42,000

Standard costing makes it relatively easy for management to evaluate what has happened because it reduces the number of values that should be investigated. Management need not be concerned with every income statement item. Rather, it should investigate those areas where actual results differ from the plan. There is no need to investigate the cost of goods sold at standard, the major cost category, because it is always based on management's plan. Those areas that should be investigated are sales and the variances. Variance analysis might reveal that current standards are no longer applicable and in need of revision.

Other Applications of Variance Analysis

The variance analysis concepts developed here can serve management in areas other than standard costing. We will illustrate this by comparing planned and actual contribution margins.

	Planned		Actual
Sales (20,000 units)	$200,000	(22,000 units)	$198,000
Variable costs ($6)	120,000		132,000
Contribution margin	$ 80,000		$ 66,000
Fixed cost	40,000		40,000
Net Income	$ 40,000		$ 26,000

In this illustration we are looking for the reasons for the contribution margin and net income being $14,000 less than planned. The analysis follows the two-step process used in earlier illustrations.

Step 1.

Planned contribution margin:	20,000 units at $4.00	or $80,000
Actual contribution margin:	22,000 units at $3.00	or $66,000
Variances	2,000 units $1.00	$14,000 (U)

Step 2.

Price variance	22,000 units at $1.00	or $22,000 (U)
Quantity variance	2,000 units at $4.00	or 8,000 (F)
Net variance		$14,000 (U)

Selling 2,000 more units than planned had the potential of increasing contribution margin by $8,000, but, due to a lower selling price and contribution margin, a lower profit resulted. Selling at $9 per unit caused a $22,000 reduction in the contribution margin; selling 2,000 more units should have increased the contribution margin by $8,000, but the increase was only $6,000. The $66,000 contribution margin actually earned can be explained as follows:

Planned contribution margin (20,000 units x $4)	$80,000
Loss of contribution margin (20,000 units x $1)	20,000
Balance	$60,000

Gain in contribution margin from additional units sold (2,000 units x $3)	6,000
Total Contribution	$66,000

SUMMARY

The control process requires that actual events be compared with some benchmark. In cost control the benchmark is a standard cost or an indication of what costs should be. The difference between actual and standard cost is called a variance. Variances can be analyzed to determine why they exist, and this analysis can provide a basis for taking corrective action.

Meaningful cost control depends on the development of standards that are realistic—standards that really state what costs should be. Standards that are too tight or too loose will do more to confuse than facilitate the process of cost control.

Cost standards are established for all variable manufacturing costs. We exclude fixed costs from standard costing because for control purposes the notion of a standard fixed cost per unit of production has little meaning. Standard costing allows management to pinpoint the reasons for actual costs deviating from the standard—a foreman was lax in the management of materials or a buyer was able to save the firm money through astute purchasing practices.

Standard costing facilitates the management by exception concept because costs need to be investigated only if actual costs deviate "too much" from the standard.

KEY TERMS

currently attainable standard

favorable variance

ideal standard

management by exception

price variance

quantity variance

spending variance

standard

unfavorable variance

variance

variance analysis

QUESTIONS

1. What steps are involved in the control process?
2. How much control should management exercise over an activity?

3. What is an ideal standard?

4. Why do some managers advocate ideal standards?

5. What major advantage does a currently attainable standard have over an ideal standard?

6. Are standard costs and budgets one and the same? Explain.

7. Illustrate an ideal material standard.

8. Illustrate a currently attainable material standard.

9. Should there be a fixed overhead standard per unit of production? Explain.

10. If each wheel of an automobile is held on by five lug nuts, how many lug nuts should be allocated per 1,000 automobiles? Explain.

11. Define a price variance.

12. Define a quantity variance.

13. What is a favorable variance?

14. In a standard cost system where do all variances come to rest? Why?

15. Describe the flow of cost in a standard cost system.

16. When is a variance significant?

17. "Any unfavorable variance indicates that some manager is not doing his job." Do you agree? Explain.

18. Is the net income shown under standard costing standard net income or something else? Explain.

19. What impact does an unfavorable price variance have on the cost of goods sold?

20. What impact does a favorable price variance have on the cost of goods sold?

PROBLEMS

1. Standard costs

The purpose of this exercise is to review a number of concepts that relate to standard costs. The Mortise Company has established the following standards for a unit of production:

Direct materials, 3 lb of X at $1.50 per lb
Direct labor, 2 hr at $7.50 per hr
Variable overhead, $3.50 per direct labor-hour

Required:

a. The standard cost per unit of production is
(1) _____ for direct material
(2) _____ for direct labor
(3) _____ for variable overhead

b. If production is 10,000 units, the total of costs charged to work in process (exclusive of fixed overhead) is _____.

c. The company employs 12 direct laborers who work an 8-hr day. The standard output per day is _____ units; the direct materials that should be used per day are _____ lb costing _____, and the variable overhead cost should be _____.

d. If 45,000 lb of material are used, the direct labor cost should be _____ and the cost of variable overhead should be _____.

2. **Variance analysis**

The Capricorn Company has established the following standards for producing an item called Bango.

Material, 2 lb of X costing $5 per lb
Labor, 1 hr at $7 per hr
Variable overhead, 1 hr at $3 per hr

Last month the firm produced 8,000 Bangos and incurred the following costs:

Material, 15,900 lb of X costing $81,090
Labor, 8,100 hr costing $55,890
Variable overhead costing $25,110

Required:

a. What is the standard cost for one Bango?
b. Identify and analyze all variances.

3. **Labor cost standard**

Oak 'n Spruce Mills has given you the following data relating to the assembly of a cabinet.

Average time taken by a worker to assemble a cabinet, 15 min

Worker efficiency rating, 12 percent above average

Personal allowances, 19 percent of adjusted time

Base rate of pay for this class of work, $6 per hour

Required:

a. How many minutes should a worker be allowed to assemble a cabinet?

b. Calculate the standard output per hour.

c. What labor standard would you establish for this job?

4. Revision of standards

The following is the current standard cost for a unit of production at the Bellows Corporation:

Material	$24.00
Labor, 10 hours at $6 per hr	60.00
Variable overhead, 10 hr at $2 per hr	20.00

Management anticipates a number of changes in the period ahead that could impact on this standard cost. They are

a. Material costs will increase by 8 percent.

b. Labor rates will increase by 10 percent.

c. Negotiated work methods changes will reduce the labor input by 1 hr per unit.

d. Increases in the cost of power and indirect labor will cause the variable overhead rate to increase by 15 percent.

Required:

a. A revised standard for a unit of production.

5. Variance analysis

The Jug End Chair Corporation produces an aluminum frame lawn chair. The following standards have been established for a unit of production:

Direct material, 40 ft of tubing at $0.24 per ft	
30 yd of webbing at $0.08 per yd	
Direct labor, 1 hr at $5 per hr	
Variable overhead, $2.40 per direct labor-hour	

During the month of January 80,000 chairs were started in production and completed with the following results:

Direct material used, 3,220,000 ft of tubing costing $740,600

2,395,000 yd of webbing costing $196,390

Direct labor used, 81,000 hr costing $413,100

Variable overhead, $190,350

Required:

a. Identify and analyze each cost variance.

b. How is it possible to have a favorable material usage variance?

6. Standard costs and variances

The Samoset Corporation operates on a standard cost system. Normal capacity for the firm is 50,000 units per month. The standard costs for this level of production are

---

Material (2 lb per unit)	$120,000
Labor (½ hr per unit)	150,000
Variable overhead (½ hr per unit)	80,000

During a recent month the firm produced 52,000 units and incurred the following costs:

Material, 105,000 lb costing $128,100

Labor, 25,500 hr costing $155,550

Variable overhead, $79,050

Required:

a. What is the standard cost for a unit of production?

b. Identify and analyze all variances.

7. Labor standards and variances

Baker Brothers' methods engineer has complied the following data regarding a machining operation in the foundry.

Average time required to machine a unit, 55.5 min

Efficiency rating of worker observed, 90 percent

Personal allowances, 20 percent of adjusted time

Base pay for the operation, $7.20 per hr

During March 8,000 units were machined requiring 8,100 hr of labor costing $57,510.

Required:

a. Determine the labor cost standard.

b. Identify and analyze all variances.

8.   Contribution margin variances

The Planter Company sells a single product. Last month planned sales were 35,000 units and $350,000. Total variable costs were planned at $210,000. Actual sales were 40,000 units and $360,000. Unit variable costs were incurred as planned.

Required:

a. What is the difference between planned and actual contribution margins?

b. Prepare a report to management which explains and analyzes this difference.

9.   Cost flow and variance analysis

The following data was taken from the records of the XYZ Corp:

Standard:	
Material, 10,000 lb at	$1.00
Labor, 20,000 hr at	$6.00
Variable overhead,	$3.00 per labor-hour
Actual:	
Material, 11,000 lb at	$0.95
Labor, 19,500 hr at	$6.10
Variable overhead,	$2.90 per labor-hour

Required:

a. Identify and analyze all variances.

b. Record this data using the following T-accounts assuming that all units starting in production were completed.

Material inventory	Work in process	Finished goods
$100,000		

Cost of goods sold	Direct labor	Variable overhead

10. Variance analysis

The labor standard for a unit of production is 3 hr at $6 per hour. Last month when the firm produced 40,000 units it used 125,000 direct labor-hours costing $720,000. Because the standard cost and actual cost of direct labor are each $720,000, is there any reason for action? Explain and be specific.

11. Variances and the income statement

The following is a partial income statement for a firm that used a standard cost system:

Sales (30,000 units at $30)		$900,000
Cost of Goods Sold at Standard:		
Direct materials (30,000 at $6)	$180,000	
Direct labor (30,000 at $7)	210,000	
Variable overhead (30,000 at $4)	120,000	
Fixed overhead	100,000	610,000
Standard gross margin		$290,000
Variances:		
Direct material	4,000 (U)	
Direct labor	8,000 (F)	
Variable overhead	5,000 (F)	9,000
Gross Profit		$299,000

Required:

a. What was the actual cost of direct material, direct labor, and variable overhead?

12. Variance analysis and income statement preparation

The following data was taken from the records of Bass River Industries for the past year:

Standards Per Unit of Production:
  Direct material, 5 lb of X at $3
  Direct labor, 7 hr at $7
  Variable overhead, $4 per direct labor-hour

Actual Results:	
Sales (10,000 units at $120)	$1,200,000
Production (units)	10,000
Direct materials used (51,000 lb)	155,550
Direct labor used (68,000 hr)	482,800
Variable overhead	265,200
Selling and administrative	185,000

Required:

a. Identify and analyze all variances.

b. Prepare an income statement using Table 12-1 as a guide.

13. Labor standards

Given the following:

Average time taken by a worker to do a job, 120 sec
Worker effort and efficiency rating, 1.10
Allowance for personal, etc., 20 percent
Base rate for the job, $7.20 per hr

Required:

a. What is the standard output per hour for this job?

b. What piece rate would apply to this job?

c. Express the standard labor cost for this job.

14. Variance analysis

Formfit, Inc. manufactures slip covers for furniture. The standard cost for one slip cover style A-16 is

Direct material,	4 yd at $8
Direct labor,	6 hr at $6
Variable overhead,	$4 per direct labor-hour

Last month 5,000 units were started and completed with the following results:

Direct material used, 21,000 yd costing	$170,100
Direct labor used, 29,000 hr costing	174,000
Variable overhead	121,800
Total actual cost	$465,900
Standard cost	460,000
Difference	$ 5,900

Required:

a. What was the actual cost per unit?

b. Prepare a report to management wherein you identify precisely the reasons for the differences in cost.

c. What is the magnitude of all variances?

15. Contribution margin variances

The following are the planned and actual income statements for the Rhebus Corporation:

	Planned	*Actual*
Sales	$100,000	$107,800
Variable cost	60,000	66,000
Contribution margin	$ 40,000	$ 41,800
Fixed cost	30,000	30,000
Net Income	$ 10,000	$ 11,800

Planned sales were 20,000 units and variable costs per unit were incurred as planned.

Required:

a. How many units were sold and at what unit price?
b. Analyze the contribution margin variances.
c. What was the magnitude of the contribution margin variances?

PART 5

Additional Considerations

13 Short-Term Decisions

CHAPTER OVERVIEW

In this chapter we are concerned with a number of short-term decisions that most managers, at one time or another, must make. For our purposes the short term is a time span during which the resources of the firm remain unchanged, that is, a time span during which no new machines, buildings, and the like are acquired.

The purpose of the discussions is to show how management can maximize the utilization of existing resources. This could involve dropping a line of products, adding a line of products, selling to new and different markets, or making component parts that, in the past, have been purchased.

In this chapter we will draw on a number of concepts that were developed earlier in this text.

QUESTIONS FOR CONSIDERATION

1. Can profit be increased when goods are sold at a price that is lower than cost?
2. What factors must be considered in a decision to drop a product line?
3. What are the basic reasons for firms to produce component parts rather than to buy them in the market?
4. What is the significance of average cost in short-term decisions?
5. Can an objective of minimizing losses be justified?

The purpose of this chapter is to apply some of the concepts developed earlier to a number of short-term decision areas. The designation short term has little meaning by itself because it does not necessarily denote a specific span of time. Rather, it denotes a time span wherein the resources of the firm are unchanged. Short-term decisions are concerned with maximizing the utilization of existing resources as opposed to long-term decisions which are concerned with the acquisition of new resources such as machinery, buildings, and the like. The distinction between short term and long term is important because in the short term the best decision could be a course of action that would minimize losses; this could never be the best long-run course of action.

Simply stated, decision making is a process whereby managers bring together as much data as possible that bears on a problem, identify options regarding courses of action, and finally decide on the course of action that will be taken. In this process there is no certainty (1) that all possible courses of action will be known to the decision makers or (2) that all the data needed to make an intelligent decision will be available. Good, poor, and in-between decisions are a fact of life in all organizations.

The data to which we refer is both quantitative and qualitative. Cost data used in decision making such as "the cost savings of machine A over machine B will be $5,000 per year" is quantitative. With respect to quantitative data there are the ever-present dangers of assuming that they are accurate and relevant. Data that accurately portrays one set of conditions may not accurately portray another; data that is relevant to situation A may not be relevant in situation B. A machine that cost $100,000 and has depreciated $30,000 has a book value of $70,000—this is accurate. Financial statements will show the "worth" of this machine as $70,000. The production manager might express the worth of this machine as something greater or less than this figure, and the worth of this machine in the marketplace could be still another figure. Thus an accurate expression of worth depends on the vantage point from which it is being viewed.

The book value of a machine is relevant to a firm's financial statements but may be irrelevant to specific decisions. If a firm is considering replacing an existing piece of equipment with another, the book value of the existing equipment is not relevant to the decision. The monies spent for the machine are a "sunk" cost, and nothing can be done to alter the situation. Only activity over which management can exercise control such as incurring variable cost or discretionary fixed costs are relevant to short-term decisions.

Qualitative data is important in many decision situations. If analysis shows that the cost to make something is identical to the cost of buying it from a supplier, the "make" or "buy" decision may have to be made on qualitative grounds. Qualitative data may lack precision and be intangible, yet it can be the force that swings a decision from one direction to another. For example, economic analysis dictates that a firm should replace an old machine with a newer, more automated model. The change would eliminate a number of jobs and make remaining jobs more menial. This was contrary to management philosophy, and the new machine was not purchased.

The situations we will discuss utilize only quantitative data, but you will be able to see in a number of instances how qualitative data can influence decisions. We exclude qualitative factors because very often a person must be on the scene or must have "lived with" a firm to assess the probable impact of qualitative influences.

MARGINAL OR INCREMENTAL COST

These are the same terms and they involve the same concepts that you may have studied in an economic principles course. Accountants generally prefer to use the terms incremental or differential cost instead of marginal cost.

Incremental cost is the increase in total cost resulting from the production of one additional unit. For example,

	10 units	*11 units*
Variable cost	$100	$110
Fixed cost	500	500
Total cost	$600	$610

The cost of producing the eleventh unit is $10; this is the incremental cost. Note that $10 is also the unit variable cost. Frequently variable cost and incremental cost are the same, but sometimes they are not. It is possible that one additional unit of output could extend activity beyond the relevant range and cause both unit variable and total fixed costs to increase. Note that "one additional unit" could be just that, a batch of production, or a special order.

The incremental cost concept is especially important in decision making when a firm is operating below the upper limit of its relevant range. The reason for this is that, as stated so many times, within the relevant range unit variable cost and total fixed costs are constant regardless of the volume of activity. Within the relevant range only variable costs change in total amount. Thus any selling price that a firm can get for a product that is greater than variable cost is a "good" price. We say "good" because any contribution in the short run is better than no contribution at all.

THE SPECIAL ORDER

The Ace Motor Works produces a 3-horsepower outboard motor that it sells for $150. Projected production and sales for next year is 120,000 units, but the firm's normal rate of production is 200,000 units per year. The only opportunity Ace has to operate at capacity is to accept an offer from Sears, Roebuck to purchase, for a special promotion, 80,000 motors bearing the Sears trade name. Sears will buy the motors only if the price is "right." Determining the "right" price is the decision that Ace management must make. Ed Flinkey, the firm's cost clerk, has developed the following cost data.

	120,000 units	*200,000 units*
Variable cost	$ 9,600,000	$16,000,000
Fixed cost	5,000,000	5,080,000
Total cost	$14,600,000	$21,080,000
Average cost	$121.67	$105.40

An $80,000 increase in fixed costs will be incurred if the Sears offer is accepted because special dies must be made to emboss the Sears trade name on the motor cover.

The average cost of a motor will decline if the Sears offer is accepted because unit fixed costs decline as volume increases. Is $105.40 the lowest price that Ace can quote to Sears and not lose on the deal? Absolutely not. We introduce average cost here for another reason. Earlier, it was mentioned that data can be accurate but irrelevant to a particular decision. The average cost of $105.40 is irrelevant to this pricing decision because the $5,000,000 of fixed cost will be incurred regardless of the Sears offer. The only relevant costs are those costs that will be incurred if motors are produced for Sears. Thus the only relevant costs are $6,400,000 variable and $80,000 fixed.

Ace can sell motors to Sears for less than average cost and, at the same time, improve its profit position. The following is the budgeted income statement if 120,000 units are produced and sold.

Sales revenue (120,000 x $150)	$18,000,000
Variable cost (120,000 x $80)	9,600,000
Contribution margin	$ 8,400,000
Fixed cost	5,000,000
Net Income	$ 3,400,000

Suppose that Sears offers to pay only $85 per motor. Should the offer be accepted? The following income statement provides a basis for making a decision.

Sales revenue (120,000 x $150)	
(80,000 x $85)	$24,800,000
Variable cost (200,000 x $80)	16,000,000
Contribution margin	$ 8,800,000
Fixed cost	5,080,000
Net Income	$ 3,720,000

Selling an additional 80,000 motors at $85 each would result in an increase of $320,000 in net income. This can be calculated in a different way. Each unit sold at $85 contributes $5 to fixed cost and net income. The total increase in contribution of $400,000 is reduced by $80,000 due to the increase in fixed cost. Actually, any selling price above $81 ($6,480,000 ÷ 80,000) will improve the profit picture.

Suppose, however, that Sears' best offer is $80 per motor. Should Ace reject this offer? If the decision is based solely on the quantitative data available, the offer should be rejected because net income would decline by $80,000. If qualitative factors are introduced, the logical decision could be to accept the offer. Operating at capacity may have advantages that Ace feels are more important than $80,000. The firm may be able to avoid layoffs and their attendant problems, relations with suppliers and banks may be maintained, or management may just hate to see idle facilities.

SEGMENT ANALYSIS

The magnitude of a firm's management of cost problems depends to a great degree on the variety of activity that takes place "under one roof." If a business deals with a single product at one location, cost management problems are relatively simple. All costs are incurred for that product, all revenue is earned by that product, and all profits and losses belong to that product.

Most business firms—in fact, most institutions—are a composite of many segments each of which must bear cost and each creates certain values. These values may be sales revenue, or they may be values for other segments of the organization. Each department in a supermarket can be a segment, each product in a firm's line can be a segment, as can each branch office. As segments increase in number, it becomes increasingly difficult to isolate the costs that should be borne by each segment, and the revenues that are generated by each segment. But it is imperative that management continuously appraise each segment to determine whether it should be expanded, reduced, or eliminated. A&P uses segment analysis to determine which, if any, stores should be closed. The drugstore uses segment analysis to determine the future of its soda fountain, and the newspaper discontinues its evening edition because of what it learned through segment analysis.

Analyzing the profitability of a single segment of a firm is difficult. It is difficult because very often the revenues and expenses of a single segment are not mutually exclusive. Sales of one product may depend on the existence of another product; a money-losing product may cause another product to be profitable. This is nothing more than an application of the loss-leader concept. Many institutions cannot engage in, or reap the benefits of segment analysis because revenues and costs cannot be isolated. "Does this course break even?" is a question raised in Chapter 1. It is impossible to answer this question unless certain assumptions are made. A review of the assumptions made in answering this question will shed some light on some of the problems associated with segment analysis.

A segment of a firm should be dropped if costs can be reduced more than revenue is reduced. The impact on cost if a segment is abandoned depends on the nature of the costs involved. The variable costs associated with a segment will disappear if a segment is dropped, but total fixed costs may or may not be affected. Fixed costs may be classified as separable or joint. A separable fixed cost exists only because a segment exists—do away with the segment and the cost goes too. The rent paid for the Starve Rock sales office is separable. Whether it is separable immediately or at a later date depends on the conditions of the lease agreement. Costs that are incurred for the benefit of more than one segment are joint costs. Thus the salary of the sales manager is a joint cost that is allocated to each of the sales offices. Doing away with the Starve Rock sales office may have no effect on this cost.

Whether a cost is separable or joint depends on the vantage point from which it is viewed. If five products are sold through the Starve Rock sales office, rent is a joint cost for these products. Yet it is a separable cost from the sales manager's point of view. Over time it is quite possible for separable costs to become joint and vice versa. If enough sales offices are closed the sales manager's salary probably would be reduced.

DROPPING A SEGMENT

The following are the divisional income statements for the Ajax Company and are typical of activity for the past three years. The firm does not expect costs and revenues in any of the divisions to change significantly next year. The problem facing management is division 2, which has been operating at a loss. Should the division be dropped and will net income increase as a result? If division 2 is dropped, $70,000 of revenue will be lost. Therefore cost savings must be in excess of $70,000 to justify the move. We will use two approaches to measure the impact of dropping division 2.

	Div. 1	Div. 2	Div. 3	Total
Sales	$80,000	$70,000	$150,000	$300,000
Variable costs	52,000	56,000	90,000	198,000
Contribution margin	$28,000	$14,000	$ 60,000	$102,000
Fixed Cost:				
Joint	$ 8,800	$ 7,700	$ 16,500	$ 33,000
Separable	9,000	8,000	22,000	39,000
Total	$17,800	$15,700	$ 38,500	$ 72,000
Net Income	$10,200	$(1,700)	$ 21,500	$ 30,000

If division 2 is abandoned,

Revenue will drop		$70,000
Variable cost will drop	$56,000	
Separable cost will drop	8,000	64,000
Net income will drop		$ 6,000

Joint costs remain the same in total and must be absorbed by the remaining divisions. Thus division 2 should not be abandoned based on the data available. The same conclusion can be reached through the revised income statements.

	Div. 1	Div. 3	Total
Sales	$80,000	$150,000	$230,000
Variable costs	52,000	90,000	142,000
Contribution margin	$28,000	$ 60,000	$ 88,000
Fixed Costs:			
Joint[a]	$11,478	$ 21,522	$ 33,000
Separable	9,000	22,000	31,000
Total	$20,478	$ 43,522	$ 64,000
Net Income	$ 7,522	$ 16,478	$ 24,000

[a]Allocated based on sales volume.

Suppose it could be predicted that dropping division 2 would cause sales in division 3 to increase by 15 percent. Would this change the previous decision? If division 2 is dropped, net income will increase by the amount of contribution margin yielded by the additional sales in division 3 or $9,000 ($22,500 x .40). This would be true only if no additional fixed costs resulted from the increased volume of activity. Net income would increase to $33,000 and dropping division 2 would result in an improvement in net income.

SERVICE SEGMENTS

Waste in organization is most apt to occur in service segments rather than in line segments. There are many reasons for this, but two will be identified. First, service segments may not produce tangible goods —items whose ingredients can be precisely measured. Frequently these divisions are concerned with mental rather than manual work. Thus it may take a long time to determine the value of a given service segment. A second reason for waste is that the size—cost—of a service tends to remain relatively fixed, yet the need for service may fluctuate significantly. The problem is to equate size and need for service. Suppose that a firm has not hired an employee for three months. Should the employment office be closed? If not, at what size should it be maintained? This question is difficult to answer because there are so many intangibles involved. But this is no excuse for letting service segments go unmonitored.

Cost Centers and Profit Centers

We look at cost centers and profit centers at this point to see how they relate to service segment analysis. A cost center is any segment of a firm that has control over the incurring of cost. Cost centers do not have control over producing revenue although they do create values. Thus in cost centers it is not possible to compare costs and revenues. Rather, control is maintained by establishing standards and comparing them with actual performance. This is effective where production-type activity is being performed but quite ineffective in many service segments. What, for example, constitutes a day's work for a manager of purchasing?

Profit centers are different because they have control over both revenue and cost. Here it is relatively easy, as we saw earlier, to determine whether division 2 should be dropped. In a sense, every segment of a firm produces a form of revenue. Every service segment creates values for other segments of the firm. Wherever possible service segments should be treated as profit centers. For example, a maintenance department could be a profit center. Its "revenue" would come from the budgets of those segment that it serves. This approach can be effective especially when the service involved has a market value or when the service can be performed by an outside agency.

MAKE OR BUY DECISIONS

The phrase "make or buy" is somewhat misleading because every business must depend on outside sources for some of its needs—there is no such thing as a completely integrated firm in American business. This applies to the industrial giants as well as to the local repair shop. Many firms are committed to a high degree of vertical integration; that is, they acquire or build basic supply sources. The problem is to determine the best degree of vertical integration for the firm. The best degree depends on a number of factors, each of which is subject to change, and what is best for one firm may not be best for another. In addition, what is best today may not be best tomorrow.

For many years Sears, Roebuck owned or controlled many firms that supplied Sears' retail outlets. Today, Sears is far less involved with manufacturing. Henry Ford, the founder of the Ford Motor Company, decided years ago that certain of the firm's steel requirements would be satisfied by a company-owned steel mill. Incidentally, it still operates and is one of the nation's larger steel mills. General Motors, on the other hand, buys most of its steel from firms such as U.S. Steel.

Make or Buy Policy

Make or buy decisions are quite easily resolved when the only factors needing consideration relate to short-term costs. Cost may be but one consideration. Make or buy decisions are usually utilization of resources decisions. General Motors could, given time, produce the steel it needs, but G.M. management feels that its resources will be better utilized in other areas of activity. There may be a tendency on the part of some managers to lean toward a policy of self-support and independence, but this could be very dangerous because it could rule out the opportunity to take advantage of favorable market conditions should they exist. A policy which states "we will always make these classes of goods" or "we will always buy these classes of goods" is also dangerous and for the same reason. Perhaps the best make or buy policy is to judge each case on its merits at the time a decision must be made.

Because no American business can be self-sufficient and because all businesses have limited resources, top management must frequently answer two very important questions relating to this topic.

1. Just what is our business? This question is often overlooked because, on the surface, the answer may seem obvious. Here we are concerned for such issues as what is it that we can do better than others? What are the reasons for our successes and failures? What are our areas of expertise and how unique are they? Answers to these questions will to some degree facilitate make or buy decisions. Over the long haul, every successful business must have something better than the next guy. During the past decade more than 100 firms turned out skimobiles. Most of these firms were not manufacturers; rather, they were assemblers who purchased component parts and assembled them into a finished product that was merchandised in a market where supply and demand relationships were, for several years, favorable to them. When supply and demand relationships reversed, most of these firms were shaken out of the field—they could no longer compete. The reason that they could no longer compete is that they had no uniqueness. Most of the firms remaining in this field are manufacturers who have a well-balanced make or buy program.

2. Are we making the best use of our resources? Managers frequently fall into the we-can-do-it-cheaper trap when handling make or buy decisions. The firm is currently making a component for $10 per unit and the best market price is $11. Because of this the firm gives no consideration to buying the component. Thought should be given to the utilization of resources. It could be that the resources used to make this component can be used in some other manner that would provide a return great enough to justify purchase.

Economic Factors

The economics of the make or buy question must be considered from two sides. A firm may be making a component and is considering the use of outside sources, or it may be buying a component and is considering manufacturing it.

To illustrate the point, suppose that a firm has been making a component part for many years. Currently it costs the firm $50 to produce a unit in lots of 10,000 units. A potential supplier has offered to meet the firm's requirements for this component at a cost of $40 per unit delivered and with no sacrifice in quality or reliability of supply. Should the firm take advantage of the offer? The basic question relates to savings. Will the firm save at a rate of $10 per unit if it buys the component? We cannot answer this question with the information at hand. Two specific areas of inquiry warrant consideration. The first area is the $40 price. Is this price realistic? Is this a price that will hold in the future? If the supplier is operating below capacity and is seeking any business that will make "some" contribution, it should be expected that this may be a short-term price. Make or buy decisions should be based on future as well as current conditions. The second area involves the firm's cost structure. The approach we will use to analyze is the same as was used in segment analysis.

Make or Buy—An Illustration

The following is a summary of the costs associated with the manufacture of the component part referred to earlier.

	Unit cost	*Total cost*
Direct material	$15	$150,000
Direct labor	10	100,000
Variable overhead	10	100,000
Fixed Overhead:		
Joint	11	110,000
Separable	4	40,000
Total	$50	$500,000

The cost to make 10,000 units must be compared with the costs that would be incurred if the part was purchased. The following shows how the comparison can be made:

Cost to make (10,000 x $50)		$500,000
Cost to Buy:		
10,000 x $40	$400,000	
Joint costs that will continue	110,000	510,000
Saving if component is made		$ 10,000

Whether the firm makes or buys, the joint costs will continue. The $10,000 saving should not be a source of joy for management. Rather, management could closely examine its cost structure because the existence of joint cost may have prevented a total saving of $100,000.

Frequently make or buy decisions must involve factors other than those used in the previous illustration. Reciprocity is common in business—you buy from me and I will buy from you. Thus the lowest unit cost may not be the best cost. For example, it costs a firm $100,000 to make 10,000 units of a component each year. A supplier offers to make these units for $120,000 and will buy 5,000 units of another component from the firm having a contribution margin of $5 per unit. We do not have all the data needed to assess this proposition, but on the surface, at least, buying at a higher price could be the better course of action.

Why Firms Make Rather than Buy

All manufacturers produce certain of their components and buy certain of their components. But there are times when buying is better than making and vice versa. At one point in time American Motors produced V-6 engines for General Motors, and for many years Polaroid bought film from outside sources. Today, Polaroid makes its film. What are some of the reasons for firms' deciding to make rather than to buy?

1. *It is less costly.* We do not mean less costly as explained in the previous illustration where the firm was committed to $100,000 in joint costs. Rather we mean that because of superior engineering and design capabilities, superior manufacturing expertise, superior control systems, and the like, the firm can outperform other manufacturers, and it decides to make the component. If a firm can produce as economically as potential suppliers, it can save the profit that suppliers would expect to earn.

2. *Greater certainty of quality and delivery.* In theory, at least, if a component is made in the firm, there should be a greater degree of certainty that it will be available to the using department when needed and of the specified quality. Those who have worked in industry know that this theory often does not apply. The department producing the component may be poorly managed, or it may give a low priority to the component because it has "more important" things to do. This, then, could be a poor reason to make rather than buy. Certainty of quality and delivery is a by-product of a well-conceived and operated manufacturing facility.

3. *To maintain uniqueness.* Every firm should have some attribute that gives it identity in the marketplace. Frequently, but not always, the differentiating factor is found in the product or the process by which it is made. For years Polaroid did not manufacture film or camera boxes; there is little unique about these items. Treating and packaging film was the source of Polaroid's uniqueness, and it did perform these functions. Today Polaroid makes both camera boxes and the film for its SX 70 camera series. The reason for this change is that just about everything that this camera has to offer is unique. The point we are making is that a firm should weed out those things that others can do just as good or better and concentrate on those areas of activity where it has unique capabilities.

PARTIALLY COMPLETED PRODUCTS

There are times when products can be sold at varying degrees of completion. A textile mill can weave cloth and sell it or it can process the cloth further and sell it to garment manufacturers. A chicken farmer can raise broilers and sell them live to someone who will process and distribute them, or the farmer can do the processing and distribution himself as Frank Perdue has done so successfully.

Similarly a manufacturer may produce a product that can be sold in different markets. A spark plug manufacturer can sell his product to the automobile industry or process it further—package, promote, and distribute—for the spark plug replacement market. In each of these situations the same basic concepts apply. There is a decision point which is referred to as the split off. Broilers can be split off when they reach marketable weight; spark plugs can be split off when the manufacturing process is completed. The basic short-term decision facing management in these situations is whether an item should be sold at split off or be processed further and sold.

On the surface the problem is simple. If the revenue that can be obtained by further processing is greater than the cost of further processing, then the decision should be to process further. Note that the costs incurred up to the split-off point are irrelevant to the decision; they will not be affected by the decision. To illustrate this concept, a broiler can be sold live today for 25 cents per pound or it can be processed further and sold for 43 cents per pound. At which point should the broiler be sold? The answer depends on additional processing costs. Potential additional income is 18 cents per pound. Therefore additional processing costs would have to be less than this amount to make additional processing worthwhile.

There is an additional factor to consider. If the broiler is sold live today, both revenue and cost are known. If the decision is made to process further—sell at a later date—uncertainties enter the picture. Will additional processing costs be less than 18 cents and will there be a market for further-processed broilers at 43 cents per pound?

Capacity Utilization—Linear Programming

In many firms a single set of facilities is used to produce a variety of products. A bakery uses the same facilities to make cookies, brownies, and pastries; a stamping department produces parts for Cadillacs and Chevrolets; and the same foundry facilities are used to produce 4-, 6-, and 8-cylinder motor blocks. A problem arises when facilities are used for multiple purposes because different products require different inputs as shown in the following illustration.

| | Capacity per day | |
Department	Product A	Product B
Casting	1,200	800
Machining	1,000	1,400
Finishing	1,500	1,500
Painting	1,800	1,800

Two products, A and B, are produced via a process that uses the services of these four departments. The problem is to determine the best balance between these two products—that is, how many units of A and how many units of B should be produced per day. The best balance to maximize contribution margin may not be the best balance to maximize production or achieve some other objective. Let us assume here that we want to maximize contribution margin and that each unit of A has a contribution margin of $5 and each unit of B has a contribution margin of $6.

There would be no problem if each product required the same inputs and yielded the same contribution margin, but most often this is not the case. An obvious question at this point is why a firm would create a production facility having such a great imbalance of capacities. Our answer is that products A and B are but two of many products using these facilities and that on an overall basis capacities are balanced. Also, we have limited our illustration to two products to simplify the capacity utilization problem. If more than two products are involved, the problem becomes multidimensional and requires more mathematics than we care to discuss.

We solve this problem through graphic analysis although it can be solved mathematically. Figure 13-1 plots the capacities of each department for each of the products. This plotting allows us to narrow the combinations of product mix to the solid white area in the lower left-hand corner. Each function in the process under the right circumstances could be a constraint on possible product mixes, but in our illustration only casting (C) and machining (M) are con-

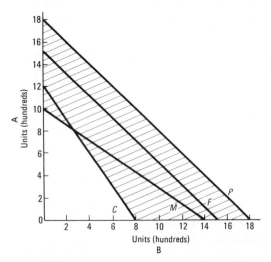

FIGURE   13-1   Linear Programming

straints. Any combination of A and B that lies within this white area is possible. No more than 1,000 units of A or 800 units of B can be produced, but this is not necessarily the best product mix. The optimal product mix always falls at one of the corners in the solid white area. We need merely measure the contribution margin at each corner to determine the optimal mix. This is shown below.

Corner		Contribution margin		Total
A	B	A	B	contribution margin
0	8	0	$48.00	$48.00
10	0	$50	0	50.00
8	2.7	40	16.20	56.20
0	0	0	0	0

Thus the optimal product mix is 800 of A and 270 of B because it yields the largest contribution margin.

SUMMARY

In this chapter we have shown how management can handle a number of short-term decisions. We have also indicated that the solutions to many problems are easily obtained provided the relevant information is available. In practice things are far less cut and dried than we have shown them to be. Our discussions, therefore, show the potential of accurate and relevant information.

In the short run management may at times have unused capacity. Any use of unused capacity that yields revenue in excess of variable costs is better than no use at all. Management should continuously monitor each segment of the firm to see if it is pulling its weight. Segments should be dropped when it results in a reduction of cost which is greater than the loss of revenue. Segment analysis is a necessary function, but its usefulness depends on the extent to which costs can be accurately allocated to each segment. Segment analysis is important for another reason. Most firms face make or buy decisions which can be a form of segment analysis—should the firm stop making component X? This question cannot be accurately answered unless component X can be segmented.

KEY TERMS

average cost	segment analysis
incremental cost	separable fixed costs
joint fixed cost	short-term decision

1. What is the meaning of short term as it relates to short-term decisions?

2. How does the long term differ from the short term?

3. Provide an illustration of both qualitative and quantitative data as it applies in decision making.

4. What is marginal or incremental cost?

5. "Incremental cost and variable cost are always the same." Do you agree? Explain.

6. "Any price that a firm can get for a product that is greater than variable cost is a good price." Do you agree? Explain.

7. "My average cost is $4.00 per unit and this guy wants me to up production and sell to him at $3.75. He must think I am crazy." Comment.

8. Why is it that the magnitude of a firm's management of cost problems depends to a great degree on the variety of activity that takes place in the firm?

9. Can all business firms successfully apply the segment analysis concept? Explain why or why not.

10. Distinguish between a separable fixed cost and a joint fixed cost.

11. Whether a cost is separable or joint depends on the vantage point from which it is viewed. Explain.

12. Why is it that waste in organizations is most apt to occur in service segments rather than in line segments?

13. Distinguish between a cost center and a profit center.

14. Is it possible for a service segment of a firm to operate as a profit center? Explain.

15. If it costs a firm $30 to make a component that an outsider can make for $25 delivered, the firm should buy the component and save $5 per unit. Comment.

PROBLEMS

1. Selling at less than average cost

Radio Hut, Inc., a chain of stores specializing in electronic products, is in the market to buy 200,000 hand calculators. The manager of purchasing approached Vermont Instruments, Inc. to see if the company would supply them at $10 each. Vermont Instrument's cost clerk provides you, the decision maker, with the following data:

	800,000 units	1,000,000 units
Variable cost	$6,400,000	$ 8,000,000
Fixed cost	3,200,000	3,400,000
Total cost	$9,600,000	$11,400,000
Average Unit Cost	$12.00	$11.40

Required:

a. If Vermont Instruments has planned production at 800,000 units and 1,000,000 units is within the relevant range, should the Radio Hut offer be accepted?

b. What impact would acceptance of this order have on the net income of Vermont Instruments?

2. The special order

The budgeted income statement for Hides, Inc., a manufacturer of hiking boots, follows:

Sales (50,000 pair)	$2,000,000
Variable cost	1,500,000
Contribution margin	$ 500,000
Fixed cost	600,000
Net Income (loss)	$ (100,000)

Mountain Trail Stores offers to buy 30,000 pair of boots for $1,200,000. If the offer were accepted, Hides would then operate at capacity.

Required:

a. Should Hides accept the offer? Explain.

b. Prepare an income statement to show the impact of accepting the Mountain Trail offer on net income.

c. If Mountain Trail Stores offered to buy 40,000 pair at the same price, would your answer be the same? Explain.

3. Special order involving overtime

The Flagstaff Corp. plans to operate at 80 percent of capacity next year and has prepared the following budgeted income statement:

Sales (80,000 Machos)		$800,000
Less Production Costs:		
Variable		
Material (160,000 lb)	$160,000	
Labor (40,000 hr)	280,000	
Variable overhead (40,000 hr)	80,000	
Total variable cost	$520,000	
Fixed overhead	96,000	
Total production costs		616,000
Gross margin		$184,000
Fixed selling and administrative		150,000
Net Income		$ 34,000

Flagstaff has been approached by a representative of the Banner Corp. to produce 40,000 Machos for them at a price of $7.00 per unit. If the offer is accepted, Flagstaff will have to work some overtime at time and a half. Fixed cost will remain the same.

Required:

a. Should Flagstaff accept the Banner Corp. offer? Explain.

b. Prepare a revised income statement which includes the impact of the Banner Corp. offer.

4. Product mix

The Wildwood Company works an average of 170 hours per month and has 10 direct laborers. The plant can produce two different bird houses, the Flicker and the Cardinal. 300 Flicker bird houses can be produced per hour or 400 Cardinal bird houses. The Flicker sells for $15 and has a variable cost of $6 per unit. The Cardinal sells for $12 and has a variable cost of $7 per unit.

Required:

a. Which of these bird houses should be produced, all other factors being equal?

5. Selecting a line of products

Several years ago Bill Thornton took an early retirement and bought a general store in a small New Hampshire town. Over several years he eliminated a number of lines of goods that just were not selling, so at the present time he deals almost exclusively in grocery-store items. The reduction in the line of goods has left a good-size portion of the store unused, and Bill now wants to make this area a revenue producer. After considerable inquiry he has narrowed his choices of how this area should be used to packaged hardware items or to beer and wine. Bill is currently analyzing the following data to determine which, if either, line should be added:

	If hardware	If beer and wine
Additional sales	$15,000	$50,000
Contribution margin	40%	22%
Additional annual fixed cost	$ 1,000	$ 5,000
Increase in grocery sales due to increased traffic	5%	12%

In addition to this data, Bill also has last year's income statement for the grocery business:

Sales		$80,000
Cost of goods sold	$48,000	
Other variable costs	8,000	56,000
Contribution margin		$24,000
Fixed costs		16,000
Net Income		$ 8,000

Required:

a. Which, if either, of the product lines should be added to utilize the available space?

b. Prepare income statements showing the impact of adding each product line.

6. Dropping a product line

One year ago Millie Frank, owner of Frankie's Pizza Parlor, decided to open early in the day and serve breakfasts. Because this was an experiment the proprietor kept accurate records for the year and reports the following:

	Breakfasts	Pizza	Total
Sales	$30,000	$90,000	$120,000
Variable cost	10,500	36,000	46,500
Contribution margin	$19,500	$54,000	$ 73,500

Fixed Costs:			
Separable	$ 8,000	$14,000	$ 22,000
Joint	12,000	26,000	38,000
Total fixed cost	$20,000	$40,000	$ 60,000
Net Income (loss)	$ (500)	$14,000	$ 13,500

Required:

a. Should the breakfast segment of the business be discontinued?

b. How certain can the owner be that breakfasts are losing money?

7. Dropping a segment

The Armco Corporation has manufactured and sold three products for several years. The following income statement is typical of Armco's recent experience:

	Alphas	*Beta*	*Chi*	*Total*
Sales	$500,000	$300,000	$200,000	$1,000,000
Variable cost	200,000	135,000	120,000	455,000
Contribution margin	$300,000	$165,000	$ 80,000	$ 545,000
Fixed Cost:				
Joint	$120,000	$ 72,000	$ 48,000	$ 240,000
Separable	50,000	40,000	35,000	125,000
Net Income (loss)	$130,000	$ 53,000	$ (3,000)	$ 180,000

Required:

a. On a purely economic basis should Armco drop product Chi? Explain.

b. Prepare a revised income statement assuming product Chi was dropped.

c. Suppose that the sales of Alpha will increase 20 percent if Chi is dropped. Will this change your answer? Explain.

8. Make or buy decision

Tarco Pump Co. has been making a pump housing in its foundry for many years. Currently it costs Tarco $45 to produce a casting in lots of 1,000 units as shown below:

	Unit cost	Total cost
Raw material	$12	$12,000
Direct labor	11	11,000
Variable overhead	4	4,000
Joint fixed cost	8	8,000
Separable fixed cost	10	10,000
Total	$45	$45,000

Walex Foundry has agreed to make these castings for Tarco at a cost of $35 each with no sacrifice in quality or delivery.

Required:

a. Should Tarco accept the Walex offer? Explain.

9. Make or buy

Raython Electronics produces a servo mechanism that uses a gear box component. Raython has been making the gear box for many years and the following are the costs for a typical production run:

	Unit cost	Total cost
Raw material	$ 4.60	$ 460
Direct labor	24.40	2,440
Variable overhead	3.00	300
Joint fixed cost	5.00	500
Separable fixed cost	3.00	300
Total cost	$40.00	$4,000

Paragon Gear Co. has approached Raython and offered to make the gear boxes in lots of 100 units for $38 per unit.

Required:

a. Should Raython accept the Paragon offer?

b. Two days later, Paragon contacted Raython stating that it would purchase 100 Raython model S496 activating mechanisms for each 100 gear boxes Raython ordered from them. Model S496 sells for $18 and has a variable cost of $12. Raython has more than enough available capacity to satisfy Paragon's requirements. Is this a good deal for Raython? Explain.

10. Make or buy

The following are the estimated costs to produce a batch of component 19 during the next budget period at the Agar Co.:

	Unit cost	Total cost
Direct materials	$ 3.00	$ 15,000
Direct labor	9.00	45,000
Variable overhead	4.00	20,000
Joint fixed overhead	3.00	15,000
Separable fixed overhead	2.00	10,000
Total	$21.00	$105,000

The Compact Corp., a reliable supplier of other components, has offered to make component 19 for $19.50 per unit, and there would be no sacrifice in quality or delivery.

Required:

a. Compact has guaranteed this price for a twelve-month period. Should the offer be accepted? Explain.

b. Suppose that as a part of the offer, Compact agreed to lease Agar's multi-purpose punch press for a year at a rental of $7,500. Would your answer be different? Explain.

11. Split-off points

The AD Spark Plug Co. has a production capacity of 50 million plugs a year. The average unit cost of a plug is $0.15. 20 million plugs have been ordered by AD's parent company, Major Motors, Inc., for next year at a price of $0.18 per unit. Management is considering two alternatives to utilize the remaining capacity. The first alternative is to develop trade with other automobile manufacturers at home and abroad, and the second is to develop the spark plug replacement market. If the first alternative is chosen, additional "leg work" and engineering costs will boost costs by $0.045 per plug. It is estimated that the automotive trade will pay $0.235 per plug. The second alternative will require packaging, warehousing, advertising and promotion, and the establishment of a distribution organization. This will increase costs by an average of $0.22 per plug. AD would sell plugs to distributors for an average of $0.40 per plug.

Required:

a. Assuming that either alternative can generate sales of 30 million plugs per year, which alternative should be selected based on the data given? Explain.

b. What other factors should be considered in an appraisal of these alternatives?

12. Split-off points

Casco Canneries, owners of the Happy Giant brand, has two marketing alternatives for its whole-kernel corn. It can be sold unlabeled for 36 cents a can, or it can be sold under the brand name for 43 cents per can. If sold under the brand name, additional costs for labeling, distribution, and promotion will average 6 cents per can.

Required:

a. How should Casco distribute its whole-kernel corn?

13. A different type of split-off

One year ago the Gillette Corporation decided to get into the digital watch business. Soon after making a number of commitments, technological advances made it possible for other manufacturers to sell a digital watch for $15 or less. At this point in time Gillette had about 30,000 watches in production that were approximately 75 percent completed. Costs incurred to bring watches to this state of completion were

	Unit cost	*Total cost*
Direct material	$ 8	$240,000
Direct labor	9	270,000
Variable overhead	8	240,000
Total	$25	$750,000

Additional costs to process and distribute the watches are estimated to be $10 per unit.

Required:

a. Which of the following courses of action should Gillette follow?

(1) Complete production of the watches and sell them for $12 each.

(2) Declare the entire lot of watches junk and sell them for $25,000.

(3) Dismantle the watches at a cost of $8 per unit and sell the component parts for $10 per unit.

b. Can you suggest any additional alternatives?

14. A simple split-off problem

The Bicco Corp. produces three products that can be sold at split off or processed further and sold in a different market. The following data is given:

Item	Sales price at split off	Sales price with further processing	Additional processing cost
A	$ 9,000	$14,000	$ 6,000
B	12,000	21,000	10,000
C	18,000	20,000	2,000

Required:

a. Which items should be processed further? Show why.

b. Are there other factors that should be considered in addition to the above data?

15. Capacity utilization

The Carmote Company produces two products using the same production facilities. Capacities per day are

	Bumpers	Backers
Stamping	1,200	2,000
Machining	2,400	800
Finishing	1,500	1,000

Each bumper has a contribution margin of $12; each backer, $10.

Required:

a. Find the optimum number of bumpers and backers that should be produced to maximize contribution margin.

14 Capital-Budgeting Decisions

CHAPTER OVERVIEW

Sooner or later every successful business must make capital budgeting decisions, that is, decisions that involve the purchase of new facilities or equipment. Capital-budgeting decisions frequently involve large sums of money and may have a long-term impact on the firm's finances and profitability. Few firms have enough funds to approve all requests for capital expenditures that will be made. Consequently management must have the capability of evaluating investment proposals so that only the most promising are allocated funds. Funds should not be invested in new facilities unless they can either increase revenues or decrease operating costs.

In this chapter we will discuss a number of techniques that measure the return a specific investment proposal is likely to yield. Frequently management will establish minimum rates of return for investments and eliminate proposals that fail to meet this standard. The techniques discussed range from simple payback calculations to the more involved discounted cash flow concept.

QUESTIONS FOR CONSIDERATION

1. Why must all successful firms make capital-budgeting decisions?
2. What does capital-budgeting philosophy mean or imply?
3. Are capital-budgeting decisions always made based on economic analysis?
4. What is the difference between cash flow and profit?
5. Is the most profitable investment always the best investment?

Unlike short-term decisions which center around the maximum utilization of existing resources, capital-budgeting decisions are investment-related decisions that center around the acquisition of resources such as land, buildings, and machinery. As a generalization, short-term decisions have a short-term impact on profits, whereas long-term decisions have a long-term impact on profits. Once a long-term decision is made, the firm may have to live with it for a long time. In addition, the wisdom of a short-term decision may become apparent within months or less, whereas it may take several years to feel or measure the impact of certain capital-budgeting decisions. In many ways the long-range future of a firm depends on its capital-budgeting decisions.

CAPITAL BUDGETING
AND THE MANAGEMENT OF COST

Capital budgeting requires an understanding of costs, cost characteristics, and cost behavior. You learned earlier that virtually every product and every service can be produced in a variety of ways and that different approaches to production may result in different balances between fixed and variable costs. For a particular firm at a given point in time, the best investment may be one that has low fixed cost and high variable cost. For another firm it may be just the opposite. If high levels of activity are expected, relatively high total fixed costs may produce the lowest total unit cost. The best balance of fixed and variable cost, therefore, must consider the firm's long-range goals or expectations.

CAPITAL BUDGETING PHILOSOPHY

Capital budgeting should be an integral part of a firm's long-range planning. No long-range plan should be considered complete or adequate if it does not include the firm's long-range resource needs. Without long-range goals it would be difficult to determine whether a particular investment should or should not be made. There should be no other reason for acquiring resources than to achieve objectives. Objectives provide a basis for determining the types and amounts of resources that should be acquired.

You may have seen a machine shop located in a rundown building and in a slum section of town. Inside you may have seen antiquated equipment, congestion, a poor layout of facilities, and the appearance of disorder. You also may have seen a machine shop located in a modern industrial park with the most modern equipment, an optimum layout of facilities, and an appearance of order. Should we conclude from these observations that one firm is poorly managed and without a plan, whereas the other firm is well managed and has a long-range plan? Absolutely not. The first shop may be highly profitable and following its plan to the letter. It may be that its long-term assets are fully depreciated and thus a cost—depreciation—has been eliminated that the other shop must include in its pricing. Investment philosophies vary. One firm that has outgrown its rundown building may choose to relocate in a larger rundown building. Another firm may solve its growth problem by constructing a new facility. In either case, management may have made the right decision, or the wrong decision.

A UNIVERSAL PROBLEM

Sooner or later every successful firm must make capital-budgeting decisions. Eventually, every machine will wear out or become obsolete, eventually new housing must be obtained, and, if the firm is growing, additional resources will be needed. In addition, technological progress may dictate that certain long-term assets be replaced prior to the end of their planned useful life.

It is generally the case that investment opportunities for a firm will outstrip the firm's capacity to finance them. Consequently, management should have the tools needed to evaluate every investment opportunity to ascertain that its limited resources will be applied in the best possible manner. Good investment opportunities do not automatically appear on the scene when needed. Management must actively seek out investment alternatives, and good capital-budgeting decisions generally stem from good capital-budgeting alternatives. It is quite possible that the best investment alternative will never receive consideration simply because management does not know that such an alternative exists.

Requests for capital funds may originate for a variety of reasons and in a variety of locations within the firm. The responsibility for deciding which of these requests will be funded can be decentralized or centralized. In some firms, the capital-budgeting pool is allocated to the various departments or divisions, and the managers of these segments decide which requests will get the go-ahead. The bases for allocating these funds are quite variable and could include sales volume of the segments and product development programs in various segments, or there may be a desire to give some funds to every segment.

Another, a possibly better, approach to the allocation of capital-budgeting resources is to centralize investment decisions. There may be a capital-budgeting committee which screens all requests for funds and accepts only the most promising regardless of the division where they originate. The logic of this approach is that the quality of investments can be improved if every request is made to compete with all other requests. This approach to capital budgeting also provides upper management with a measure of the ability of subordinate managers to seek out and evaluate investment opportunities.

THE NATURE OF THE PROBLEM

Simply stated, capital budgeting involves a number of cost-benefit analyses. Every investment should provide a return to the firm, and every investment involves a cost. Obviously, the return should be greater than the cost, and management frequently establishes investment standards to distinguish between acceptable and unacceptable investment proposals. For example, a firm may have a policy of rejecting any investment proposal that will not yield, say, 18 percent. It should be noted that measuring the rate of return on a long-term investment is a risky undertaking. The basic purpose of making investments is to increase revenues or to reduce operating costs, the net result of which is an improved profit picture. But predicting the impact of a particular investment on revenues and expenses cannot be done with complete accuracy. Increased revenues depend on a favorable market response to the firm's line of goods, and future cost reductions depend on the proper selection and use of resources.

The time frame for many capital budgeting projects can span several years, and this magnifies the risk factor. At one point in time the Chrysler Corporation decided to invest in a new manufacturing facility. This decision was based on a perceived favorable market response to Chrysler products in the years ahead. Long before the plant was completed, it became evident that the market forecast was overly optimistic and that there would be no need for the new facility. Although completed, the new plant was never used by Chrysler. Also, it is seldom certain that a particular investment will reduce costs to the degree expected, or as much as might have been the case had a different investment alternative been selected.

Some investments, because of their nature, are very risky, and others are not. Investing in a manufacturing facility, for example, can be a low-risk venture. In today's economic environment investments of this nature can appreciate 10 percent or more per year while lying idle. Referring back to the Chrysler illustration, we should not assume that building the plant was a poor investment; it was built for the wrong reason. Chrysler ultimately sold the plant to a German firm and conceivably may have earned a handsome return on its investment. Other investments that may look good today may turn sour tomorrow. If the level of technological change is high, the investment risk is also high due to the obsolescence factor. Technological change is rapid today in minicomputers, digital watches, and copying equipment, for example. Recently one producer of copying equipment announced a machine having a capacity of 2,500 copies per hour. Within a week, a competitor announced a machine that did the same thing at the rate of 4,200 copies per hour and at little additional cost.

Later in this chapter we will discuss capital-budgeting techniques. All these techniques require an estimate of the annual flow of cash savings (to be defined later) that an investment will produce. But, as we have seen, the flow of cash savings could dry up over night because someone comes up with a better idea. Knowledge of the state of technological advancements is essential in many capital-budgeting situations. Put another way, the risk factor can be critical to the direction of capital budgeting decisions.

Regardless of the risk factor, investments must be made if the firm is to prosper. Consequently management must gather the most accurate data possible and apply the best tools of analysis to reduce the possibility of making bad investments. In essence, this is what capital budgeting is all about.

A DUAL PROBLEM

Capital-budgeting decisions involve two distinct yet interrelated areas of concern. The first, the investment decision, relates to the types of investments that the firm should make. For example, management decides that the firm should invest in a new building or machine. The second relates to the source from which the capital to finance the investment will be obtained and the price—interest or dividends, for example—that must be paid for that capital. The cost of capital is a very important consideration in capital-budgeting decisions; often it is the deciding factor.

Determining the cost of capital is more in the province of the finance function than the management-of-cost function. Consequently only a brief reference will be made to this topic. The cost of capital is defined as that rate of return on investment that will leave unchanged the value of the firm. That is, a firm will pay no more than 10 percent for capital if the expected return from investing that capital is only 10 percent.

In theory, managements apply this concept; in practice, managements may do something quite different. If a firm has a large surplus of cash that should be invested, management has considerable latitude in selecting the investments it will make because there is no out-of-pocket cost of capital. Offices will be elaborately refurbished, executives will be given company cars, and the like, simply because "we can afford it." Investments that will yield less than the desired rate of return are made on the premise that other investments will yield more than the desired rate of return, and so on. We would be remiss, however, if we did not underscore that managements should adopt the cost of capital definition given.

CAPITAL BUDGETING AND CASH FLOW

Investments are made with the expectation that long-run profits will thereby increase. However, it does not necessarily follow that top priority will be given to that investment alternative that is expected to yield the greatest profit. The reason for this is that the measurement of profit does not consider cash flow, and no firm can exist for long without cash. It is true that over the long run profit will become cash, provided that the assumptions used when income is measured actually hold true. However, it can take weeks or months to convert profit into cash. Management, therefore, may be forced to make investments based on the firm's cash position.

The immediate impact of certain types of investments might be to reduce cash requirements or to increase cash requirements. Consequently a firm may be forced to accept an investment that can generate $10,000 in cash savings in the immediate future over an investment that can generate $20,000 in cash savings over a longer time frame. Many firms are forced to forego long-term profit maximization to preserve a viable short-term cash position. Over the long run, profit is a prime consideration. In the short run, cash is of greater importance than profit.

Cash Inflows and Outflows

Cash inflows that can be expected if an investment is made include first any increase in revenue. That increase in revenue resulting from making an investment is considered a cash inflow. Note that many times it is difficult to isolate those revenues that are the direct result of a specific investment. A second source of cash inflows is the cost savings that result from an investment such as a reduction in direct labor cost. The net effect of such a savings is a reduction in cash outflow. A third source of cash inflows may come from a reduction in working capital requirements. More and more soft drink makers no longer buy and hold in inventory the cans needed in the production process. Rather, these firms have invested in machinery that makes cans as a part of the production process. Thus these firms invest in the raw materials needed to make cans, and this results in lower inventory investment. Another reason that the industry is moving in this direction is that wages in the metal industries are $1.00-2.00 per hour higher than in the soft drink industry. A final source of cash inflows comes from noncash expenses. Depreciation and some forms of amortization are charges against revenue that do not require the expenditure of cash.

Cash outflows include the dollars required to pay for the investment. This could be the entire cost of the investment made in a single payment or payments may be extended over a period of time. Other cash outflows are the cost of making the asset operative, any additional working capital requirements or operating costs, plus the cost of repairs and maintenance. A basic task facing management is an accurate estimate of both cash inflows and outflows attribut-able to the investment. Any investment should produce a net cash inflow and this cash inflow must be large enough to provide the desired rate of return both in the short-run and in the long-run.

CAPITAL-BUDGETING TECHNIQUES

A number of techniques are available to management to evaluate investment opportunities. It must be emphasized that any technique no matter how simple or complex cannot provide management with a decision base unless the data used is reliable. Incorrect assumptions are more often the cause of bad investment decisions than the capital-budgeting technique applied. Thus, as indicated, a most important aspect of capital budgeting is the amount of cash flow that can be expected and over what time span.

Another important aspect of capital budgeting is selecting the correct technique for evaluation. It would be very unwise to assume that there is one approach that is always the best. One technique might present a favorable picture of an investment alternative, and another technique might present an unfavorable picture. The wrong approach could show an obviously good investment opportunity to be bad and vice versa. Management needs to know what each tech-nique does and does not do. An examination of the more popular capital budgeting techniques follows.

Payback

Payback is the simplest of the techniques because all that it does is to express the number of years that it will take for cash savings to equal the original investment. Thus if a machine costing $100,000 promises to produce cash savings of $25,000 per year, the payback is four years ($100,000 ÷ $25,000). In general, the shorter the payback period, the better. Also, the risk of obsolescence increases with the length of the payback period.

Although simple, the payback technique has a number of weak-nesses. This technique emphasizes liquidity and ignores long-term profitability. The useful life of an investment after payback is very important because savings after payback are cash. If the useful life of the machine mentioned earlier is estimated to be five years, the investment will produce an increased cash flow of $25,000. Another investment having a longer payback may be "better" if the total savings after payback is greater. This is shown in the following illustration.

	Machine A	*Machine B*
Investment	$60,000	$80,000
Annual savings	$15,000	$16,000
Expected life	5 years	8 years

Machine A has a payback of four years; machine B has a payback of five years. However, machine A has but one year of useful life after payback and should generate only $15,000 in profit. Machine B has three years of useful life after payback and should generate $48,000 in profit. Another weakness of the payback technique is that it ignores the time value of money. This concept is discussed later in this chapter.

Accounting Rate of Return

This technique compares the average annual profit after taxes that an investment is expected to generate to the investment involved. Thus if an investment of $200,000 is expected to yield an after-tax profit of $50,000, the accounting rate of return is 25 percent. Firms that use this technique establish acceptable rates of return to evaluate investment proposals. This is a simple technique to use because the values needed are readily available, but it ignores both cash flow and the time value of money.

TIME VALUE OF MONEY

The time at which cash savings are received is an important part of capital-budgeting decisions. An investment that requires eight years to produce cash savings of $10,000 is not as good as one that will produce the same savings in a shorter span of time. The reason for this is that a dollar in hand today is worth more than a dollar in hand one year from today. The following discussion is a simplified explanation of the time value of money concept when the interest rate is 10 percent.

Year	Amount	Interest	Total
1	$1.000	$0.10	$1.100
2	1.100	0.11	1.121
3	1.121	0.121	1.331
4	1.331	0.133	1.464
5	1.464	0.146	1.610

Thus $1.00 invested today at 10 percent will be worth $1.61 in five years if interest is compounded annually. But $1.00 received at some future date is worth less than $1.00 today. If we divide $1.00 by its future value, we obtain the present value of $1.00.

Year received	Amount	Future value	Present value factor	Sum of factors
1	$1.00	$1.100	$0.909	$0.909
2	1.00	1.121	0.826	1.735
3	1.00	1.331	0.751	2.486
4	1.00	1.464	0.683	3.169
5	1.00	1.610	0.621	3.790

Thus $1.00 to be received one year from today is worth $0.909 today or $0.909 today will be worth $1.00 one year from today if interest is 10 percent, and $1.00 to be received five years from today is worth $0.621 today, and so on.

The annuity concept. The cash savings from an investment if constant from year to year are similar to an annuity. Thus receiving $1.00 per year for two years is the equivalent of having $1.735 today; receiving $1.00 per year for five years is the equivalent of having $3.790 today. These values are shown in the sum of factors column in the preceding table. Receiving $1,000 in savings per year over a five-year period is the equivalent of receiving $3,790 today (provided that interest is 10 percent compounded annually). Compound interest tables are available to show how $1.00 grows at different interest rates and over different spans of time. Similarly, present value tables (see Tables 14-1 and 14-2) eliminate the need for the calculations shown above. Note that Table 14-2 does nothing more than add the values shown in Table 14-1. The reason that we have included these calculations is to remove any mystery that may surround the present value concept.

DISCOUNTED CASH FLOW

This capital-budgeting technique recognizes that the savings produced by an investment flow into the firm over a period of time and that savings to be received in the future must be discounted so that their time value can be compared to dollars in hand today.

Suppose that an investment of $100,000 is expected to produce a stream of savings amounting to $25,000 per year for a five-year period. Suppose also that the firm desires to earn a 10 percent return on its investment. Is this a good investment? We will first use a long-way-around approach to answer the question.

$25,000 received 1 year from today is worth $22,725 today ($25,000 x $0.909)

$25,000 received 2 years from today is worth $20,650 today ($25,000 x $0.826)

$25,000 received 3 years from today is worth $18,775 today ($25,000 x $0.751)

$25,000 received 4 years from today is worth $17,075 today ($25,000 x $0.683)

$25,000 received 5 years from today is worth $15,525 today ($25,000 x $0.621)

Present value of this stream of savings = $94,750

Thus the stream of savings promised by this investment have a present value of $94,750, which is $5,250 less than the amount needed to produce a 10 percent return. Based solely on economic analysis, this investment proposal would be rejected.

A simpler way to handle this problem is to refer to Table 14-2. Go down the years column to 5 and across to the 10 percent column where you will find the factor 3.790. Multiply this factor by $25,000 and the result is $94,750.

Another Illustration of Discounted Cash Flow

A firm plans to invest $240,000 in a machine that promises annual cash savings of $80,000 per year over a five-year period. The

TABLE 14-1
Present Value of $1

PERIODS	4%	6%	8%	10%	12%	14%	16%	18%	20%	22%	24%	26%	28%	30%	40%
1	.962	.943	.926	.909	.893	.877	.862	.847	.833	.820	.806	.794	.781	.769	.714
2	.925	.890	.857	.826	.797	.769	.743	.718	.694	.672	.650	.630	.610	.592	.510
3	.889	.840	.794	.751	.712	.675	.641	.609	.579	.551	.524	.500	.477	.455	.364
4	.855	.792	.735	.683	.636	.592	.552	.516	.482	.451	.423	.397	.373	.350	.260
5	.822	.747	.681	.621	.567	.519	.476	.437	.402	.370	.341	.315	.291	.269	.186
6	.790	.705	.630	.564	.507	.456	.410	.370	.335	.303	.275	.250	.227	.207	.133
7	.760	.665	.583	.513	.452	.400	.354	.314	.279	.249	.222	.198	.178	.159	.095
8	.731	.627	.540	.467	.404	.351	.305	.266	.233	.204	.179	.157	.139	.123	.068
9	.703	.592	.500	.424	.361	.308	.263	.225	.194	.167	.144	.125	.108	.094	.048
10	.676	.558	.463	.386	.322	.270	.227	.191	.162	.137	.116	.099	.085	.073	.035
11	.650	.527	.429	.350	.287	.237	.195	.162	.135	.112	.094	.079	.066	.056	.025
12	.625	.497	.397	.319	.257	.208	.168	.137	.112	.092	.076	.062	.052	.043	.018
13	.601	.469	.368	.290	.229	.182	.145	.116	.093	.075	.061	.050	.040	.033	.013
14	.577	.442	.340	.263	.205	.160	.125	.099	.078	.062	.049	.039	.032	.025	.009
15	.555	.417	.315	.239	.183	.140	.108	.084	.065	.051	.040	.031	.025	.020	.006
16	.534	.394	.292	.218	.163	.123	.093	.071	.054	.042	.032	.025	.019	.015	.005
17	.513	.371	.270	.198	.146	.108	.080	.060	.045	.034	.026	.020	.015	.012	.003
18	.494	.350	.250	.180	.130	.095	.069	.051	.038	.028	.021	.016	.012	.009	.002
19	.475	.331	.232	.164	.116	.083	.060	.043	.031	.023	.017	.012	.009	.007	.002
20	.456	.312	.215	.149	.104	.073	.051	.037	.026	.019	.014	.010	.007	.005	.001
21	.439	.294	.199	.135	.093	.064	.044	.031	.022	.015	.011	.008	.006	.004	.001
22	.422	.278	.184	.123	.083	.056	.038	.026	.018	.013	.009	.006	.004	.003	.001
23	.406	.262	.170	.112	.074	.049	.033	.022	.015	.010	.007	.005	.003	.002	
24	.390	.247	.158	.102	.066	.043	.028	.019	.013	.008	.006	.004	.003	.002	
25	.375	.233	.146	.092	.059	.038	.024	.016	.010	.007	.005	.003	.002	.001	
26	.361	.220	.135	.084	.053	.033	.021	.014	.009	.006	.004	.002	.002	.001	
27	.347	.207	.125	.076	.047	.029	.018	.011	.007	.005	.003	.002	.001	.001	
28	.333	.196	.116	.069	.042	.026	.016	.010	.006	.004	.002	.002	.001	.001	
29	.321	.185	.107	.063	.037	.022	.014	.008	.005	.003	.002	.001	.001	.001	
30	.308	.174	.099	.057	.033	.020	.012	.007	.004	.003	.002	.001	.001	.001	
40	.208	.097	.046	.022	.011	.005	.003	.001	.001						

TABLE 14-2

Present Value of $1 Received Annually for n Years

PERIODS	4%	6%	8%	10%	12%	14%	16%	18%	20%	22%	24%	25%	26%	28%	30%	40%
1	0.962	0.943	0.926	0.909	0.893	0.877	0.862	0.847	0.833	0.820	0.806	0.800	0.794	0.781	0.769	0.714
2	1.886	1.833	1.783	1.736	1.690	1.647	1.605	1.566	1.528	1.492	1.457	1.440	1.424	1.392	1.361	1.224
3	2.775	2.673	2.577	2.487	2.402	2.322	2.246	2.174	2.106	2.042	1.981	1.952	1.923	1.868	1.816	1.589
4	3.630	3.465	3.312	3.170	3.037	2.914	2.798	2.690	2.589	2.494	2.404	2.362	2.320	2.241	2.166	1.849
5	4.452	4.212	3.993	3.791	3.605	3.433	3.274	3.127	2.991	2.864	2.745	2.689	2.635	2.532	2.436	2.035
6	5.242	4.917	4.623	4.355	4.111	3.889	3.685	3.498	3.326	3.167	3.020	2.951	2.885	2.759	2.643	2.168
7	6.002	5.582	5.206	4.868	4.564	4.288	4.039	3.812	3.605	3.416	3.242	3.161	3.083	2.937	2.802	2.263
8	6.733	6.210	5.747	5.335	4.968	4.639	4.344	4.078	3.837	3.619	3.421	3.329	3.241	3.076	2.925	2.331
9	7.435	6.802	6.247	5.759	5.328	4.946	4.607	4.303	4.031	3.786	3.566	3.463	3.366	3.184	3.019	2.379
10	8.111	7.360	6.710	6.145	5.650	5.216	4.833	4.494	4.192	3.923	3.682	3.571	3.465	3.269	3.092	2.414
11	8.760	7.887	7.139	6.495	5.938	5.453	5.029	4.656	4.327	4.035	3.776	3.656	3.544	3.335	3.147	2.438
12	9.385	8.384	7.536	6.814	6.194	5.660	5.197	4.793	4.439	4.127	3.851	3.725	3.606	3.387	3.190	2.456
13	9.986	8.853	7.904	7.103	6.424	5.842	5.342	4.910	4.533	4.203	3.912	3.780	3.656	3.427	3.223	2.468
14	10.563	9.295	8.244	7.367	6.628	6.002	5.468	5.008	4.611	4.265	3.962	3.824	3.695	3.459	3.249	2.477
15	11.118	9.712	8.559	7.606	6.811	6.142	5.575	5.092	4.675	4.315	4.001	3.859	3.726	3.483	3.268	2.484
16	11.652	10.106	8.851	7.824	6.974	6.265	5.669	5.162	4.730	4.357	4.033	3.887	3.751	3.503	3.283	2.489
17	12.166	10.477	9.122	8.022	7.120	6.373	5.749	5.222	4.775	4.391	4.059	3.910	3.771	3.518	3.295	2.492
18	12.659	10.828	9.372	8.201	7.250	6.467	5.818	5.273	4.812	4.419	4.080	3.928	3.786	3.529	3.304	2.494
19	13.134	11.158	9.604	8.365	7.366	6.550	5.877	5.316	4.844	4.442	4.097	3.942	3.799	3.539	3.311	2.496
20	13.590	11.470	9.818	8.514	7.469	6.623	5.929	5.353	4.870	4.460	4.110	3.954	3.808	3.546	3.316	2.497
21	14.029	11.764	10.017	8.649	7.562	6.687	5.973	5.384	4.891	4.476	4.121	3.963	3.816	3.551	3.320	2.498
22	14.451	12.042	10.201	8.772	7.645	6.743	6.011	5.410	4.909	4.488	4.130	3.970	3.822	3.556	3.323	2.498
23	14.857	12.303	10.371	8.883	7.718	6.792	6.044	5.432	4.925	4.499	4.137	3.976	3.827	3.559	3.325	2.499
24	15.247	12.550	10.529	8.985	7.784	6.835	6.073	5.451	4.937	4.507	4.143	3.981	3.831	3.562	3.327	2.499
25	15.622	12.783	10.675	9.077	7.843	6.873	6.097	5.467	4.948	4.514	4.147	3.985	3.834	3.564	3.329	2.499
26	15.983	13.003	10.810	9.161	7.896	6.906	6.118	5.480	4.956	4.520	4.151	3.988	3.837	3.566	3.330	2.500
27	16.330	13.211	10.935	9.237	7.943	6.935	6.136	5.492	4.964	4.524	4.154	3.990	3.839	3.567	3.331	2.500
28	16.663	13.406	11.051	9.307	7.984	6.961	6.152	5.502	4.970	4.528	4.157	3.992	3.840	3.568	3.331	2.500
29	16.984	13.591	11.158	9.370	8.022	6.983	6.166	5.510	4.975	4.531	4.159	3.994	3.841	3.569	3.332	2.500
30	17.292	13.765	11.258	9.427	8.055	7.003	6.177	5.517	4.979	4.534	4.160	3.995	3.842	3.569	3.332	2.500
40	19.793	15.046	11.925	9.779	8.244	7.105	6.234	5.548	4.997	4.544	4.166	3.999	3.846	3.571	3.333	2.500

*Payments (or receipts) at the *end* of each period.

desired rate of return is 16 percent. The question is whether the savings are adequate to yield the desired rate of return.

Investment	$240,000
Present value of savings:	
$80,000 x 3.274[a]	261,920
Net Present Value	$ 21,920

[a]From Table 14-2, present value of $1 received annually for *n* years. Read down the years column to 5 and across to the 16 percent column.

In this case the savings is more than adequate to produce a return of 16 percent. Based solely on economic analysis, this investment proposal should be accepted.

Time-adjusted Rate of Return

In a previous illustration, a flow of $25,000 in cash savings over a five-year period was not adequate to provide a 10 percent return on an investment of $100,000. Before discarding the investment proposal, management might want to know the rate of return that these savings would generate. A simple way to determine the actual rate of return is as follows. First, find that factor which, when multiplied by $25,000, equals $100,000. In this illustration the factor is 4 ($100,000 ÷ $25,000), the same as payback. Using Table 14-2, follow the five-year line across until the nearest value to 4 is located. 3.9333 is the value nearest to 4. Therefore the rate of return that this investment would generate is approximately 8 percent.

TAXES AND DEPRECIATION

Capital-budgeting decisions must consider the impact of investments on taxes and depreciation. If a given investment promises to increase profits by $100,000 per year, part of this increase will flow out of the firm to pay taxes. Thus income taxes have the effect of reducing the net cash flow of an investment.

Business expenses can be classified as cash expenses and noncash expenses. Cash expenses include materials, labor, power, insurance, and the like. These expenses reduce a firm's cash balance. Hopefully, goods or services will be sold at a price that will allow the firm to be "repaid" for these expenditures. Depreciation, on the other hand, is a noncash expense. That is, a charge is made against revenue, but the cash balance is unaffected. The journal entry to record depreciation is a debit to depreciation expense and a credit to accumulated depreciation. Thus depreciation has a positive effect on a firm's cash flow. This concept is developed in the following illustration.

A firm is contemplating an investment which promises to increase revenues by $50,000 per year. The investment is $200,000, and its useful life is estimated to be ten years with no salvage value. If the investment is made, cash expenses will increase by $20,000 per year. Taxes are 40 percent and straight-line depreciation is used. Our concern is for the net cash flow that can be expected if the investment is made.

A quick calculation shows that before-tax net income resulting from the investment is $10,000 and that after-tax net income is $6,000. However, $6,000 is not the net cash flow because only $20,000 for cash expenses plus the $4,000 in taxes have flowed out of the firm. Thus the net cash flow is $26,000, and the time-adjusted rate of return on this investment would be slightly under 5 percent. A simple method for determining cash flow is to add depreciation to net income after taxes.

This illustration underscores the importance of cash flow in evaluating investment opportunities. Neither net income before taxes or net income after taxes is a suitable value to use but cash flow is.

Consider also the impact of different depreciation methods on cash flow and ultimately the investment decision. If sum of the years' digits depreciation or accelerated depreciation is used, cash flows will be stimulated during the early life of the asset. If the firm is concerned with maximizing cash flow quickly, these depreciation methods work in that direction. If uniform cash flows are desired, the straight-line method of depreciation should be used.

A COMPREHENSIVE ILLUSTRATION

The Saramich Corporation is studying the purchase of a new machine. The machine will cost $250,000 and have an estimated useful life of five years. Saramich uses straight-line depreciation. It is estimated that the machine will increase revenues by an average of $100,000 per year. The additional cash expenses associated with this investment will average $20,000 per year. The minimum acceptable rate of return on machine investments is 10 percent per annum. Income taxes are estimated to be 40 percent of taxable income. Management wants to know if this is an acceptable investment. The analysis follows:

Gross revenue		$100,000
Less Expenses:		
Cash expenses	$20,000	
Depreciation	50,000	70,000
Net income before taxes		$ 30,000
Income taxes		12,000
Net income		$ 18,000
Add back depreciation		50,000
Cash Flow		$ 68,000

The basic question is whether an annual cash flow of $68,000 is adequate to provide a 10 percent return on investment. The answer is provided as follows:

Investment	$250,000
Present value of net cash	
inflow ($68,000 ×	
3.791)	257,788
Net Present Value	$ 7,788

If everything goes according to plan, this investment will provide a return on investment in excess of 10 percent.

This technique can be used in a number of capital budgeting situations such as

Equipment replacement where the present equipment is compared with a new piece of equipment

Comparing two or more machines which perform the same task—Xerox versus IBM copying machines, for example

Whether a new building should be constructed or the existing building remodeled

Whether an asset should be purchased or leased

WHICH TECHNIQUES ARE USED?

Table 14-3 summarizes the findings of one study of business firms to determine which techniques were most commonly used in capital-budgeting decisions.[1] Note that there has been a shift in the use of techniques and that far fewer firms are waiting until they have no alternative before making capital-budgeting decisions. It is quite possible for a firm to get into such an urgent position that it must buy specific items of equipment immediately or go out of business. These findings suggest that more firms are using discounting techniques.

TABLE   14-3

Most Sophisticated Evaluation Standard

		Percent using in	
Evaluation standard	*1970*	*1964*	*1959*
Discounting (rate of return or present worth)	57%	38%	19%
Accounting rate of return	26	30	34
Payback or payback reciprocal	12	24	34
Urgency	5	8	13
Total	100%	100%	100%

A CONCLUSION

Although the techniques described have been helpful to managers in thousands of instances, it would be wrong to infer that investment decisions are made solely on the basis of economic analysis. The amount of confidence that mana-

[1] T. Klammer, "Empirical Evidence of the Adoption of Sophisticated Capital Budgeting Techniques," *Journal of Business*, Vol. 45, (July 1972), 387-397, Table 6.

gers have in these techniques varies significantly. One assumption underlying these techniques is that managers are always interested in maximizing returns to the firm. This is not necessarily true. Divisional managers may have a goal of reasonable returns with a situation that can be easily managed. Top management may be influenced by the prestige, security, or power that will result if a particular investment is made. Finally there is the response-to-crisis capital-budgeting decision that should not occur but does. Some piece of equipment essential to meeting sales or shipment budgets falls apart and must be replaced immediately. If a business cannot function until certain equipment is purchased, management will have to abandon the approach it would like to use simply to avoid disaster.

The theme of this chapter is that there are tools available to improve the manner in which a firm utilizes its capital, but we cannot be certain that they can or will be used to provide a decision base.

KEY TERMS

accounting rate of return	long-term decisions
capital budgeting	net present value
cash flow	noncash expense
cost of capital	payback
discounted cash flow	rate of return

QUESTIONS

1. Distinguish between the short term and the long term as they relate to decision making.

2. How is capital budgeting related to the management of cost?

3. What is meant by a capital-budgeting philosophy and how does it influence capital-budgeting decisions?

4. Prepare a definition of the cost of capital.

5. Why is the cost of capital an important factor in investment decisions?

6. "We should always select that investment alternative that promises to yield the greatest amount of profit." Do you agree with this statement? Explain.

7. a. What are the basic sources of cash inflow when investments are made?
   b. What are the basic sources of cash outflow when investments are made?

8. Is there one capital budgeting technique that is better than all others? Explain why or why not.

9. "The investment that has the shortest payback is the best investment." Do you agree? Explain.

10. How much will $1.00 to be received a year from now be worth today if money is worth 12 percent? Explain.

11. Would you rather receive $1.00 today or $1.25 two years from today if money is worth 10 percent? Explain.

12. Profit and cash are equal. Do you agree? Explain.

13. What impact does depreciation have on cash flow? Explain.

14. Different depreciation methods impact differently on cash flow. Explain why this is true.

15. Do you agree with the notion that all investment decisions should be based on economic analysis? Explain.

PROBLEMS

1. Time is money

   a. You have a customer for a parcel of land you wish to sell who offers you $4,000 cash today or $5,000 cash two years from today. If money is worth 10 percent per annum which is the better economic choice?

   b. A rich aunt offers you the choice of receiving $5,000 today or $1,000 per year for six years. If money is worth 8 percent, which is the better economic choice?

   c. Sam Hill is 60 years old and his employer wants him to take an early retirement. Sam has been offered $20,000 a year for five years or $15,000 per year for eight years as an inducement. If Sam decides to accept either offer, which should it be if money is worth 14 percent per annum?

2. Instant millionaires

   The Massachusetts state lottery has a million-dollar game, and several times per year instant millionaires are selected. They are called millionaires because they will receive $50,000 per year for a period of 20 years.

Required:

a. If money is worth 8 percent per annum, would you accept $500,000 today in lieu of 20 payments of $50,000 spread over 20 years?

3. Rate of return

   An investment today of $300,000 promises to return the investor $50,000 per year for the next 20 years.

Required:

a. What is the discounted rate of return on this investment?

4.   Investment evaluation techniques

Valley Mills, Inc. has two investment proposals that it is considering. Data relating to these investments follows.

	A	B
Investment	$100,000	$160,000
Annual savings	25,000	32,000
Economic life	6 years	6 years

Required:

a. What is the payback period for each proposal?
b. What rate of return will be earned by each proposal?
c. Determine the net present value of each proposal if the cost of capital is 14 percent.
d. Which proposal, if either, would you select? Why?

5.   Investment proposals

The Backward Company has $150,000 of surplus cash. Currently it has two investment proposals under consideration. The first proposal came from the shop foreman who wants a computer-controlled milling machine complex costing $140,000. The proposal promises to yield annual savings of $40,000 per year for the next six years. The machine will have no salvage value. The second proposal came from the plant manager who wants an automated material-handling facility that would cost $150,000 and provide annual savings of $45,000 for the next 6 years. The cost of capital is 12 percent.

Required:

a. Which of these proposals would you select? Explain.

6.   Net present value

Bill Fortune has inherited $300,000 and wants to invest most of it in either of the following:

A Motel on Cape Cod:	
Cash outlay	$250,000
Annual cash inflow	35,000
Estimated life	15 yr
Cost of capital	10%

A Motel in Ski Country:

Cash outlay	$250,000
Annual cash inflow	45,000
Estimated life	15 yr
Cost of capital	14%

The cost of capital is higher in ski country because of the risk factor. Poor weather in the summer on Cape Cod does not impact on patronage nearly as much as does poor weather (no snow) in ski country.

Required:

a. What is the net present value of these investments?

b. Which investment proposal should Bill select?

7. Time value of money

The following situations are not related.

a. How much should you set aside today so that you will have $8,000 in 17 years from now to pay for your child's freshman year at Excaliber University if money earns 8 percent per annum compounded annually?

b. How much money would you have to deposit in a savings account today so that you will have $5,000 in five years if money earns 6 percent per annum? As above if money earns 8 percent per annum.

c. The Bamberger Company is considering the purchase of a new machine that will require an investment of $10,000 and promises to reduce operating costs by $2,000 a year for the next eight years. The economic life of the machine is eight years, and it will have no scrap value. What time adjusted rate of return will this investment provide?

8. Payback and net present value

The Locker Company must replace an existing machine. Two machines are being considered, and each is expected to have a useful life of ten years. Estimated data follows:

	Machine A	Machine B
Initial investment	$12,000	$15,000
Operating receipts per year	8,000	10,000
Operating costs per year	5,500	6,200

Required:

a. What is the payback period for each machine?

b. What is the net present value of each proposal if money is worth 8 percent per annum?

c. Which machine would you recommend be purchased?

9. Impact of depreciation and taxes

The plant manager of the Agate Corporation has provided the following data relative to the purchase of a new machine. The company uses straight-line depreciation.

Purchase cost	$400,000
Economic life of the machine	8 yr
No salvage value	
Additional annual revenue	$160,000
Additional annual cash cost	80,000
Income taxes	40%
Cost of capital per annum	12%

Required:

a. Evaluate this investment proposal.

10. Net present value

Lincoln Fabricators, a supplier of component parts to the automotive industry, is contemplating the purchase of a new automatic welding machine that will cost $30,000 and have no scrap value at the end of its useful life which is ten years. This machine, which costs $1,800 per year to operate, would replace a machine that costs $3,800 per year to operate. Additionally, the new machine can turn /out 40,000 more units each year than did the old machine, and each unit has a contribution margin of $0.10.

Required:

a. If the firm requires a 14 percent rate of return, is the net present value of the investment adequate to justify purchase?

15 Inventory

Management

CHAPTER OVERVIEW _____

In previous chapters we have considered a number of problem areas associated with inventory. To a great extent the discussions centered around inventory valuations and their impact on income measurement. In this chapter we consider the broad area of inventory management.

A basic inventory management problem is determining the "right" amount of inventory to have on hand at any point in time. The problem involves all categories of inventory including raw materials, component parts, work in process, and finished goods. The "right" amount of inventory is contingent on a number of factors such as price changes, fluctuations in demand, strikes, and the reliability of supply sources and transportation services.

The "right" amount of inventory is also contingent on management's willingness to run out of inventory on occasion. Contrary to popular belief, running out of inventory can be a good policy because of financial considerations. Inventory is a stagnant investment until sold, and every firm should attempt to minimize its inventory investment in such a way that relations with customers are not impaired. In this chapter we will present some ideas that indicate how this can be accomplished.

QUESTIONS FOR CONSIDERATION _____

1. What is a stock-out and why might stock-outs be good for the firm?
2. What factors are involved in deciding when to buy and how much to buy?
3. How does management determine the most economic purchase?
4. What is a safety stock and how is it measured?
5. How are inventory carrying charges computed?

The nature of inventory management and the problems associated with inventory management can be placed in perspective if we first identify the basic reasons for carrying inventory. A financial manager, ideally, would prefer a minimum of inventory. Raw materials and component parts would flow into the firm as needed by the manufacturing system, the manufacturing system would compress the time required to convert raw materials and component parts into finished products, and finished products would flow to customers as they leave the manufacturing system. This ideal is seldom, if ever, achieved although some automobile manufacturers at times come close to it. Inventories are often the largest category of current assets for a firm and consequently represent the major investment in working capital. Until inventories move out of the firm, say, as finished products, they represent a nonproductive use of funds.

REASONS FOR INVENTORY

All manufacturing and trading businesses must have inventories, but the magnitude of an inventory investment will vary depending on the reason for making it. Inventories provide management with a reserve that can be used when the need arises. There may be a sudden increase in the demand for an item within the firm. There may be a sudden increase in the demand for an item in the marketplace which could prolong the inventory replacement cycle. Transportation delays caused by strikes, the weather, and other conditions also extend replacement cycles. The trend of prices is another factor that influences inventory policy. Increased inventories can often be justified during periods of rising prices.

Not having enough inventory can be a costly situation; having inventory results in higher operating costs. The goal should be to maintain inventories at optimal levels, but optimal levels vary over time and from one inventory category to another. The basic challenge to inventory management is optimization.

INVENTORY MANAGEMENT

Inventory management involves many areas of activity. Some of these are directly related to the management of cost and others, although they impact on cost, are not of immediate concern to costing. Systems of material identification, the layout of storage areas, safe-guarding inventory from theft and deterioration, and the physical movement of goods into and out of storage are each a part of the inventory management problem, but they are not of immediate concern to this discussion.

Our concern is for two dimensions of the problem. The first deals with inventory amounts and addresses such issues as when to buy, how much to buy, and the development of a safety-stock policy. The second deals with the financial aspects of inventory management and addresses such issues as inventory valuation, costing materials as they move into production, and problems associated with the valuation of work-in-process inventory.

THE MAGNITUDE OF THE PROBLEM

Inventory management is one of the more pressing problems facing management, and there are a number of reasons why this is so. The first is the tremendous proliferation of goods and materials that are produced and merchandised. In the 1930s most food retailers could satisfy the cold-cereal demand of their customers by carrying half a dozen brands. Today there are more than 150 brands on the market from which the retailer must choose. In 1935 a retailer could satisfy the demand of most cigarette customers by carrying four brands— Lucky Strike, Camel, Chesterfield, and Old Gold. Today a North Carolina merchant advertises the fact that he carries 110 different brands, sizes, styles, and flavors of cigarettes. In 1954 Chevrolet produced a single line of cars each built on a standard frame and each powered by the same model 6-cylinder engine. Today Chevrolet produces more than a dozen different models each with a variety of options. The desire of businessmen to cater to the slightest consumer whim that will result in a sale is largely responsible for this proliferation.

The consequences of this proliferation are increased costs of production and distribution. Manufacturers must have a greater variety and volume of raw materials in inventory, production is less efficient because the variety of options that are available partially negate the economies that result from standardization, and production must be interrupted to shift from one line of goods to another. It is also worth noting that as the variety of items coming out of a particular production facility increases, the more difficult it becomes to pinpoint the cost and profitability of any one item.

A visit to any supermarket will quickly reveal how proliferation can increase distribution costs. Observe the shelf space reserved for the dozens of brands of dog food, cereals, soaps, and the like. Shelf space represents a significant investment, and one reason why supermarkets are as large as they are is the tremendous variety of goods that they must carry. Proliferation increases the number of dollars that a retailer must tie up in inventory, and in some instances it results in a slower rate of inventory turnover for individual brands. Thus the businessman must wait for longer periods of time before he realizes a satisfactory return on his investment. A complete inventory of fan belts for a Chevrolet dealer today involves dozens of different sizes and shapes. Back in 1954 there was only one.

High levels of technology can have a significant impact on inventory management, and this impact comes from at least two directions. The first is the rather obvious impact that technology can make materials and products obsolete in a short span of time. Witness the impact on slide rule sales with the advent of the hand calculator, the demise of the fountain pen, and possibly the demand for "conventional" wrist watches as the popularity of the digital watch increases. It could well be that the watch capital of the world will shift from Switzerland to the semiconductor capital in our great Southwest. As a technology develops, the costs of production and consequently selling prices can drop at an alarming rate. We have seen this in both the hand calculator and digital watch industries. Hand calculator dealers at one point in time were in the unenviable position of ordering calculators from suppliers at a cost greater than their selling price when received.

Finally, inflation compounds the problem of inventory management. Not only must larger amounts of money be invested in inventory as prices rise, but the unpredictable rate of inflation and the possibility of deflation in some segments of the economy could easily make inventory investments turn sour.

KEEPING TRACK OF INVENTORY

Many aspects of inventory management hinge on knowing how much material is in inventory at any point in time. Establishing reorder points is useless unless a system exists whereby management can obtain accurate and timely information signaling that inventory has dropped to the reorder point. Computer-based systems are helpful even for relatively small businesses, but, as a generalization, managers know far less about the status of inventories than they would like. Multiplant operations and product proliferation each make the inventory management function more complex. Basically there are two systems that management can use to keep track of inventory. They are perpetual inventory and periodic inventory.

Perpetual Inventory

The basic concept upon which perpetual inventory systems are built is very simple. All authorized additions to inventory (such as purchases) are added to the opening inventory balance. This total is reduced by the authorized withdrawals (such as material requisitions) and the difference is the amount that should be in inventory (see Figure 15-1) at a given point in time. Knowledge of what goes into and out of inventory is an absolute necessity to operate a perpetual inventory system. Thus the word "authorized" is of paramount importance.

Perpetual inventory systems have been known to break down, a major reason being the sheer volume of inventory transactions that may take place. Again, product proliferation magnifies the problem. If a firm carries 10,000 items in inventory, it will have a minimum of 10,000 inventory accounts. There is always the possibility and probability that some inventory transactions will be overlooked and that transactions will be entered in the wrong account. It is hoped

Item: Idler shaft						Code Number: 4923A	
Additions			Withdrawals			Balance	
Date	Description	Units	Date	Description	Units	Date	Balance
						1/01	5,000
			1/04	Req. #489	2,000	1/04	3,000
1/14	P.O. #318	6,000				1/14	9,000
			1/20	Req. #512	4,000	1/20	5,000
			1/26	Req. #604	1,000	1/26	4,000

FIGURE 15-1 Perpetual Inventory Record

that such omissions or errors will not significantly impair the useful-ness of the system.

The advantages of a perpetual inventory system are so great that they can overshadow the shortcomings referred to earlier. First, at any point in time management can determine the balance in any inventory account by reading the inventory card. In a computer-based system balances can be easily retrieved and viewed on a cathode ray tube. Second, perpetual inventory systems eliminate the need for a physical count of inventory at the end of the accounting period. The Internal Revenue Service permits the use of perpetual inventory values in the preparation of financial statements. Annual physical count of inventory is mandatory, but under this system management can have the physical count taken at its convenience. In some firms there are inventory teams that take perpetual counts of inventory on a rotating year-round basis. Finally, perpetual inventory provides a standard of what should be in inventory. A comparison of actual count with the standard indicates whether there are inventory short-ages or overages and the degree to which the inventory control system is working.

Periodic Inventory

Periodic inventory is based on the following concept. The amount purchased during a period is added to the beginning balance; this comprises the stock available for use. At the end of the account-ing period, a physical count of inventory must be taken. The difference between stock available and the ending inventory indicates the quantity of an item used during the period. It is possible that this system can be as effective as any inventory system, but there are both actual and potential deficiencies when compared with a perpetual inventory system. There is no way to determine inventory balances except at year's end when a physical count is made. Also, the quantity classified as "used" may have been sold, lost, or stolen.

Physical Inventory Problems

The purpose of taking a physical count of inventory is to deter-mine the actual status of inventory. This provides a basis for adjusting perpetual inventory accounts where necessary. In many instances, however, a physical count of inventory is impractical if not impossi-ble. Visualize a room 200 feet square in a textile mill in which bolts of cloth 36 inches or 42 inches in length are stacked on end. Each of the thousands of bolts are wrapped in paper and sealed. On each wrapper the quality of cloth, its color, and the yardage is indicated. Unless each bolt is unwrapped, examined, and measured there is no way to be certain what each bolt contains. The best that can be done is to take a small sample of an inventory item and hope that the sample results are indicative of the lot from which the sample was taken. If the sampling process is properly designed, it can provide a good picture of the universe from which it was drawn. In general, complete identification of inventory amounts is neither necessary or warranted. The important factor is the system that is used to control inventory and report inventory data. It takes time to develop a reliable inventory system. If, with a given inventory system, there are persistent and unplanned stockouts, if inventory turns over at a much lower rate than planned, or if the system is consistently in error, then the system needs an overhaul.

In most instances, where firms carry thousands of items in inventory, there will always be discrepancies between what is and what should be in inventory. These discrepancies are in the form of overages or shortages. A discrepancy may or may not be a signal for corrective action; this action depends on the magnitude of the deviation both in terms of units involved and the value of the inventory item. The rule of thumb to apply is that discrepancies should be investigated only if the predicted benefit from investigation seems to be greater than the cost of the investigation.

WHEN TO BUY MATERIALS

On the surface this appears to be a simple situation to handle. In job-order production materials may not be purchased until a job is received because the job identifies the materials that will be needed and the date when the job must be completed. In process production, inventories are usually replenished based on a predetermined reorder point. When inventory of an item falls to a given low limit, this is a signal to reorder. In practice, there is a problem in determining the appropriate time to buy, and the major reason for this is the inability to forecast with a high degree of reliability. Every time a businessman purchases merchandise, it should be in anticipation of a need. In many instances this need arises sooner than anticipated or later than anticipated, or it may never materialize.

When everything goes according to plan, determining when to buy specific materials can be determined systematically. In job-order production, each job in the shop is scheduled according to machine and manpower availability. This schedule identifies the times when specific materials will be needed. If accurate lead times for procuring materials have been established, it is a relatively simple task to determine when orders should be placed. In practice, determining lead times is a difficult task for most buyers. Once the decision to make a purchase is made, there is a significant amount of paperwork and prepurchasing activity that must take place. It could be days or weeks before a purchase order leave the firm, and there will be a time-consuming paperwork routine at the supplying firm. If we add to this the possibility of stock-outs and delays in transportation, there is ample evidence to conclude that lead times can be quite variable. One way to avoid this dilemma is to plan well into the future. If General Motors tells Firestone in July that it will need 10 million tires during the first quarter of the following year, the odds are greatly increased that G.M. will have what it needs.

In theory, at least, determining when to buy in process production requires three bits of knowledge:

1. the mean rate of use of the material
2. the time required to replenish an inventory item (lead time)
3. the required safety stock

To illustrate, let us assume the following:

1. the mean rate of use of an item is 10,000 units per week.
2. the time required to replenish the inventory item is three weeks.
3. the safety stock is set at 20,000 units, or a two-week supply.

With this data we establish the "when to buy" for this item at 50,000 units or a five-week supply. This is the reorder point. During the three weeks it takes to replenish inventory, 30,000 units will be used in production leaving the safety stock of 20,000 units when the replacement order is received.

Other factors such as the probability of a strike at a supplier's plant, transportation interruptions, price hikes, and the like can also affect the when-to-buy decision. The process described establishes the time to buy when management is concerned only for meeting production requirements—this is the reason for inventory.

The reader may wonder whether determining when to buy is as easy in practice as we have shown. The fact is that if the actual rate of consumption is 10,000 units per week the actual time required to replace inventory (lead time) is three weeks, then the when-to-buy point is 50,000 units. But, if the actual course of events were known in advance, there would be no need to discuss safety stock.

In practice, variations in the rate of use from week to week and variations in lead time are as much the rule as they are the exception. Safety stock is an extra inventory that is carried to reduce stock-outs when there are variations in the rate of use of a material and when lead time is longer than anticipated. The size of safety stocks depends on a number of factors. If management establishes a policy of no stock-outs, safety stocks of necessity would have to be greater than if occasional stock-outs are permitted. The trick is to operate with a minimum of safety stock and a minimum of stock-outs. A second factor that bears on safety stock is the variation in rate of use and variation in lead time that may be anticipated. If variations here are high, safety stocks will tend to be high. Without these two inputs, safety-stock determination must be hit or miss.

Safety-stock Illustrated

Suppose that we have a large number of experiences regarding a particular material and have established 2,000 units as the mean rate of use per week and three weeks as the mean lead time. Whether these mean values are good indicators of what can be expected in a "typical" situation depends on the distribution of values that resulted in these means. Two thousand is the mean of 3,999 and 1 as well as 1,999 and 2,001. If the actual values that produced these means are clustered close to the mean, there is a good probability that future rates of use and lead times will also be close to the mean unless new variables are involved. The statistical measure, standard deviation (σ), describes how the individual items in a distribution are dispersed around the mean. A small standard deviation tells us that the bulk of the items in the distribution are relatively close to the mean.

The standard deviation concept permits us to draw certain conclusions that anyone who has taken an elementary course in statistics should remember. Suppose that the mean rate of use is

2,000 units per week with a standard deviation of 50 units. There is a probability that 68.28 times out of 100 the actual rate of use was between 1,950 and 2,050 units per week; a probability that 95.45 times out of 100 the actual rate of use was between 1,900 and 2,100 units per week; and a probability of 99.73 times out of 100 the actual rate of use was between 1,850 and 2,150 units per week. This represents plus and minus 1, 2, and 3 standard deviations, respectively. We also conclude that these probabilities will continue in the future if the same conditions prevail then as in the past. Thus management is almost certain that actual usage will not exceed 2,150 units per week.

Suppose also that the mean lead time is three weeks with a standard deviation of 0.2 weeks. Using the logic applied above, management can be almost certain that lead times will not exceed 3.6 weeks (3 weeks plus 3σ x 0.2). Thus management can be virtually certain that the amount of this material used during lead time will not exceed 7,740 units (3.6 weeks x 2,150 units per week). Management can be virtually certain that a safety stock of 1,740 units (7,740 – 6,000) will eliminate stock-outs. However, the odds are just as great that the actual rate of use can be 1,850 units per week and the actual lead time can be as low as 2.4 weeks. Thus the material used during lead time could be as little as 4,440 units, and there would be no need for any safety stock.

Management probably would not set a safety stock as high as 1,740 units for a number of reasons. There is little probability that maximum use and maximum lead time will coincide; the maximum rate of use could come when lead time is at a minimum, and so on. In addition, it is generally poor practice to minimize stock-outs through large safety stocks because there may be better—less costly—alternatives. Some of these alternatives are covered later in this chapter in the section dealing with safety-stock policy. In practice, management might establish a safety stock for this item at, say, 800 units and increase or decrease this amount as experience dictates.

Maintaining safety stocks is a costly endeavor. It could well be that determining safety stocks by the process given earlier would require more inventory investment than the firm could afford. For this reason many firms use a selective approach to safety-stock determination.

THE ABC METHOD

The ABC method of selective control provides a means for reducing safety-stock investment without increasing the probability of stock-outs. The logic behind this approach is that for most products there are a few components which account for most of the material cost and a large number of components whose total cost is low. Visualize an automobile or a TV console set, and you will see that this idea has merit. The ABC method operates as follows. All stock items are given a value which is the product of units used over a period of time and the unit cost of the item. All items are arrayed in order of magnitude (see Table 15-1). The first 10 percent of the items are classified as A items, the next 20 percent as B items, and the final 70 percent are C items. Characteristically, however, the top 10 percent of the items involve the greatest number of dollars of investment and the bottom 70 percent the least. In our illustration, 70 percent of cost is in the A group, 20 percent in the B group, and 10 percent in the C group.

TABLE 15-1

Value of Materials Used

Component number	Usage (units)	Unit cost	Value
2146	700	$50.00	$ 35,000
2150	1,000	22.00	22,000
2161	1,300	10.00	13,000 A
0920	2,400	4.00	9,600
0875	2,000	2.80	5,600
2111	1,600	3.00	4,800 B
5597	6,000	0.75	4,500
4701	5,000	0.50	2,500
5700	5,000	0.31	1,550
8417	3,000	0.29	870
1976	2,000	0.29	580 C
Total	30,000		$100,000

To carry this concept one step farther, let us assume that a firm carries 1,000 items in inventory. The number of items in each class, the average inventory investment, and the investment in safety stock (30 percent) is as follows:

Class	No. of items	Avg. inventory investment	Safety stock investment	Stock-outs	Revised safety stock investment	Revised stock-outs
A	100	$ 70,000	$21,000	3	$10,500	6
B	200	20,000	6,000	6	6,000	6
C	700	10,000	3,000	21	9,000	7
Total	1,000	$100,000	$30,000	30	$25,500	19

Now let us assume that with this investment the firm experienced 30 stock-outs during the year. Assume that these are distributed at random as shown and that each is equally capable of disrupting production. Note the discrepancy in the cost of stock-out protection. Seven times the investment is used to protect A items from one-seventh the stock-outs of C items.

Arbitrarily we will decrease the investment in A items by 50 percent which will double the possibility of stock-outs to 6. We will add $6,000 to our safety-stock investment of C items and thereby decrease the possibility of expected stockouts to 7. Thus we have significantly decreased the probability of disrupting production due to stock-outs and at the same time reduced our safety-stock investment. We have not attempted to identify the optimum safety-stock investment through this illustration; we have merely shown the potential of this concept.

Because stock-outs result from variations in delivery time also, it is in order to suggest that, by exercising greater control over deliveries and perhaps by reducing the number of purchases, the possibility of stock-outs can be reduced. If a firm purchases an item ten times a year, there is the possibility of ten late deliveries and ten stock-outs, but if only three purchases are made, there are only three chances of stock-outs.

STOCK-OUT POLICY

The ideal size of inventory depends, among other things, on the firm's stock-out policy. Stock-out policy refers to the frequency of stock-outs that management will accept. Seldom will a business firm attempt to eliminate all stock-outs. It should take steps to reduce the causes of stock-outs wherever feasible such as

1. stabilizing levels of production
2. developing more dependable sources of supply
3. developing reliable transportation sources
4. reducing the frequency of purchase

Having a no stock-out policy is impractical and often unnecessary in most businesses. It is impractical because of the larger inventory investment, and unnecessary because the impact of some stock-outs may be minimal. A stock-out that occurs at 4:50 P.M. on Friday may have less impact than a stock-out at 10:30 A.M. on Tuesday. Certain stock-outs may not stop production; they may only require an adjustment in the production process.

Stock-out policy should hinge on a comparison of two costs. Stock-outs are reduced by increasing the size of the safety stock. The increased cost of carrying more inventory must be compared with the cost of not being able to perform. If a firm has a $50,000 investment in safety stock which costs 30 percent per annum to carry, the cost of not being able to perform must be greater than $15,000 per year to justify the safety stock.

HOW MUCH TO BUY

There are a number of factors that affect this decision. Some of these were identified earlier in the discussion of material standards. It is impossible to answer this question specifically unless the objectives management seeks through its materials management program are known. Some such objectives are

1. to meet production requirements
2. to minimize the investment in materials inventory

3. to obtain the lowest possible acquisition cost

4. to obtain the most economic purchase lot

The last three objectives must be considered "in addition to" the first and overriding objective. The how-much-to-buy problem could have significantly different answers depending on the combination of objectives that management seeks to attain. We will see why this is true later on.

To a great extent, the better a firm can forecast or predict, the better it can answer this question. Forecasting here involves both usage and price. A somewhat different approach to this question is required when job-order production is involved as opposed to process production.

Job-order Purchasing

Job-order production varies from a one-of-a-kind situation to situations that closely resemble process production. A precision machine shop might produce a one-of-a-kind valve or a boatyard might produce to your order a skiff having just the length, beam, freeboard, and other features that you desire. In the first instance, the material used by a machine shop could vary with each order. In the second instance, the same types of materials could be involved in every order. In the first instance, material purchases will probably wait until orders are received. In the second, inventory problems could be similar to those encountered in process production.

Whether the how-much-to-buy question is easy or difficult to answer in a job-order situation depends on a number of variables. At times customers will supply the raw materials; the raw material may be a stock item that is readily available at suppliers; or the material may be an intricate component part. It is in this last situation that the problem of how much to buy could be sticky.

To illustrate, a job-order machine shop has an order to produce one highly specialized valve which will be used to control the flow of certain chemicals. The major component of the valve is a casting which the firm must have specially made at a foundry. The casting will be subjected to about 100 machining operations, many of which are very precise. A mistake in any machining operation will render the casting useless. The firm can sell only one valve, but, because the probability of error is so high, it plans to buy several castings and bring them through the machining cycle simultaneously. The problem is to decide how many castings to buy and machine to wind up with just one acceptable valve.

There is no simple answer to this problem, but, if management has a good idea of the probability of loss or success at each stage of the machining process, a reasonable, but not foolproof, decision can be made. If management has no idea of the probabilities of success or failure, it should not even consider accepting the job. These probabilities can be used to reach such conclusions as

1. If only one casting is machined, there is a 40 percent probability that it will meet specifications.
2. If 5 castings are machined, there is a 90 percent probability that one casting will meet specifications.
3. If 10 castings are machined, there is a 95 percent probability that one casting will meet specifications.
4. If 25 castings are machined, there is a 99 percent probability that one casting will meet specifications.

The basic issue here is the optimal risk among these or other alternatives. Costs increase as more castings are machined, but the probability of getting a satisfactory casting also increases. Machining a single casting will involve the least production cost, but the risk

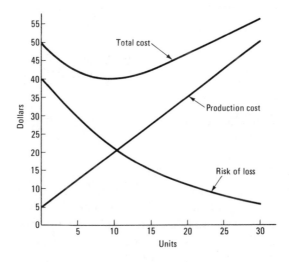

FIGURE   15-2

factor, which must be translated into dollars, is the highest. The reverse is true if 25 castings are machined. The optimal number of castings to buy and machine depends on the movement of these two costs as shown in Figure 15-2.

The best alternative here is to buy and machine 10 castings because the sum of the cost is lowest. But there is no guarantee that one of the ten will emerge from the process in an acceptable condition. The purpose of this illustration in addition to the concept involved is to underscore the fact that there are uncertainties and that it may be unwise or impossible to eliminate all risk. Knowing how much risk to accept and when to accept it is a trait of a good manager. If there were no uncertainties, the manager's job would be routine and a bore. Any manager who is afraid of losing a battle now and then will probably win few big battles.

PURCHASING FOR PROCESS PRODUCTION

We will first answer the how-much-to-buy question when the objective is simply to meet the needs of production. The basic data needed to answer the question and the process for using the data is

Mean rate of use	10,000 units per week
Delivery time	3 weeks
Safety stock	20,000 units
Maximum inventory	10-week supply, 100,000 units

The amount that should be purchased in this situation is 80,000 units. This is the difference between the maximum inventory and the safety-stock levels. This item should be ordered when inventory drops to 50,000 units. During the three weeks that it takes to replenish inventory, 30,000 units will be consumed in production. Inventory will be at the safety-stock level (on an average) when the 80,000 units are received. The 80,000 units will bring inventory up to the maximum level. Maximum inventory is a predetermined quantity. It is determined by considering such factors as storage space, deterioration, obsolescence, purchase price, investment, and delivery costs.

ECONOMIC PURCHASE LOTS

Here we answer the how-much-to-buy question when the objective is to establish the most economic purchase lot size. In the previous illustration 80,000 units had to be purchased at a time to meet production needs. In theory, at least, buying less than this amount could jeopardize production schedules. Therefore this approach to how much to buy considers the question of when it would be advisable to buy more than 80,000 units at a time. Quantity discounts, transportation and handling savings, lower purchasing costs, and a reduced probability of stock-outs are the types of savings that can accrue through large-scale purchasing. But larger purchases result in larger inventory carrying charges.

Inventory Carrying Charges

It is common practice in business to charge department and division managers for the inventory investment that they maintain. The logic behind such a charge is sound because managers, in an attempt to reduce their costs, may consider optimizing their inventory investment. Measured on an annual basis, it costs about 30 percent of the value of an item to carry it in inventory. Thus a department manager having an average inventory investment of $100,000 would be charged $30,000 per year. The inventory carrying charge includes interest on the investment, obsolescence, taxes, insurance, storage, handling, depreciation, paperwork, and the like and is applied to the value of the average inventory. Obviously there are tremendous variations in the suitable inventory carrying charge. Pig iron stored in a field would have a much lower carrying charge than sterling silver that must be kept under lock and key.

To illustrate this concept, suppose that a firm plans to purchase 50,000 units of a material during the next year. Consumption of the material will average 1,000 units per week for the 50 weeks that the firm will operate. The supplier has quoted the following:

Lot size	Unit price delivered	Total cost of acquisition
5,000 units	$1.95	$97,500
10,000 units	1.90	95,000
25,000 units	1.85	92,500
50,000 units	1.80	90,000

To obtain the lowest acquisition cost the firm would have to buy a single lot of 50,000 units, but this purchase quantity also involves the largest inventory and, consequently, the largest inventory carrying charge. Thus as acquisition costs go down, carrying costs rise. We seek to find the lot size where the sum of these two costs— acquisition and carrying charge—is the lowest. The process for doing this is shown in the table following. Note that total costs go down and then rise. The reason that total costs go down is that the downward "pull" of quantity discounts is greater than the upward "pull" of the increased carrying charge. But the rate of discount must eventually decrease and stop while the carrying charge continues to increase as lot sizes increase. The most economic lot size is 10,000 units because total cost is lowest.

Alternative lot sizes (units)	5,000	10,000	25,000	50,000
Acquisition cost	$97,500	$95,000	$92,500	$ 90,000
Inventory carrying charge	1,463	2,850	6,938	13,500
Total cost	$98,963	$97,850	$99,438	$103,500
Calculation of carrying charges				
Maximum inventory	5,000	10,000	25,000	50,000
Average inventory	2,500	5,000	12,500	25,000
Value of average inventory	$4,875	$9,500	$23,125	$45,000
Inventory carrying charge (30%)	$1,463	$2,850	$6,938	$13,500

A number of assumptions should be explained. Maximum inventory is the lot size; we have assumed the same safety stock for each lot size. Average inventory is one-half the maximum inventory; we have assumed a constant rate of use.

ECONOMIC ORDERING QUANTITY

Even when the unit purchase price does not vary with the lot size, it is necessary to determine the order quantity. If a firm purchases 50,000 units of an item during a year in a lot size of 1,000 units, the cost to purchase 50,000 units would be greater than if a single purchase was made. It is common practice to consider the cost of making a purchase when determining purchase lot sizes. For example, suppose that a firm plans to purchase 50,000 units of an item next year at a unit cost of $2. The cost to place an order is $50 and the inventory carrying charge is 30 percent. The following formula is frequently used to determine order quantities:

$$\text{EOQ} = \sqrt{\frac{2 \times \text{units used per year} \times \text{cost of placing an order}}{\text{Unit cost} \times \text{carrying charge}}} = \sqrt{\frac{2 \times 50{,}000 \times \$50}{\$2 \times 0.30}} = 2{,}887 \text{ units}$$

Economic Order Quantity— Another Dimension

There are times when the quantity of a material to be purchased is expressed in dollars rather than in units. The process for determining the most economic purchase lot size is basically the same as the process described on page 394, but there are a number of modifications that we will identify.

A firm plans to purchase $90,000 of a given material next year. The firm plans to operate 300 days during the year and will use the material at a constant rate. The cost to process a purchase order and receive and store a delivery is set at $250. The inventory carrying charge (ICC) is 30 percent (based on the value of the average inventory), and the safety stock is set at $5,000. The planned lead time is 15 days. We will use this data for two purposes. First, the reorder point is ($90,000 ÷ 300) x 14 plus safety stock, or $9,200.

Next we will determine which of several purchase lot sizes should be used:

| | Number of purchases | | | | |
	2	3	5	6	10
(a) Purchase lot size	$45,000	$30,000	$18,000	$15,000	$9,000
(b) Average inventory	22,500	15,000	9,000	7,500	4,500
(c) ICC	6,750	4,500	2,700	2,250	1,350
(d) Cost of purchasing	500	750	1,250	1,500	2,500
Total of (c) and (d)	$ 7,250	$ 5,250	$ 3,950	$ 3,750	$3,850

Thus the most economic way to purchase this material is to place six orders of $15,000 each during the year.

INVENTORY COSTING

When raw materials, component parts, supplies, and the like move from inventory into production or elsewhere, a cost must be assigned to them. Whether the cost assigned to an item is the actual price paid for it or some other value depends on the costing techniques that is applied. In job-order production when a specific purchase is made for a specific job, the actual cost of the material is known and can be applied to production. In process production especially, no attempt may be made to identify the cost of specific inventory items. Rather, a number of assumptions are made regarding the flow of cost out of inventory. The two most common cost flow assumptions are first-in, first-out (FIFO) and last-in, first-out (LIFO). Note that we are referring to cost flow and not the physical movement of goods. Wherever practical, the physical movement of goods should be on a first-in, first-out basis. We refer to these as assumptions because the cost assigned to an item is probably not the cost paid for it.

First-in, First-out Assumption

This approach to cost flow assigns the oldest price paid first, then the next oldest, and so on as materials move from inventory. At the end of the accounting period, the items in inventory will carry the most recent price(s) paid. During periods of rising prices this approach results in an ending inventory value that is high in relation to the cost of the items issued during the period. Thus during periods of rising prices FIFO will cause a higher net income to be shown than will be shown with the LIFO cost assumption.

Last-in, First-out Assumption

This approach charges the most recent price paid first, then the next newest, and so on as materials move out of inventory. At the end of the accounting period, the items in inventory will carry the oldest price(s) paid. Conceivably, the value of an ending inventory today could be based on prices paid 5, 10, or more years ago. During periods of rising prices LIFO causes the value of an ending inventory to be smaller than under FIFO. Thus this approach has the effect of suppressing net income and is the principal reason that businessmen apply the LIFO concept during periods of rising prices.

FIFO and LIFO Compared

If a firm had a material inventory of $80,000 at the beginning of a year and purchases of $420,000 during the year, there is $500,000 of materials to account for. At year's end the sum of materials issued plus the sum of materials in inventory must equal $500,000. The difference between these two cost flow assumptions is the amount that is charged to each category.

In periods of rising prices FIFO charges less of the $500,000 to production than LIFO because FIFO charges the oldest and lowest prices first whereas LIFO charges the latest and highest prices first. The net result is that ending inventory under FIFO carries the latest and highest prices and LIFO carries the oldest and lowest prices. This is the reason why LIFO suppresses net income during periods of rising prices.

Work-in-process Inventories

Of all classes of inventory, raw materials are the easiest to value because they are obtained in a market. The same may be true of certain component parts. This is not the case of work that is in process.

By definition, work in process is material to which some direct labor and overhead has been applied. The more direct labor and overhead that is applied to a given amount of material, the higher is the cost of work in process. Unlike raw materials and component parts, work-in-process inventories have no market value that can be used as a guide for evaluation. Consequently there is considerable risk that these inventories will be overvalued. (This was noted in the discussion of job-order and process costing.) We repeat that in cost accounting, the cost of direct material, direct labor, and overhead become an asset—work-in-process or finished goods inventory—and are not expensed until actually sold. Thus a low level of efficiency can result in high inventory values and possibly a high net income. The day of reckoning comes when the inventories are sold.

Valuation of work-in-process inventory always involves a degree of uncertainty because the value of in-process inventory is contingent on its ultimately becoming a revenue-producing commodity. A particular in-process inventory may be given a value for end-of-year purposes, and two days later it may be worthless because of spoilage or other factors. Thus accurate valuation of work in process depends on knowing the reliability of the production processes. In job-order production every job may contain an element of newness—an operation not previously duplicated—and consequently the certainty of success will be less than with process production. For example, in a previous illustration it was stated "if 10 castings are machined, there is a 95 percent probability that 1 casting will meet specification." Supposing that these 10 castings are one-third completed and that each casting passed all inspections, what is the value of this work-in-process inventory? In process production where each operation may be repeated thousands of times, the probability of success can be accurately measured. Thus it is possible to accurately value work-in-process inventory.

Standard costing provides a means for giving work-in-process inventories a reasonable value. Because all costs are charged to production at standard, the value of work-in-process inventory will reflect these standards. If the standards are reasonable, the value given to inventory will be reasonable.

SUMMARY

In this chapter we have identified the magnitude of the inventory management problem. We have also shown how outside forces such as market demand and technology can give rise to problems that management may not anticipate.

The two basic inventory problems are determining when to buy and how much to buy. If a firm knows what the future holds, answering these problems is simple, but the odds are that few firms can control the future and avoid the basic inventory problems. The consequence is that most firms will have either too much or too little inventory at any point in time. Too much inventory is bad because it ties up dollars that might be used more productively in some other investment. Too little inventory can, in some instances, cause production shutdowns and, in other instances, the loss of customers.

Managers of inventory have a difficult time satisfying all members of the management team because some managers want large inventories and others want small inventories. Finding the right balance between inventory investment and user satisfaction will continue to be a major problem area.

KEY TERMS

economic ordering quantity

first-in, first-out

inventory carrying charge

perpetual inventory

physical inventory

safety stock

last-in, first-out   stock-out
lead time   stock-out policy
periodic inventory.

QUESTIONS

1. How does product proliferation increase production costs?
2. How does product proliferation increase distribution costs?
3. How does technology impact on inventory management?
4. What information is needed to answer the when-to-buy question in process production?
5. What is a safety stock?
6. What factors are involved in the determination of a safety stock? How are these factors related?
7. Explain the logic behind the ABC method of selective control.
8. What steps can management take to reduce the possibility of stock-outs besides increasing the safety stock?
9. Should management permit stock-outs? Explain.
10. The how-much-to-buy question cannot be answered without an indication of the material management objectives. What are some of these objectives?
11. Purchasing for job-order production can be similar to purchase for process production. Explain how this can be true.
12. What data is needed to answer the how-much-to-buy question in process production when the objective is simply to meet the demands of production?
13. "The more we buy at a time, the cheaper it is." Do you agree? Explain.
14. Explain the first-in, first-out cost flow assumption.
15. Explain the last-in, first-out cost flow assumption. Why do we call these assumptions?
16. "Raw materials are the easiest of inventory items to value." Do you agree? Explain.
17. Work-in-process inventories are difficult to value. Explain.
18. Running out of inventory is always bad for any business. Do you agree with this statement? Explain.

PROBLEMS

1. Reorder issues

The following data relates to inventory item No. 2829:

Mean rate of use per week	5,000 units
Mean lead time	3 weeks
Safety stock	2-week supply
Maximum inventory level	20-week supply

Required:

a. At what level of inventory should this item be reordered?

b. How many units should be ordered at a time?

2. Economic purchase lot

The Sharon Company plans to use 200,000 lb of X during the next year. Consumption will be 4,000 lb per week for the 50 weeks the firm operates. The purchasing manager has received the following price schedule for this item:

Lot size	Unit cost
10,000	$3.00
20,000	2.95
40,000	2.90
50,000	2.87
100,000	2.85

A charge of $100 is made for each purchase order to cover paperwork and receiving. In addition, there is an inventory carrycharge of 30 percent based on the value of the average inventory.

Required:

a. What lot size will result in the lowest cost to the firm?

3. Safety-stock determination

The Apex Corporation annually consumes 150,000 units of material X. The mean rate of use is 3,000 units per week with a standard deviation of 60 units. The lead time is maintained at exactly two weeks.

Required:

a. If management wants to be 95.45 percent certain that there will be no stock-outs, how much inventory should be on hand when this material is reordered?

b. As in (a), if management wants to be 68.28 percent certain that there will be no stock-outs.

c. A unit of material X costs $10 and the inventory carrying charge is 30 percent per annum. How much will it cost the firm to be 27.17 percent more certain that there will be no stock-outs?

4. Reorder points and inventory carrying charges

The following data relates to material Y:

Mean rate of use	3,200 units per week
Maximum rate of use	3,600 units per week
Mean delivery time	3 weeks
Maximum delivery time	4 weeks

Required:

a. At what level (units) should this material be reordered if there are no variations in the rate of use or lead time?

b. At what level (units) should this material be reordered if maximum variations in use and lead time might occur?

c. If material Y costs $5 per unit and inventory carrying charges are 30 percent per annum, how much does it cost the firm per year to avoid stock-outs?

5. Inventory valuation

The following transactions relate to part No. 456, Snitzer valve:

Balance, July 1	2,000 units at $12
Purchase, July 6	3,000 units at $14
Issued, July 14	4,000 units
Purchase, July 20	3,000 units at $15
Issued, July 26	2,000 units

Required:

a. Determine the cost of materials issued during the month using (1) the FIFO cost flow assumption and (2) the LIFO cost assumption.

b. Determine the cost of inventory on July 31 using each of these cost flow assumptions.

6. Economic purchase lot

One material used by the Bambi Corp. is called Deerflex. Next year the firm plans to purchase $150,000 of this material. The firm will operate 300 days and use this material at a constant rate. The cost to place and receive an order is $400 and the inventory carrying charge is 30 percent of the value of the average inventory. Lead time is 12 days and the safety stock is $9,000.

Required:

a. Determine the reorder point for this item.

b. What is the most economic purchase lot size? (Use the following number of purchases: 2, 3, 4, 5, 6, and 10)

7.   The ABC method

The Bismark Corporation has developed a new product which requires ten component parts each of which is purchased from outside suppliers. The identification of parts, the estimated annual usage, and the estimated unit costs follow:

Part	Estimated use (units)	Estimated unit cost
BX 101	120,000	$ 0.050
BX 102	72,000	0.100
BX 103	68,000	0.750
BX 104	144,000	0.050
BX 105	24,000	17.500
BX 106	192,000	0.040
BX 107	138,000	0.500
BX 108	216,000	0.080
BX 109	240,000	0.049
BX 110	96,000	0.030

Bismark uses the ABC method to assist in managing inventories and has established the following categories of parts according to their total value:

A: the top 10 percent of items
B: the next 20 percent of items
C: the bottom 70 percent of items

Required:

a. Which parts belong in each category?

b. The company maintains a safety stock at all items equal to 20 percent of the annual dollar usage of each category and normally experiences 40 stock-outs per year which occur at random. What recommendations do you have for reducing the safety-stock investment and the probability of stock-outs?

8. Safety stock levels

The mean rate of use for an inventory item is 5,000 units per week with a standard deviation of 50 units. The lead time for this item is 3 weeks with a standard deviation of 0.2 weeks.

Required:

a. Show how this data can be used to establish a safety-stock level.

9. Inventory costing

The Peltzer Company operates a perpetual inventory. The following transactions pertain to inventory item NJ 43-23:

August 1, Balance	5,000 units at $1.20
August 8, Purchased	10,000 units at $1.30
August 12, Issued	11,000 units
August 18, Purchased	14,000 units at $1.35
August 27, Issued	15,000 units

Required:

a. Determine the cost of material issued using (1) the FIFO cost flow assumption and (2) the LIFO cost flow assumption.

b. Determine the cost of inventory on August 31 using each of the above cost flow assumptions.

10. Inventory valuation

Flocking is a process whereby various types of material such as paper, cloth, and plastic are coated with an adhesive. Then fine bits of material are allowed to fall on the material to produce a number of suede effects. Major customers are the garment trade and the packaging trade.

Bython, Inc. a job-order flocking plant uses more than 300 different types of flock each year. The company usually has a significant backlog of orders and therefore can wait until it receives an order before it must purchase flock.

Frank Parker, the office manager, has been buying flock for many years, and the following illustrates a very common buying practice. A job is received that requires 360 lb of flock No. 48763-W. Frank made a check and came up with the following schedule of prices:

Lot size	Price per pound
Up to 100 lb	$2.50
100 to 199 lb	2.40
200 to 299 lb	2.30
300 to 399 lb	2.20
400 to 499 lb	2.05

He decided to buy 400 lb to take advantage of the greater discount. The unused 40 lb would be stored in the loft in case the firm got an order in the future requiring this flock.

Required:

a. What value would you place on the 40 lb of flock which remained in inventory? Explain.

b. How much would you charge this job for the 360 lb of flock used? Explain.

11. Finished goods inventory

This problem involves production scheduling and consequently the size of the finished goods inventory. If a firm produces a year's supply of an item in January and sells off the inventory over the next eleven months, the size of the finished goods inventory will be much greater than it would be if one-twelfth of the yearly requirement were produced each month.

Pilgrim Engineering Company, a job-order machine shop, has received an order to deliver 300 gyroscope housings to a customer on the first of each month for the next twelve months. The shop's level of production will be at the rate of 600 units per month with a minimum production run of one month. A unit costs $100 and setting up for a production run costs $3,000. Inventory carrying charges are 30 percent of the value of the average inventory. The shop foreman is currently considering a number of production scheduling alternatives:

Produce the 3,600 units in a single production run lasting six months.

Produce the 3,600 units in two production runs of three months each.

Produce the 3,600 units in three production runs of two months each.

Produce the 3,600 units in six production runs of one month each.

Required:

a. Which of these alternatives will yield the lowest cost? *Note:* In this problem, units are being delivered as they are being produced.

12. Economic order quantity

The Maxwell Company plans to purchase 240,000 units of material X next year. The supplier has quoted the following delivered prices:

$3.00 per unit in lots of 20,000 units

$2.95 per unit in lots of 60,000 units

$2.85 per unit in lots of 120,000 units

The costs associated with each purchase order is $100 and the inventory carrying charge is 30 percent per annum.

Required:

a. In which lot size should the purchase of 240,000 units be made to achieve the lowest total cost?

16 Organization, Control, and Responsibility Accounting

CHAPTER OVERVIEW

The purpose of this chapter is, in a sense, to qualify some of the concepts and practices discussed in previous chapters. It is all too easy to assume that, if certain actions are taken, certain results will be forthcoming. We fail many times to emphasize that a good accounting system depends more on people than on procedures.

In this chapter we will look again at organizations and how the performance of organization members is evaluated. We review the common bases for evaluating managerial performance and point out their strengths and weaknesses.

Finally we discuss responsibility accounting. This is a reporting process that is designed to assure that all costs incurred by a firm become the responsibility of some manager. Its purpose is to make the control process more effective.

QUESTIONS FOR CONSIDERATION

1. What guidelines are there for developing evaluation criteria?
2. Why are the bases selected for the evaluation of managerial performance important?
3. Is net income earned by a manager a good basis for evaluating performance?
4. Why might return on investment or residual income be better bases for evaluation than net income?
5. What is responsibility accounting and how does it facilitate the control process?

Throughout this text we have emphasized that, if certain actions were taken, certain known results would be forthcoming. Whether the expected results will be achieved does not depend on concepts and their application; it depends on people doing what they are expected to do, and frequently this does not happen. We stated, for example, that a particular safety stock would eliminate stock-outs and interruptions of operations due to the want of materials. A safety stock can provide an adequate cushion against planned variations from normal, but the breakdown of a control system due to poor management can neutralize the value of a safety stock. Every accounting system must be designed with the firm's organization in mind because the firm's organization structure dictates the information needs of each manager and it impacts on the nature and types of controls that are needed. An accounting system that works well in organization A may fail to meet the needs of organization B.

SOME MISCONCEPTIONS ABOUT ORGANIZATIONS

The fact that many institutions, business and otherwise, develop and circulate organization charts suggests that management expects them to serve some useful purposes. They can serve useful purposes, but there is a tendency to expect them to do more than should be expected. The organization chart (see Figure 16-1) identifies the functions and subfunctions necessary to achieve objectives, and it establishes the relationships between the various functions; that is, accounting is established as a subfunction of finance and transportation is a subfunction of marketing. In theory, the organization chart identifies what is to be done and how functions should blend or relate to one another.

The presence of boxes and solid lines on an organization chart may lead one to believe that each functional division is finite and that communication will follow the solid lines. The presence of a chain of command may lead one to believe that leadership, direction, and motivation are moving through the organization. Things just do not happen this way.

Organizations are people, and any organization takes on the character of those who are responsible for getting things done. As the goals, aspirations, abilities, and confidence of these people

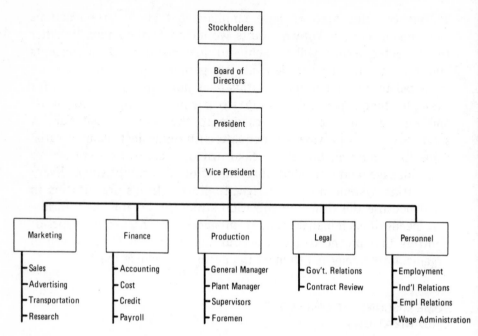

FIGURE   16.1   Organization Chart

change, so does the organization. When new managers are brought in to head up functions, the organization again changes. Over time managers may assume additional authority on their own, or they may ignore areas of responsibility. Thus there may be several managers who try to exercise authority over a function—purchasing, for example—and there may be areas of activity that are devoid of monitoring. Whenever there is a question regarding the locus of authority and responsibility, the control process is weakened. The use of profit centers as opposed to expense centers can eliminate much of this problem at the divisional manager level, but there will always be subordinate levels of management to contend with.

PERFORMANCE EVALUATION

How will a particular manager perform? Will this person try to enlarge his or her job or live by the job description? Will this person allow waste to continue because the budget appropriation is sufficient to pay for waste? Will this person attempt to build the job to serve his or her purposes, or will this person be dedicated to the objectives of the firm? The answers to these and other similar questions depend on the things that motivate a manager. Motivation, in turn, depends on the consequences of certain actions. If a given action, favorable or unfavorable to the firm, provides a reward for a manager, he or she may be motivated to take that action.

The bases for evaluating managerial performance are an important part of the management of cost process. The entire planning and control process may be influenced by evaluation criteria. If a production manager is evaluated on the sole criterion of unit production costs, the manager may intentionally do a number of things at the expense of other managers and the firm so that his performance will get a favorable rating. If a student's grade in a course is based solely on a final examination, he or she will manage the course quite differently from the case of the multiple criteria of attendance, participation, homework, in-term exams, plus a final. The instructor may prefer the single-criterion approach because it is much easier to administer than a multiple-criteria approach.

Guidelines for Evaluation Critiera

The overriding concern here is that criteria be such that they motivate managers to achieve the firm's objectives. Thus it is imperative that every manager understand and hopefully be motivated by the objectives that have been established for his or her function. Specific guidelines include the following:

1. Criteria should include only those factors over which the manager has control. If a manager has no control over the amounts spent in a department, spending should not be an evaluation criterion. This is consistent with the management principle dealing with authority and responsibility. Authority should be commensurate with responsibility. The range of evaluation criteria therefore is a function of the firm's management philosophy. If a firm is highly centralized, that is, if most authority and responsibility is held by upper management, there will be fewer areas of activity over which lower levels of management have exclusive control. If the firm is highly decentralized, lower levels of management may have considerable authority and decision-making power, and consequently there will be more criteria for performance evaluation.

2. Criteria must be measurable. Evaluation criteria should be capable of timely, specific, and unquestioned measurement.

Frequently this is not possible, and the consequence is a generalized performance evaluation. Evaluating a course instructor is difficult because evaluation criteria are not easily measured.

Evaluation criteria are standards that are used to control managerial performance. Control requires, among other things, a comparison of actual performance with the standard. Thus there must be (a) a means of measuring performance as it relates to the criterion and (b) a reporting system that brings this information to the manager being evaluated and his or her superior so that "variances" can be analyzed and corrective action taken.

3. Criteria should be such that they encourage—positively motivate—rather than discourage managerial performance. Evaluation criteria should lead to personal development as well. This guideline is a by-product of the first two guidelines.

PERFORMANCE MEASURES

The performance measures that we discuss here are net income, return on investment, and residual income. These measures are used to evaluate managerial performance at the level of chairman of the board and the president, and they can be applied to several subordinate levels provided the organization structure and managerial philosophy permit. Conceivably these measures could be applied to the first level of management—the shop foreman, for example. If the organization is decentralized and the foreman operates a profit center, net income could be the criterion for measuring his performance. It is desirable to apply these performance measures throughout the organization to obtain maximum control.

Net Income

Earning a profit is a basic objective of all businesses, and it can be a good measure of performance. We know that top management in many firms is rewarded and penalized based on profit performance; we know that profit-sharing plans are used to reward employee performance at all levels of organization. Generally, however, we hear of profit sharing only in those instances where it has been successful and are unaware of the thousands of failures that this approach to evaluation and reward has experienced.

Net income may be a good measure of performance provided those being evaluated have control over the ingredients of profit. In theory, and in practice, top management does have control over both the revenues and expenses of the firm and therefore can be evaluated on this basis. Whether this condition exists in regard to individual segments of the firm depends on the organization structure and the philosophy of management. If the structure requires the allocation of costs (see Chapter 10) and the transferring of cost from department to department (see transfer pricing), many costs may not be under the control of the manager being evaluated. There is also the problem of ascertaining the revenues attributable to a single segment of the firm. Decentralized organization and profit centers can be used to increase the controllability of revenue and expense at the segment level.

Rather than using net income to evaluate performance, some firms use contribution margin or gross margin. The gross margin criterion is commonly used to evaluate managerial performance in retail businesses. The logic is that managers can control contribution margin or gross margin but not net income.

Return on Investment

Even if we can overcome the problems involved in measuring net income at either the firm or segment level, this criterion should not necessarily be taken at face value. We know that there may be a difference between profit shown and profit earned; we know that it is possible for one segment of the firm to show a profit at the expense of another segment; and we know that it is possible to show short-run profit at the expense of long-term profit.

Return on investment (ROI) considers another factor that bears on the significance of a particular net income. Top management is vitally concerned with the dollars of investment that are required to earn a particular amount of net income. Net income of $100,000 in one division of the firm may reflect a better performance than a net income of $200,000 in another. ROI is concerned for the relationship between net income and investment. Thus, if one division earned $100,000 with an investment of $400,000, ROI is 25 percent. ROI provides a means for measuring and evaluating performance where different investments are involved. For example,

Division	Net income	Investment	ROI
A	$ 80,000	$ 286,000	28%
B	140,000	580,000	24
C	300,000	1,500,000	20
D	400,000	2,500,000	16

From this it is easy to see that the firm's investment was more effectively used in division A, where net income was the lowest, and least effectively in division D, where net income was the highest. A basic management goal is to maximize the net income that can be generated per dollar of investment. Had division D used its investment as effectively as division A, only $1,429,000 of investment would have been required, or alternatively division D should have had net income of $700,000.

Again, measuring investment at the firm level is much easier than at the segment level. At the segment level it is necessary to determine what we call applicable assets. The investment in inventory needed to generate a given net income could be quite clear. Measuring the investment in long-term assets is less clear because of traditional approaches to asset valuation. A division requiring new and highly sophisticated equipment very likely would show a lower ROI than a division using equipment that is fully depreciated. In addition, the investment in cash and receivables attributable to a given segment must somehow be measured. Net income and ROI can be excellent bases for evaluating managerial performance, but their measurement is far from being cut and dried.

Residual Income

The residual income (RI) criterion utilizes both net income and ROI. Because it would be normal for some areas of activity to show either a relatively high or low ROI, managements establish a target ROI for each segment being evaluated. RI is that net income in excess of the target ROI percentage multiplied by the investment. If investment was $1,000,000, net income was $200,000, and the desired ROI was 18 percent, RI would be $20,000, that is, $200,000 − ($1,000,000 × 0.18).

RI brings managerial performance into clearer focus than either net income or ROI as shown in an extension of a previous illustration.

Division	Net income	Investment	Target ROI	Target return	RI
A	$ 80,000	$ 286,000	20%	$ 57,200	$ 22,800
B	140,000	580,000	18	104,400	35,600
C	300,000	1,500,000	16	240,000	60,000
D	400,000	2,500,000	22	550,000	(150,000)

Thus we can conclude that division C is by far the most valuable division, based on this measurement, and that division D is considerably less effective than it should be. The manager of division D might argue that his target ROI is too high, but targets are the result of management expectation.

Neither measure is without weakness, and this tells us something about performance appraisals. A particular measure could very well work to one manager's advantage more than it could to another manager. Regardless of the performance measure, it should be so designed and defined that high ratings reflect a high contribution to the firm's objectives.

RESPONSIBILITY ACCOUNTING

A basic purpose of using performance standards is to assure goal congruence, that is, to establish an environment where the operational goals of subordinate managers are aimed at the goals of the firm. Another way to achieve goal congruence is to design the organization structure so that it facilitates the control process. To be effective, responsibility accounting requires an organization structure in which it is certain where the responsibility for each expenditure lies.

The term "responsibility accounting" is something of a misnomer because it does not involve accounting in the traditional sense. Rather, it involves reporting of cost data to those people who are responsible for the control of cost.

This new approach to accounting and reporting is ... designed to control expenditures by directly relating the reporting of expenditures to the individuals in the company organization who are responsible for their control ... which is another way of saying that expenditures must be reported on the basis of where they were incurred and who had responsibility for them. Hence comes the term responsibility accounting.[1]

As the term implies, there must be responsibility centers for this system to operate. The number and location of responsibility centers is a function of organizational philosophy. Decentralization is a prerequisite for responsibility accounting.

We will use a portion of an organization to explain how responsibility accounting operates and how it aids in the control process. Figure 16-2 is the segment of an organization that we will use. We assume that there are a number of foremen who report to a lesser number of supervisors who report to the production manager, and so on.

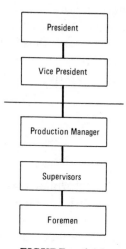

FIGURE   16-2

Responsibility accounting is a reporting function that provides each level of management with the information it needs to control costs. The several foremen report the results of their activity to their supervisor. Each supervisor combines the data from each of his departments, adds the cost of his function, and reports this to the production manager. The production manager in turn repeats the process for his area of responsibility and reports to the vice president, who repeats the process.

[1]John A. Higgins, "Responsibility Accounting," *The Arthur Andersen Chronicle,* 12 (April 1952), p. 94.

Table 16-1 outlines this process using only the two lowest levels of responsibility, foremen and supervisors. The only costs included in these reports are those that are controllable by the responsible manager. The process is based on two main concepts. First, a manager, such as the production manager, can effectively control only the immediate subordinate area of activity. Generally, the third level of responsibility (production manager) does not have the capacity to control the first level of responsibility (foreman) and consequently receives only a summary of the costs involved at the foreman level. It is the supervisor who is responsible for the control of cost at the foreman level.

Second, the only costs that are included in these reports are those over which the responsible manager has control. Under responsibility accounting, managers at every level of organization are truly managers of cost. Each manager has his budget or standard costs and he is responsible for all variances. It is imperative that each manager view the budget or standards as his or hers and therefore subject to his/her control.

TABLE   16-1

	Standard cost or budget	Actual cost	Variance (unfav.)
	Supervisor 1 **Cost summary, July**		
Foundry cost	$166,000	$169,500	$(3,500)
Machining cost	240,000	245,000	(5,000)
Assembly cost	120,000	118,000	2,000
Supervisory cost	20,000	21,000	(1,000)
Total cost	$546,000	$553,500	$(7,500)
	Foundry cost summary, **month of July**		
Direct material	$ 28,000	$ 30,000	$(2,000)
Direct labor	82,000	80,000	2,000
Variable overhead	48,000	52,000	(4,000)
Foundry supervision	8,000	7,500	500
Total cost	$166,000	$169,500	$(3,500)

The intent of this process is twofold. First, it reduces the data flow to superior managers. The only data that is transmitted up the line is that which is useful to upper levels of management. The vice president should not be concerned with material or labor costs in the foundry. This is a concern for the foreman of the foundry.

Second, this process gets away from job-order cost sheets, cost of production reports, and the like as reporting emphasizes the control of cost. Each level of management has only that data needed to control those areas for which he is responsible. Job and product cost measurement are essential, but, if costs are adequately controlled, costs should be in line with expectations.

SUMMARY

Control, the process of assuring that actual events conform to the plan is a basic management function. Whether the control process will be easy or difficult, effective or ineffective, depends on the firm's organization structure and the ability of managers at all levels to manage their subordinates. If the delegation of authority and the assignment of responsibility is uncertain, the process of control will be difficult and ineffective.

Both the control of managerial performance and the control of cost can be facilitated by subjecting managers to a variety of performance evaluation measures. The effectiveness with which managers employ the firm's resources can be measured by establishing standards for net income earned, return on investment, and residual income.

Responsibility accounting provides the means for a continuous monitoring of activity by reporting budget and standard cost variances to the responsible manager.

KEY TERMS

function

performance evaluation

residual income

responsibility accounting

return on investment

QUESTIONS

1. What can an observer learn from an organization chart? Are there things that cannot be shown on a chart regarding a firm's organization? Explain.

2. Why are performance evaluation bases important to the management of cost process? Illustrate.

3. If you are a manager, would you rather use a single criterion or multiple criteria when evaluating subordinates?

4. "The range of evaluation criteria is a function of management philosophy." To what does management philosophy refer? Why is this a true statement?

5. Why is the measure net income easier to use at the top management level than at low levels of management?

6. The criterion net income should not necessarily be taken at face value in measuring managerial performance. Why is this so?

7. What values does ROI consider?

8. ROI provides a means for measuring performance where different investments are involved. Explain and illustrate.

9. What problems are involved in measuring ROI at the segment level?

10. What is investment as it applies to ROI?

11. What is residual income?

12. In what respect is RI a better criterion for evaluation than ROI?

13. What is responsibility accounting?

14. Why is decentralization a prerequisite for responsibility accounting?

15. Explain the responsibility accounting process.

16. What is the twofold intent of responsibility accounting?

PROBLEMS

1. Cost allocation

The computer division of the Montrose Insurance Company is set up as a profit center. At the end of each month, those departments served by the computer division are billed a portion of the division's cost based on the number of hours of computer time they have used. The rate charged by the computer division is calculated by dividing total cost of operation (plus profit) by the actual hours worked. The capacity of the computer division is such that it can serve the firm's needs while operating at 80 percent of capacity.

Required:

a. Many department managers are disturbed over this policy because they feel that it is unfair to them. Do you agree? Explain.

b. Suggest an alternative method for charging departments for the computer service that they receive.

2. Responsibility centers

Figure 16-3 is a partial organization chart for the Mako Corporation:

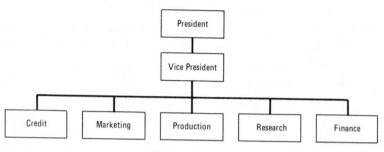

FIGURE   16-3

Credit is a functional division at Mako; that is, it has final say in all credit extensions. Before marketing can book an order with production, credit must first approve. On June 1 Jim Powers, a sales engineer for Mako, finally landed an order that he had been working on for nearly six months. The order called for the delivery of 3,000 electric motors per month for the next 12 months. The motors sell for $40 each and yield a contribution margin of $12 per motor. Landing this order put Jim over the top as far as his sales quota for the period was concerned. On June 4 the credit department rejected Jim's customer as a credit risk and would not approve the order.

Required:

a. Evaluate a policy that gives the credit department such absolute authority over credit sales.

b. Might it be better to have a credit department that only advises the marketing group and leaves the final decision to them?

c. As a result of the credit department's decision Jim failed to meet his sales quota. Who should accept the responsibility for this? Explain.

3. Cost allocation

For a number of years Argyle Electronics has had a policy that requires all departments to use Argyle's machine shop for machining work provided that the shop can promise delivery within four weeks from the date the work order is placed. If the backlog of work is such that a four-week delivery cannot be made, departments may then go to outside sources to have the work done. The hourly rates for direct labor and overhead are established by the accounting department for all work done by the machine shop, and these rates are reviewed every four weeks.

Required:

a. Appraise this policy.

4.   Responsibility accounting

Figure 16-4 is a partial organization chart for the Mysto Corporation:

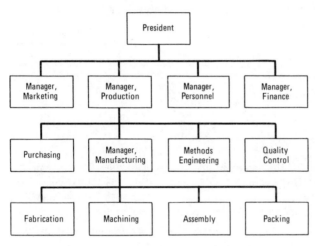

FIGURE   16-4

The following data relates to budgeted and actual activity for the departments during the month of March.

	Budget	*Actual*
Fabrication	$44,000	$46,000
Machining	76,000	72,000
Assembly	32,000	34,000
Packing	18,000	20,000
Purchasing	12,000	10,000
Manager, manufacturing	19,000	18,000
Methods engineering	9,000	10,000
Quality control	13,000	12,000
Manager, marketing	28,000	34,000
Manager, production	18,000	16,000
Manager, personnel	6,000	8,000
Manager, finance	9,000	10,000

Required:

a. Prepare responsibility accounting reports for the president, manager, production, and manager of manufacturing.

5. Performance evaluation

At the end of last month the production supervisor received the following report summarizing the costs of the assembly department:

	Standard cost	Actual cost
Direct labor	$126,000	$124,250
Overhead	72,000	73,500
Total	$198,000	$197,750

The manager of the assembly department was called in by the production supervisor to review the month's performance. When he was shown these figures, the manager of the assembly department was dismayed because he had tried his best to beat the standards by a wide margin.

The production supervisor presented the following data to show why there was only a small favorable variance:

a. Normal capacity, 10,000 units; actual production, 9,000 units

b. Direct labor standard, 2 hours per unit at $7 per hour

c. Overhead rate, $4 per direct labor-hour; actual direct labor-hours, 17,500

d. Overhead cost at normal capacity; variable—$44,000, fixed—$36,000; fixed overhead costs were incurred as planned.

Required:

a. Evaluate the performance of the assembly department, assuming that the manager has no control over wage rates or the volume of production.

b. Would your appraisal differ if the manager had control over wage rates?

Glossary

A

Absorption costing: A costing process that charges both variable and fixed manufacturing costs to production. Compare with variable costing.

Accounting cycle: The process of journalizing and posting business transactions, making the necessary adjustments, and preparing financial statements.

Accounting equation: Assets minus liabilities equals owner equity.

Accounting rate of return: The increase in annual net income expected from an investment alternative divided by the increase in investment required to produce that income.

Accounts payable: The amount owed by a firm for goods and services purchased.

Accounts receivable: The amount owed to a firm by customers who have purchased goods and services on account.

Accrual basis of accounting: An approach to accounting where revenues are matched with the costs of producing that revenue. Compare with the cash basis of accounting.

Acid-test ratio: Current assets minus inventory divided by current liabilities. Also called the quick ratio.

After-tax profit: Gross net income less provision for income taxes. The amount of profit that may be added to retained earnings.

Allocation bases: Measures of activity such as hours worked or units produced used to assign indirect costs to segments of the firm that benefit from these costs.

Applied overhead: The amount of overhead charged to work in process. It is the product of actual activity and the estimated overhead rate per unit of activity.

Average cost: Total cost of an activity divided by the units of activity.

B

Balance sheet: A financial statement that summarizes assets, liabilities, and owner equity at a specific point in time.

Bill of materials: A statement of the types and amounts of material that should be requisitioned for a job or batch of production.

Book value: The value at which an asset is carried in the balance sheet. The book value of a machine costing $100,000 with cumulative depreciation of $40,000 is $60,000.

Break-even analysis: The process of studying the relationship between variable costs, fixed costs, and revenue at various levels of activity.

Break-even chart: A graphic presentation of the relationships between total cost and total revenue at various levels of activity.

Break-even point: That volume of activity measured in units or dollars where total cost equals total revenue.

Budget: A quantifiable plan.

Budgeting: The process of preparing and administering a budget.

C

Capital budgeting: A plan for the acquisition of long-term assets.

Cash basis of accounting: An approach to accounting where expenses are recorded when paid and revenues are recorded when received. Contrast with the accrual basis of accounting.

Cash budget: A schedule of cash receipts and disbursements for a period of time. It is derived largely from the firm's operating budgets.

Cash flow: The inflow and outflow of cash due to operations, borrowing, and the like.

Centralization: A management philosophy where the bulk of authority and responsibility is held at high organization levels.

Constant dollars: The result of adjusting dollar values to a common base to counter the impact of inflation or deflation. Dollars are thus expressed in terms of their current purchasing power.

Contribution margin: The difference between sales revenue and variable cost. Contribution can be expressed on a per unit basis or as a total. If selling price is $10 and variable costs are $6, contribution is $4.

Contribution margin ratio: The difference between sales and variable cost divided by sales. If selling price is $10 and variable costs are $6, contribution margin is 40 percent.

Controllable cost: A cost that a specific manager can regulate in either the short run or the long run.

Cost: The amount, measured in money, paid in consideration of goods or services received or to be received.

Cost accounting: That portion of an accounting system concerned with the recording, analysis, and reporting of costs incurred in the operation of a firm.

Cost allocation: The process of charging indirect costs to segments of the firm that benefit from the cost incurred.

Cost balance: The relationship between variable cost, fixed cost, and total cost.

Cost behavior: Costs are classified as fixed, variable, or mixed based on how they respond to changes in the volume of activity that takes place.

Cost center: A segment of a firm that is responsible for incurring costs but not revenue. Contrast with a profit center.

Cost flow: The movement of variable and fixed costs into production and out of production in the form of goods ready for sale.

Cost of capital: That rate of return on investment that will leave unchanged the value of the firm. A firm will not pay more than 12 percent for capital if the use to which it is put produces a 12 percent return.

Current asset: Cash plus those assets that normally will become cash during the year or the firm's normal operating cycle.

Current liability: Obligations that will become due during the current year or the firm's normal operating cycle if it is longer than a year.

Currently attainable standard: A standard that can be met if the firm operates with a high degree of efficiency and effectiveness. Compare with an ideal standard.

Current ratio: Total current assets divided by total current liabilities. The result is a measure of the firm's short-term debt-paying capacity.

D

Decentralization: A management philosophy where significant amounts of authority rest at relatively low levels of organization.

Depreciation: The allocation of the decrease in value of long-term assets (except land) to an accounting period or to units of production.

Direct cost: A cost such as direct material or direct labor that can be traced logically and practically to some cost object such as a unit of production.

Discounted cash flow: The process of converting dollars to be received at some future time into their equivalent present value. A dollar to be received a year from today is worth less than a dollar in hand today.

Discretionary cost: Costs that are subject to current control by management such as the amount that will be appropriated for an advertising budget. Compare with committed costs which cannot be changed in the immediate future.

E

Economic order quantity: The amount of material that should be purchased to obtain the lowest cost of acquisition, purchasing, transportation, and carrying charges for inventory.

Expense: In cost accounting, an expired cost; that is, a cost that has been charged to revenue.

F

Financial accounting: The part of a firm's accounting system that is concerned for transactions that affect the income statement, the balance sheet, and other formal financial statements.

Finished goods: Goods that are ready for sale. These goods have had all material, labor, and overhead charged to them.

First-in, first-out: An inventory costing procedure that charges the oldest inventory cost first.

Fixed cost: A cost that remains the same in total regardless of the volume of activity as long as it is within the relevant range.

Fixed budget: A budget in which allotments are designated for each expense category and these allotments are allowed to stand regardless of the actual level of activity attained.

Fixed overhead: That portion of indirect costs that remains the same in total regardless of the actual level of activity attained.

Flexible budget: A budget of indirect costs for any level of actual activity within the relevant range. Costs are expressed as unit variable and total fixed.

Function: Any activity in a firm that has organizational status and for which a manager is responsible. Every firm has personnel activity, but, until personnel is given a place in the organization structure and has a person responsible for it, it is not a function.

Future costs: Costs which are likely to be incurred at some future time.

G

Goodwill: The amount paid for, say, a business that is in excess of the value that would normally be given to the individual assets purchased.

H

High-low method: A simplified method for separating a mixed cost into its unit variable- and total fixed-cost components.

Historical cost: A cost already incurred. It is therefore irrelevant in the decision-making process.

Horizontal analysis: A form of financial analysis in which like items for different periods of time are compared, such as a comparison of this year's inventory with last year's inventory.

I

Ideal standard: A standard based on the assumption that nothing will go wrong.

Income statement: A statement that shows revenues and expenses for a period of time. The bottom line of an income statement shows the profit or loss for the period.

Incremental cost: The added cost of producing one more unit.

Indirect cost: A cost incurred to serve more than one segment of an organization such as depreciation on a building.

Information overload: A situation in which the volume of data funnelled to a manager is so great that time is lost in the process of separating relevant from irrelevant information.

Inventory carrying charge: A charge made to cost or profit centers for the inventory carried. It is a percentage applied to the value of average inventory.

Inventory policy: The relationship established between inventory levels at a point in time and the volume of activity they are expected to support. Management may, for example, require an inventory on October 1 that will cover sales for the next two months.

Inventory-turnover ratio: The cost of goods sold divided by the value of average inventory.

J

Job order production: A production system that is structured to provide a variety of services. A job order machine shop can produce many products but does not have a line of products.

Joint costs: Costs that are common to more than one segment of a firm or one product. Costs that must be allocated.

L

Last-in, first-out: An inventory costing procedure that charges the most recent cost first regardless of the actual cost of the material units involved.

Lead time: The interval between the time a decision is made to place an order for material and receipt of that material.

Least squares regression: A statistical measure that can be used to isolate the unit variable and total fixed cost components of a mixed cost.

Line functions: Functions that are directly involved with the generation of revenue such as production and distribution.

Long-term debt: Obligations that will become due more than one year from the date in question. That portion of long-term debt that must be paid in the current year is considered a current liability.

Long-term decisions: Decisions that effect the firm for years to come.

M

Management by exception: An approach to management in which only the exceptional situations are brought to the attention of upper management. If, for example, actual and standard costs are in harmony, there is no need to involve upper management.

Managerial accounting: A phase of accounting concerned for the decision-making process.

Market price: The price that must be paid to acquire a good or service in the market at a given point in time.

Marketable security: A security such as a government bond that can readily be converted to cash.

Material requisition: A form usually prepared by the production department that authorizes the issuing of specific types and amounts of material needed to complete a job.

Mixed cost: A cost that is neither fixed or variable but contains an element of each type of cost.

N

Net present value: The difference between the dollars required for an investment and the present value of the flow of savings that the investment is expected to generate.

Net working capital: The excess of current assets over current liabilities.

Noncash expense: An expense chargeable against revenue, such as depreciation, that does not involve the expenditure of cash.

Not-for-profit enterprise: An organization that has no ownership group such as a private university. Any excess of revenue over expenses earned by the organization must remain in the organization.

O

Organization by function: An approach to organization that emphasizes the basic functions performed such as production, marketing, and finance.

Organization by product: An approach to organization that emphasizes the products produced and sold. Product managers are responsible for all activity that relates to the production and sale of the product.

Overapplied overhead: The amount by which overhead applied to production exceeds actual overhead costs.

Overhead: The total of all indirect and fixed costs.

Overhead rate: Estimated overhead divided by estimated activity. Used to apply overhead costs to work in process.

Owner equity: Assets minus liabilities equals owner equity.

P

Payback: A measure of the time required to recoup the cost of an investment through the cash savings that the investment creates.

Period cost: Those costs that are charged, not to products, but to the accounting period involved. The amount of a one-year lease could be a period cost that is written off as an expense.

Periodic inventory: A method for determining the amount of materials used. Materials available for use minus the amount of actual inventory on hand at the end of the period equals the amount of materials used.

Perpetual inventory: A continuing record for each inventory item that shows the beginning inventory, authorized additions to inventory, and authorized withdrawals. The ending balance is a measure of the amount that should be in inventory.

Physical inventory: Used with periodic and perpetual inventory methods. A physical count of inventory.

Plant-turnover ratio: Sales revenue divided by the investment in plant. It measures the sales revenue generated by each dollar invested in plant.

Price variance: The difference between a standard price and the actual price paid for a good or service multiplied by the actual number of units purchased.

Process costing: A method for determining the average cost of a unit produced. Used where homogeneous production is involved.

Product cost: All costs that can be reasonably associated with getting a product ready for sale. These costs are treated as assets until goods are sold. Compare with period cost.

Production order: The authorization to produce a certain quantity of a product. It may also provide authorization to use materials, labor, and overhead.

Profit center: A segment of an organization that is responsible for incurring costs and generating revenue.

Profit earned: Net income resulting from the sales of goods and services. Compare with profit shown.

Profit shown: The net income that results from charging fixed costs to inventory. If more units are produced than sold in a period, net income shown will be greater than net income earned.

Profit-volume chart: A graph that permits reading the profit/loss at various levels of activity.

Pro-forma financial statements: A forecast of financial statements.

Q

Quantity variance: See volume variance.

R

Ratio analysis: A form of financial analysis that established relations between items. A current ratio of 3 to 1 shows that current assets are three times current liabilities.

Receivable turnover ratio: Credit sales divided by the average amount of accounts receivable. It provides a measure of the average age of receivables.

Relevant range: The range of activity in which costs behave as expected; that is, unit variable cost and total fixed cost are constant.

Residual income: The net income of a segment of a firm that is in excess of the cost of capital times the assets used to generate the income.

Responsibility accounting: A system of accounting that makes every expenditure the responsibility of some manager.

Return on investment: The relation between an investment and the net income that the investment will generate.

S

Safety stock: A reserve inventory held to minimize stock-outs caused by variations in the rate of use of a material or variations in the lead time.

Sales mix: The percentage of total sales of each product class when several products make up total sales.

Separable fixed cost: A fixed cost incurred to serve a single segment of the firm. Compare with joint cost.

Service function: A function whose purpose is to serve line functions and other service functions. Personnel is a service function. Compare with line function.

Short-term decisions: Decisions relating to the use of existing resources.

Staff function: Staff functions are service functions. Staff managers have the authority to advise but not the authority to act.

Statement of changes in financial position: A financial statement that shows the sources and uses of working capital or cash during a period of time.

Stock-out: The running out of inventory.

Stock-out policy: Management's attitude toward stock-outs. This policy is generally determined by comparing the costs of having a stock out with the cost of carrying safety stocks.

Step variable costs: Variable costs that increase in steps rather than in direct proportion to the volume of activity. The variable cost of labor could jump $60 per day each time a new employee is hired.

T

Transfer price: The amount charged by one segment of a firm to another for goods or services provided.

Trial balance: A listing of the balances of all ledger accounts. Debit balances must equal credit balances.

U

Underapplied overhead: The amount by which applied overhead is less than actual overhead. It increases the cost of goods sold.

V

Variable cost: A cost that increases in total amount in direct proportion to the volume of activity. It is, therefore, fixed per unit of activity.

Variable costing: An approach to costing where only variable costs are charged to production and fixed costs are charged off as a period cost.

Variable overhead: That portion of indirect costs that tends to increase and decrease in total amount as the volume of activity increases and decreases.

Variance: The difference between actual events and planned events. Used in standard costing and budgeting.

Variance analysis: The process of breaking a variance into price and volume (quantity) components.

Vertical analysis: A form of financial analysis where each item is compared with the total. Expressing each item in an income statement as a percentage of sales is a form of vertical analysis.

Volume variance: That difference between planned and actual cost that can be attributed to the difference between planned and actual volumes of material, labor, or overhead used. It is calculated by multiplying the difference in volume by the planned (standard) unit price.

W

Work-in-process inventory: Raw materials to which some direct labor and overhead have been applied. Partially completed products.

Z

Zero-base budgeting: An approach to budgeting where every year the budget starts from scratch rather than adding to or subtracting from previous budgets.

Index